HISTORY OF THE LABOR MOVEMENT

IN THE UNITED STATES

VOLUME VIII

HISTORY OF
THE LABOR MOVEMENT
IN THE UNITED STATES

VOLUME VIII: Postwar Struggles, 1918-1920

BY PHILIP S. FONER

INTERNATIONAL PUBLISHERS, New York

Library of Congress Cataloging-in-Publication Data
(Revised for vol. 8)

Foner, Philip Sheldon, 1910—
    History of the labor movement in the United States.

    (New World paperbacks)
    Includes bibliographical references and index.
    Contents: —v. 2. From the founding of the American Federation of Labor to the
emergence of American imperialism.   —v. 5. The AFL in the progressive era, 1910-
1915.   —v. 8. Postwar struggles, 1919-1921.
    1. Trade-unions—United States—History.   2. Labor and laboring classes—United
States—History.   I. Title. II. Series.
HD6508.F57   1975   331.88'0973   75-315606
ISBN O-7178-0092-X
ISBN O-7178-0388-0 (pbk.)

CONTENTS

ACKNOWLEDGEMENTS

As in the case of previous volumes, this work could not have been completed without the generous assistance of numerous libraries and historical societies. I am again indebted to Dorothy Swanson and her staff at the Tamiment Institute, Elmer Bobst Library, New York University, for kind assistance and cooperation. I also again wish to thank the staff of the State Historical Society of Wisconsin for assistance in the use of the Archives of the American Federation of Labor. I also wish to thank the staffs of the Library of Congress, National Archives, New York Public Library, U.S. Department of Labor, Bancroft Library, University of California, Berkeley, the interlibrary loan department of the University of Pennsylvania; and the libraries of New York University, Duke University, Columbia University, University of Wisconsin, Catholic University of America, Cornell University, University of Virginia, Swarthmore College, Temple University, Haverford College, University of Pennsylvania, University of Maine, Farmington; University of Chicago, Washington University, St. Louis; University of Washington, Seattle; University of Florida, Northwestern University, University of New Mexico, Wayne State University, University of Oklahoma; and Lincoln University, Pennsylvania. Finally, I wish to thank my brother Henry Foner, who read the entire manuscript, helped prepare it for publication, and made valuable suggestions, and Jules Chazin of Madison, Wisconsin, who helped in obtaining material from the University of Wisconsin and the State Historical Society of Wisconsin.

Philip S. Foner
Professor Emeritus of History,
Lincoln University, Pennsylvania

PREFACE

This is the eighth volume of my *History of the Labor Movement in the United States*. The seventh volume of the series dealt with the position of the Socialist Party of America and organized labor, especially the American Federation of Labor (AFL), the Industrial Workers of the World (IWW), and the Railroad Brotherhoods toward the outbreak of World War I in Europe in August 1914. It carried the story to America's entrance into the war in April 1917, the experiences of organized labor and the Socialist Party during the war, and closed with the situation of the labor movement at the armistice in November 1918.

Volume 8 concentrates on the postwar years, 1918-1920, a period of unprecedented labor struggles and political developments. It was my original intention to include a discussion of the role of the labor unions and the Socialist Party towards Latin America, culminating in the formation of the Pan-American Federation of Labor in 1919. However, this discussion is included in a separate volume of mine, *U.S. Labor Movement and Latin America*, volume I, 1846-1919, published by Bergin and Garvey.

In 1928, the labor writer J.B.S. Hardman looked back at the strike wave of 1919 and observed: "The language that was used then no longer sounds familiar to our ears. The emotions that overwhelmed people in those momentous days fail to excite us today."* It would take less than a decade for another great wave to make Hardman's observation dated. It is true, however, as we shall see in the present volume, that rarely has labor in the United States exploded with such fury as in the aftermath of the Great War. In 1919 American workers staged an unprecedented series of uprisings which, if only temporarily, vigorously challenged employers' control of the workplace. During 1919 labor unrest swept across the United States as four million workers walked off the job in order to consolidate wartime victories and win new gains. The "strike craze" affected more workers than during any previous period in American history. The scale and intensity of the labor struggles reflected not only the wartime growth of union strength, but also the determination of employers to wipe out labor's wartime gains and to set the pattern for postwar relations on an entirely different basis than they had been often forced to adopt during the war years. In this determination, they were most often fully supported by the authorities—national, state and municipal—and a media which most often backed the industrialists and joined them in disseminating anti-Bolshevik propaganda that denied the legitimacy of labor's protests.

Historians such as David Brody, Arnon Gutfield, and Melvyn Dubofsky have argued that the combined power of the state and of the corporations was sufficient in itself to defeat many of the efforts of labor to hold its own and to advance in the postwar period.** But as the present volume demonstrates, there were important exceptions which proved that given the correct structure, a militant rank-and-file and leadership, and labor unity, the unions were able to overcome these obstacles and triumph. While not in any sense negating the role played by the state in aiding monopoly capitalism to defeat organized labor, this volume demonstrates that the recent tendency of labor historians to regard any workers' struggles in an environment of conservative political domination to be doomed, is both too negative and cynical.

*J.B.S. Hardman, *American Labor Dynamics in the Light of Post-War Developments*, New York, 1928, p. 10; reprinted, New York, 1968.
**David Brody, *Labor in Crisis—The Steel Strike*, New York, 1965; Arnon Gutfield, *Montana's Agony—Years of War and Hysteria, 1917-1921*, Gainesville, Fla., 1979; Melvyn Dubofsky, "Abortive Reform: The Wilson Administration and Organized Labor, 1913-1920," in James E. Cronin and Carmen Sirianni, *Work, Community and Power: The Experience of Labor in Europe and America, 1900-1925*, Philadelphia, 1983.

HISTORY OF THE LABOR MOVEMENT

IN THE UNITED STATES

VOLUME VIII

CHAPTER 1

The Setting I:
The Struggle For Control

The Armistice of November 11, 1918 brought a profound change in the thinking of rank-and-file members of the labor movement. Even during the war, appeals to patriotism and for the destruction of the Kaiser had not sufficed to prevent strikes.* Once the war was over, these appeals would be unable to persuade workers that they must do the bidding of either their government or the leaders of their unions.

CAUSES OF LABOR UNREST

The year 1919 was one of the most militant in United States labor history. During its twelve months, 3,630 strikes were called involving 4,160,000 workers, an increase of 2,933,000 over the number of workers involved in strikes in 1917.[1] the *Literary Digest* called it a year characterized by "an epidemic of strikes,"[2] and the *Outlook* lamented: "Everywhere strikes. . . . The strike fever is in the air. . . . The situation changes kaleidoscopically. The disease that has struck our industrial systems breaks out in one place as it subsides in another; one strike is scarcely over when another one begins."[3]

The main cause of labor unrest was the continued rise in the cost of living, which had advanced inexorably throughout the war period. In November 1918, the month of the Armistice, the index stood at 169, or 69 percent above the 1914 level. With the end of the war, the increase continued, month by month. The highest peak was reached in July 1920, when the index read 212, an increase of 112 percent within four and a half years!

Studies reveal that workers in manufacturing industries doubled their average earnings between 1914 and 1919. Real wages for all industrial

*See Philip S. Foner, *History of the Labor Movement in the United States* 7 (New York, 1987): 150-70.

workers in 1919 were 19 percent above the average in 1915.[4] However, most workers were able to meet the wartime increase in living costs only through full employment supplemented by overtime pay and bonus payments.[5]

When the war industries ceased to be important, even these alleviating factors were eliminated. On November 12, within twenty-four hours of the Armistice, a directive issued jointly by the chairman of the Shipping Board and the secretaries of the Navy and War called for the immediate cessation of Sunday and overtime work under all government-supervised contracts. For many workers this meant wage reductions of as much as 50 percent.[6]

Within three months of the Armistice, the U.S. economy entered a recession brought about by the transition from war to peacetime production. But the cost of living continued to rise so that by the end of the year, workers' living standards were very seriously affected. In fact, in April 1919, the National Industrial Board expressed the view that "a substantial reduction in the cost of living would do more for industrial peace than seems possible by any program of reconstruction."[7]

Of the 3,630 strikes in 1919, 1,115 or approximately 31 percent, had a wage increase as their basic demand. In an additional 921 strikes, or 25 percent, wage increases figured in the demands. Thus a total of 56 percent of all the strikes in 1919 demanded wage increases.[8]

Second in importance to the cost of living as a cause of labor unrest was the matter of working hours. In many industries, the eight-hour day was still a dream in 1919. On the street railways, among operating engineers, in the oil fields, in canneries, in printing shops, in clothing factories, in textile mills and steel mills, workdays of ten, twelve or more hours prevailed. In steel, canning, oil, municipal transportation and domestic service, the seven-day week, too, persisted for hundreds of thousands of workers.[9] As Grace Hutchins wrote: "The very workers most in need of a strong union to demand shorter hours are often too exhausted at night to attend . . . meetings. The writer has seen silk workers, keenly interested in the union, fall asleep at a meeting . . . after the day's work."[10]

In the strike wave of 1919, workers in those industries that had the longest hours of work tried to remedy the situation through a series of organizing drives and job actions centering mainly on the length of the working day and on union recognition. How strongly the workers felt about gaining union recognition is evidenced by the fact that of the 3,630 strikes in 1919, 860, or 24 percent, were called to achieve that demand. Together, the demands for higher wages, shorter hours and union recognition caused 80 percent of all the strikes.[11]

Although labor had achieved advances during the war, a major cause of industrial unrest was the feeling among many workers that, in contrast to the capitalists, they had not received what they were entitled to as a result of their wartime sacrifices. World War I brought U.S. monopoly capital immense profits. Between 1914 and 1918 the income of U.S. corporations rose from $3,711 million to $9,500 million. Profits also spiralled. In his "Letter to American Workers," first published in the United States in *Class Struggle*, a left-Socialist journal, in December 1918, V.I. Lenin wrote of American monopoly capitalists: "They have profited more than the rest. They have converted all, even the richest, countries into their tributaries. They have grabbed hundreds of billions of dollars."[12]

This is not to say that labor had not made some gains. During the war, largely to prevent strikes, under the guidance of the National War Labor Board, the Ordnance Bureau, the Railway Administration, and other agencies, shop committees were promoted to resolve workplace disputes, union wage and hour standards were set in many local industries, and union growth was encouraged. This was one of the reasons, as we have seen in our previous volume, that between 1915 and 1920, membership in railway, streetcar, and sailors' unions expanded by 111 percent, by 67 percent in building trades, 113 percent in clothing, 280 percent in metal fabricating, and 368 percent in textiles.[13]

Pointing in January 1918 to these and other gains, Professor John R. Commons of the University of Wisconsin*, warned American labor not to be influenced by those who claimed that "this is a capitalistic war." On the contrary: "This is an American workingmen's war, conducted for American workingmen, by American workingmen." He continued: "All labor in this country is benefitting because organized labor is actually 'On the Inside' in running the Government." Commons concluded: "Never before was a war carried on by workingmen. Never before was the voice of labor so powerful as it is now in America. It will continue to be so in peace."[14]

PROMISE AND REALITY

When workers questioned whether the wartime gains would continue in postwar America, the *Labor Herald* of Kansas City, Missouri published Commons' assurance, as well as that of Rabbi Stephen S. Wise, which urged the workers to continue to put their trust in President Wilson, "because labor knows that the President will never, never consent to

*The famous *History of Labor in the United States* (volumes 1 and 2) by John R. Commons and Associates was published in 1918.

any elimination of the gains labor has achieved during the war."[15] At the same time, the official organ of the Central Labor Union of Kansas City noted that much was being said of the "industrial democracy" that would follow the end of the conflict, in which labor would receive its full reward. From every quarter came statements giving credence to this assertion. Josephus Daniels, Secretary of the Navy, wrote of the "Golden Age" of labor that would follow the war, and assured the workers: "The world after peace . . . will not go back to conditions such as existed prior to our entrance into the mighty struggle." George W. Perkins of the House of Morgan foresaw the time when "the tool user will be part tool owner."[16] Charles M. Schwab, chairman of the Emergency Fleet Corporation and president of Bethelehem Steel, declared: "We are at the threshold of a new social era. . . . It means . . . that the man who labors with his hands . . . is the one who is going to dominate the affairs of this world. . . ."[17]

Similar statements came from Frank A. Vanderlip, president of the National City Bank of New York; John D. Rockefeller, Jr.; Elbert H. Gary, chairman of the United States Steel Corporation; and Thomas L. Chadbourne, counsel for Midvale Steel and Ordnance Corporation.[18] The most significant statement came from President Wilson in his message to Congress on May 20, 1919. He asserted that industrial democratization was predicated upon the "full recognition of the right of those who work, in whatever rank, to participate in some organic way in every decision which directly affects their welfare or the part they are to play in industry."[19]

It is not surprising then that workers looked forward to an era of "democracy in industry" in which labor would enjoy not only a decent standard of living and the recognition of its right to bargain collectively, but also a stronger voice in industrial affairs. It soon became evident, however, despite all their eloquent phrases, that employers were determined to operate without unions and with much lower wages than they had granted workers under government pressure and as a patriotic gesture in order to win the war. They made it clear that what they really had in mind for labor all along was the "open shop," and that if workers were to be represented at all, they should be represented by company unions.[20] In short, not only was labor to be denied benefits it had been led to expect during the war years, but the employers were coordinating their efforts to eliminate whatever wartime gains workers had made. Small wonder that a group of steel workers in Steelton, Pennsylvania declared:

During the war we fabricated munitions plants, small arms plants. . . '

We did the work cheerfully, without strikes or trouble of any kind. We were so exhausted after a day's work that we fell asleep at the supper table. We pared to the bone in order to buy Liberty Bonds, to give to the Red Cross and similar organizations. For what? To make the world safe for democracy. . . .

The whole industrial world is in chaos and it is up to the Industrial Kings of America to grant their employees industrial democracy.[21]

The lack of government concern for wage earners was an important factor in the great strike wave of 1919. Returned soldiers, seeking to achieve a better life in peacetime, were often attacked by the armed forces they had recently left. When Anaconda Copper announced that as of February 7, 1919, all wages would be reduced from $5.75 per day to $4.75 per day, the Metal Mine Workers Union (Independent) and the Industrial Workers of the World (IWW) immediately responded with a call to strike. The craft unions joined in a sympathy strike and various veterans' organizations endorsed it. But U.S. troops were rushed into Butte, Montana, and in a number of instances, soldiers patrolling Butte "seized veterans who were picketing and stripped them of their army uniforms." A protest telegram to the War Department read: "Hundreds of returned soldiers home from France among striking miners of Butte—the strikers peacefully picketing which we believe is their legal right. Regular troops this morning arrested returned soldiers and severely bayonetted many—is this authorized by War Department?" The protest was ignored.[22] Indeed, in a special dispatch from Butte, the *New York Times* reported on February 11, 1919 that Major Jones, in charge of the U.S. troops in the city, did not rebuke the soldiers for "the use of the bayonet against strikers," but lectured "discharged soldiers for participating in the strike."

The brutal action led one labor paper to tell the "homecoming soldiers" that "the fight is not ended, that there is a great task ahead . . . and that if the present status is to be held and bettered, all who dream of better things and long for a fairer adjustment will have to join hands and go on fighting."[23]

But in "fighting," labor would find itself handicapped by the fact that the government shed any responsibility it had toward the workers. As David Montgomery points out:

Immediately after Germany signed the armistice . . . industrialists launched a campaign to dismantle the Railway Administration, the War Labor Board, the Fuel Administration, and other regulatory agencies. Their success in getting the Labor Board out of business by June 1919, and returning the railroads to private hands in February 1920 stripped the unions of governmental protection, while business embarked on a militant crusade to roll back the union tide.[24]

When strong appeals for the continuation of the War Labor Board proved unavailing, labor realized that if it were at least to maintain "war standards," it would have to rely solely on its own power.[25]

Black workers felt the special sting of government policy. The House Committee on Appropriations initially approved continued funding of the Division of Negro Economics in the Department of Labor, headed by George Haynes of the National Urban League and Fisk University, along with funds for the Women's Bureau and the U.S. Employment Service. All three agencies were to aid in finding work for the unemployed during the postwar job crisis, but funds for all three were excluded from the House Sundry Civil Appropriations Bill on a point of order raised by Rep. Thomas L. Blanton (D-Texas). The Senate restored the funds for the Women's Bureau and the Employment Service, but not for the Negro Economics office, even though Black workers were suffering the most from postwar unemployment at a time of rising living costs.

The Senate, like the House, had been convinced by Rep. Blanton's argument, in which he bitterly denounced the Division of Negro Economics for having sent Black organizers into Georgia, Alabama, Mississippi, and the Carolinas "to unionize colored domestic workers and farm hands and to encourage them to demand wages ranging from $75 to $100 a month for only seven to eight hours of work per day." Blanton also charged these organizers with stirring up domestic workers against their employers, the "best friends the Negroes ever had on God's given earth." Determined not to sanction any expenditures for the purpose of promoting unrest among Black workers, Congress lost all interest in supporting a special agency to deal with the severe problem of Black unemployment. When Secretary of Labor William B. Wilson tried to continue the Division of Negro Economics by including an allowance in the department's budget, Congress eliminated that, too.[26]*

THE INDUSTRIAL CONFERENCE

In a Labor Day message, delivered in the midst of the great strikes of 1919, Wilson announced that he was calling a conference of employers, labor and the public to "discuss fundamental means of bettering the whole

---

*The United States Railroad Administration also abandoned its former policy of upholding the rights of Black workers on the railroads when it capitulated to the white switchmen who went on a wildcat strike demanding that the USRA revise certain work rules "so that Negro switchmen would in effect be barred from their jobs." Rather than risk the spread of the strike, the USRA bowed to the wishes of the racists in the Switchmen's Union of America. (Allen La Verne Shepherd, "Federal Railway Labor Policy, 1913-1926," Unpublished Ph.D. dissertation, [University of Nebraska, 1971], pp. 162-63.)

relationship of capital and labor and putting the whole question of wages upon another footing." He added later that if industrial strife continued, it would be an "invitation to national disaster."[27]

The conference was to be made up of forty-five members. Fifteen public members were to be selected by the President, fifteen labor representatives to be selected by Samuel Gompers, and fifteen representatives of business to be selected in the following manner: five by the National Industrial Conference Board, two by the Investment Bankers' Association, one by the American Society of Equity, one by the National Grange, one by the National Farmers' Union, and five by the U.S. Chamber of Commerce.[28] Later, seven members were added to the public group and four more to the labor group.[29]

Gompers announced the names of fifteen men chosen by the AFL Executive Council to represent organized labor, and four were added later representing the Railroad Brotherhoods. Nine members of the labor delegation were also members of the AFL Executive Council. All nineteen were conservative trade unionists—"the leaders of 'pure and simple' unionism," as Haggai Hurvitz points out in his study of the Conference.[30]

The employers' delegation included James A. Emery of the National Association of Manufacturers, J.W. O'Leary of the National Metal Trades' Association, and executives of great corporations such as Bethlehem Steel, the Dupont companies, General Motors, International Harvester, General Electric, and Standard Oil of New Jersey—all notorious as bastions of anti-unionism. Added to this group were John D. Rockefeller, Jr. and Elbert H. Gary, chairman of the U.S. Steel Corporation, who had been appointed to represent the public interest.[31]

Viewing the composition of the delegations, the *New Republic* commented: "Neither the President's list of delegates nor Mr. Gompers' inspires confidence in the national labor conference that is to be held...."[32] On the other hand, the *New York Times* was most upset by the presence of Charles Edward Russell and John Spargo, former Socialist Party activists who had left the party to support America's entrance into World War I. Both had been appointed by Wilson to the public delegation, which led the *Times* to comment: "It is more than a little curious. . . . Does anyone believe that two-fifths of the public is Socialist? The Socialists are entitled to be heard; but it would have been a grave mistake to open the door to all sorts of private whims and projects."[33]*

---

*The *Times* changed its mind after Spargo submitted a resolution "insisting that the right to strike, while not subject to denial, should not be used to stop vital services or government operations." (*New York Times*, Oct. 16, 1919.)

The Conference opened on October 6, 1919 in the Hall of the Americas of the Pan-American Building in Washington, D.C. Thirteen members of the AFL and four from the Railroad Brotherhoods sat at a table with fifteen members of the employers' group and twenty-five of the public group. Absent were John L. Lewis of the United Mine Workers and Frank Duffy of the Brotherhood of Carpenters and Joiners.[34] A short welcoming address by President Wilson was read on his behalf by the Secretary of Labor.* In it Wilson expressed the hope that the delegates "will make a searching investigation into those ways and means by which peace and harmony have been secured in a large number of our industries that their methods may be extended more universally."[35]

The labor group presented an eleven-point program that included the right to organize in trade and labor unions; the right of workers to representatives of their own choosing; the eight-hour day and one day of rest per week plus overtime pay at time-and-a-half; a living wage for all workers, skilled and unskilled; equal pay for women; prohibition of labor of those under 16 years of age; and restriction of immigration "at least two years after peace shall have been declared."[36]** Fundamentally, the labor delegates sought to achieve a transformation of the wartime right of workers to organize, affirmed by the National War Labor Board, into a permanent principle of American industrial life. This included the Board's declaration that the right of workers to organize "should not be denied or abridged, or interfered with by employers in any manner whatever." Gompers declared that "We shall never again go back to prewar conditions and concepts."[37]

On October 16, a resolution on collective bargaining was introduced by a Committee of Fifteen, which had been appointed to decide for or against all resolutions to be admitted to the Conference, and which was made up of five members from each of the three groups. It read:

> The right of wage earners to organize in trade and labor unions, to bargain collectively, to be represented by representatives of their own choosing in negotiations and adjustments with employers in respect to wages, hours of labor, and relations and conditions of employment is recognized.
>
> This must not be understood as limiting the right of any wage earner to

---

*President Wilson suffered a severe breakdown while on a western tour. The stroke that was to leave him an invalid for the remainder of his life occurred on October 2. (*New York Times,* Oct. 3, 1919.)

**The U.S. did not formally sign a peace treaty with Germany until August 1921.

refrain from joining any organization or to deal directly with his employer, if he so chooses.[38]

To the surprise of the entire Conference, and especially of the labor group, John D. Rockefeller, Jr. supported the resolution. He declared that "representation is a principle which is fundamentally just. . . . This is the principle upon which the democratic government of our country is founded. Surely it is not consistent for us as Americans to demand democracy in government and to practice autocracy in industry." This, coming from the multi-millionaire who had bitterly fought unionism in the Colorado coal strike of 1914 and the Bayonne oil strike of 1916, was indeed surprising. However, Rockefeller revealed that he meant that workers' representatives were to be selected "by the parties concerned in the light of facts in each particular instance," a position opposed by organized labor, which insisted that its members should be permitted to deal with any employer.[39]

In any event, the majority of the employer group not only rejected the resolution, but asserted that under no circumstances would they deal with unions. Indeed, they announced a campaign "to extirpate unionism, root and branch, from the United States and establish the 'open shop' throughout all of industry.[40] Moreover, they demanded that the government not only refuse to revive the National War Labor Board, but also do its part to "curb the unions' drive for additional power."[41]

The employers' spokespersons were supported by telegrams from leading industrialists and corporations demanding that the "open shop be maintained in full vigor."[42] In response to this advice, the employer group submitted a statement of principles that it insisted should govern employment relations in industry. One of these principles was entitled "THE OPEN SHOP" and declared that

> the right of the employer and his men to continue their relations on the principle of the "open shop" should not be denied or questioned. No employer should be required to deal with men or groups of men who are not his employees and chosen by and from among them.[43]

In its statement of principles as well as in a position statement it issued, the employer group did recognize the right of all men to "associate voluntarily," and the right of workers to organize on a shop basis, where the representatives of the workers would be selected from among the plant employees. But under no circumstances would they recognize the right of collective bargaining through trade unions.[44]

It was useless for the labor delegates to warn the employers' representa-

tives that if they destroyed or weakened the AFL and the Railroad Brotherhoods, they would have to face "the Bolsheviki." To the employer delegates, Hurvitz points out, "it was the unions and not a handful of Reds
who posed the real danger to the American system."[45]

As a result of the determination of the employers' representatives to
insist upon the open shop as the only possible solution to the industrial
unrest, it was inevitable that the Industrial Conference would be paralyzed. The Conference broke up after two weeks of debate without passing
a single resolution.[46]*

Two weeks after the breakup, the National Industrial Conference Board,
which had five representatives at the Conference, issued a pamphlet entitled *The Vital Issues in the Industrial Conference at Washington, D.C.* The
conclusion stated:

> "In the final analysis, the stand taken by the Employers' Group was predicated
> on the maintenance of the open shop, which they regarded as a vital American
> principle and which they saw endangered by the adoption of the type of collec-
> tive bargaining insisted upon by the Labor Group."[47]

The failure of the Industrial Conference aggravated the deepening labor-
capital conflict, and, as we shall see, gave strength to the development of a
vigorous open shop movement.

STATUS OF WOMEN WORKERS

Not only were the fifteen labor representatives at the Industrial Conference all men, but not even one of them was the head of a union made up
predominantly or largely of women workers, such as the International
Ladies' Garment Workers' Union or the Amalgamated Clothing Workers.** Yet women played an important role during the wave of postwar
militancy, either as strikers themselves or as allies of their striking husbands, sons, and other male relatives. In both cases, they revealed that the
war experience had had the effect of raising their consciousness as to the
material basis of their oppression. Having found employment in the factories or as office workers in the rapidly expanding category of white col-
lar employees, they had also found that they could compete with men as
equals in these areas—and they therefore felt less dependent on male

---

*A fair amount of this time was spent discussing and rejecting a proposal by Samuel Gom-
pers calling for immediate arbitration of the steel strike by the Conference. The employers'
representatives and a number of those from the public group opposed this resolution. (*New
York Times,* Oct. 12, 13, 14, 20, 1919.)

**Two women were present among the public group of twenty-five: Ida Tarbell and Lillian
Wald. (*Survey,* Oct. 15, 1919, pp. 35-36.)

breadwinners. However, their wages rarely equaled the scale received by men for the same work. And they saw more clearly than before what exploitation of women workers at the point of production meant.

Moreover, the postwar rise in the cost of living hit women workers especially hard since their wage scales were so low. In a report on women's wages in 417 factories in New York, the State Industrial Commission revealed that for the *week* reported, 3,305 women, or 10 percent of the 32,881 women on the payrolls, earned less than $6 a week; 6,434 (20 percent) earned less than $8; 11,377 (35 percent) earned less than $10; 17,593 (53 percent) earned less than $12; 22,426 (68 percent) earned less than $14; 10,455 (32 percent) earned $14 or more; and only 2,711 (8 percent) earned $20 or more. Commissions and bonuses were included in earnings, and all data used in the investigation applied to weeks with six working days.

The commission commented that it could not understand how the majority of these workingwomen could maintain decent living standards in view of the prices they had to pay for necessities. This was also the conclusion of a 1919 master's thesis at Columbia University by Elizabeth Rhodes Butler, entitled, "A Study of the Cost of Living in New York City in 1918, as It Affects the Low-Wage Working Women." After discovering from a study of the classified weekly earnings of New York City workingwomen that "there are more girls [*sic*] grouped under wages between $10 to $12 than in any other category," the author concluded: "The astonishing fact is that there should be any who are able to cope with the difficulties such incomes presented."[48]

Women were angered by the failure of the government to fulfill its wartime pledges. Many had worked in war industries and had become financially independent of men for the first time in their lives. They felt deep resentment toward a government that had urged them to abandon home and the traditional women's occupations to help win the war, only to advise them, when the war was over, to return to their subordinate role as housewives.[49]

Women workers fought back on their own, or in conjunction with male workers. Indeed, one of the features highlighted in press coverage of the 1919 strikes was the "class solidarity" demonstrated by male and female workers—a feature "heretofore rarely present in our labor struggles."[50] Many newspapers commented on the militancy of women strikers. For example, one hundred scrubwomen employed at the Mutual Life Insurance building in New York City struck for shorter hours on July 21, 1919, "and at 4:30 o'clock in the afternoon threatened to storm the building with sticks and stones asserting

that strikebreakers had been hired to take their places." A reserve police force
was rushed to the building, whereupon the scrubwomen turned their weapons
on the scab protectors. Several women were arrested, but the building owners
granted their demand for shorter hours.[51]

An outstanding example of women's militancy and solidarity was contributed by Helen Keller, who was scheduled to speak at the Lyric Theater
in New York City on August 18, 1919, at the premiere of a motion picture
depicting her triumph over the childhood disease that had left her deaf,
blind, and mute.* Helen Keller refused to appear because the theater was
connected with the Producing Managers' Association, against which the
Actors' Equity Association was on strike for recognition and better conditions. "I would rather have the picture fail," she declared, "than consent
to aid the managers directly or indirectly." Instead, she spoke to the
strikers and rode in the automobile heading the strikers' parade down
Broadway, signifying by her presence that "she favored the cause of the
actors." She also favored the cause of the chorus girls who were in the
parade line and had been organized as a special branch of Actors'
Equity.[52]

The first victory in the actors' strike of 1919 was won by the chorus
girls. On August 30 the management of the Hippodrome granted all their
demands. It immediately "raised the minimum pay of chorus girls from
$25 to $35 a week, and recognized the right of Actors' Equity Association
to bargain collectively." On September 6, the victory was completed: the
management agreed to all of Equity's demands, covering actors, actresses,
and chorus girls, and including union recognition.[52]**

As we shall see, there were also several major strikes in 1919 in which
women played an important role.

THE NEW UNIONISTS

As early as December 17, 1918, the *Literary Digest* pointed out that
"beginning with the *Wall Street Journal* and ending with the San Diego

---

*Although she could not speak clearly, Helen Keller did learn to talk and often addressed
meetings in a voice that one who heard her described as "indescribable." (Hattie Schlossberg
in New York *Call*, May 4, 1913, reprinted in Philip S. Foner, editor, *Helen Keller: Her
Socialist Years*, [New York, 1967], p. 9.)

**The demands included wage scales of $30 a week in New York and $35 on tour, based on
eight performances a week, and *pro rata* payment for any performances in excess of that
number. The performers agreed to rehearse for four weeks without charge, but they
demanded half-pay for the next two weeks of rehearsal and full payment thereafter. They also
asked for Pullman berths for chorus girls while traveling. (*New York Times*, Aug. 18, Sept.
7, 1919.)

Union, a considerable proportion of the American press is convinced that 'the rocks of Bolshevism loom menacingly ahead.'"[53] Soon the press would be explaining the rash of strikes in 1919 as the consequence of revolutionary agitation aimed at the overthrow of the government and the establishment of Bolshevism in the United States. Although a series of bombing outrages throughout the country coincided with the 1919 strikes and were used to further the charge of "Bolshevism," in reality the alarms reflected the fears in economic ruling circles that the great strike wave had inspired significant new currents of radical thought among workers, especially those in the large group of immigrants. The membership of the trade unions had doubled between 1915 and 1920, and this unprecedented growth had occurred mainly among the unskilled and semiskilled, a high percentage of them immigrants, in such previously unorganized industries as meatpacking, clothing, textiles, and metal trades.[54]

These new unionists considered their labor unions as more than bargaining agents within the prevailing capitalist system. They viewed them as primary instruments for fundamental change.[55] Such phrases as "workers' control" and "the democratization of industry" were voiced in these circles,[55] and the view was popular that "workers should take charge of their machines, their workplaces, and their companies, until finally all the means of production were controlled by the working class."[56]

Many strikes of this period were marked by worker determination to achieve more than wage increases and shorter hours.[57] Strikers at meatpacking plants in the midwest appealed to President Wilson to take the factories under federal control if the employers displayed intransigence.[58] The joint call of metal trades councils from the various works of General Electric for a strike included the following objectives: official recognition of the shop committees, reinstatement of laid off employees and planned sharing of the available work, release of all political prisoners, and reconstitution of all delegations to the Paris Peace Conference so that half their members would be workers.[59] Striking copper miners in Butte, Montana were directed by a Workers, Soldiers, and Sailors' Council, while unions in Portland, Oregon joined together in a council whose aim was "to strike the final blow against the capitalist class."[60] Shop committees, hailed as "militant tribunes of the union members and non-members within the firm" spread through American industry.[61] These types of demands had been advanced previously by the syndicalist-oriented IWW, but with the weakening of the Wobblies during and immediately after the war, they were now advanced by workers who were often members of the AFL.[62]

Between January 14 and 17, 1919, representatives of 1,100 unions met in Chicago at the National Labor Congress on the Tom Mooney case.* One delegate reported back to the Central Labor Union of his city that "this was without doubt the most remarkable convention of workers ever recorded in the annals of organized labor. The great majority of the delegates present came direct from the mines, the mills and the shops, members of the rank and file, and the great labor leaders in the country were conspicuous by their absence."[63] They were absent because when they learned that Samuel Gompers did not approve of the Congress, top AFL officials, including most of those from California, did not attend the great meeting.[64]

The National Labor Conference discussed a proposal for a nationwide general strike of all labor organizations in the United States should efforts to free Mooney by federal intervention fail. The general strike was to take place on July 4, 1919, and the conference proposed that "a referendum vote be taken by the rank and file of labor at an early date and that all forces be united for a final and crucial test."[65]

But Gompers was adamantly opposed to the proposal for a general strike. "It would destroy all that American labor has won in fifty years," he told Lucy Robins.[66] Gompers arranged for Secretary of Labor Wilson to speak out against the idea of a general strike at the AFL convention in June 1919. Wilson urged organized labor "to refuse to support the nationwide strike which has been proposed as a protest against the conviction of Thomas Mooney," and echoed Gompers' warning that the strike would destroy labor's wartime gains.[67]

The general strike movement was effectively undermined by Gompers and the top AFL leadership,** but between July 4 and 9, 1919, political strikes swept a number of communities demanding freedom for the imprisoned Tom Mooney. A strike by Illinois coal miners was set off as roving "Crusaders" shut mines in protest against the punishment of earlier Mooney strike participants. It culminated in a convention of insurgent delegates from 141 miners' locals. Dissatisfied with the United Mine Workers' earlier appeal for nationalization of the mines, the convention called for "the mines for the miners."[68]

Many of these workers were influenced by the British shop stewards'

*For a discussion of the Mooney-Billings frame-up, see Philip S. Foner, *History of the Labor Movement in the United States* 7 (New York, 1987): 78-95.

**For the role of Gompers in crushing a move for a general strike in 1916-1917 to free Tom Mooney and Warren K. Billings, see *ibid.*, p.92.

movement,* and by *Labour and the New Social Order,* the manifesto of the British Labor Party for the reconstruction of English society after the war. The manifesto envisioned the creation of a socialist commonwealth and urged specifically that the state recognize its responsibility to prevent unemployment and to provide maintenance for those out of work. It also called for "common ownership of the means of production," the complete overhauling of the taxation system so that the main burden would fall on private business and those with substantial income, and appropriation by the state of all the "surplus wealth" of the nation.[69]

But it was the Bolshevik Revolution in Russia on November 7, 1917 that largely inspired the militancy of the new unionists, especially the immigrant workers.** Many workers in the United States, not only Socialists and Communists, were greatly influenced by this momentous event. Its impact could be seen during many of the 1919 strikes, as strikers came to view the struggles both as battles for union recognition, higher wages, fewer hours, and improved working conditions—and as part of a worldwide revolutionary movement in which they now had a chance to participate. At a meeting during the great Lawrence textile strike of 1919 (which John A. Fitch called "a strike for wages carried on in a revolutionary atmosphere"[70]) a strike leader told workers: "You are fighting for a great cause. . . . You should learn to work together. You should learn the business because you will soon take it over for your own, like the Russians are doing in Russia."[71]

Commenting on the "Great Steel Strike of 1919," the *Nation* observed: "This is no mere squabble over wages and hours and collective bargaining and the open shop. These are the shibboleths, the battle cries, but the real question is, who shall control our steel industry, our mines of coal and iron, our roaring furnaces, our giant steel mills."[72] All this, the *Nation* insisted, was not solely a "Soviet inspired event" proving the existence of the "insidious Bolshevik menace," but the result of new radical thinking among workers in the United States, particularly the foreign-born.[73] In an

*The shop stewards' movement made the shop the unit of industrial representation. Under this plan, each workshop would set up a committee whose function was to confer with the employer about production and the conditions of labor. Decisions were to be arrived at in a "democratic" manner. (Leland Olds, "The 'Temper' of British Labor," *Nation* 108 [April 19, 1919]: 803.)

**David Montgomery achieves the near impossible when he discusses the militant strikes of 1919 without once mentioning the impact of the Bolshevik Revolution. His only mention of Russia is in the proposal of progressive AFL leaders to "trade with revolutionary Russia and Mexico." ("Immigrants, Industrial Unions, and Social Reconstruction in the United States, 1916-1923," *Labour/Le Travail* 13 [Spring, 1984]: 101-13.)

address to the 1919 AFL convention, Margaret Bondfield, a delegate from
the British Trade Union Congress, noted that the outlook of the strikes in
the United States and England was characterized more by "the determination of labor to challenge the whole existing structure of capitalistic industry, than in the more special and smaller grievances which come to the
surface at any particular time." Like British workers, U.S. workers
seemed to be "penetrated with the Bolshevik idea."[74]

THE PLUMB PLAN

To many spokespersons for big business, concrete evidence of this trend
was the "revolutionary" Plumb Plan championed by the usually conservative Railroad Brotherhoods. It was drawn up in 1919 by Glenn E. Plumb,
a Chicago attorney who represented various labor unions, including rail
unions, and who was a great admirer of the Bolshevik Revolution and the
nationalization of industries and resources in Russia.

Plumb urged that the United States follow Russia's example and nationalize its major industries, but he was willing to limit the action to the railroads. Plumb realized that the Railroad Brotherhoods were growing
increasingly alarmed that return of the railroads to private industry would
threaten the gains they had achieved during the wartime government operations, so he proposed to them a plan under which all railroad property
would be purchased by the federal government through an issue of United
States bonds.[75] The property would then be leased to a national corporation created for the express purpose of running the nation's railroad system. From its operating income, the corporation was to pay rental fees to
the government. A fifteen-member board of directors, divided equally
among representatives of the public, management and labor, would manage the enterprise. The Interstate Commerce Commission would be
retained, along with its rate-fixing powers. One-half of annual net earnings would be divided among classified employees and the other half
would be retained by the corporation for investments and the improvement
of railroad facilities. Labor disputes were to be settled by a central wage
board, with appeal to the board of directors in case the wage board failed
to reach an agreement.[76]

The Plumb Plan was attractive to the Brotherhoods because it represented a way of preventing the railroads from forcing unfavorable
revisions in work rules and procedures that had been achieved during wartime. This fear was strengthened when the Cummins Bill was introduced
in the Senate on September 2, 1919, providing for return of the railroads
to private enterprise and effecting a ban on strikes by railroad workers

through compulsory arbitration.* The Plumb Plan also appealed to the railroad workers because it would enable them to participate directly in the management of the carriers and to have a voice in the policy-making that would directly affect them. In short, the unions "would gain a direct participation in the nation's railroad system."[77]

Actually, the railroad workers, both in the Brotherhoods and the AFL unions, wanted to go beyond the Plumb Plan, and called upon Congress to accept a plan for government ownership and "operation of railroads by workers." In a brief submitted to the Senate Interstate Commerce Commission in February 1919, the four Railroad Brotherhoods, the AFL Railway Employes' Department, the Brotherhood of Maintenance of Way Employes and Trackmen, and the Order of Railway Telegraphers—14 organizations representing approximately 1,900,000 workers—urged the adoption of a plan under which a federal corporation would take and operate the railroads under the full regulatory power of the government, to whom it would account for all its operations and expenditures. The corporation would be managed by a board of directors, two-thirds of which would represent the workers and one-third would be men appointed by the President of the United States. The earnings of the corporation would be paid to the labor which it employed. Thus the proposal, said the brief, would

> supplant the old system of competition under which the profits of the laborer's industry went to another, and in which he could never hope to share, by a new system where the profit of his industry accrued to himself alone.[78]

But it soon became clear that this proposal stood no chance of being adopted, so, with the exception of the Trainmen, the Railroad Brotherhoods enthusiastically endorsed the Plumb Plan. So did other labor organizations. The Wisconsin Federation of Labor and the United Mine Workers supported it, while the Ohio State Federation not only did the same, but called for nationalization of the telegraph lines, the merchant marine, the coal mines, and oil production as well.[79] To the surprise of many and the discomfiture of Samuel Gompers, the 1920 AFL convention, after a year of discussion, put its stamp of approval on the Plumb Plan. Gompers at-

*The bill passed the Senate, but in the House the anti-strike provision was dropped. The Esch-Cummins Bill, or Transportation Act of 1920, provided for a United States Labor Board of nine members—three each representing the public, labor, and the railroads—to hold hearings on disputes concerning wages, grievances, rules, and working conditions voluntarily brought before it. Railroad workers were not prohibited from striking nor the companies form engaging in lockouts. (*Congressional Record*, 66th Congress, 2nd Session, pp. 3316, 3350.)

tempted to prevent endorsement with the argument that the right to strike would disappear in a nationalized railroad industry. But the fact that the Cummins Bill—which proposed that the railroads be returned to private interests—also called for a ban on strikes by railroad workers, weakened his argument. And for once the Gompers machine failed, and the AFL convention endorsed the Plumb Plan. In fact, the Railway Employees Department of the AFL became one of the main supporters of the Plan.[80]

A group of diverse elements, including the railway unionists, AFL members, Socialists, the Public Ownership League, independent reformers such as Frederick C. Howe, Amos Pinchot, and George L. Record, and radical farmers, members of the Non-Partisan League and the Farmers' National Council, began to work together in support of the Plumb Plan. Many were interested only in nationalization of the railroads, but others saw the Plan as a first step that would establish a model for the steel industry, utilities, coal mines, and oil production. The Socialist New York *Call* predicted that "nothing less than the foundations of private ownership of every public industry are menaced by the Plumb plan. . . ."[81]

To publicize the Plumb Plan, a newspaper, *Railroad Democracy* [soon renamed *Labor*] was established and distributed to members of the newly formed Plumb Plan League. The League sold annual memberships for one dollar to finance the campaign to win supporters for the Plan and to influence Congress to enact the necessary legislation.[82] In advertisements in the labor, liberal, and radical press, the League asked: "Is it Worth, ONE DOLLAR to You to have the Railroads of the United States Operated Not For *Private Profit* But For *Public Service?*" This was followed with the assertion that "The Plumb Plan League Proposes that the Railroads Shall Be Managed by Human Beings for Human Beings, and Not Solely for Money." Samuel Gompers was listed as honorary president, and Warren S. Stone, Chief Engineer, Brotherhood of Locomotive Engineers, as president.[83]

But the campaign immediately ran into the "Red scare." The enemies of the Plumb Plan—leading corporation spokesmen and major newspapers and magazines—tarred it with the stigma of Bolshevism. "Bolshevism, pure and simple," cried the New York *Sun*. According to the *New York Times*, it was "a very long step toward the principles of Lenine [*sic*] and Trotsky and of *Soviet* government." A group of Boston businessmen passed resolutions characterizing the Plumb Plan as "the most serious menace to the welfare of the nation of any legislation presented to Congress since we became a republic."[84]

When Glen Plumb, testifying before the House Commerce Committee on August 7, 1919, admitted to admiring the Bolshevik plan for national-izing resources in Russia, and followed this up with the statement: "My God, if we can't get this plan there's going to be a revolution," the anti-Red maniacs had a field day. Republican Rep. Everett Sanders of Indiana cried out that the Plan was aimed at "the soviet control of industry." Dem-ocratic Sen. Atlee Pomerene of Ohio charged that the Plan "has nothing akin to it outside of Bolshevik Russia. It is worse than socialism." The Republican Club of Detroit resolved that " the railroad brotherhoods' sug-gestions are entirely along class lines and their demands carry a threat of revolution."[85]

On August 2, 1919, in the midst of the Red scare and the labor mili-tancy that was sweeping the United States, Rep. Thetus W. Sims of Ten-nessee introduced a bill to put the Plumb Plan into effect. It was promptly referred to Chairman John J. Esch's Commerce Committee where it died without receiving serious consideration.[86]

In 1920, the leaders of the Railroad Brotherhoods and Railroad shop-men's unions polled their members' views on the Plumb Plan. Ninety per-cent of those polled voted to strike to force Congressional enactment of the nationalization plan.[87] But nothing came of the whole operation because of the increasingly reactionary climate in Washington.

CHAPTER 2

The Setting II:
Red Scare and Red Summer

While a Siberian Expeditionary Force was dispatched from the United States as part of an international endeavor to overthrow the Soviet government, a Red Scare was unleashed in the United States. At the height of the Red Scare, Thomas H. West, the well-known labor poet, published his version of what lay behind the unprecedented hysteria:

The Bolshevist Breeders
The Bolshevist breeders are busy, it seems.
In trying to further their underhand schemes.
Though wealthy, they're anxious to pile up some more.
Meanwhile keeping the wolf at the workingman's door.
They oppose every movement the workers uphold.
They bribe everybody they can with their gold.
It is they and their methods make Bolshevism grow
These are facts which the world is beginning to know.

The Bolshevist breeders are big profiteers.
For the laws of the land they have nothing but jeers.
When they furnish the music the law-makers dance,
And bills for the workingmen don't stand a chance.
They're the real labor crushers, who grab for it all,
Making life for the workers as bitter as gall.
If with torment and trouble the world is aflame.
The Bolshevist breeders are surely to blame.[1]

Another poem pointed out that the Red specter was used not only as a union-busting and strikebreaking device but also as a weapon against all forms of liberalism, and that allegations of "bolshevism" were used to counter any attempt at reform:

> *You believe in votes for women? Yah!*
> *The Bolsheviki do.*
> *And shorter hours? And land reforms?*
> *They're Bolshevistic too.*
> *"The Recall" and other things like that,*
> *are dangerous to seek;*
> *Don't tell me you believe 'em or I'll*
> *call you Bolshevik!*
> *Bolshevik! veek! veek!*
> *A reformer is a freak!*
> *But here's a name to stop him, for it's*
> *like a lightning streak.*[2]

HYSTERIA

Reinforced by the press and a combination of business groups and superpatriotic societies, the anti-Red crusade claimed that the labor uprising of 1919 was essentially the product of left-wing ideologies sown by the Bolshevik Revolution and borne into the American labor movement by "outside agitators" who had their greatest influence among the foreign-born workers. When Robert W. Dunn and Evan Thomas (brother of Norman Thomas) attempted to establish a local of workers in Paterson affiliated with the Amalgamated Textile Workers of America, they immediately came up against the Red Scare. "We had scarcely signed the lease on the union office," Dunn recalled, "when the local silk manufacturers snapped their fingers and the police raided the place, closed it down and threw us into the Paterson jail along with two leading silk workers. The formal indictment against us was that we had conspired to overthrow the government of the State of New Jersey. The 'evidence' was that the first national convention in the new union a few months before had sent fraternal greetings to the textile union of Soviet Russia—a typical solidarity message of workers in one country to those of another."[3]

In a full-page advertisement in the *Toledo Blade* of May 9, 1919, the Merchants and Manufacturers Association, the banks of Toledo, and the local Kiwanis and Rotary clubs explained the strike of auto workers employed by the Willys Overland Company for a wage increase and a 44-hour week as follows:

Outside agitators, having no interest in the welfare of our city or our citizens are seeking to stir up trouble in the ranks of labor, harass and interfere with the production of our factories and by their revolutionary doctrine, ferment in the minds of many misguided foreigners a class hatred and a disregard for all law and authority.

The strike of 6,000 auto workers was defeated as a result of a restraining order issued by Judge Killits, which was expanded into a permanent injunction. It limited the number of pickets to 150, only 50 of whom could be used at one time. It further stated, for the first time in U.S. labor history, that all pickets had to be citizens of the United States. The injunction was enforced by hundreds of former soldiers sworn in as policemen by the mayor of Toledo. The soldier-police arrested and imprisoned many of the pickets on the ground that they were foreign born and had thus violated the injunction. The fact that a picket looked Polish was enough to cause his arrest.[4]

Late in April 1919, newspapers all over the country headlined "Reds Planning to Overthrow U.S. on May Day." The American Legion announced that it had information pointing to a revolution that would follow May Day demonstrations. The scare was intensified on the eve of May Day by the discovery of bombs in some post offices, said to be addressed to thirty-six wealthy individuals. The *Liberator,* a left-wing Socialist journal, charged that the so-called May Day bombs were "a frame-up by those who are interested in 'getting' the leaders of radicalism, and feel the need of a stronger public opinion before they can act." But A. Mitchell Palmer, Attorney-General of the United States, charged that the bombs were part of a "Bolshevik plot" to overthrow the government on May Day. "Reds Plan May Day Murders," blared the headlines in the nation's press.[5]

Despite threats, radicals and unionists staged rallies, held mass meetings, and conducted parades on May 1. In Boston the police attacked 1500 marchers in a parade sponsored by the Lettish Workmen's Association, and during a battle in which the police were aided by a mob of bystanders, one police officer was mortally stabbed and one civilian was wounded. Mobs then proceeded to demolish the Boston Socialist headquarters while vigilantes all over the city went on a rampage against Socialists. Ultimately 116 May Day paraders were arrested, charged with rioting and resisting the police. Fourteen were found guilty of disturbing the peace and sentenced to prison terms ranging from six to eighteen months. Not a single member of the mob was arrested.[6]

In Detroit, where 12,000 workers were on strike, the police stopped the workers from holding a parade. In Chicago too the police stopped a May

Day demonstration. In New York no parade was permitted, but a May Day rally was held in Madison Square Garden as a Tom Mooney protest meeting.[7] Signs around the Garden read: "We demand freedom for our Comrade Tom Mooney" and "We demand freedom for our Comrade Eugene V. Debs."[7]*

Headlines in the press on May 2, 1919, read: "Soldiers and Sailors Break Up Meetings in New York." The reference was to the attacks on the Russian People's House, and the offices of the New York *Call*, the Socialist daily, by 400 soldiers and sailors (aided by some civilians). The mob confiscated literature and smashed office furniture. At the Russian People's House the vigilantes forced the May Day gathering to sing the "Star Spangled Banner," and at the *Call's* office they broke up a May Day reception of 700 people, and drove them into the street with such violence that seventeen had to receive first aid.[8]

The anti-May Day rioting reached its peak in Cleveland. A peaceful parade, led by Charles E. Ruthenberg, left-wing Socialist leader, was halted by a mob led by an army lieutenant, who demanded that the soldier leading the parade drop his red flag. When the paraders refused, the lieutenant tore the flag from the soldier's hands, and during the mob attack that followed, twenty Socialists were injured. More than 20,000 workers continued the parade to the public square where they were augmented by thousands more. Here the police and more vigilantes attacked several Socialist soldiers who refused to surrender the red flags they wore on the breasts of their uniforms. Five demonstrators were so severely beaten that they "required treatment by ambulance surgeons."[9]

The Socialist Party headquarters were then raided and completely wrecked by the mob of soldiers and civilians. By the time the raids had ended, one person was killed, over fifty were wounded, and 106 Socialists were arrested and charged with responsibility for the riots. Not a single soldier or civilian vigilante was arrested.[10] The following report, published in the *New York Times* on May 3, 1919, reveals the hysteria that was sweeping the nation:

> Federal troops with two machine-gun companies, equipped with motor trucks, were mobilized outside of Cleveland to suppress any disorder resulting from the Socialist May Day demonstration in the event the police proved incapable to cope with it.

As might be expected, the *Times* justified this action with the argu-

---

*For opposing U.S. entrance into World War I, Debs was sentenced to twenty years in federal prison.

ment that the May Day demonstrators were "foreign-agitators" acting on behalf of the Bolsheviks in Russia.[11] The fact that May Day had originated in the United States in 1886* was of no consequence!

The charge of foreign influence was made in every 1919 strike. The instigators were always characterized as either foreigners or of foreign-born parentage, who operated as agents of a seemingly worldwide Communist upheaval and represented a threat to American life.[12] Denver Rabbi William S. Friedman returned from touring the Eastern states to warn that "the greatest and gravest crisis" in American history was at hand, and that unless something was done to quell the industrial unrest, chaos was sure "to descend upon us" within our own borders as "Bolshevism and the possibility of a Soviet regime endangered the nation."[13] General Leonard Wood offered a solution to the danger: Here was how he would deal with the Reds:

> S.O.S.—ship or shoot. I believe we should place them on all on ships of stone, with sails of lead and that their first stopping place should be hell. We must advocate radical laws to deal with radical people.[14]

And the anti-Red mania did produce a whole series of laws against these supposed foreign "Bolsheviks" and their "native-American dupes." Several states passed new and stronger versions of the criminal syndicalist statutes, providing for harsher punishment for persons associating with organizations advocating "the doctrines of criminal syndicalism," while these and other states passed a "Red flag law" which usually stated that

> . . . the displaying of the Red Flag, the emblem of anarchy, in public, or in any place where the public tends to congregate . . . tends to foment and cause trouble . . . encourages riots and lawlessness and inculcates disrespect for the laws of the United States . . . as well as for the Flag of our Country, and thus endangers the peace and safety of our people. . . .

Violators would be guilty of a felony, the penalty for which was usually from one to ten years in prison.[15]

"DEPORTATION DELIRIUMS"

Under the existing immigration law, deportation of undesirable immigrants was the responsibility of the Immigration Bureau, which arrested and tried the immigrants. The Commissioner General of Immigration

*See Philip S. Foner, *May Day: A Short History of the International Workers' Holiday 1886-1986* (New York, 1986), pp. 3-49.

reported his findings to his superior, the Secretary of Labor, who made the final decision. The alien had no right to appeal the decision to any higher authority.

As we saw in our preceding volume, after the United States entered World War I in 1917 the right of free speech and expression was sharply curtailed by the Espionage and Sedition Acts. War critics, pacifists, draft resisters, and socialists were arrested, prosecuted, and jailed for violations of these repressive laws. When the cases of IWW aliens reached him for review, Secretary of Labor Wilson ruled that membership in the IWW alone was not sufficient grounds for deportation. Wilson held that individual acts in violation of the immigration law would be the only criteria used to determine the fate of the alien held for deportation.[16]

Angered and frustrated by the release of two-thirds of the Wobblies arrested, the Immigration Bureau and the Justice Department drafted and supported the Immigration Act of 1918, which for the first time in U.S. history made membership in radical organizations a deportable offense. "The membership provision alone," William Preston writes, "made possible the mass character of the red raids of 1919."[17]*

PALMER RAIDS

In June 1919, following a series of bombings at the homes of Attorney General Palmer and other government officials, the Senate pressed the Justice Department to investigate charges of a conspiracy to overthrow the government. Congress appropriated funds for comprehensive investigations of radical activities. Palmer reported that on August 1, 1919, a General Intelligence Division (GID) of the Bureau of Investigation was formed "with the purpose in view of collecting evidence and data upon the revolutionary and ultradical groups." Palmer appointed J. Edgar Hoover, a young clerk with the Bureau, as head of the GID. Hoover's immediate task was to organize the anti-radical division of the Bureau. For this purpose he set up a master file of all radical activities which, Palmer reported, "makes it possible to determine or ascertain in a few minutes the numerous ramifications or individuals connected with the ultra-radical movement."

*Two years later, Congress passed the Immigration Act of 1920 which the chairman of the Senate Committee on Immigration, Sen. Thomas R. Hardwick, "proposed restricting immigration as a means of keeping out Bolshevism." Fusing racist theories of Anglo-Saxon superiority with anti-Bolshevik hysteria, the law aimed to encourage Anglo-Saxon immigration from Central and Northern Europe, and to discourage immigration from Southern and Eastern Europe. A quota system was instituted that would admit to the U.S. annually a number of immigrants from any country equal to no more than three percent of the total already part of the U.S. population in 1910.

By the end of 1919 Hoover, Palmer, and Commissioner General of Immigration Anthony J. Camminetti had developed elaborate procedures for dealing with the "Red Menace." These included sudden and simultaneous dragnet raids, secret testimony from undercover agents and informants, seizure of correspondence, mailing lists, and membership cards, cross-examination of aliens without the presence of defense lawyers, and detention of radicals incommunicado with excessive or no bail.[18]

The first application of these procedures came in December 1919 when 240 deportees—aliens and suspected anarchists, including Emma Goldman and Alexander Berkman—were deported on the U.S. Transport *Buford* (called the "Soviet Ark") from Ellis Island in New York to Finland to preserve "America and the human race." On January 10, 1920, while aboard the *Buford*, Emma Goldman and Alexander Berkman wrote in a letter that the deportation had been surrounded by secrecy and had taken place during the darkness of night.

> To be sure, the Government could not afford to take us from Ellis Island in broad daylight. The condition of the first group of American deportees, most of them destitute and half naked, among them a number who had been rushed to Ellis Island direct from the jails of Buffalo, Detroit, Youngstown, Bridgeport, etc., and arrived only a few hours before their deportation, would have aroused the indignation of even the most callous American citizen. The Government, which waxed so indignant over the German atrocities in Belgium, did not dare to let the people see that it was committing similar atrocities at home, on people more helpless and defenseless than the Belgians were. It did not dare. Therefore our kidnapping in the dead of night, in mad haste, with a military force armed for murder and bloodshed at the least provocation.[19]

On December 31, 1919, while Secretary of Labor Wilson was ill and absent from Washington,* "acting" Secretary John Abercrombie signed three thousand warrants for the arrest of aliens throughout the nation, charging them with membership in the Communist Party or Communist Labor Party.

On the night of January 2, 1920, agents of the Bureau of Investigation, with the aid of local police, arrested 10,000 "members" of the Communist and Communist Labor parties in simultaneous raids throughout the country. During these operations scant attention was paid to legal proce-

*Many contemporaries argued that Secretary of Labor Wilson left Washington because he did not want to interfere with the hysterical attacks on aliens, but W. Anthony Gengarelly, who is very critical of Wilson's early approval of these vicious tactics, insists that he was actually ill. ("Secretary of Labor William B. Wilson and the Red Scare, 1919-1920," *Pennsylvania History*, [Oct., 1980] pp. 325-27.)

dure. Behind banner headlines like "2000 Reds Arrested in 56 Cities . . .," one atrocity after another was perpetrated on the men and women rounded up during the dragnet operations. It was days before a suspect alien was permitted access to counsel or friends, and it was weeks before the case was decided. Meanwhile, the victim languished in jail, unable to raise bond money that ranged close to $10,000.[20]

Newly opened records in the National Archives reveal that many persons not affiliated with Communist parties and not mentioned in arrest warrants were seized simply because they "had attended lawful and political and social functions that (J. Edgar) Hoover and his staff regarded as subversive."* In Nashua, New Hampshire, for example, 141 men and women were arrested at a Socialist party rally. In Manchester, Bureau of Investigation agents arrested everyone at a dance sponsored by the "Tolstoi Club." They were taken to the Manchester police station where immigration inspectors tried "to connect them with the warrants." Sedar Serachuch, one of those arrested in New Hampshire, asked the agent to show his warrant. Serachuch later testified: "He showed me his fist, and said, 'This is your warrant,' and continued to search the room."[21]

Evidence obtained in the raids supposedly proved the existence of the most "menacing revolutionary plot yet uncovered;" fortunately, according to the Department of Justice, it was nipped in the bud at the right time.[22] In general, the press accepted this ludicrous statement and applauded the raids. On January 5, 1920, three days after the raids, the *New York Times* exclaimed: "If some or any of us, impatient for the swift confusion of the Reds have ever questioned the alacrity, resolute will, and fruitful, intelligent vigor of the Department of Justice in hunting down these enemies of the United States, the questioners and doubters now have cause to approve and applaud."

But there were dissenting voices. On January 12, 1920, Francis Fisher Kane, the United States Attorney for eastern Pennsylvania, resigned in protest against the arrests. In an open letter to the Attorney General, Kane warned Palmer that "the policy of raids against large numbers of individuals is generally unwise and very apt to result in injustice." Raising their voices collectively to criticize the actions of the Justice Department, a loose coalition of lawyers, labor organizers, union members, Congress-

---

*In 1977 the National Archives acquired the investigative records, 1908-1922, of the Federal Bureau of Investigation (FBI). The file includes field agents' reports, summaries of various investigations, and intradepartmental and interdepartmental memorandums. (*See* "Accessions and Openings," *Prologue* 9 [Spring 1977]: 48; James Gregory Bradsher, "Historians, Archivists, and the FBI's Archives," *OAH Newsletter* [August 1986]: 9-12.)

men, and journalists led the opposition to the deportation raids.[23] The right to free speech and assembly is fundamental to American constitutional government, declared the *Nation,* and the Justice Department had subverted these constitutional guarantees during the raids.[24] The *New Republic* compared the raids to the witchhunts of the seventeenth century, and charged that "the nation, solid and imperturbable, has been wracked by persecution, by cowardice, by mistrust. Its great problems are postponed; its great tasks are undone; its houses turned into bedlam, the humble oppressed, its ideals flouted and the light it held to the oppressed of mankind extinguished."[25]

In May 1920, the National Popular Government League published a documentary account of the raids entitled *To the American People: Report Upon the Illegal Practices of the Unites States Department of Justice.* A group of twelve lawyers, including some of the most respected jurists in the United States, signed the pamphlet, which was a devastating condemnation of the Attorney General, and accused the Justice Department agents of illegal search and seizure, "third degree" torture, and subversion of the judicial process.[26]*

The violations of civil liberties committed during the raids were ignored by Secretary of Labor Wilson, but were successfully challenged by Louis F. Post, Assistant Secretary of Labor in charge of deportations.** Post was convinced that the government's assault on the immigrant population "was an unnecessary suppression of basically innocent and hard-working Americans." He wrote in his diary on January 1, 1920:

> At present . . . there are signs of an overthrow of our government. It is going on under the vigorous drive against "anarchists," an "anarchist" being anybody who objects to government of the people by Tories and financial interests.[27]

On April 10, Post went public and commented on what his study of several hundred cases had revealed. He released to the press his findings in a case involving a Polish clothes presser, Thomas Truss. Post declared that illegal affiliation in this case was nonexistent, and that although Truss was neither a communist nor an anarchist, he had been victimized because

---

*The Justice Department's Bureau of Investigation investigated the League, its officers and financial backers and compiled dossiers on the twelve lawyers who signed the *Report*. They included Dean Roscoe Pound and professors Felix Frankfurter and Zachariah Chaffee, Jr. of Harvard Law School; Frank P. Walsh and Francis F. Kane.

**Post had been a disciple of Henry George, editing the *Standard*, a single-tax weekly, until 1898 when he founded the *Public*, a progressive journal published in Chicago through 1920

of a bogus membership in a defunct branch of the Communist Party of America. Post then commented on the summary procedures that had attended the several hundred cases he had determined over the past month:

> As a rule, the hearings show the aliens arrested to be workingmen of good character who had never been arrested before, who are not anarchists or revolutionaries, not politically or otherwise dangerous in any sense. Many of them, as in this case, have American-born children. It is pitiful to consider the hardships to which they and their families have been subjected . . . by arbitrary arrest, long detention in default of bail beyond the means of hard-working wage earners to give, for nothing more dangerous than affiliating with friends of their own race, country, and language, and without the slightest indication of sinister motive or any unlawful act within their knowledge or intention. To permit aliens to violate the hospitality of this country by conspiring against it is something which no American can contemplate with patience. Equally impatient, however, must any patriotic American be with drastic proceedings on flimsy proof to deport aliens who are not conspiring against our laws and do not intend to.[28]

Two days after this public release, on April 12, right-wing Republican Congressman Albert Johnson attacked Post on the House floor, accusing the assistant secretary of usurpation of authority and left-wing sympathies. On April 15 a resolution of impeachment was introduced and referred to the House Rules Committee.[29]

But Post did not lack support. Felix Frankfurter offered him free legal counsel in the upcoming impeachment battle, and most important, Secretary of Labor Wilson, having returned to Washington and changed his position during his absence from supporting to opposing the witch-hunters, extended Post his unqualified support. In this new situation, the reactionary Congressmen retreated and impeachment proceedings against Post were dropped.[30]

Post decided 1,600 cases during his tenure of a little more than a month. He ordered 460 aliens deported and cancelled 1,140 deportations.[31] During his brief tenure, he had halted the "deportation deliriums" and, along with other progressive and labor forces, had alerted the people to the way in which American democracy was being undermined in the interests of, as he had put it, "Tories and financial interests."

BERGER, CONGRESS, AND THE RED SCARE

As we saw in the preceding volume,* in the midst of his campaign for United States Senator from Wisconsin, on March 9, 1918, Victor Berger,

*See Foner, *History of the Labor Movement in the United States* 7:329-31.

the first Socialist Congressman, was indicted for violating the Espionage Act. Although the war was over by then, Berger was tried with four other Socialists on December 9, 1918 in Chicago before Kenesaw Mountain Landis.* They were charged with conspiracy against the war effort. The trial lasted four weeks, and resulted in conviction of the defendants on January 8, 1919. Landis sentenced each of the four to twenty years of imprisonment at Fort Leavenworth, but all were freed in a total bail of $625,000 and the case was appealed to higher courts.

Prior to his conviction, indeed just six days before the armistice was signed, Berger had been elected Congressman from the Fifth District, largely the city of Milwaukee. When he came before Congress on May 9, 1919 to be sworn in, his right to a seat was challenged, and a resolution was passed without dissent suspending Berger from all rights as a member of the House until final action was taken. On October 24, 1919 the committee appointed to hear the charges against Berger reported to the House. An eight-man majority agreed that "Victor Berger . . . did obstruct, hinder, and embarrass the Government of the United States in the prosecution of the war and did give aid and comfort to the enemy," and declared him to be "absolutely ineligible to membership . . . in the House of Representatives. . . ."

On November 10, 1919 the House voted to exclude Berger; the vote was 311 to 1. Like many other papers, the *Baltimore Sun* decried the fact that even one vote had been cast for Berger. The Milwaukee Socialists immediately renominated Berger for Congress in a special election called for December 1919. The Democrats and Republicans fused behind one candidate, to defeat a man "associated with the Bolshevism of Lenin and Trotsky." But a majority of the electorate of the Fifth District voted for Berger.

When Berger appeared before Congress on January 10, 1920, he was again excluded; this time the members refused even to hear him, and by a vote of 330 to 6 barred him from Congress for a second time. But again he was immediately renominated by the Milwaukee County Executive Committee, which issued the statement that "We'll keep on nominating Berger until Hades freezes over if that un-American aggregation, Congress, continues to exclude him."

In 1922 Berger was reelected to Congress. A year before that the Supreme Court had, on a technicality, thrown out his conviction for violating the Espionage Act, and when Berger appeared in Congress in Decem-

---

*Judge Landis had been the presiding judge in the Federal trials of the IWW and on August 31, 1918 handed down the severe sentences against the Wobblies. (*Ibid.*, pp. 310-12.)

ber 1923 to take the oath of office he was warmly welcomed. He was reelected until 1928.[32]

In January 1920 as Berger was being denied his seat in Congress, five New York state assemblymen had their seats challenged. They were excluded in April 1920 solely because of their membership in the Socialist Party.[33]

Nevertheless, the high tide of the Red Scare had passed with the notorious Palmer Raids of January 2, 1920, and more and more communities were joining Milwaukee in expressing their discontent with repression and intolerance.* In January and February, proposals for a peacetime sedition law bogged down in Congress despite lobbying on its behalf by Attorney General Palmer. Later in the spring, Palmer's dire prediction of revolutionary violence on May Day failed to materialize. By the summer of 1920, the Red Scare was just about over.[34]

SACCO AND VANZETTI

The heritage of the madness and persecutions of the Red Scare remained, however, in the form of jail cells filled with political prisoners. Among them were two immigrant Italians, Nicola Sacco and Bartolomeo Vanzetti, the former a skilled factory worker and the latter an itinerant, unskilled laborer and fish peddler. Neither had come to America as a radical, but both were later attracted to anarchism. Both men were involved in strikes and war resistance. In 1917, Sacco, Vanzetti, and other New England anarchists fled to Mexico for a year to avoid the draft and possible deportation for anti-war activities. After Sacco and Vanzetti returned to the United States, they resumed their radical activities.

On April 15, 1920 a robbery took place in South Braintree, Massachusetts. In the course of stealing a $15,000 payroll, the robbers shot and killed the paymaster and his guard. Three weeks later Sacco and Vanzetti were arrested for the crime on a policeman's hunch that anarchists were responsible. They were arrested in Brockton, a shoe factory town, as they were organizing a protest meeting. In Vanzetti's pocket was the Italian text of the announcement of a meeting to be held on May 9. It read (in English translation):

---

*The expulsion of the five Socialist members of the New York State legislature was a factor in the decline of the Red Scare since it aroused widespread public anger. (Thomas E. Vadney, "The Politics of Repression: A Case Study of the Red Scare in New York," *New York History* 45 [January 1968]: 56-75.)

Fellow Workers: You have fought in all the wars. You have worked for all the capitalists. You have wandered over all the countries. Have you harvested the fruits of your labors, the price of your victories? Does the present smile on you? Does the future promise you anything? Have you found a piece of land where you can live like a human being? On these questions, on this argument and on this theme, the struggle for existence, Bartolomeo Vanzetti will speak.[35]

Neither Sacco nor Vanzetti was told the reason for the arrests until many weeks had passed.[36]

Vanzetti had just been to New York, where he had investigated the two-month detention of the Italian anarchist Andrea Salsedo, who had been held incommunicado for over a month by federal agents. After Vanzetti left New York, Salsedo died "falling" from a fourteen-story window. Anarchists believed that Salsedo had been pushed from the Justice Department office.

Vanzetti warned his anarchist comrades that his visit to New York had convinced him that a federal net was closing in on them. Upon learning of Salsedo's death, Sacco and Vanzetti, as well as other anarchists, armed themselves and prepared for arrest and deportation. The Palmer raids were very much on their minds when they were arrested in Bridgewater on May 5, 1920.

The celebrated trial of Sacco and Vanzetti for the South Braintree crimes* began on May 31, 1921 and lasted six weeks. The prosecution presented eyewitnesses and ballistic experts to connect the two men with the crime. The defense presented alibi witnesses and its own ballistics experts, who contradicted the prosecution. The jury found Sacco and Vanzetti guilty, and they were sentenced to death in the electric chair.

Even before the trial, unions in Boston and the surrounding mill towns had protested the arrests, charging that the men were being persecuted for being anarchists and because, as foreign-born radicals, they were viewed as the symbol of evil by self-appointed defenders of "the American way." The labor movement knew from recent experience in the strikes of 1919 that the government, the press, and the business community were indifferent to the civil liberties of anyone who dared to challenge the status quo.*

After the trial and the conviction, the defenders of Sacco and Vanzetti believed that the judge was deeply prejudiced against the anarchists and that the jury was influenced by his prejudice and by the patriotic hysteria that began with World War I and culminated in the Red Scare of 1919-20.[37] In our next volume we will study "the case that will not die," and

*In the first of two trials (the one on May 31, 1921 was the second) Vanzetti was accused of participating in a failed holdup in Bridgewater, Massachusetts on December 24, 1919.

the seven-year ordeal endured by Sacco and Vanzetti before they were executed by the Commonwealth of Massachusetts in 1927 for a crime they did not commit. But we should note here that on August 23, 1977, on the fiftieth anniversary of the real crime in the case of Sacco and Vanzetti, namely, their execution, Governor Michael Dukakis of Massachusetts declared that "any stigma or disgrace should be forever removed" from their names. Yet he refused to assess their guilt or innocence.[38] But in 1985, in *Postmortem: New Evidence in the Case of Sacco and Vanzetti*, William Young and David E. Kaiser established their innocence beyond a reasonable doubt, in an excellent investigation of evidence never before part of any previous evaluation. So after sixty years of scholarly debate about the guilt or innocence of Sacco and Vanzetti, the definitive study has appeared decisively establishing their innocence.[39]

UNIONS AND THE RED SCARE

In the spring of 1919 the Lusk Committee of the New York legislature (named after its chairman, Senator Clayton R. Lusk) was set up to expose "revolutionary activities" of all types, and stamp them out. The committee not only investigated scores of organizations but conducted raids on the socialist Rand School of Social Science and sent spies to cover meetings in Harlem and to disclose activities of Black radicals.[40] In its investigation of the American Federation of Labor, the Lusk Committee found "suspicious tendencies" in certain unions but declared "the policies of Gompers and the national A.F. of L. to be free from the taint of revolutionary radicalism." The committee praised the AFL for declining to form a labor party "as British labor has done."[41]

One large AFL union, however, the International Ladies' Garment Workers' Union, was castigated in the report. "It is organized along industrial lines," declared the committee's report, "and shows marked

---

**The first pamphlet on the Sacco-Vanzetti frame-up, *Are They Doomed?* by Art Shields and illustrated by Robert Minor, appeared before the trial and was widely distributed among trade unionists with "the help of trade union leaders." Shields, a reporter for the commercial press, had been sent to Boston by Elizabeth Gurley Flynn, head of the Workers' Defense League, to write a pamphlet about the case, which was not understood in many circles, and begin a publicity campaign for Sacco and Vanzetti. (Art Shields, *On the Battle Lines, 1919-1939*, New York, 1986, pp.84-87.)

"From the beginning in 1920," Gary R. Mormino and George E. Pozzetta point out, "leftists (in Ybor City, Florida) . . . collected money for defense funds, held rallies, sent telegrams and petitions, and staged protest strikes in support of the two anarchists in Massachusetts." (*The Immigrant World of Ybor City: Italians and Their Latin Neighbors in Tampa, 1885-1985* [Urbana and Chicago, 1987], p. 160.)

radical tendencies . . . it is founded upon the principles of class struggle
. . . it adopts the One Big Union idea and seeks to bring about the overthrow of society." The committee further found that the union was guilty
of un-American education practices in classes held for members of the
ILGWU. "There is a manifest purpose of getting before the membership
of the organization the principles of government and of industrial organization which are the basis of Socialist psychology."[42]

Many AFL leaders hailed the Lusk investigation as proving that, with
the one exception noted, the Federation had been absolved of radicalism.
John Golden, president of the United Textile Workers (whose class-
collaboration policies we noted previously and will meet again below),
congratulated the Lusk Committee "on the splendid work being done . . .
in getting at real facts in connection with the seditious activities of such a
large number of the foreign element." James P. Holland was proud of the
fact that the Lusk Committee cited him in its report because he had testified before the committee that "over" 90,000 AFL members were "Bolsheviks or ultra-radicals."[43]

However, the *Garment Worker,* a fervent supporter of the policies of the
Gompers-AFL Executive Council machine, especially their policy concerning Russia, argued that the Lusk Committee had underestimated the
degree and extent of radicalism in the American labor movement. "We do
not believe," the *Garment Worker* editorialized, "there is a union in any of
our large cities, but that is feeling the influence of revolutionary radicalism. There need be less to fear from hostile employers than from the revolutionary elements in our unions."

This approach was endorsed by J.E. Roach, in charge of the AFL's New
York office, who told David J. Saposs that the Red Scare was beneficial
since "there is no room for radicalism in the labor movement." Roach
pointed to the preamble to the AFL's constitution, adopted in 1881 and
repeated every year thereafter, which emphasized: "A struggle is going on
in all the nations of the civilized world, a struggle between the capitalist and
laborer, which grows in intensity from year to year, and will work disastrous
results to the toiling millions if they are not combined for mutual protection." "It is ridiculous," Roach continued, "to have a preamble calling for
the abolition of the capitalistic system and at the same time expecting to deal
with the employer and also expecting him to improve your condition thereby
helping himself out of business ultimately." "It won't be good for the labor
movement in general to have too many radicals," Roach concluded,
expressing the hope that investigations such as that conducted by the Lusk

Committee would help solve this problem.[44]*

These approaches were sharply criticized by trade unionists and trade union publications for aiding and abetting the anti-union employers. *The Carpenter*, organ of the Brotherhood of Joiners and Carpenters, insisted that the capitalists were attributing social unrest to Bolsheviks in order to advance the Open Shop movement,** and that *"our own unions are accepting and fostering the union hating employers' propaganda."*[45]

No one more effectively tore the curtain aside and revealed the real aims of the Red Scare than did J.G. Wright, president of the Central Labor Union of Kansas City, Missouri, when he said in late February 1919:

> We hear much of late about Anarchists and Bolsheviki. All these laws for the suppression or deportation of the Bolshevists are made by the capitalist class so that when men are ground down to the last notch and strike because they cannot stand it any longer the employer may cry "Bolsheviki" and drive them out of the country.[46]

It is indeed tragic that sections of the labor movement cooperated in these endeavors.

"RED SUMMER"

The summer of 1919, which marked the beginning of the hysterically anti-radical "Red Scare," also witnessed the terrible "Red Summer." When Black intellectual and civil rights leader James Weldon Johnson originated the expression "Red Summer," he was referring to the race riots that bloodied the streets of twenty-five towns and cities throughout the country in the six-month period from April to early October 1919.

Most Afro-Americans had patriotically supported the war "to make the world safe for democracy," and 40,000 had served in the armed forces. There they had met with discrimination and segregation, and when they came home they had to face lynching, Jim Crow, and unemployment caused by the slackening demand for labor during postwar demobilization.

*In his interview with Saposs, Roach delivered a number of attacks on foreign-born workers. "Foreigners as a rule," he declared, "do not make good unionists as they keep themselves isolated and un-Americanized. One of the faults is that they have too many isms. The Jews are the worst offenders, altho it is true of the others also. . . . (I) don't believe in printing anything in foreign language or using foreign language organizers. Foreigners should be forced to learn English. . . ." (Interview with J.E. Roach, in charge of New York office, American Federation of Labor, Feb. 17, 1919, David J. Saposs Papers, State Historical Society of Wisconsin.)

**For a discussion of the relationship between the Red Scare and the Open Shop drive in Ohio, *see* Raymond Boryczka and Lorin Lee Cary, *No Strength Without Union: An Illustrated History of Ohio Workers, 1803-1980* (Columbus, Ohio, 1982): 158-67.

Black veterans who were fortunate enough to find work were given only the most menial and lowest-paid jobs. Even those with college degrees ended up as common laborers.[47]

Some improvements had occurred in the conditions of life for the hundreds of thousands of Black migrants from the agricultural regions of the South to the industrial centers of the North. But these were not sufficient to compensate for the bitter experiences of being herded into Northern ghettoes with crowded, substandard homes, forced to pay exorbitant rents and high food prices, and subjected to continuing discrimination on the job and in everyday life. The 1919 report of the Research Bureau of the Associated Charities of Detroit told a typical story:

> There was not a single vacant house or tenement in the several Negro sections of the city. The majority of Negroes are living under such crowded conditions that three or four families in an apartment is the rule rather than the exception. Seventy-five percent of the Negro homes have so many lodgers that they are really hotels. Stables, garages and cellars have been converted into homes for Negroes. The pool rooms and gambling clubs are beginning to charge for the privilege of sleeping on pool tables overnight.[48]

When Blacks sought to break out of the ghettoes and achieve a better life, they were subjected to attacks, lynchings, and race riots in both North and South. Lynch mobs murdered seventy-eight Black people in 1919, an increase of fifteen over 1918 and thirty over 1917.[49]

The first of the race riots of the Red Summer erupted in Charleston, South Carolina on May 10, and when it was over, two Black men were dead and seventeen Blacks and eight whites were wounded. Then race violence exploded in Longview, Texas; Washington, D.C.; Knoxville, Tennessee; Phillips County, Arkansas; Omaha, Nebraska; and, worst of all, Chicago.[50]

On a Sunday afternoon, July 27, with the temperature in the 90's, a group of white bathers at one of the Chicago city beaches stoned a Black youth, Eugene Williams, causing him to drown. Outraged Blacks, whose patience had been stretched thin by a series of anti-Negro actions since early spring, insisted that a policeman, who was white, arrest the alleged murderer. He not only refused but stopped a Black policeman from arresting the white youth. Racial conflict erupted as angry Blacks and whites swarmed to the beach, and it spread throughout the southern section of the city.

The rioting that began on July 27 raged virtually uncontrolled for the greater part of five days. Chicago was embroiled in the worst race riot in its history, and the toll was fearful. Police officers fatally wounded seven

Black men during the riot. Mobs and lone gunmen brutally murdered an additional sixteen Blacks and whites. Well over 500 Chicagoans of both races sustained injuries.[51]

In Knoxville, Tennessee, on August 30, 1919, white mobs intent on lynching an alleged Black murderer inflicted considerable damage in the downtown area, while national guardsmen joined in the attack on the Black community. The riot took several lives, injured scores of people of both races, and cost thousands of dollars in property losses. Nineteen whites were indicted on felony charges, but the jury acquitted fourteen of the defendants and the other five went free because of a mistrial.[52]

THE ELAINE MASSACRE

One of the riots of the Red Summer was a massacre. This occurred in Elaine, Phillips County, Arkansas. Phillips County was part of what was commonly referred to as the "Black Belt," since there was a high concentration of Black people, many of whom were sharecroppers and tenants on numerous plantations in that region. In 1910 the county had a population of 26,354 Black and only 7,176 white people. The land, devoted to the growing of cotton on the plantation system, was owned by whites and most of the labor was performed by Blacks.

According to the arrangement that prevailed before the massacre, Black sharecroppers and white landowners shared the profits from the sale of the cotton. Between the time of planting and time of sale of the crop, the sharecroppers were advanced food, clothing, and necessities, at excessive prices, from the plantation store owned by the planter. At the end of the year the landowner sold the crop at his discretion, showed no records to the Black workers, and settled with them unilaterally so that most Negroes lived in constant debt to the landlord. The system led to abuses against which the Blacks feared to protest because of rank intimidation and the threat of bodily harm. Although permanently in debt to the landlords, they were unable, because of written laws and unwritten laws of the cotton country, to leave a plantation until their "debts" were paid.[53]

Many Blacks in Phillips County whose cotton was sold in October 1918 did not get a settlement until July 1919. With no other recourse available to them, Black farmers, sharecroppers, tenants, and laborers of both sexes in 1918 formed the Progressive Farmers and Household Union of America, at Winchester, Arkansas. The union's objective was "to advance the interests of the Negro, morally and intellectually, and to make him a better citizen, and a better farmer." In addition, "to further advance the cause, uniting the race into a perfect union in various counties."[54]

Between April and August of 1918, lodges of the Progressive Farmers and Household Union were established in Ratio, Elaine, Hoopspur, Old Town, Ferguson and Mellwood. Secrecy was maintained and fines and expulsion for exposing the secrets were provided for in the union's constitution. In its campaign for members, the union quoted Biblical passages that supported its demand "for economic justice and social equality." Members were required to affirm their belief in God, and to pledge to "defend this Government and her Constitution at all times."[55]

Union members began to withhold their cotton so that they might receive higher settlements and rates. Influenced by the union, many Blacks in the area refused in 1919 to pick cotton unless paid the price they demanded, and at Elaine, Black sawmill workers refused to allow their wives and daughters to pick cotton or to work for a white man at any price. In general, Blacks declared they were tired of being exploited and "forced to act as children."[56] To protect themselves from the inevitable attack by the white landowners, union members armed themselves with rifles and pistols, and each member pledged to protect other members "as they sought to obtain their rights as citizens." The union members knew that

> to acquire these rights in Phillips County they need to protect themselves and their families for the white man's law would not protect them against the abuses of the white men.[57]

In the evening of September 30, 1919 the Hoopspur branch of the union held a regular meeting in a Black church, to discuss a plan for withholding all cotton, thereby "forcing their landlords to make equitable settlements with them." At 11 P.M. the meeting was fired on by white men from an automobile outside the church. In the shootout that followed, lasting until 12:30 A.M., one white man was killed and another wounded.

The Blacks at Hoopspur immediately reported to the authorities that the white men had fired first to break up the union meeting, and that they had returned the gunfire. But reports of the shooting spread and whites prepared to attack all union members. When a force of whites from Helena arrived at Elaine and began to search and ransack the homes of Blacks, arresting men and women indiscriminately, they were resisted by armed Blacks who exchanged gunfire with the posse. Men were killed on both sides. As the fighting spread from Elaine throughout the southern part of the county, white men from other sections of Arkansas and from Tennessee and Mississippi streamed into Phillips County to join the fight against what the *Arkansas Gazette,* speaking for most whites, called the "black insurrectionists."[58]

The Black sharecroppers, tenants, and laborers fought back so fiercely that Governor Charles H. Brough was urged to send federal troops from Camp Pike. The governor not only complied, but himself accompanied five hundred United States soldiers, armed with twelve machine guns and other weapons, to Elaine and Helena. Elaine was placed under martial law, and the Blacks were attacked by the soldiers, rounded up, and held in a stockade.[59]

A secret committee of seven, made up of local leaders, including two plantation owners, appointed by the governor to investigate the cause of the riot, issued a report asserting that the shooting at Hoopspur "nipped a mature plan of insurrection by members of the Progressive Farmers and Household Union against the white population of Phillips County." The alleged uprising was to have taken place on October 6, and twenty-one white men were said to have been marked for death. The issuance of this incendiary, utterly false report served only to exacerbate the situation.[60]

A news release went out all over the nation portraying the Blacks as "murderers" and "insurrectionists" who had plotted to massacre the white population. All Black people within the vicinity of Elaine were arrested and released only upon the word of a white citizen. Those with union membership cards and those not vouched for were detained. All Black people, male and female, were required by the federal troops to have a pass for identification purposes. Over a hundred were jailed at Helena.[61]

A month later sixty-five Blacks were indicted by the Phillips County grand jury—eleven for murder in the first degree. After a farcical trial, in which the only evidence produced by the prosecution was the report of the Committee of Seven, and following a few minutes of deliberation, the jury found all guilty. Eleven Blacks were sentenced to death, and fifty-four were given penitentiary sentences, ranging from one to twenty-one years. A twelfth Black, indicted for murder, was apprehended and tried later. He too received a death sentence.[62]

On December 7, 1919, the People's Movement of Chicago unanimously passed a resolution offered by Ida B. Wells-Barnett and sent it to Governor Brough. It read:

> Whereas, the press dispatches bring the news that twelve Negroes have been condemned in Helena, Ark., to die in the electric chair for the alleged killing of five white men after a deliberation of eight minutes by the jury which found them guilty, and
>
> Whereas, it would appear that this riot arose over a determination of those Negroes to form a union for the protection of their cotton crop, therefore, be it
>
> Resolved, That we demand of Governor Brough that he exert his influence to

see that those men are goven a new trial or chance to present their cases to the Supreme Court. Hundreds of Negroes have left Arkansas because of unjust treatment, and we pledge ourselves to use our influence to bring thousands away if those twelve men die in the electric chair. Arkansas needs our labor but we will never rest till every Negro leaves the state unless these men are given justice.

The Chicago *Defender* of December 13 carried an appeal from Ida B. Wells-Barnett to Blacks throughout the country to raise funds to help the condemned men carry their cases to the Arkansas Supreme Court, and to the U.S. Supreme Court if necessary.* Wells-Barnett received a touching letter from one of the twelve condemned men in Arkansas thanking her for the appeal. "Because we are innocent men." he wrote, "we was not handle with justice at all in Phillips Couty court. It is prejudice that the white people had agence we Negroes. So I thank God that thro you, our Negroes are looking into this trouble...." After receiving the letter, Wells-Barnett departed for Little Rock, and spent a day interviewing the prisoners. She reported that since the first week in October when they were imprisoned, the men had been "beaten many times, and left for dead while there, given electric shocks, suffocated with drugs, and suffered every cruelty and torment at the hands of their jailers to make them confess to a conspiracy to kill white people. Besides this a mob from the outside tried to lynch them."

With the support of the NAACP, the unjust verdict and sentences were appealed. After a stay of execution, the cases were carried through the courts of Arkansas to the U.S. Supreme Court and back to the Arkansas court, which dropped prosecution. After two terms of the court went by without trial, six of the men were released on June 25, 1923. The other six were granted indefinite furlough by Governor McRae on January 14, 1925.[63]

An indeterminate number of Black farmers—at least one hundred—had been killed, and a number of their fellow sharecroppers had been forced to spend years in prison. As explained by one student of the massacre: "The audacity of the Negroes to organize a union and to attempt through it to secure economic justice led inevitably to the charge of "insurrection."[64] An Arkansas lawyer who was involved in the case put it concisely when he wrote that there was no insurrection, but "only a preconceived plan to put

---

*Ida Bell Wells-Barnett (1862-1931), journalist, lecturer, and civil rights leader, was a militant fighter in the crusade against lynching and exposed it in her pamphlet, *A Red Record* (1895), and as chairperson of the Anti-Lynching League. She was a founder and charter member of the NAACP. On June 27, 1895, she married Ferdinand Lee Barnett, a Black lawyer and editor of the *Chicago Conservator*. For an excellent discussion of Ida B. Wells's battle against lynching, *see* Herbert Shapiro, *White Violence and Black Response: From Reconstruction to Montgomery*, Amherst, MA (1988) pp. 53-65.

a stop to the negro [*sic*] ever asking for a settlement, which ended in the slaughter of so many negroes and some whites."[65]

BLACK RESISTANCE

The exact figures of the casualties in the Washington riot are not available, but it is known that on the afternoon of July 21, when some of the most severe fighting took place, four people were killed and eleven seriously or fatally wounded. Ten of the dead and injured were white, five were Black.[66] In a moving letter to the editor of *The Crisis*, "A Southern Colored Woman" told of her happiness when she learned that Black people in Washington had fought back:

> No woman loves a weakling, a coward, be she white or black, and some of us have been near thinking our men cowards, but thank God for Washington colored men! All honor to them, for they first blazed the way and right swiftly did Chicago men follow. They put new hope, a new vision into their almost despairing women.[67]

Black men and women were thus not mere passive victims. These "new Negroes" fought back in Chicago, Washington, Phillips County, and elsewhere:

> If we must die—oh, let us nobly die,
> So that our precious blood may not be shed
> In vain; then even the monsters we defy
> Shall be constrained to honor us though dead![68]

So wrote Claude McKay in the Red Summer of 1919.

As might be expected at a time when the Red Scare was getting under way, the militant Black resistance to the white rioters, and their readiness to use retaliatory violence, were attributed to a "Bolshevik plot" and to the intrigues of "Bolshevik agents."[69] But it was actually an expression of Black frustration that grew out of their U.S. experiences. As William M. Tuttle, Jr. points out, the attacks on Black men and women during the summer of 1919 did not occur because they were radicals and foreign-born,

> but because they threatened the nation's race system of white superiority and black inferiority. Having helped as soldiers and war workers to win the war for worldwide "democracy," blacks entered the year 1919 with aspirations for a larger share of democracy at home. Tensions mounted and racial violence erupted as these aspirations collided with the general white determination to reaffirm the black people's prewar status in the bottom rung of the racial ladder.[70]

CHAPTER 3

The U.S. Labor Movement and the Bolshevik Revolution

For decades before the revolution of 1917, tsarist Russia had been a symbol in the U.S. of reaction, tyranny, injustice, and persecution. That such a country would be the scene of the most sweeping revolution in the history of the world was something few Americans would have dared to predict. Certainly it was too much to expect that a land with a semifeudal structure and with an underdeveloped bourgeoisie and a relatively small working class would be the one in which the first socialist state would be established.*

Nevertheless, there were Americans who had confidence that despite the tsarist tyranny, the Russian workers and peasants would ultimately overthrow the autocracy and usher in a socialist society. When the unrest that gripped Russia exploded in rebellious students' demonstrations, strikes, and widespread acts of peasant violence that culminated in the revolution of 1905, some radical journals were convinced that the revolution would triumph—if not immediately, then eventually. "The Russian people are demanding industrial liberty, and the fires of revolution will never be quenched until the people are supreme," the *Miners' Magazine*, organ of the militant Western Federation of Miners, predicted on November 9, 1905. The *Industrial Worker*, official journal of the newly organized Industrial Workers of the World (IWW), ventured the prediction in March

*Contrary to the opinions of Marx and Engels, and of Lenin himself, it was the more or less common view among American Socialists that Russia was not ready for socialism and that before the working class could take over the government, the country would first have to go through the stage of fully developed capitalism. (For the views of Marx and Engels, *see The Selected Correspondence of Karl Marx and Frederick Engels, 1846-1895*, New York, 1942, pp. 301, 349, 434, 438, 501. For those of Lenin, see his *Two Tactics of Social Democracy in the Democratic Revolution* [1905], U.S. edition, New York, 1935.)

1906 that "The sun of the socialist republic will first cross the horizon of the Slavic empire." The *International Socialist Review* was convinced in its January 1906 issue that if the revolution were successful in Russia, it might usher in an era of "European revolutions that will end with the dictatorship of a Socialist society."

Even after the 1905 revolution was crushed, radicals were not completely discouraged. Their great hope had to be postponed, but only for a while. The revolution had clearly demonstrated the great potential power of the Russian workers, and in due time that power would achieve victory. When World War I broke out, some radicals were certain that in Russia the reaction against the war would provide the impetus for a successful revolution. "At the risk of shocking some of our readers," declared *Solidarity,* the IWW journal, on September 12, 1914, "we are offering to bet on Russia as the hope of Europe." The Tsar had led Russia into the war, but the workers would lead the nation out of the conflict and into a new social system. By 1916, as the strain of the war opened ever increasing cracks in the Russian economy, and tsarist failures aroused widespread discontent both in the army and on the home front, many American radicals anticipated the coming of the revolution. On April 13, 1918 the *Industrial Worker* noted that after the 1905 revolution, it had expected another one in ten years. "And it came. Not in 1915, nor in 1916, as we expected, but in 1917—it came." But the long-awaited explosion came with a suddenness that surprised even some of the radicals.

THE FEBRUARY REVOLUTION

In February 1917 spontaneous strikes swept Petrograd and Moscow as workers complained of lack of bread, mounting inflation, and the terrible toll of lives in the war against Germany. On February 27 the Tsar ordered the workers back to the factories and shops, but when the Petrograd garrison joined the strikers the Tsar abdicated, and on March 1, 1917 a Provisional Government under Prince George E. Lvov, a liberal nobleman, assumed power. Alexander Kerensky, soon to become Minister of War and Premier of the Provisional Government, occupied the post of Minister of Justice under Prince Lvov. At the same time, the Petrograd Soviet of Workers' Deputies was created,* and began to function as a sort of separate government, issuing its own proclamations.

The February revolution in Petrograd (March 9-14, 1917, by the West-

---

*The name was soon changed to Petrograd Soviet of Workers' and Soldiers' Deputies. The word "soviet" means "council." A Soviet of Workers' Deputies was first formed in St. Petersburg on October 26, 1905, in which each deputy represented 500 workers.

ern calendar) aroused widespread rejoicing in the United States. "The most corrupt government, the most detestable despotism which has survived among the nations of the modern world, is by way of perishing," the *New Republic* cheered on March 24, 1917. At its national convention in April 1917 the Socialist Party of the United States sent "fraternal greetings to the Socialists and workers of the Russian republic, and hearty felicitations upon their glorious victory in behalf of democracy and social progress." The American Federation of Labor hailed the revolution and saluted "freedom in Russia," while the tiny Knights of Labor heralded the revolution as "the most wonderful step out of the darkness of absolutism towards the light of freedom and democracy ever known to human history."[1]

Samuel Gompers, president of the AFL, sent a cable to the "representatives of the working people of Russia," cautioning the Russian workers to solve their problems "practically and rationally" and not attempt further revolutionary activity. Freedom could not be "established by revolution only—it is the product of evolution," Gompers wrote.[2] But the *New Republic* noted on March 24 that it would require more revolutionary activity "to eradicate the old regime in Russia," and a meeting of radicals in New York City on April 29 declared that the February revolution "had solved the political problem only, and has yet to solve the most important social and economic ends of said Revolution." To achieve these ends a second revolution, a real revolution would be required.[3]

Despite widespread evidence of the longing for peace in Russia and the demoralization of the army, the United States put pressure upon the Provisional Government to keep Russia in the war. To arouse enthusiasm among the Russians to continue the fight, and to survey the situation and make policy recommendations, the Wilson Administration sent a mission to Russia headed by Elihu Root, former Secretary of War and Secretary of State and a leading spokesman for big business. Wilson wanted the mission to include a labor representative, but feared that "Gompers and the leaders immediately associated with him are known to be pronounced opponents of Socialism and would hardly be influential in the present ruling circles in Petrograd. And yet we shall have to be careful, if we are to send a real representative of American Labor, not to send a Socialist." The dilemma was solved by choosing a Gompers-type bureaucrat, 79-year-old James Duncan, president of the Granite Cutters' International Union and AFL vice-president. Also chosen was Charles Edward Russell, the prowar right-wing Socialist. The other members of the mission were representatives of business, finance, the army and philanthropy.

The Elihu Root mission spent the latter part of June and the beginning of July 1917 in Petrograd, "wined and dined by all sorts of respectable elements." Russell had been expelled from the Socialist Party for his stand on the war and for accepting a place on the Root mission. This did not stop him from holding up his red card of the Socialist Party when he addressed the Soviets and told the Russians: "I come . . . from the plain people of America, from the workers, the radicals, the American socialists, the champions of democracy." Russell urged the Russian workers to give up their opposition to the war, arguing that only "through victory against Germany" could socialism be built.[3] Duncan, viewing the Russians as children who with childlike enthusiasm were seeking to build a better world, lectured the Petrograd workers about the union label. But Elihu Root got down to the real purpose of the mission. He told the Provisional Government that unless Russia continued to fight in the war, no money would be forthcoming from the United States. "No fight, no loan," he declared in Petrograd.[4]

Bowing to this pressure (as well as more from London and Paris) the Provisional Government launched the summer offensive into Galicia, which ended in appalling disaster.[5] The decision to continue the war caused a series of violent demonstrations in Petrograd. Soldiers refused to be sent back to the front. On July 16-18 the Kronstadt sailors, the Petrograd workers, and soldiers demonstrated against the Provisional Government. Urging the end of dual power, the crowds in the streets shouted Lenin's slogan, "All power to the Soviet!"[6]

TRIUMPH OF THE BOLSHEVIKS

On November 7 (October 25 by the old-style Russian calendar), under Lenin's leadership, the Bolsheviks captured the Winter Palace and overthrew the Provisional Government in Petrograd. Lenin wrote his famous proclamation, "To the Citizens of Russia," which read:

> The Provisional Government has been deposed. State power has passed into the hands of the organ of the Petrograd Soviet of Workers' and Soldiers' Deputies, the Revolutionary Military Committee, which heads the Petrograd proletariat and the garrison.
>
> The cause for which the people have fought, namely, the immediate offer of a democratic peace, the abolition of landed proprietorship, workers' control over production, and the establishment of Soviet power—this cause has been secured.
>
> Long live the revolution of workers, soldiers and peasants!

On November 22, 1917 the headline in the New York *Call* read: "John Reed Cables The Call News of Bolshevik Revolt He Witnessed," and the subheading: "First Proletarian Republic Greets American Workers." The dispatch, dated Petrograd, November 13, but delayed by the censor in the United States, carried the stunning words: "This is the revolution, the class struggle, with the proletariat, the soldiers and peasants lined up against the bourgeoisie. Last February was only the preliminary revolution. . . . The extraordinary and immense power of the Bolsheviki lies in the fact that the Kerensky government absolutely ignored the desires of the masses as expressed in the Bolsheviki program of peace, land and work-?rs' control of industry."

News of the Socialist revolution, the real revolution in Russia, was met with undisguised hostility by the Allied governments, including the United States. Appalled by the rise to power of the Bolsheviks, the Allies set out to isolate the Soviet government, sever it from all contacts with the West, and destroy it. An Allied blockade of Soviet-controlled territory began soon after the October Revolution. The formal Allied intervention in Siberia began in August 1918 with the landing of their men of war in Vladivostok. Soon there were some 25,000 Allied troops, half of them Japanese, stationed in that city.

U.S. INTERVENTION IN RUSSIA

Two contingents of American troops were landed at Vladivostok in August 1918. A month later, approximately 2,000 more men under the command of General William S. Graves arrived. At the same time, a company of infantry, a company of engineers, and some hospital units were landed in North Russia at Archangel. By late 1918 the United States had approximately 7,000 soldiers on duty in Russia.[8]*

The bulk of the U.S. forces arrived at Archangel in September 1918. They were Americans who composed the 339th Infantry Regiment, made up of 4,487 men who were nearly all from Michigan. They had been drafted in June 1918 to fight in France; that they were sent to fight Bolsheviks instead came as a complete surprise to them. Ill-equipped for the bit-

---

*The standard work on the intervention is Leonid I. Strakhovsky, *Intervention at Archangel: The Story of Allied Intervention and Russian Counter-Revolution in North Russia, 1918-1920*, Princeton, 1944. More recent studies are George F. Kennan, *Soviet-American Relations, 1917-1920* vol. II: *The Decision to Intervene*, Princeton, 1958; Richard H. Ullman, *Anglo-Soviet Relations 1917-1921*, vol. I: *Intervention and War*, Princeton, 1960, and vol. II: *Britain and the Russian Civil War*, Princeton, 1968. The Russian view is summarized in N.V. Swachev and N.N. Yakolev, *Russia and the United States*, Chicago, 1977, pp. 42-62.

ter Russian winter and decimated by a virulent strain of influenza that had broken out on two of the British transports, they arrived at Archangel only to fall victim to the general lack of sanitation at that city and the poor and inadequate hospital facilities. Instead of finding themselves facing a negligible force of poorly-trained, ill-equipped Bolsheviks,* they were up against trained and highly-motivated fighting men deep in the interior of North Russia. As the Bolsheviks effectively used their superiority in long-range artillery, the Allies were forced to withdraw. The interventionists failed to recruit support among the Russian population, and, infuriated, Allied commanders ordered the execution of Russians unwilling to cooperate, without even the pretense of a trial.[9]**

In the United States, the *New York Times* and other leading papers published reports based on War Department sources stressing that the U.S. forces were "bearing up splendidly," their morale was "excellent," and "the troops are being well taken care of in every way, and the Allied command is capable of taking care of itself against the whole Bolshevist army."[10]

But accounts of the poor morale of U.S. troops began appearing in the same press, based on letters and statements of wounded soldiers. These were smuggled out of Russia, and then printed in the *Congressional Record* by critics of the intervention such as Senators Charles E. Townsend of Michigan, Robert LaFollette of Wisconsin, and Hiram Johnson of California. In April of 1919 reports began to appear in the press that a number of U.S. troops stationed at Archangel had staged a "mutiny," refused to fight, and were asking such questions as "Why are we being sent to the front now that the war on the Western front has ended?" As the Associated Press reported from Archangel:

> The men contended that they were draft men selected for the war with Germany which was finished now; that America was not at war with the Bolsheviki, that the entire Bolshevist question was the subject of much political debate and indecision in the United States and that so far as they were concerned they

*Later British General R.G. Finglason noted that the Bolsheviks were mistakenly dismissed as "a great rabble of men armed with staves, stones and revolvers who rushed about foaming at the mouth in search of blood and who are easily turned and broken by a few well directed shots." (Benjamin D. Rhodes, "The Anglo-American Intervention at Archangel, 1918-1919: The Role of the 339th Infantry," *International History Review* 8 [August 1986]: 369-70.)

**According to Soviet authorities, 111,720 people were murdered or killed by diseases caused by the Allied occupation. This included 12,805 tortured or beaten, 20,201 wounded or mutilated, and 3,116 women raped. (Albert Sirotkin, "A Bitter Memory in the Soviet Union," *People's Daily World,* March 25, 1987.)

were unable to see why they should be fighting if there was no war.[11]

The Associated Press reporter added: ". . . since the armistice with Germany was declared, the soldiers have been subjected to constant Bolshevik propaganda which together with their desire to return home after the end of the war for which they were drafted and the hardships and loneliness of the Arctic winter, has caused them to lose their spirits." Calling the Bolsheviks "the world's best propagandists," the AP reporter wrote that they hung "large red banners, printed in English, to trees. These banner blazoned forth in great white letters on their red backgrounds that 'The workingmen of France and England and Germany Have Made Peace,' and urged the Americans to come and do likewise." Their propaganda, he added, "placed great stress on the claim that the Bolsheviki are workingmen, fighting against the capitalists of the world and inviting the Americans to come and join their fight."[12]

This situation, added to the total disarray of the U.S. forces in Russia, caused such alarm in the Wilson administration that the necessity of extricating the United States became a major priority. On June 7, 1919 two transports evacuated 4,500 "disillusioned U.S. troops" while an eight-man graves registration unit remained for another two and a half months "collecting U.S. corpses in hermatically sealed coffins."[13] On February 19, 1920 the northern provisional government set up by the Allies fled to Great Britain. Two days later, without firing a shot, Bolshevik forces entered Archangel "to the acclaim of the population."[14]

The United States insisted throughout the intervention that its troops were not to be used for interference in Russia's domestic affairs,* but the troops did what they could to assist the White Armies. Large supplies of war material were sent to Admiral Alexander Kolchak's counterrevolutionary forces, while private banks in the Unites States helped to finance his war against the Soviets. In November 1918 the U.S. treasury allowed the payment of $1,239,000, from funds accredited to the Kerensky government, for printing paper money to be used by Kolchak. Boris Bakhmetev, officially recognized by Washington as the Russian representative until June 1922 even though the government he represented had been over-

---

*In his instructions of July 17, 1918, agreeing to participate in the Anglo-American intervention at the Russian port of Archangel, President Wilson supposedly limited the use of U.S. troops to guarding military stores and assisting the Czechoslovak Legion—an anti-Communist group of former prisoners of war that was fighting its way across Siberia to Vladivostok. (Eugene Trani, "Woodrow Wilson and the Decision to Intervene in Russia: A Reconsideration," *Journal of Modern History* 48 [1976]: 440-61; John W. Long, "American Intervention in Russia: The North Russian Expedition, 1918-1919," *Diplomatic History* 6 [1982]: 45-48.)

thrown, supported the White forces with funds derived from the sale of supplies purchased with American credits.[15]*

THE AFL AND THE NEW SOVIET REGIME

Although Gompers and other top American labor leaders had hailed the Russian Revolution in February 1917, they shared the Wilson administration's hatred of and hostility to the Bolshevik Revolution. Regarding the new regime as the most "monstrous or degrading government ever . . . set up anywhere in the world," the AFL leadership allied itself with a succession of administrations in Washington in efforts to isolate and destroy the Soviet government. As they saw it, any anti-Soviet act, including military intervention and blockade, was justified.

The AFL leadership did not merely oppose the new government in Russia as an undesirable political institution; it regarded Bolshevism as the substantive evil in the world, which should be extirpated at any cost. "As a result," concludes one student of the subject, "opposition to the Soviet government became the cornerstone of AFL foreign policy. Furthermore, the AFL's unrelenting hostility to Bolshevism and radicalism, broadly defined, grew so pervasive that it significantly affected AFL domestic policy and became a common issue in internal affairs."[16]

It did not take long for the AFL leaders to show their hatred for the October Revolution. "The industrial and commercial life of Russia has broken down," Gompers wrote in July 1918. "It is our imperative duty to help the Russian people rehabilitate themselves. . . . The Allies must go to the rescue of Russian democracy."[17] When the Allies did intervene to overthrow theSoviet government, Gompers justified the policy as "morally right with incidental strategic, practical and military advantages."[18]

Gompers was in Paris when he learned that President Wilson had sent William C. Bullitt to Moscow on a special mission to see what was happening after the Bolshevik ascent to power. He complained to the American Peace Commissioners about treating with the Bolsheviks, arguing that enough was known of actual conditions in Russia, and he cited press re-

---

*The entire May 1987 issue of *U.S. Farm News,* published in Hampton, Iowa, was an answer to the vicious anti-Soviet ABC-TV series "Amerika," which dealt with a supposed invasion and occupation of the United States by the Soviet Union. The issue was entitled, "The America of 1918-1920, the U.S. invasion of the Soviet Union," and the headlines said: "Russia Invaded by Allies; America, Great Britain, France Land at Vladivostok and Archangel: Local pro-soviet people murdered or fled; millions of American taxpayers' dollars aiding monarchists; foreign exploiters hope to regain mines and factories from Bolsheviki."

ports that told of cruelty of all sorts against the Russian people by the Bolsheviks, of the existence of a "Bureau of Free Love" with which all women over the age of eighteen had to register. The women were then to be parcelled out among various men. And he cited reports of the institution of a total dictatorship.[19]

Gompers made the AFL's Russian policy crystal clear by late 1919: the AFL condemned the Bolshevik Revolution and its offspring, the Soviet Union, completely and for all time. The president of the Federation and its Executive Council would oppose U.S. recognition of the Soviet Union now and forever. Actually, "forever," he noted, was simply for the record, for it was his belief and that of the Executive Council that it would be only a comparatively short time before the Soviet government would either be overthrown or fall of its own contradictions and the fact that it was solely "a dictatorship of a self-appointed committee."[20]

But Gompers' and the Executive Council's Russian policy encountered significant opposition in the American labor movement; indeed, the "Russian question" stood on the order of the day. It was actively debated in every postwar AFL convention. Despite Gompers' bitter opposition, delegates to these conventions insisted on voicing their members' support for the Soviet republic.[21]

At the 1919 AFL convention in Atlantic City, resolutions were introduced calling for recognition of Soviet Russia, for the lifting of the blockade, and for an end to the intervention. The one introduced by the central labor union of Portland, Oregon, urged withdrawal of American troops from Russia; another proposed on behalf of the central labor unions of Cleveland and Akron, Ohio, asked that all American troops be withdrawn as speedily as possible, and that the Russian people "be left to regulate their own affairs."[22] The strongest expression was that of the delegation representing the Seattle Central Labor Council. It read:

> The workers of Russia are endeavoring to establish in their country a government of, by and for the workers; and the capitalists of the world are seeking to annul their efforts . . . we believe the workers of America have the power to prevent the capitalists of the United States from carrying out their part in the plan for the destruction.

The resolution requested that Congress withdraw U.S. troops from Russia and that the Soviet government be recognized by the U.S. government. The resolution proposed that the question of recognition be referred by ballot to all members of the AFL, so that policy might be determined by the rank and file.[23]

These three resolutions were rejected by the committee on resolutions. However, bowing to the sentiment of the delegates, the committee reported out a resolution that mildly recommended withdrawal of American troops "at the earliest possible moment," but reflecting the viewpoint of the AFL leadership, refused to endorse the Soviet government until the people of Russia had established "a truly democratic form of government." John P. Frey, secretary of the committee on resolutions and regarded as the theoretician for AFL policies, gave an astounding explanation for the committee's refusal to endorse the Soviet government: since the Russians claimed that their government represented only the workers, such a government was unrepresentative of the nation as a whole. The committee on resolutions could not approve of sending food to the Russian people because "it would simply strengthen the Bolshevik government that controls the transportation of food." A delegate from the International Ladies' Garment Workers' Union bitingly asked: "I would like to know if this resolution is adopted, whether the A.F. of L. will approve sending ammunition to the Kolchak government to kill the Russian workers." Gompers indignantly replied: "I think that question is an insult to this convention." The committee resolution was then carried by voice vote.[24]

The *American Federationist,* edited by Gompers, triumphantly announced the convention vote. "Bolshevism and its kindred manifestations of error have been firmly set aside"; the verdict was that "principles of dictatorship [are] without any redeeming qualities."[25] Writing in the *Federationist* a month later, William E. Walling, a prowar Socialist and coauthor with Gompers of a book viciously attacking the Soviet Union, echoed his collaborator. "Bolshevism in America was buried on the 17th of June (by the AFL convention)." He went on to write that those who agitated for aid to Russia were asking "to grant them (the Russians) what we refuse their teachers and allies, the Huns. For the Bolsheviks are the Hun Kultur of the Gutter."[26]

At the 1920 Montreal convention of the AFL, resolutions on Russia were again placed before the delegates. Delegate Luigi Antonini of the ILGWU introduced a resolution praising the people of Russia for having established a government which was "based on the universal duty to work and the right of all toilers to have and enjoy the full produce of their labor, thereby doing away with industrial slavery and economic injustice, the elimination of which we hold to be the ultimate aim and finality of the organized labor movement." The resolution called for lifting the blockade against Russia, the resumption of trade relations with her, and recognition of the Soviet government by the United States. James Duncan of the Seattle Central Labor Council introduced a resolution that called the Russian workers "the most slandered in the world," and expressed admiration for "the noble defensive fight waged against tremendous odds by the workers of Russia for the right to work out their salvation, without outside interference." It called upon the government to urge the immediate withdrawal of all foreign troops from Russia, to lift the blockade, and to furnish credits to the Russian government.

Once again the machine-controlled committee on resolutions rejected these resolutions. Instead it recommended a resolution that not only failed to call for withdrawal of foreign troops but went beyond the 1919 resolution in criticizing the Soviet government. It added to the previous charges an indictment of Russia's attempt "to create revolutions in the well-established, civilized nations of the world" and to interfere in the functioning of trade unions. Duncan announced himself "astounded" by the report, and urged the delegates not to be taken in by imperialist propaganda against the workers' republic. "I know that possibly it is unpopular in an American Federation of Labor convention, at least, to say one word in behalf of my Russian brothers, but regardless of the cost I am going to undertake at least one sympathetic voice in this convention." Duncan expressed the hope that the convention would go on record in a very definite way as being opposed to any further blockade, for the resumption of trade with Russia, and for the right of the Russian people to have the opportunity "to work out their own salvation without outside interference."

But the AFL leadership refused to budge. Frey, speaking again for the committee on resolutions, disclosed the fact that during the convention, Gompers had wired Secretary of State Bainbridge Colby asking if the government sanctioned trade relations between the United States and Russia. Colby had replied that "there is no licensed or regular trading between the United States and Russia at present," and added hypocritically that while the government "had no desire to interfere with the international affairs of the Russian people or to suggest the kind of government they should have," it could not approve of "the existing regime in Russia" nor recommend trade relations with it. The AFL leadership emphasized that Colby's stand was sufficient to justify the convention's refusal to recommend relations with Russia. The convention then proceeded to adopt the resolution proposed by the committee on resolutions.[27]

One-third of the votes cast, however, were in favor of trade relations with Russia, and *Justice,* official organ of the ILGWU, reported in its issue of July 2, 1920 : "The Negroes (at the convention) in general voted to extend the helping hand to the Russians."* The Philadelphia *Public Ledger*, conservative Republican organ, hailed the AFL leadership for having defeated the rising tide in the labor movement for recognition of and support for the Russian Soviet government. "It is a matter for congratulations," it declared enthusiastically on June 17, 1920.

THE ILGWU AND AMALGAMATED CLOTHING WORKERS

While the national AFL refused to take a stand in support of Soviet Russia and instead allied itself with the interventionist drive to destroy the Socialist republic, many international unions, local unions, city centrals and state federations of labor rallied to the support of the embattled Russian workers and peasants. The International Ladies' Garment Workers' Union and the Amalgamated Clothing Workers of America, a large percentage of whose membership were Jewish immigrants from tsarist Russia and identified themselves with the Socialists in the United States, took the lead.** At the ILGWU's 14th convention in May 1918, the delegates pledged themselves to the following program: "The members of the International Ladies' Garment Workers' Union will follow the struggle of their brothers in Russia with intense interest and sympathy, not only because many are linked to them by ties of kinship and sentiment, but also because the fate of the first great working class republic in the world cannot but be a matter of prime concern to the organized and progressive workers of all countries."[28]

The ILGWU condemned the blockade and called for the reestablishment of trade relations with Russia. The union attacked Wilson's policy toward Russia as "pathetic and lacking in vision," and condemned the AFL's stubborn opposition to the Soviet government. It called the resolution adopted by the 1920 AFL convention "condescending" to the workers' republic.

President Benjamin Schlesinger of the ILGWU spent several weeks in

---

*This is only one of a number of examples of the widespread support of the October Revolution among Black Americans, especially Black Socialists. Both *The Messenger* and *The Crusader*, Black Socialist journals, praised the October Revolution, and in October 1919 *The Crusader* declared: "If to fight for one's rights is to be Bolshevist, then we are Bolshevists, and let them make the most of it." The Black press gave considerable coverage to the national policy conducted by the Soviet Union, contrasting it with the racial discrimination prevalent in the United States. (*See* Philip S. Foner, *The Bolshevik Revolution: Its Impact on American Radicals, Liberals, and Labor* [New York, 1967] pp. 22, 99-101, 181, 206-07.)

**For the response of the Socialist Party to the Bolshevik Revolution, *see* Foner, *The Bolshevik Revolution*, pp. 20-24.

Russia prior to attending the International Federation of Trade Union's conference in Copenhagen. On his return to the United States in November 1920, he predicted that the Soviet government would "not fall before the blows of international capitalism," and declared that the "great suffering in Russia is not due to failure of the workers' Republic, but is due to the blockade that has kept Russia from importing necessaries." Schlesinger praised the admirable attempts to regenerate the poorer classes, the absence of exploitation of labor, and the magnificent role of the trade unions in determining the nation's destinies.[29]*

The Amalgamated Clothing Workers were even more firm in support of the Russian Revolution. "The interest in Russian affairs among our members is intense," Joseph Schlossberg, general secretary of the union, declared in June 1918. "Many of them have been citizens of Russia in the past, and they are familiar with conditions there and know what the revolution means to the great mass of the Russian people." At its convention that same month, the Amalgamated hailed "with joy free Russia" and sent her its "most fraternal greetings." "It is our fervent hope," the union resolved, "that our own country and all other civilized nations will come to the assistance of free Russia by recognizing the Russian people's Soviet government, and giving the Russian people all aid in working out their own destinies."[30]

The Amalgamated endorsed the Russian Soviet Recognition League, formed in June 1918 to influence the government to establish relations with the Soviet republic. It opposed intervention on the ground that the Bolshevik government was supported by a majority of the Russian people and was successfully establishing order. The union denounced American participation in the blockade against Russia, and at its 1920 convention called upon the government to enter into friendly relations with Russia to offset the untold hardships created by the blockade.

The Amalgamated felt that it was the duty of all American workers to stand by Russia because, regardless of certain faults, the Soviet republic embodied the principle of a workers' government. The union viewed Russia's struggle against her capitalist enemies as an industrial strike on a vast scale, and insisted that world labor should adopt the same attitude toward Soviet Russia as it would toward any sister organization in the industrial

---

*Schlesinger spent five weeks in Russia, and made his report in a series of nine articles in *Justice*, the official organ of the ILGWU. He was critical in several of the articles, but he found many things to praise, especially the improvements made by the Soviet government in working hours, protection of women workers, abolition of child labor, and sanitary and safety conditions in the factories.

world. The enemies of Russia were also the enemies of labor. The Amalgamated regarded the Russian experiment as a test of whether labor was able to take over the reins of government or whether it must resign itself to a secondary position. It admired Russia's progress in the face of a hostile world, believing that the workers' republic held out the promise of a better day for workers everywhere.[31]

The Amalgamated's fervent support of the Soviet Union brought a barrage of criticism down on the union by supporters of the Gompers-AFL Executive Council Russian policy. Especially was it the target of vicious attacks by the *Garment Worker,* organ of the United Garment Workers of America, the union from which the Amalgamated split in 1914 because of its corruption, class-collaboration policies, and indifference to and contempt for the Yiddish-speaking Eastern European garment workers.* Denied affiliation with the AFL for many years, the Amalgamated Clothing Workers was free of domination by the Gompers-Executive Council machine.

To the *Garment Worker* the Amalgamated's Russian policy was not surprising since, it charged, "90 percent of the leaders and 75 percent of the workers are Bolsheviks." The paper headlined an Amalgamated victory in a Rochester strike: "Sovietism in Clothing Factory in Rochester."[33]**

THE SEATTLE LABOR COUNCIL

No labor body was a more consistent defender of the Bolshevik Revolution than the Seattle Central Labor Council. Its official journal, the *Seattle Union Record,* published and distributed 20,000 copies of Lenin's speech, delivered in April 1918 to the Congress of Soviets, on the next task of organizing power. It was "avidly read by radicals up and down the Pacific coast as well as in Seattle's shipyards."[33]

The Russian freighter *Shilka* steamed into Seattle's harbor on December 21, 1917. The cargo included beans, peas, and licorice bound for Baltimore. But rumors said that the hold contained munitions and gold destined to aid enemies of the U.S., especially $100,000 in gold to help the IWW. The sixty-three men crew was said to have mutinied just outside of Vladivostok, formed a soviet (governing committee) aboard ship, seized control from the captain, and placed decision-making in the hands of the committee.[34]

See Philip S. Foner, *History of the Labor Movement in the United States 5* (New York, 1980) 260-64 .
**Further activities by the Amalgamated Clothing Workers in support of the Soviet Union will be discussed in our next volume.

The Seattle Central Labor Council launched a campaign to defeat the reactionary forces seeking to imprison the *Shilka's* crew and impound the ship. It proved that the munitions and gold rumor was a fabrication, and invited the crew to meet Seattle workers, including both AFL and IWW members. Through the aid of a Russian interpreter, the Central Labor Council learned of conditions in what the *Seattle Union Record* called the "world's newest and most advanced democracy."[35]

When the *Shilka* left Seattle harbor on January 8, 1918 it carried a letter from the Central Labor Council to the workers of Russia. Entitled "To the Workers of All Russia, Who are Sincerely Endeavoring to Establish Democracy, in Care of the Crew of the Russian Steamship *Shilka*," the letter contained fraternal greetings in the name of more than 40,000 organized workers of Seattle who were also "an integral part of the American Federation of Labor, whose membership is composed of 2,000,000 men and women." The Central Labor Union wished the Russian workers success in "your efforts to make of Russia a free republic conditioned upon both political and industrial democracy."[36]

Since little or no authentic news about Russia was printed in the Seattle commercial press, the *Union Record* opened a Bureau of Russian Information, which from time to time published reports of constructive work under the Bolsheviks. The educational work conducted by the *Union Record* helps explain the fact that while most unions opposed intervention against Russia through speeches and resolutions, the workers of Seattle went further. In September 1919 the longshoremen of the city noticed a mysterious shipment by rail—50 freight cars destined for Vladivostok and labeled "sewing machines." When a longshore crew suspicious of the cargo allowed a crate to crash on the dock, out came stacks of rifles, bound for the Kolchak counterrevolutionary government. The longshoremen's union announced that its members would not touch the cargo, and that any dock that attempted to move it would be put under permanent ban. The union notified other ports of their action. The Central Labor Council backed up the longshoremen.[37]

On September 20, 1919 the *Seattle Union Record* reported: "Pacific Coast longshoremen will tie up the coast from Seattle to San Diego before they will load rifles or munitions for Siberia or any part of Russia. . . ." Soon reports appeared in the press that longshoremen in Pacific coast ports and in Baltimore had refused to load arms for the interventionists; the Baltimore longshoremen had staged a work stoppage in protest against arms shipment to Russia.[38]

The *Shilka*, which left the United States carrying a message from the

Seattle Central Labor Union and its members who were "an integral part of the American Federation of Labor," also carried a more emphatic message sent by the Tacoma IWW. The Tacoma Wobblies wrote of themselves as "co-workers . . . in our attempt to establish the world wide Industrial Commonwealth. . . ." The message continued:

> You no doubt realize that we, the revolutionists of America, being still in the minority, are unable as yet to follow your example in freeing ourselves from the terrible slave system in which we are enthralled, but confidently look forward to the time when we can reach across the Pacific Ocean and grasp the hands of our Progressive Fellow Workers in Russia and say WE ARE WITH YOU.[39]

As the message makes clear, the IWW saw in the victory of the Bolsheviks the triumph of the very class and principles for which the Wobblies were working. Thus an IWW publication (*Defense News Bulletin*) concluded a month after the Bolshevik Revolution that "in broad essentials, the now famous Bolsheviki stand for about the same thing in Russia as our IWW stands for in America," specifically, workers' control of industry through industrial unions.[40] On January 26, 1918 the *Industrial Worker* announced: "The trend of events in Russia sustains the IWW contention that the power of the workers lies in industry and in their unions on the economic field. None but actual producers can function there and the laws that are passed in the union hall have behind them the strength of the organized toilers." Noting that the Bolsheviks were a minority, the *Industrial Worker* held that they represented, nevertheless, the majority, the peasants, workers, and soldiers, who, because they were the wealth producers, were "the only groups which can and do control the situation. . . . It is they who are the revolution, not Lenin and Trotsky as the capitalist press would try to have American workers think." From this truly democratic society a new freedom would arise, based on the sturdy backs of the Russian workers who, because they controlled the all important element in society, the means of production, would be able to develop the new freedom.[41]

The Bolshevik emphasis on political action and the necessity of capturing the institutions of the state went against IWW insistence that only economic activity was important since the state is only a reflection of "the economic." But although the Soviets and the formation of a Bolshevik government were "admittedly political (and) not the establishment of a society of labor based on the principles of industrial administration," this was regarded as necessary "for the time being."

In any case, the IWW did not condemn the Soviets:

We understand them, we understand why they acted so, and moreover, we approve of their actions. It was impossible to act otherwise. We think that while it is necessary for the workers to participate in political questions, and while at the heads of foreign nations there are capitalists and autocrats, the working class of Russia must have a government of its own, based on strictly working class lines.[42]

It was too much to expect, many Wobblies noted, for the Bolsheviks, facing military invasion and blockade, to institute the "correct" economic organization. But on January 24, 1920, *The New Solidarity*, official journal of the IWW published in Chicago, ended an editorial entitled, "All Hail to the Bolsheviki," with the observation: "With all military resistance practically ended and the blockade raised, Soviet Russia now enters the second period of the revolution—the period of construction. And the working plan of the new social order which it shall build will be—the industrial unionism of the IWW."

But the Soviet Union did not proceed to base the first Socialist state solely "on the industrial unionism of the IWW." As a result, a strong anti-Soviet faction that dominated the IWW General Executive Board was no longer willing to accept "the state character of the Soviets." The Board banned further distribution of Harrison George's pamphlet, *The Red Dawn: The Bolsheviki and the I.W.W.*, extolling the Bolshevik Revolution and explaining its background.[43] But many Wobblies still continued to show their enthusiasm for the Bolshevik Revolution by singing the new chorus for the famous IWW song, "Don't Bite the Hand That's Feeding You":

> *All hail to the Bolsheviki*
> *We will fight for our Class and be free.*
> *A Kaiser, King or Tsar, no matter which you are*
> *You're nothing of interest to me.*
> *If you don't like the red flag of Russia,*
> *If you don't like the spirit so true,*
> *Then just be like the cur in the story*
> *And lick the hand that's robbing you.*[44]

"HANDS OFF RUSSIA!"

Despite the positions of the leaders of the AFL and IWW, the mass of the membership of both organizations had a single stand: support of the Bolshevik Revolution. Moreover, a strong feeling permeated these two groups of American workers—that it was not enough to extol the Russian revolution—it was also necessary to protect it. They joined with members of the Socialist Party, the Socialist Labor Party, the newly founded Communist Party and Communist Labor Party,[45] liberals, and many others to conduct a tireless campaign to end the intervention against Soviet Russia. The Communist Party of America made its first campaign "the struggle to arouse the workers against the blockade of Soviet Russia." All branches were urged to hold mass meetings from November 7 to 9, 1919, adopt resolutions against the blockade, and distribute a "Break the Blockade of Russia" declaration issued by the Central Executive Committee of the party. The declaration stated boldly:

> The war against Russia, the blockade of Russia, is an expression of the international class struggle between the workers and the capitalists. Force is used against the Russian workers, but force is also used by these governments— British, French, Italian, Japanese, American—against their own workers. The war against Soviet Russia is a war against the workers of the world.
>
> Let the workers determine: We must break the blockade of Soviet Russia....
>
> Workers, men and women! Come to the aid of your fellow-workers! Break the blockade of Soviet Russia![46]

The Communist Labor Party entered the campaign against the blockade and intervention, distributing its "Hands Off Soviet Russia" appeal, which urged American workers to emulate their brothers in Britain, France, and Italy who were "refusing to load ships with ammunition and provisions destined for the foes of Soviet Russia."[47]

In the second half of 1919, more and more important unions and labor organizations were not only backing the "Hands Off Soviet Russia!" movement, but calling for recognition of and trade with the Soviet Union. The September 1919 convention of the United Mine Workers of America adopted a resolution calling for U.S. diplomatic recognition of Soviet Russia. Resolutions supporting the Soviets were adopted by New York trade unions of metal workers and engineers, the Chicago Federation of Labor, and many others. The International Congress of Working Women in November 1919 in Washington passed a resolution protesting against the economic blockade of Russia and demanding the removal of all restrictions on sending food supplies to Russia.[48]

The Allied intervention and blockade caused widespread suffering in Russia, but for the purpose of overthrowing the Bolshevik government they proved fruitless. To be sure, the anti-Soviet press repeatedly reported the intervention to be a success, and the fall of the Bolshevik government was a regular weekly feature. "It fell with a regularity that in time became tedious," writes Christopher Lasch. "Altogether, if the *New York Times* was to be believed, it fell or was about to fall 91 times in a period of two years from November 1917 to November 1919."[49] But by the beginning of 1920 the failure of the intervention was obvious, and in January the blockade against Russia was lifted by the Allied powers. The United States, however, waited until July 7, 1920, before announcing the nominal lifting of the blockade. Later that year Allied warships and troops, including American troops, were withdrawn.[50]

Although many reasons were advanced for the failure of the intervention, there was general agreement that the "Hands Off Russia!" campaign by American radicals, liberals, and trade unionists (and similar campaigns in other countries) had contributed to ending the intervention. Yet there was still more work to be done—such as achieving U.S. recognition of Soviet Russia and the reestablishment of trade relations between the two countries. The latter received considerable impetus when, following the wartime boom, business suffered a severe setback. In mid-1920, an economic crisis began in the United States that continued until late 1921.* The industrial production index dropped 23 points with coal, iron, steel, and copper industries leading the decline. The number of unemployed mounted, and business and labor urged trade with Russia because it would serve a two-fold purpose: alleviate famine conditions in Russia and reduce unemployment in the United States. "We have come to realize now," declared Schlossberg of the Amalgamated Clothing Workers late in 1920, "because the hundred and thirty million human beings in Russia are badly in need of the things which we can produce for them, that they will be excellent customers and give us employment if Washington will permit us to work for them."[51]

AMERICAN LABOR ALLIANCE

On November 21, 1920 a conference of authorized delegates of New York's labor unions founded the American Labor Alliance for Trade Relations with Russia. (Originally the organization was called the American Humanitarian Labor Alliance.) The delegates, representing 800,000 organized workers, chose Timothy Healy of the International Association of Firemen and Oilers as chairman of the Alliance, and Alexander Trachtenberg of the ILGWU as secretary. A resolution adopted by the conference stated:

---

*The full impact of the postwar depression will be discussed in our next volume.

Resolved, that we demand that the State Department take immediate steps to remove all obstacles to trade with Russia, to establish communication by post, cable, and wireless, to restore the right to travel between the United States and Soviet Russia, and to permit the transfer of funds from Russia to be used in the purchase of American goods, to allow authorized representatives of the Soviet government to act in its behalf regarding all commercial transactions and otherwise establish complete and unrestricted relations with Russia.[52]

The objectives of the Alliance were endorsed by 12 international and national unions, more than a score of state federations of labor, and the central labor unions of 72 cities in 29 states, all of them affiliated with the American Federation of Labor,* and representing a membership of 2,500,000 workers. (When one realizes that the total membership of the AFL was about 4,000,000, it is clear that the aims of the Alliance received the endorsement of a substantial section of the Federation.) Leaders in support of the Alliance's program included the Central Trades and Labor Council of New York City (600,000 members), the Chicago Federation of Labor (400,000 members), the ILGWU (115,000 members), and the Amalgamated Clothing Workers (175,000 members). All these except the Amalgamated were affiliated with the AFL.[53]

During the summer of 1920, when the American Woolen Company and the Pennsylvania Railroad laid off thousands of workers, and other companies were set to do likewise, Gompers denounced these actions as "nothing less than an indictment of management and a heinous offense against a people in need of every possible ounce of production." "The

---

Labor, the weekly newspaper of the Railroad Brotherhoods, with almost a half-million circulation, gave favorable front page treatment to the activities of the American Labor Alliance for Trade Relations with Russia. (*See* issue of December 11, 1920.)

However, Donald F. Wieland, on the basis of a study of *Labor*, as well as the publications of the Trainmen, Railway Conductors, and Railway Expressmen, found that "in all four papers there were only thirteen direct references that can be given as showing an attitude toward Russia." He states therefore that "Russia did not take up much of the Railroad Brotherhoods' time during the 1917-1925 period. Problems at home—the Plumb plan for one— took most of their attention." But he concludes that the "Brotherhoods would not have objected to Russian recognition by the United States. . . ." ("American Labor and Russia," unpublished M.A. thesis, University of Wisconsin, Madison, 1948, p. 76.)

**The national and international unions endorsing the objectives of the Alliance were International Association of Machinists; Amalgamated Clothing Workers: International Ladies' Garment Workers; International Fur Workers; United Cloth, Hat and Cap Makers; International Brotherhood of Firemen and Oilers; International Jewelry Workers; International Woodcarvers Association; International Federation of Hotel Workers; Grand Division of Sleeping Car Conductors; Amalgamated Textile Workers; Eastern Federation of the Brotherhood of Railway and Steamship Clerks.

nation," he insisted, "needs production."[54] But when informed of the huge meeting leading to the formation of the American Labor Alliance for Trade Relations with Russia and of the demand of so many AFL members for the State Department to "take immediate steps to remove all obstacles to trade with Russia," his reply was that the proposal proved that these workers were the unwitting tools of American business, which put profits above the nation's interests. For "free resumption of trade would be an unlimited opportunity [for the Bolsheviks] to corrupt the world with propaganda."[55]

On the second anniversary of the October Revolution, Ludwig C.A.K. Martens, the Soviet government's official representative in the United States, hailed American labor for its support of his country. "I wish to thank the American workingmen and women in behalf of Soviet Russia for the sympathy and helpfulness which they have shown during the past year in their protests against the attacks on Soviet Russia. I feel confident that the more the American workers learn the truth about the republic of the Russian workers, the stronger will be our bonds of sympathy and solidarity."[56]

In the Soviet Union, Lenin noted that "in the Unites States, the strongest and youngest capitalist country, workers have tremendous sympathy with the Soviets." He added: "America, naturally, is at the head of the states where the workers can help us, are already helping us, and will help I am profoundly confident—on a far greater scale."[57]

Among the central labor unions endorsing the Alliance were the central labor bodies of Barstow, San Diego, Taft, Calif.; Denver, Col,; Bridgeport, Hartford, Meriden, New Haven, Conn.; Wilmington, Del.; Washington, D.C.; Council Bluffs, Iowa; Chicago, Springfield, Ill.; Portland, Shelbyville, Terre Haute, Ind.; Frostburg, Baltimore, Md.; Boston, Salem, Mass.; Albert Lea, Minn.; Omaha, Neb.; Berlin, N.H.; Fort Edward, Schenectady, N.Y.; Cincinnati, Ironton, Ohio; Altoona, Harrisburg, Jeannette, Philadelphia, Pittsburgh, Reading, Warren, Wilkes-Barre, Pa.; Charleston, S.C.; Ogden, Utah; Newport News, Richmond, Va.; Seattle, Tacoma, Wash.; La Crosse, Milwaukee, Wis.; Cheyenne, Greybill, Wyo.; Central Trades and Labor Council of New York. United Hebrew Trades of New York, Women's Trades Union League of Philadelphia, Women's Trades Union League of New York, and Italian Chamber of Labor of New York were also among the supporters of the Alliance's program. *Relations with Russia. Hearings before the Committee on Foreign Relations United States Senate, Sixty-Sixth Congress, Third Session, on S.J. Res. 164, A Resolution Providing for the Establishment of Trade Relations with Russia, And So Forth,* Washington, D.C., 1921, pp. 29, 55-60.)

CHAPTER 4

General Strike: Seattle and Winnipeg

The year of strikes, 1919, had barely begun when the Seattle general strike started. Although it was neither a revolution nor a rebellion, *the Seattle strike was one of the key events in post-World War America.

SEATTLE SHIPYARDS' STRIKE

The causes of the general strike were linked to the long radical and militant traditions of Seattle's labor movement. As one study of that movement put it: ". . . the Seattle labor movement . . . stood for everything Samuel Gompers rejected: labor in politics, industrial unionism, and nationalization of key industries."[1] Indeed, the Seattle labor movement was so distinctive that even the Industrial Workers of the World characterized it as a movement "affiliated—more in form than in spirit—with the American Federation of Labor."[2]

Many radical unionists in Seattle held both IWW and AFL cards. Since Seattle was essentially a closed shop city, a worker without a valid AFL card could not get work. "I belong to the I.W.W. for principle and the A.F. of L. for a job," one Wobbly declared.[3]

The radical nature of the Seattle labor movement was further advanced by the Bolshevik Revolution. The triumph of the Russian workers intensified the determination of Seattle workers to find radical solutions to the question of labor's place in society, even though there was no agreement how this would be achieved.

*Despite the dramatic title of his book, *Revolution in Seattle,* Harvey O'Connor concedes that, in the case of the general strike, the Seattle workers "were launched on a trade union trial of strength, and not a revolution." (New York, 1964), p. 110. As one who was personally involved in the strike, O'Connor's testimony is significant.

Harry Ault, editor of the *Seattle Union Record,** put it succinctly:

> I believe 95% of us agree that the workers should control the industries. Nearly
> all of us agree on that but very strenuously disagree on the method. Some of us
> think we can get control through the cooperative movement, some of us think
> through political action, and others think through industrial action. . . .[4]

The direct cause of the general strike of 1919, however, was not a desire
on the part of the Seattle labor movement to achieve workers' control of
the city's industries. Rather it was the result of a strike in the shipyards,
Seattle's most important industry. With the tremendous expansion in wartime shipbuilding, the shipyards became the largest employer in Seattle.
As a result, the shipyard unions grew enormously in membership, and the
yards were almost 100 percent organized. The Metal Trades Council, a
combination of twenty-one craft unions in the shipbuilding industry, was
the major force in Seattle's Central Labor Council.[5]

The shipyard workers had been greatly disappointed and outraged by
the decision handed down in the fall of 1917 by the Shipbuilding Labor
Adjustment Board of the Emergency Fleet Corporation. (The EFC had the
responsibility of building shipyards and ships and supervising the use of
the ships.) The Board, a wartime agency created to adjust disputes over
hours and wages, used the wages paid on June 1, 1916 as a base point and
from it granted a 31 percent pay increase. The basic rate for skilled workers was set at \$5.25 for an 8-hour day. These wages were not only lower
than the Seattle shipyard workers had expected, but they became the maximum wages that could be paid. Moreover, while increasing the wages of
some crafts, the Board's award decreased the wages of others—"some
twenty-two cents per day below the level of wages granted in other [non-
contract] work in the same city."[6]

During the war the Seattle Metal Trades Council, while protesting the
wage award (known as the Macy award) and appealing in vain for its
reversal, did nothing to disturb labor relations. Although the shipyard
workers were bitter and dissatisfied, they accepted the appeals of their
union leaders to their patriotism. The leaders also pointed out that a strike
would be a violation of their union agreement.[7]

---

*The *Seattle Union Record* was the only labor-owned daily in the country. It was a complete
daily with all the features of a large paper: wire-service coverage of major national and international stories, a women's section, and coverage of the arts. After World War I, circulation
boomed and for a time the newspaper had a daily readership of 112,000. (Robert L. and
Robin Friedheim, "The Seattle Labor Movement, 1919-1920," *Pacific Northwest Quarterly,*
[October 1964] p. 150.)

The Council awaited news of the armistice in order to take more vigorous action, and in November 1918, less than two weeks after the war had ended, Council officials asked their locals to vote on an authorization to strike. The vote was secret, but the metal trades officials announced that authorization to call a strike had been voted by the required two-thirds majority of the affiliated unions. The Council was authorized to demand a new wage scale ranging from $5.50 to $8 per day, graduated on the basis of skill, plus an 8-hour day and a 5½-day week.[8]

Since the war was not yet legally ended, the federal government still played a decisive role in the settlement of the wage dispute that had precipitated the strike vote. The employers' committee announced its willingness to offer a raise in wages to the skilled mechanics, but refused any increase for the less skilled and lower-paid workers. But Charles Piez, director of the Emergency Fleet Corporation, threw the full weight of the government against any concession. Piez ordered the shipowners not to yield to any union demands under threat of the loss of their steel allotment. Since the wartime demand for ships had ended, the shipyards would not be able to pass the increased cost of higher wages on to the United States government, and the employers were only too happy to comply with Piez's demand.[9]

On January 18, 1919, two days after the employers had responded favorably to Piez, formal strike notices were distributed to the managements of the various yards, notifying them that all work would cease on January 21. All work did stop in the shipyards on that day as about 35,000 workers walked out—24,300 in the metal yards, 3,250 in the wooden yards, and the rest in the allied trades.[10]

Three days later, in an effort to put pressure on the wives of the strikers to get their husbands back to work, the Seattle Retail Grocers' Association voted to discontinue the granting of credit for food purchases to idle workers.[11] The Machinists' Union responded with a circular that was distributed to the wives of all shipyard workers. It opened with a sentimental appeal:

> The best part of your husband's life has been spent in grinding toil for you. Through the bitterness of winter nights, through the heat of summer days, he has gone into the merciless treadmill of capitalist industry to wrest therefrom with his bare hands, a living for you; while he has suffered abuse and galling injustice at the hands of the masters of industry—he has toiled on day after day with mute lips for you.

Now, the leaflet went on, the "masters of industry" had decreed that these men should not be able to bring home "a living wage" to their wives—but they did not know with whom they were dealing:

> The manhood in your husband was swelled within his breast. He has flung back his manly answer—NO. He has struck. When he laid down his tools his thoughts were all of you. Full well he knew that the hardships and miseries of a strike would fall most heavily on you. Of himself he did not think. The masters know this well, while they protect their own families from any sign of want with the profits they have wrung from your husband's toil. They hope to make him yield through his fear of seeing you suffer. On this they base their hope of driving him back to work at their own terms—to crack the cruel whip of capitalism over his head forevermore.

The appeal concluded on an even more emotional note:

> The eyes of the working class of America today are turned on you. On you they base their hopes, their fears. Stand by your man in this, his hour of trial. Fight by his side in the age-long fight for freedom. Courage, hope—it is always darkest before the dawn. Already a new day is breaking overseas.* Be brave, be firm, and the vicious wolves of want will be forever driven from the doors of the homes of the working class. [12]

Mrs. Eric Lindquist, the wife of one of the strikers, penned her own appeal to the women, which was distributed by the strike committee:

> This is not the first time I've been called to stand beside my husband and his fellows and uphold their hands in a labor contest. My message is to the women—the mother, wife, daughter, sister, sweetheart, of the man in Seattle who aligns in battle for the right to live. Tell these women to raise their eyes on high and when they feel like crying just to smile and be cheerful. History tells of no greater bravery than that of the Spartan mothers. What was the task of these noble women? To hold up the hands of their men fighters; to encourage them on the one hand, and on the other to make them understand that the only way to win their approval was to win in battle. When the soldiers left for the front did the Spartanesses droop and wither? They did not. They swallowed all misgivings and sent their men away with recollections of mothers and wives smiling bravely. That's the big duty the working women of Seattle have cut out for them today, tomorrow and the next day, and the next till the war our men are waging for a living wage is won. [13]

So widespread was the response to this appeal that the Seattle Central Labor Union credited Lindquist with having almost single-handedly defeated the strategy of the Seattle Retail Grocers' Association. [14]

*This is undoubtedly a reference to the Bolshevik Revolution and the establishment of the Soviet government, which, as we have seen, was widely supported in Seattle.

Confronted with the employers' charge that the metal trades workers did not support the strike, Boilermakers' Local 104, the largest striking union, held a mass meeting on January 26. Six thousand members of the union voted unanimously to support the Metal Trades Council in its calling and handling of the strike.[15] But the employers received renewed support from the federal government as EFC officials, led by Piez, declared publicly that the unions had violated their agreement with the government. They ordered the shipowners "to make no effort to resume operations unless the men were willing to accept the Labor Adjustment Board's decision." [16] This prompted the *Seattle Times* to declare in alarm: "The Emergency Fleet Corporation's intervention in the local shipbuilding strike has developed an entirely new situation."[17]

There was good reason for the newspaper's concern. Seattle labor saw the EFC intervention as the beginning of a joint employer-government conspiracy to break the power of the city's militant labor movement and to start an open shop drive.[18]

On January 22 at its regular weekly meeting, the Seattle Central Labor Council adopted a resolution proposed by the Metal Trades Council calling upon the affiliated locals to poll their members on the proposal to call a *general* strike of all organized Seattle workers in sympathy with the shipyard workers. (At about the same time, one thousand delegates attending a Chicago conference called by the International Workers' Defense League to protest the imprisonment of Tom Mooney,* voted that if Mooney were not granted a new trial by July 4, 1919, the delegates would act to have their locals call every organized worker in the land out on strike.[19]**)

On the evening of January 29, at the regular meeting of the Seattle Central Labor Council, 24 locals, constituting approximately 27 percent of the locals eligible to vote, reported that their members were willing to strike. The unions voting to strike were the painters, barbers, blacksmiths, boilermakers, building laborers, carpenters, cigarmakers, cooks and assistants, foundry workers, garment workers, hotel maids, hod carriers, housebuilders, housepainters, jewelry workers, laundry workers, longshoremen, milk wagon drivers, newsboys, plumbers, riggers, structural iron

*Tom Mooney, a militant San Francisco labor organizer, had been convicted on perjured testimony (along with Warren K. Billings) of murder in connection with the bombing of a Preparedness Day parade in 1916. The original death sentence had been reluctantly commuted to life imprisonment by Governor William D. Stephens at the request of President Woodrow Wilson, but labor, convinced that Mooney was the victim of a colossal frameup, continued to demand his release from prison. (For the story of the Mooney case, *see* Foner, *History* . . . 7: 78-95

**Twenty-five of the delegates were from Seattle.

workers, tailors, teamsters, and truck drivers. While the delegates from these locals indicated that support for the metal trades workers had been the major factor in the vote in favor of a general strike, they also made it clear that members of these unions had their own grievances over wages, hours, and working conditions, and that past experience had indicated that actions of individual unions were ineffective and inadequate. However, the meeting voted not to add the demands of the individual unions to those of the Metal Trades Council and not to make the yielding to these demands and those of the Council a condition for ending the proposed general strike.[20]

In an effort to prevent a general strike, new mediation schemes for the settlement of the shipyard dispute were quickly proposed by Seattle bankers. However, Piez quickly scotched this effort by notifying the employers that the Emergency Fleet Corporation "cannot consent to outside mediation that would involve a revision of the decision of the Shipbuilding Labor Adjustment Board." Going even further, Piez inserted full-page advertisements in the Seattle newspapers urging shipyard workers to return to their jobs "to preserve the sanctity of contract." He warned them that if they continued to strike, the government "might choose not to continue the building of ships." The strikers did not respond. Upton Sinclair, the Socialist novelist, wired Piez expressing the hope that no government money was used to pay for the advertisements. "If it is your personal money," he wrote, "all right. If it is mine, I protest with utmost vigor."[21]

STEPS LEADING TO A GENERAL STRIKE

The shipyard strike was now taking second place to the developing momentum for a general strike. On February 4 the *Seattle Union Record* published what has been called the most famous editorial in its entire history. Written by Anna Louise Strong, then a reporter for the newspaper, it was entitled "No One Knows Where," and said in part:

ON THURSDAY AT 10 A.M.
There will be many cheering, and there will be some fear.
Both these emotions are useful, but not too much of either.
We are undertaking the most tremendous move ever made by LABOR in this country, a move which will lead—NO ONE KNOWS WHERE.
We need not hysteria.
We need the iron march of labor.

LABOR WILL FEED THE PEOPLE.
Twelve great kitchens have been offered, and from them food will be

distributed by the provision trades at low cost to all.

LABOR WILL CARE FOR THE BABIES AND THE SICK.

The milk-wagon drivers and the laundry drivers are arranging plans for supplying milk to babies, invalids and hospitals, and taking care of the cleaning of linen for hospitals.

LABOR WILL PRESERVE ORDER.

The strike committee is arranging for guards, and it is expected that the stopping of the cars will keep people at home. . . .

Labor will not only SHUT DOWN the industries, but Labor will RE-OPEN, under the management of the appropriate trades, such activities as are needed to preserve public health and public peace. . . .

Strong stressed that it was not "the withdrawal of LABOR POWER, BUT THE POWER OF THE STRIKERS TO MANAGE THAT WILL WIN THE STRIKE." She also referred to "the taking over of POWER by the workers." Robert C. Freidheim, in his detailed history of the Seattle general strike, criticizes Strong for this language, arguing that the mere mention of "the taking of power by the workers" frightened the public, leading them to believe that a strike in which Seattle labor wished only to enable the ship-yard workers to secure higher wages and shorter hours had been converted into a revolution to overthrow the American system.[22] Yet Strong's was at most a generalized comment. Much more specific was a handbill written by young Harvey O'Connor entitled "Russia Did It" and distributed after the general strike was announced. In it, O'Connor urged the workers "to take over the management of the shipyards." He continued:

The Russians have shown you the way out. What are you going to do about it? You are doomed to wage slavery till you die unless you wake up, realize that you and the boss have no one thing in common, that the employing class must be overthrown, and that you, the workers, must take over control of your jobs, and through them, the control over your lives instead of offering yourself up to the masters as a sacrifice six days a week, so that they may coin profit out of your sweat and toil.[23]

The leaflet was quickly disavowed by the strike leaders, but nevertheless a report circulated that it was an official statement issued by the General Strike Committee, leaving the distinct impression that "the general strike was the first stage of a revolution. . . ."[24]

The General Strike Committee had been formed on February 2 and consisted of three representatives from each union that had voted to set February 6 as the day the general strike was to begin. An executive committee of 15 members was chosen by the larger committee to plan the details of the strike.[25]

The Committee of Fifteen devoted most of its time to preparing the city to operate at a certain level during the general strike. A Labor War Veterans Guard was established to maintain law and order, and three hundred returned veterans, all union members, responded to the committee's call for enlistments in the Guard. Requests for exemptions from striking of workers considered essential for health and safety were evaluated. School janitors requested exemption to keep the school plants running but were refused and told to respond to the strike call. Auto drivers were given permission to carry "mail only" and to dispatch vehicles on emergency calls for hospitals and funerals if the requests came through union headquarters. Organized firemen and garbage collectors were exempted from participation in the strike. One of the most interesting statements issued by the Committee of Fifteen concerned the telephone operators:

> In conformity with the spirit of the law and order committee's desire to prevent rowdyism by disinterested persons, it is the earnest desire after conferring with the officials of the telephone operators' union that they cooperate with the strikers' police division in maintaining order by placing their entire membership, which voted 100 percent strong for the general strike, at the disposal of organized labor (this not to include telephone men), who desire to postpone the entire shutdown of telephone dispatching wires for the reason that the continuance of same is so essential in the dispatching of our committee work.

Those receiving exemptions were to carry large signs reading: "Exempt by the Strike Committee."[26]

A troublesome issue facing the Committee of Fifteen involved the question of furnishing power and light for the city during the general strike. After Leon Green, business agent of Electrical Workers Local 77, threatened to turn off the publicly owned City Light plant and plunge the city into darkness, the Committee of Fifteen overruled him and assured Mayor Ole Hanson that light and power would continue to be supplied. But the electrical workers insisted that they would not allow light and power to be supplied, maintaining that in this way they could bring the strike to a victorious end within a few days. However, when Mayor Hanson threatened to invoke martial law and operate the City Light plant with soldiers, the electricians yielded. The Committee of Fifteen informed the mayor that except for commercial service the light plant would operate at full capacity.[27]

Mayor Hanson was not satisfied. He swore in extra police and requested Governor Ernest Lister to send the National Guard to Seattle. But Henry

Suazallo, president of the University of Washington, and Vaughn Thomas, the state attorney general, who had informally taken over the duties of the ailing Governor Lister, telephoned Secretary of War Newton D. Baker, asking for federal troops. Baker immediately authorized Major General John F. Morrison, Western Department Commander, to take personal charge. Morrison ordered elements of the First Infantry's Thirteenth Division to be dispatched to Seattle.[28] Meanwhile, "businessmen took out riot insurance on their property; householders laid in heavy stocks of groceries; hardware stores unearthed lamp supplies and sold them at considerable profit; the press alternately appealed to the workers not to ruin their city and threatened them with penalties if Bolshevism showed its head."[29]

THE GENERAL STRIKE

At 10 A.M. on Thursday, February 6, 1919 the Seattle General Strike began. More then sixty thousand AFL workers quit work when the ten o'clock whistle blew. Other workingclass organizations joined the walkout. Japanese unions, composed mostly of hotel and restaurant workers segregated by union practice, joined the strike with the approval of the General Strike Committee, which even allowed segregated unions to send nonvoting delegates to its sessions. Thirty-five hundred IWW members also walked off their jobs, and to assure the General Strike Committee they would not create disorders the Wobblies promised not to hold any demonstrations nor make any soapbox speeches. Moreover, IWW headquarters announced that any Wobbly who disobeyed the order would be expelled from Seattle.

When the strike began, 40,000 other workers in addition to the strikers were off their jobs, making a total of well over 100,000 workers—men and women—who stopped working. With public transportation facilities completely shut down, even those who may have wanted to work could not get to their places of employment.[30]

Downtown shops, theaters, and restaurants were closed, and Seattle's 88 public schools closed voluntarily. Butcher shops and food markets remained open. Those government employees who could get to work did so, since they had been warned that if they joined the strike they would be subject to imprisonment. Three newspapers—the *Post-Intelligencer,* the *Star,* and the *Daily Bulletin*—printed abbreviated editions but with no one to deliver the papers they had to be given away at the plants. Unfortunately, the *Seattle Union Record* decided to suspend publication for the duration of the strike. While this was understandable, it deprived workers of pro-labor reporting and interpretation of events, a service that was sorely needed and that could not be adequately performed by the daily strike bulletins.[31]

The following letter from Seattle describes the situation in the city one day after the general strike began:

> I have just returned to my room in the hotel in its sixth story, made accessible by walking the six flights of stairs. The room is exactly as I left it at noon. . . . I fail to discern the soft touch of a painstaking chambermaid upon anything. The bed is as I left it, soiled clothes are where I threw them. . . .
>
> Among the many female employes of the hotel, the only union girl among them pulled all the others out with her yesterday at ten. Several large posters in the hotel lobby announce to guests that as a result of the strike all employes had walked out, and they are requested to take the inconveniences cheerfully.
>
> I went uptown at noon to get a meal at one of the 21 union eating houses, practically the only ones in the city, maintained by the unions themselves in their entirety operating under a three-hour shift. But going there I must pass through the Japanese section. What a sight!
>
> The streets are noiseless with the exception of the clatter of feet along the sidewalks, and here and there a private automobile. Every commercial establishment is closed with the exception of two drug stores. Signs on doors and windows tell the reason. "Unfair to organized labor"; "Closed for duration of strike"; and some simply have it "Closed." One Japanese restaurant has on the door a permanent sign, "We Never Close," but underneath a temporary one saying, "We Believe in Labor's Cause, So We Have Closed." The two adjoining stores have the sign "So Do We."
>
> The Jewish quarter tells a similar story.
>
> On Yesler Way a funeral procession passed. On the windshields of the hearse and ten hired automobiles following, there was the sign in red letters, "Exempted by Committee."
>
> Above Yesler Way most of the stores are open for business, but there is no business to do. Restaurants, soft-drink places and candy stores are closed. The sidewalks are not crowded by any means. There are no yelling newsboys and the silk stocking brigade is notable for its absence. . . .[32]

The care with which the General Strike Committee had prepared for the strike paid off in the orderliness of the city. The 300 men inducted into the War Veterans Guard kept order, even though they served without legal authority, carried no weapons, and wore only a white armband to identify themselves. No one, striker or opponent of the strike, was arrested on any charge related to the walkout. Strikers not assigned to police duty remained at home as requested by the Strike Committee. Whereas before the strike there was an average of 100 arrests per day, the docket decreased during the strike to an average of 30 per day.[33] Major General J. D.

Leitch, whose troops of the Thirteenth Division were on their way to suppress the expected disorder, publicly acknowledged that he was impressed. So, too, was the Seattle chief of police. Nevertheless, federal troops did arrive in Seattle after the first day of the strike, and Mayor Hanson ordered special police to patrol the streets.[34]

Although there was no disorder, the mayor issued a proclamation on the second day of the strike that gave a completely opposite impression:

> I hereby guarantee to all the people of Seattle absolute and complete protection. They should go about their daily work and business in perfect security. We have 1,500 policemen, 1,500 regular soldiers from Camp Lewis, and can and will secure, if necessary, every soldier in the Northwest to protect life, business and property.
>
> The time has come for the people of Seattle to show their Americanism. Go about your daily duties without fear. We will see to it that you have food, transportation, water, light, gas and all necessities.
>
> The anarchists in this community shall not rule its affairs.
>
> All persons violating the laws will be dealt with summarily.[35]

In another declaration issued on February 9 Hanson claimed that the "sympathetic revolution was called in the exact manner as was the revolution in Petrograd," and that it was the first phase of a revolution that was "to spread all over the United States." He called on the entire nation to "clean up the United States of America. Let all men stand up and be counted."[36]

While Hanson was demagogically capitalizing on the national hysteria, the press joined him in characterizing the general strike as an "attempted revolution." No matter that the New York *Tribune's* correspondent in Seattle reported that the city was completely calm and that "there was absolutely no violence."[37] "The whole thing," declared the *Outlook*, "had been planned by the IWW and Bolshevist elements as the beginning of a revolution. The Seattle hold-up was to extend to the entire state and then to other states, until it had spread over the entire country. The government was to be conducted by the Workmen's and Soldiers' Delegates, as in Russia."[38]

The general level of reporting by the press was expressed by the Cincinnati *Times-Star,* which called the general strike "a revolution, a deliberate attempt by agitators, many of them foreigners, to start a disturbance on the Pacific Coast, which they hoped would spread and eventually result in the overthrow of the Government at Washington."[39]

Shortly after the Seattle general strike, Alexander M. Bing observed:

To-day there is a great deal of difference of opinion as to the extent to which an industrial revolution was contemplated; there can be no doubt, however, that there were some of the workers who hoped that the upheavals of Europe would be duplicated in the United States and that the Seattle strike was only the beginning. As a matter of fact the strike committee did adopt as one of its maxims that of revolutionary socialism (from the old international manifesto)—'you have nothing to lose but your chains and the world to gain.' Yet radical as many of the leaders of the strike undoubtedly were, it does not appear that revolutionary opinions and motives animated either their calling or their conduct of the strike. Certainly, the actions of the strike committee were not those of a body of men who seriously contemplated revolution. (*War-Time Strikes and Their Adjustment*, [New York, 1921]: 29.)

Robert L. Friedheim, who has studied the general strike more fully than any other historian, concludes that the strike "was not a revolution, but it was a revolt—a revolt against everything and therefore a revolt against nothing. There were too many enemies to thrust out against for labor to be able to define the goals of the strike." He also notes that separately, the various causes of discontent among Seattle workers "could not have provoked the general strike; rather, it was the combination of extraordinary events and the condition of Seattle labor."*

Arne S. Swabeck,** a participant in the general strike, agrees that it was "not an attempt at revolution," but emphasizes that it was permeated by the revolutionary spirit of the time, and above all by the spirit of the Bolshevik Revolution and the subsequent revolutionary upheavals in Europe." Both Friedheim and Swabeck agree that the Central Labor Council was the dominant force behind the general strike.

On February 7, Mayor Hanson delivered an ultimatum to the General Strike Committee, warning that unless the "sympathy strike is called off" by eight o'clock the next morning, he would "take advantage of the protection offered this city by the national government and operate all essential enterprises."[40] Knowing Hanson's penchant for issuing endless threats that were usually followed by little or no action, the Committee did not react to the ultimatum. However, on the morning of February 8, the first crack appeared in the remarkable solidarity the strikers had thus far demonstrated. The streetcar men began to return to work and six cars started to run, enabling some residents to get downtown. By that afternoon other union workers had returned to their jobs. Stores, including Bon Marché,

*"The Seattle General Strike," *Pacific Northwest Quarterly* 52 (July 1961) :98.
**"The Seattle General Strike of 1919: A Participant Remembers," in Paul Buhle, *et al.*, editors, *Free Spirit: Annuals of the Insurgent Imagination*, San Francisco, 1987, p. 92.

one of Seattle's leading department stores, began to open.[41]

END OF THE STRIKE

Pressures to end the strike were now increasing. The strongest came from the top leadership of the AFL and the international officers of its affiliated unions. Even before the general strike had begun it was denounced by the AFL as a "violation of [its] rules and regulations." Leaders of international unions whose locals in Seattle were involved wired and telephoned orders forbidding them to participate.[42] Some of these officers even came to Seattle in person to prevent their locals from joining the walkout, but only the printing trades locals yielded to the pressure. Once the strike began, however, the pressure increased. The return to work by a number of unions was attributed to the influence of the international officers present in Seattle.[43]

By a margin of thirteen to one (with one absence), the executive committee voted to request the General Strike Committee to end the strike at midnight on Saturday, February 8, and to instruct all workers except the shipyard strikers to return to work, "holding themselves in readiness to respond to another call from the General Strike Committee in case of failure to secure a   satisfactory adjustment of the Metal Trades' demands within a reasonable length of time. . . ." When the General Strike Committee, after a lengthy debate, submitted this proposal to a vote, it was overwhelmingly rejected. The strike would continue, the Committee explained, because it had not been empowered to call it off by the unions that had originally voted to strike.[44]

However, this was only a temporary reprieve. More and more union workers were returning to work, some openly and some surreptitiously. On February 10, the General Strike Committee met again, and, with the shipyard workers excluded from voting, accepted a new date to end the strike—February 11. Those local unions that had returned to work were asked to walk out again so that all trade unionists could return together. The resolution ending the historic Seattle General Strike read:

Whereas, this strike committee now assembles in the midst of the general understanding of the true status of the general strike; and

Whereas, the Executive Committee is sufficiently satisfied that regardless of the ultimate action that the rank and file would take, the said committee is convinced that the rank and file did stand pat, and the stampede to return to work was not on the part of the rank and file, but rather on the part of their leaders. (However, be it understood that this committee does not question the honesty of any of the representatives of the general movement).

Therefore be it

Resolved, that the following action become effective at once, February 10, 1919:

That this strike committee advise all affiliated unions that have taken action to return their men to work, that said unions shall again call their men to respond immediately to the call of the rank and file until 12 noon February 11, 1919, and to then declare this strike at a successful termination, and if developments should then make it necessary that the strike be continued, that further action be referred to the rank and file exclusively.[45]

Some unions, including the auto drivers, newsboys and teamsters, did go out again, but most did not respond to the second strike call. In any case, by noon on February 11, all organized workers except those in the shipyards had returned to their jobs.[46]

The American Federation of Labor greeted the end of the general strike with the comment: "Born in a spirit of insubordination, disregarding all rules and regulations adopted by trade unions for orderly procedure . . . the strike was from its inception destined to die an early death."[47] The AFL, moreover, proudly took credit for having brought the general strike to an end:

It was the advice and counsel and fearless attitude of the trade union leaders of the American International Trade Unions and not the United States troops, or the edicts of a mayor, which ended this brief industrial disturbance of the Northwest.[48]

The press, however, gave Mayor Hanson the credit for ending the strike and praised him for his "patriotic" conduct. The newspapers even lauded Hanson's action in placing dozens of picked marksmen on rooftops, ready to "take care of those Reds," after the strike was already over and people were calmly going about their business. He was hailed as the "new American hero" who had furnished "one of the finest examples of patriotism and courage, both physical and political, in our history."[49] The *New York Times* editorialized: "In one splendid moment, Ole Hanson, a man two or three days ago quite unknown . . . has made himself known and beloved through the United States."[50]*

*Hanson decided to take advantage of his sudden popularity and resigned his office to conduct a lucrative speaking tour, lecturing on how he beat the Reds in Seattle, on "Americanism" and "law and order," before Chambers of Commerce, women's clubs, American Legion posts, and other groups. He told the veterans that the only way to guarantee that they did not "fight the good fight in vain" was to launch a vigorous campaign to achieve the "deportation, incarceration, annihilation" of all radicals, socialists, Wobblies, anarchists,

The Seattle General Strike demonstrated an amazing solidarity of workers—skilled and unskilled, men and women, and of all nationalities. It extended to the Japanese, who struck in sympathy with the very unions that had in the past discriminated against them. The IWW also struck in solidarity with the AFL unions, making for an almost totally united strike.

The strike also revealed an effective and efficient strike machinery. It lasted five working days, and each day was characterized by a total lack of disorder and violence. As one contemporary commentator noted, it was "the most complete walkout that has ever occurred in America. At the same time it was the most peaceful."[51]

But whereas the General Strike Committee spent a great deal of time organizing the walkout down to the most minute detail, it did nothing to provide the public with information as to the reasons for the general strike, other than describing it as a "strike of solidarity" in support of the shipyard workers in their quest for higher wages. The General Strike Committee never clarified why such a "strike of solidarity" was crucial to the welfare of all workers in Seattle. Robert Friedheim believes that this was the key weakness of the strike: "Labor's inability to state reasons and goals for the strike was the major reason for its subsequent collapse."[52] Most other labor historians agree with this conclusion.

It was thus not too difficult for an opportunist like Mayor Hanson to capitalize on Seattle labor's mistakes and equate a "sympathy strike" with "a plot to establish a Bolshevist society." The press eagerly picked up this theme, but of course, it is altogether likely that regardless of what the General Strike Committee may have done, the newspapers would have insisted on calling the general strike a "Bolshevik plot." The *Literary Digest* found that "all over the country, papers congratulate the nation on what they consider the complete collapse of our first general strike, a complete victory in our first open grapple with Bolshevism in America."[53]**

and enemy aliens. The fact that the AFL national leadership had played a conspicuous role in breaking the general strike did not prevent Hanson from charging the Federation with disloyalty. In addition to his lectures, Hanson also published *Americanism Versus Bolshevism*, a pamphlet.

Carried away by his sudden popularity, Hanson let it be known that he would allow himself to be persuaded to become President of the United States. But his period of popularity lasted only a few months. As we shall see, his place as the "American hero" was soon taken over by Calvin Coolidge after the governor of Massachusetts broke the police strike in Boston. (*See New York Times,* Sept. 28, 1919; Robert L. Friedheim, *The Seattle General Strike,* [Seattle, 1964]: 174-76).

**The *Commercial and Financial Chronicle* called the general strike "the first endeavor to apply so-called Bolshevist methods in an American community." (108 [Feb. 15, 1919]: 642).

The *Digest* was incorrect in calling it the "first general strike." It was actually the ninth in U.S.* history. But it was correct in describing the end as a "complete collapse" of the strike. To be sure, for five days a major American city had been paralyzed by the power and solidarity of its workers. Nevertheless, the strike ended in confusion, with some unions returning to work before it was called off and others remaining out. Moreover, the strikers returned without having attained their objective—to enable the shipyard workers to get an honorable settlement of their demands. Indeed, while most Seattle workers returned to their jobs, many of the shipyard workers never did. The Emergency Fleet Corporation, in keeping with its warning against a general strike, suspended all construction of vessels being built in Seattle yards and followed this up in April by cancelling contracts for the construction of 25 vessels. Thousands of shipyard workers were permanently laid off, and the membership of the unions in the yards was drastically reduced. That of Boilermakers' Local 104 was cut by two-thirds.[54]

On February 11, the day the general strike ended, the nation's newspapers carried an article distributed by Associated Press entitled "OPEN SHOP STRIKE SEQUEL." It reported that Seattle unionists returning to their jobs were working alongside nonunion men. Two months before the general strike, the Seattle waterfront had been a "closed shop," but, the dispatch reported, as a result of a program inaugurated by the Waterfront Employers' Association, "Now the docks and wharves are again operated on the 'open shop' plan . . . and this policy will be continued."[55]

Continued—and extended. In March, the Waterfront Employers' Association, along with other business and professional groups and independent employers, organized the Associated Industries of Seattle, whose primary purpose was the promotion of the open shop.[56] In an advertisement published in the Tacoma *Leader* and the Seattle *Post-Intelligencer,* the Associated Industries of Seattle spelled out its aim even more precisely. The general strike, it declared, pointed to but one solution:

> We must smash every un-American and anti-American organization in the land. We must put to death the leaders of this gigantic conspiracy of murder, pillage, and revolution. We must deport all "aliens," Socialists, Non-partisan Leaguers, "closed shop unionists," Syndicalists, "agitators," "malcontents"—all these must be outlawed by public opinion and hunted down and hounded until driven beyond the horizon of civic decency.[57]

*Preceding general strikes occurred in Philadelphia, 1835 and 1910; St. Louis, 1877; New Orleans, 1892; Springfield, Illinois; Waco, Texas; Billings, Montana; and Kansas City, Missouri, 1918.

In the end, this vicious objective was not achieved.* But after the defeat of the 1919 general strike, the Seattle labor movement "became easy prey for a virulent open-shop drive, and it slid into a long period of decline."[58]

BACKGROUND OF THE WINNIPEG GENERAL STRIKE

Three general strikes took place in Canada in 1919, each generated by local industrial struggles. They occurred in Amherst, Nova Scotia, in Toronto, and in Winnipeg.[59]** This wave of general strikes was dubbed "Winnipegitis" by Canadian trade unionists, in tribute to the greatest general strike in Canadian history.[60]

For several dramatic weeks during the early summer of 1919, a general strike that involved even the police paralyzed Winnipeg. As in Seattle, the Winnipeg upper class immediately linked the strike to world revolution and charged that the "Bolsheviks" were deeply entrenched in the city.

Described as "one of the most complete withdrawals of labor power ever to occur in America,"[61] the Winnipeg general strike has been perhaps the most widely studied event in Canadian workingclass history. Although it is rarely mentioned or discussed in studies of American history, it was associated with U.S. labor because the same international unions with affiliates in Canada were involved. The leaders of these unions and of the AFL and the Railroad Brotherhoods played the same role in Winnipeg that they had in Seattle.

The Winnipeg general strike occurred in a year when union membership in Canada increased from 248,887 to 378,047—over 50 percent—and during which almost 150,000 workers engaged in 336 strikes and lockouts. Many of the same conditions caused the wave of strikes in Canada as in

---

*The businessmen were enraged that a charge of sedition brought by the U. S. government against the editorial staff members of the Seattle *Union Record,* including Anna Louise Strong, had been dropped. While she was under arrest, Strong's bail was furnished by the Boilermakers' Union, which turned over its Liberty Bonds for the purpose. (Anna Louise Strong, *I Change Worlds: The Remaking of an American,* [New York, 1935]: 84-85).

**In Amherst the local Federation of Labour led the general strike, which spread from the Canadian Car and Foundry Workers' demands that they receive pay equal to that which their 4,000 Montreal co-workers had won in a three-day strike in early May 1919. The company's rejection of the demand led to a citywide walkout involving all of Amherst's major employers.

In Toronto the metal trades fight for the eight-hour day led the Toronto Trades and Labour Council (TTLC) to demand that metal trades employers negotiate. On May 13, 1919, 44 unions, meeting at the TTLC, voted for a general strike to begin on May 30 unless the right of collective bargaining and the 44-hour week was granted to the Metal Trades' Council. The general strike began on May 30, and lasted until June 4, when it was called off by the Central Strike Committee at the request of the Metal Trades' Council. (Gregory S. Kealey, "1919: The Canadian Labour Revolt," *Labour/Le Travail* 13, [Spring 1984]: 25-28.)

the United States: the rising cost of living while business profits were mounting, unemployment resulting from war demobilization and the return of soldiers, and bitterness over the failure of business to live up to its wartime promise that Canada would be a happy place for workers to live in once the Kaiser was defeated. In Canada, too, the impact of the Russian Revolution of November 1917 was influential in heightening workingclass consciousness and confidence. In fact, in his study of the Winnipeg general strike, David Jay Bercuson points out that Western Canada and Winnipeg workers were influenced by reports of the revolutionary movement in Germany and Hungary as well as that in Russia, and that "they became more certain than ever that they themselves were part of a great world tide of change."[62]

Postwar radicalism was even more pronounced in the Canadian labor movement than it was in the United States. At the convention of the British Columbia Federation of Labour, held in Calgary in March 1919, labor delegates attended from all western cities, including 29 from Winnipeg. The convention came out for a 6-hour day to be won by a national general strike that was to take effect no later than June 1, 1919. A vote to ratify this decision was to be held among all Canadian locals. The convention also endorsed a resolution submitted by Victoria Lodge 456 of the International Association of Machinists AFL, which declared that "Full acceptance of the principle of proletarian dictatorship is absolute and sufficient for the transformation of private property [into] public or communal wealth." Finally, the convention went on record as "favoring the immediate reorganization of the workers along industrial lines, so that by virtue of their strength, the workers may be better prepared to enforce any demand they consider essential for their maintenance and well-being."[63]

That same month the Western Canada Labour Conference took place, attended by 250 delegates representing most of the important local unions between Winnipeg and Victoria. The convention adopted resolutions that (1) urged "the abolition of the present system of production for profit, and the substitution for it of production for use"; (2) establishment of a "system of industrial soviet control by selection of representatives from industry," a system, it declared, that was "superior to capitalistic parliamentarianism," and (3) expressed "full accord and sympathy with the aims and purposes of the Russian Bolshevik and German Spartacus revolutions." The convention also called for "immediate reorganization of workers along industrial lines." Lastly, the Western Canada Labour Conference decided on a general strike to begin on June 1, 1919 for these demands: (1) the 6-hour day; (2) the release of political prisoners; (3) the removal of restrictions on workingclass organizations; (4) the immediate withdrawal of Allied troops from Russia, and (5) the defeat of Allied attempts "to overthrow the Soviet administration in Russia or Germany."[64]

At both the British Columbia Federation of Labour convention and the Western Canada Labour Conference, delegates were present who supported the concept of "One Big Union," or OBU, which was soon to be formally established, and the general strike was "a weapon much favored by the OBU."[65]*

At a conference in March 1919 of Western trade unionists, called for the purpose of forming a left-wing caucus within the Trades and Labour Congress, the idea of secession from the American Federation of Labour and the Congress was pushed by several key militants and won wide support. The delegates decided to withdraw from the AFL and the Trades and Labour Congress, and to create a new organization, based on a Marxist analysis of society and designed to unite all workers in Canada into a single union. Three months later, at the beginning of June 1919, their work reached fruition with the founding of the One Big Union.**

From the day of its birth the OBU expanded rapidly across the West. Lodges, trades councils, and provincial federations withdrew from the international unions and threw in their lot with the OBU. By the end of the year the OBU's membership reached almost fifty thousand.[66]

The upsurge in militancy of Canadian unionism following the Armistice was especially evident in Winnipeg, where many workers were earning only $12 or $15 a week when "a dollar could buy only a quarter or third of what it bought before the war."[67] Small wonder that James Winning, president of the Winnipeg Trades and Labour Council, noted just before the general strike that "more workers had been added to the organized labor movement . . . than during the past 15 years."[68] With the growth in membership came a great increase in the spirit of labor solidarity.

The general strike grew out of this spirit of solidarity, and its develop-

---

*Although the Amherst General Strike was conducted under the influence of the One Big Union, and the strikers identified themselves with the OBU, a number of Canadian historians argue that although it advocated general strikes in industrial disputes, the OBU said nothing about the revolutionary strike, which is an essential feature of revolutionary syndicalism. This in spite of the fact that the One Big Union was born as a syndicalist movement. Syndicalism may be defined as a doctrine that espouses the ownership by workers of all means of production and distribution in society. This was to be achieved through massive general strikes waged by highly centralized trade federations. (David Jay Bercuson, "Western Labour Radicalism and the One Big Union: Myths and Realities," *Journal of Canadian Studies*, May 1974, pp. 2-19.)

**Bercuson, *Ibid.*, p.3

ment resembled that which took place in Seattle. It started as a result of action taken by the Winnipeg Trades and Labour Council in response to a request for support from the metal and building trades councils in their strikes. The metal trades workers had organized a council to overcome the weakness of separate craft locals, but the employers had refused to deal with the council, insisting on meeting with shop committees from individual shops. On May 2, 1919 the metal workers went on strike, demanding recognition of their trades council, the 8-hour day and 44-hour week, double pay for overtime, a one-hour premium for the night shift, and new hourly rates for machinists, boilermakers, electrical welders, laborers, and apprentices.

The building trades unions had also formed a council and demanded recognition. Since the workers were earning about $900 a year when they claimed the head of a family of five needed $1,500, they also asked for a substantial wage increase. When the Builders' Exchange, representing the employers, rejected these demands, the building trades union's went on strike.[69]

Upon receiving the appeal from the metal and building trades councils for support, the Winnipeg Trades and Labour Council responded by holding a general strike vote among its affiliated unions. The strike ballot contained three demands on behalf of the metal and building trades councils: (1) a living wage, (2) the eight-hour day, and (3) the right to organize—to be confirmed by a signed agreement. The vote was overwhelmingly in favor of strike action.[70]

THE STRIKE BEGINS

The general strike began on Tuesday morning, May 15, at 11 A. M. Twelve thousand organized workers walked out, followed by an equal number of unorganized men and women. Construction came to a halt. Streetcars stopped running. Telephone and telegraph workers walked out. Hotels and banks and buildings, deprived of servicemen and elevator operators, ceased functioning. Bakery and dairy delivery men joined the strike, and within 48 hours bread and milk were no longer being delivered. Restaurants closed, and no newspaper was published in Winnipeg except the strike committee's *Strike Bulletin*. The municipal police and firemen and the federal post office workers continued on the job, but they indicated that they were ready to go on strike if called upon. This soon happened, and they, too, joined the general strike. Within 48 hours 35,000 workers were on strike in a population of 200,000. More joined the strike every day as workers signed up in unions in every trade.[71]

The Labour Temple was the strike headquarters. There the Central Strike Committee directed an event unprecedented in Canadian history. The committee was composed of 290 members—three delegates from each of 95 local unions, plus five from the Trades and Labour Council. Subcommittees were appointed for food, press, organization, and other functions. The Central Strike Committee elected an executive committee of fifteen, but decisions on basic policy remained in the hands of the larger body.[72]

Originally the strike had been called to support the recognition of the metal and building trades councils and for the granting of their wage and hour demands. In a resolution adopted on May 22, the committee added two new demands: (1) all strikers must be reinstated without discrimination, and (2) employers and government must recognize the right to organize. Specifically, the provincial and federal governments were asked to enact legislation requiring employers to recognize trade union bodies—whether they were craft or industrial, and whether locals, councils or federations.[73]

Early in the strike Winnipeg's employers organized the "Citizens' Committee," ostensibly to provide milk for babies and to ensure an uninterrupted supply of water, bread, and milk for the public. But it showed its real purpose when it organized between three and five thousand "volunteers" into a militia body. Another purpose of the "Citizens' Committee" was to promote the view that the strike was a revolution; that a "soviet regime" had been installed in the Labour Temple, and that Winnipeg was "under red rule." The general strike was said to have been organized by agents of the One Big Union, which, the "Citizens' Committee" declared, was "Bolshevism Pure and Simple." The Canadian press also charged that Winnipeg was the second phase of the general strike begun in Seattle, that "radical leaders, having failed in Seattle, had come to Canada to try their luck and that the strike in Winnipeg had been financed and led by radical groups from the United States."[74] No proof was offered to substantiate these charges, since there was none.

Early in the strike the Canadian government sent the Royal Canadian Mounted Police to Winnipeg, and on May 2 when General Ketchem, the general officer commanding the Winnipeg Military District, wired Ottawa for help, the government immediately sent in a battalion of troops and two Lewis machine guns. Four days later the Canadian government, in conjunction with the provincial and municipal authorities, ordered the postal workers to go back to work, to sign an agreement pledging never again to go out on a sympathy strike, and to sever their affiliation with the Winnipeg Trades and Labour Council. The provincial government issued a similar ultimatum to the telephone workers. The Winnipeg City Council then informed the firemen and policemen that they must either return to work or be fired. The policemen were also ordered to sign the following agreement:

> I further agree that I will not join or remain a member of any union or association with whose orders, directives or recommendations . . . we as members are obliged to agree. . . . I will not take part in or support or favor what is known as a sympathetic strike. . . . Upon a breach of the above conditions, I shall be liable to instant dismissal from the force. . . . [75]

The Central Strike Committee rejected the federal-provincial-municipal ultimatums to the government employees. The Committee also announced: "Not a single worker goes back until all are reinstated."[76]

"BLOODY SATURDAY"

A major feature of the strike was the support it received from the returned soldiers. Delegates from the Great War Veterans Association sat on the strike committee, along with 20 other returned soldiers who were delegates from local unions. On May 31, 10,000 ex-servicemen demonstrated before the legislature, demanding an immediate settlement of the strike, withdrawal of the ultimatum to the police, and the enactment of legislation to compel employers to bargain collectively with unions. A delegation met with Premier Norris of Manitoba and asked him to promise that he would settle the strike and bring in legislation for collective bargaining. The answer was: "Call the strike off first!"[77]

Dissatisfied, the soldiers returned on June 2, and this time they were told by Premier Norris that he was not sure the government had the authority to call a special session of the legislature to enact collective bargaining legislation. The soldiers then demanded that the government resign, and challenged Norris to take the issue to the people in a referendum.[78]

On June 9, after the striking police to a man had rejected the ultimatum, the municipal authorities dismissed the regular police force and replaced it with "specials"—a private force recruited by the "Citizens' Committee." Two thousand of these strikebreakers were sworn in.[79]

On June 17 the top strike leaders were arrested. The Labour Temple and the office of the *Western Labour News* were raided, as was the Ukranian Labour Temple. The offices were wrecked and files and records were strewn on the floors.[80] A silent parade to protest the arrests and raids was arranged for Saturday, June 21.

That afternoon a large crowd of men, women, and children assembled at the City Hall on Winnipeg's main street, preparing to parade behind a large contingent of ex-servicemen. Then the Royal Canadian Mounted Police opened fire on the unarmed strikers and their sympathizers. The officer in command of the RCMP later described "Bloody Saturday":

> About 120 bullets in all were fired into the crowd of men, women and children. They were not marching round the streets, but standing in front of the City Hall. Many were running away when we fired on them. I didn't wait to see if they would run on our charge, but fired.

Two were killed and thirty injured.[81]

Winnipeg was immediately placed under military control and 100 strikers were arrested. Public meetings within the city were abandoned; the strike committee explained that because of military control, meetings would be held outside city limits.[82]

END OF THE STRIKE

The strikers had more than the employers and the government opposing them. The presidents of AFL affiliates and officials of the Federation were assisting the anti-strike forces. Gideon Robertson, international vice president of the Commercial Telegraphers Union, AFL, had been appointed Minister of Labour in 1917. On May 29, 1919, he wrote to Samuel Gompers:

> In my opinion, the prestige and authority of the international unions whose local membership is participating in the strike . . . should receive the rather serious consideration of the executives of the various organizations concerned. . . . The motives are undoubtedly support of the One Big Union movement. . . .[83]

This was all that Gompers had to hear. Soon after he received the message, officers of the international unions with locals in Canada began to oppose the general strike movement. When the Canadian locals that were not on strike asked their international headquarters what they could do to help the strikers, they were informed that their constitutions forbade sympathy strikes, and that in any case the locals could not strike without permission from international headquarters. Some international officers in the United States even recommended strikebreaking. The Brotherhood of Railway Trainmen sent the following order from its Cleveland headquarters to its Canadian members:

> In view of illegal strike of members of the Winnipeg lodge, resulting in terminals in that city being tied up, it is deemed necessary that our organization use every effort to furnish members of the brotherhood willing to accept positions

made vacant by the illegal strikers, and that members of the organization be called upon to furnish such assistance to handle business of the road affected....

Members of the Brotherhood striking in defiance of international leaders were taken off the membership rolls, and locals defying headquarters had their charters revoked.[84]

Fred Tipping, a member of the strike committee, later summed up the attitude of the international unions based in the United States as "unsympathetic to the strike":

> I spent some time in Chicago during the strike, trying to raise some money for the relief of the men who were in need. We were looked upon as a bunch of rebels by the union headquarters. Their attitude was what I should have expected: the strike should never have taken place because they were not official. I got no help from them. As it turned out, I met Bill Haywood of the IWW and he gave me the contacts I needed.[85]

All serious students of the Winnipeg General Strike dismiss the upper-class fears of revolution as groundless. The strikers, they agree, were not revolutionaries. But the repressive measures of the municipal and national governments, in response to the charges of a revolutionary strike to establish a Soviet Winnipeg, doomed the strike to defeat. As David Jay Bercuson puts it: "When the federal government decided to involve itself in countering a revolution which never existed, the workers were lost."[86] Or as D. C. Master writes: "Intervention by the Dominion Government smashed the strike."[87]

On June 26, 1919, the general strike was ended by the Central Strike Committee.[88]

The metal trades and building trades workers returned to their jobs. The former gained a partial victory. In the metal trades, hours were reduced from 55 to 50 per week, with the same pay, and the companies committed themselves to deal with the shop committees instead of only the top local committees. Building trades workers, however, had to content themselves with the understanding that a wage increase would be left for settlement by negotiation.[89]

But not one of the major demands of the workers who joined in the general strike was won—neither recognition of the building and metal trades councils, nor recognition of all Winnipeg unions by the employers, nor a guarantee that all strikers would get their jobs back. On the contrary, thousands of the strikers were locked out, blacklisted, dismissed, or otherwise discriminated against. Members of the Municipal Firemens' Union were locked out, and some firemen and policemen lost their jobs. Raids on union halls and offices by the Dominion government military police took place in Winnipeg and in other Canadian cities where strikes also had broken out.* George S. Kealey lists general strikes in sympathy with Winnipeg in 31 Canadian cities in May-June 1919. The strike in Brandon (May 20-July 2) was the longest of all the sympathy strikes.[90]

Years later, strike committee member Tipping told interviewers: "I wouldn't say that the strike failed. I would say that the direct objectives of the strike were not reached at the time."[91]

Reorganization got under way immediately. The Trades and Labour Council set up a committee on July 8 to visit unions. Assistance was organized for unemployed workers, and a program of mass meetings was arranged. The *Western Labour News,* the Council's official organ, declared on July 10, 1919: "The spirit of labour was in no way crushed; it has been but a setback."

The "setback" on the economic front was to be followed by victories in the political arena. All the men who had been imprisoned and others active in the strike received some public recognition. Several were elected to the legislature, one was elected mayor of Winnipeg, and one had a public school named after him. More labor representatives were sent to the provincial legislature in the election following the strike than in any other period in Canadian history.[92]**

---

*The strike wave had spread to Vancouver, where 60,000 workers walked out; to Alberta, where railroad shop workers and expressmen struck; and to Calgary, where streetcar, hotel, and restaurant workers walked out; as did miners at Drumheller and Lethbrigge.

**In Seattle, unlike Winnipeg, labor was defeated at the polls after the general strike. In 1920, James Duncan ran for mayor as candidate of the Triple Alliance, in which labor was the major participant, and defended the general strike. Hugh M. Caldwell, Duncan's Republican opponent, denounced the general strike as "a revolution." Caldwell won a landslide victory, receiving the largest majority of any candidate for mayor up to that time. (Robert L. Friedheim, *The Seattle General Strike,* pp. 166-69).

CHAPTER 5

The Boston Telephone and Police Strikes

GRIEVANCES OF TELEPHONE OPERATORS

One of the most important strikes in 1919 involved Boston's telephone operators. This was hardly surprising, since of all the workers seriously affected by the rising cost of living, probably none felt it more than the telephone operators. The average annual earnings of an operator amounted to about half that of the government clerk and about 65 percent of the average for a female worker in manufacturing. In fact, with the exception of those areas where operators had raised their wages by strikes, the 1919 earnings of telephone operators, alone of all the workers under government control during the war, remained at their prewar level.[1] On the other hand, telephone rates had been increased repeatedly.

Several months before the Boston telephone operators' union agreement expired on December 31, 1918, union president Julia O'Connor had proposed a new wage scale to William E. Driver, general manager of the New England Telephone Company. The union's demands illustrate the low level of wages paid the operators:[2]

	Old Weekly Wage Scale	New Scale Demands
Assignment of duty	$ 6.00	$10.00
First month's service	7.00	11.00
Three months' service	7.50	12.00
Six months' service	8.50	13.00
Nine months' service	9.00	14.00
First year's service	10.00	15.00
Eighteen months' service	10.50	17.00
Second year's service	11.00	18.00
Third year's service	12.00	20.00
Fourth year's service	13.00	22.00
Supervisors	17.50 to 19.00	22.50 to 25.00

Driver informed O'Connor that he had no power to act on general wage increases and that the issue would depend on a government decision. After O'Connor had been assured by a representative of Postmaster General Albert Burleson that the government had jurisdiction, the new schedule was presented to the Ryan Commission in Washington.* On December 20, 1918 the commission's chairman assured O'Connor that he could "definitely promise" that the commission would order a percentage wage increase retroactive to October and would establish a committee, on which the telephone workers would be represented, that would adjust any matters not satisfactorily settled under the percentage increase. But by the time the contract expired on December 31, the Ryan Commission had not even met to deal with the promised increase.

For the next three months, Burleson kept promising to act but did nothing. The telephone company, of course, would not change the wage scale unless ordered to do so by the government. On April 11, 1919 the union finally asked outright if the company would accept the new wage scale. When general manager Driver replied that he would not accept it, the Boston local ordered a strike, to begin on April 15. In a long statement to the public, Julia O'Connor related the experiences of the telephone operators since the service had been taken over by the government. In spite of all efforts, including her own resignation from the government commission, to get Burleson or President Wilson to act on their demands for increased wages and improved working conditions, the Boston Telephone Operators' Union was compelled to conclude "they could expect no justice under the present system and the only way they could get it was to fight for it."[3]

THE TELEPHONE STRIKE

Although the walkout of the 6,000 Boston operators who were members of the union and those in nearby Massachusetts communities had been expected, no one had anticipated that the strike would shut down all of New England's telephone service. But over 3,000 operators in 90 exchanges in Massachusetts, New Hampshire, Maine, Vermont, and Rhode Island also walked out. Of the many telegrams that poured into the Boston strike headquarters, one read: "One hundred percent out, all four of us. Picketing since yesterday morning at seven. Very hungry. Send relief." The strike committee wired back: "Call it a day's work and get something to eat."[4]

On the second day of the strike, 12,000 cable splicers, test room men and other workers belonging to the New England Joint Council of Electri-

*Established to investigate the working conditions and wages of telephone and telegraph employees.

cal Workers joined the walkout. "All N.E. Telephone Plant Men in Maine Walk Out," read the headline in the *Kennebec Journal* of April 18, 1919. The story began: "Practically every union man employed in the plant department of the New England Telephone & Telegraph Co. in Maine struck today in sympathy with the telephone operators, according to the officials of the company." "Men Join Girls at Brockton" and "Male Employees Join the Girls on Picket Lines in Providence" were other headlines in the press. All over New England, the unity of the operators and the "inside and outside men" were reported to be "remarkable," presenting the "most spectacular demonstration of the power of organized labor to force attention upon their grievances."[5]

With the cooperation of the presidents of Harvard University and the Massachusetts Institute of Technology, the New England Telephone Company recruited male college students to scab at struck telephone exchanges. Nine Smith College girls were also strikebreakers "as a patriotic duty," but Smith President William Allen Nelson ordered them to quit until they had obtained permission from their parents to do such work. The college, he said, was neutral in the controversy.[6]

Police wagons transported students from Harvard Yard to Boston to take switchboard positions. The students told reporters that they were eager for "a little excitement" and "sport and diversion" while earning extra money. But the student scabs got more excitement than they had anticipated. They were attacked by the striking operators and several had their teeth knocked out as women shouted, "He is taking our bread! Give it to him!" All the scabs went hungry, for when they were taken to nearby hotels to be fed, the Cooks and Waiters Union declared that none of its 2,000 members would serve the strikebreakers.[7]* "The Chinese were wonderful during the strike," Rose Norwood, a striker, recalled later. "They put a long table against the door so that the company could not bring strikebreakers in through the back entrance. They said, 'We keep scabs out.'"[8]

In several cities the central labor unions endorsed the strike, praised the operators for their militancy, and publicly announced "moral support and financial assistance." The International Brotherhood of Electrical Workers (IBEW) threatened a nationwide walkout if Burleson delayed in recognizing the telephone employees' union and their demands. Only the national AFL refused to come out in favor of the striking telephone workers. Several months before the strike began AFL Secretary Frank Morrison had announced support of the telephone operators in their dispute with Burle-

---

*The same union also pledged $28,000, its total funds, for use in winning the strike, if necessary.

son and called "on organized labor to give these telephone girls every aid."[9] But on the eve of the strike Samuel Gompers, while conceding that the operators had patiently endured their grievances, urged them not to walk out but "to maintain self-control" and let the issues be settled by arbitration. "You're only girls," he reminded the operators, "and such strikes have an awful record."[10]

Burleson, however, seemed to have more respect for the "record" of women's strikes, for he reacted swiftly to the strike. To the amazement even of the commercial press, he declared that both the company and the government had been willing to receive the operators' demands, but "for some reason, they have refused to submit their matters and have gone on strike without any cause existing." But he agreed to forgive all past errors and to act, as he put it, "for the telephone girls myself."[11]

END OF THE STRIKE

At a conference of strikers and company officials held on April 20, the wage scales demanded by the operators were accepted, with details to be worked out after the women went back to work. Although the men had walked out without any demands of their own and solely out of sympathy with the striking operators, they were to receive an increase of 30 cents a day. Julia O'Connor told the press: "It is the best agreement ever reached by the telephone operators."[12] "When we went back to work," Rose Norwood recalled, "we got back pay, better wages and better hours. After that, they put cafeterias in some of the exchanges and we got food at cost."[13]

On June 14, 1919, Burleson issued a directive recognizing the right of

> employees of telephone companies to organize or to affiliate with organizations that seem to them best calculated to serve their interests, and no employee shall be discharged, demoted, or otherwise discriminated against because of membership in any such organization....
>
> Where requests or demands are now pending, the telephone companies shall immediately proceed to negotiate a settlement.[14]

On the heels of this announcement, Julia O'Connor began a nationwide organizing tour. Wherever she spoke, she told the story of the New England strike and "how the girls back there won their fight for real recognition of their union and better wages." However, she was quick to add, no thanks to Burleson, and she warned against relying on the Postmaster General's June 14 directive to secure union recognition. "Autocrat Burleson," she pointed out, had clearly demonstrated himself to be a friend of the telephone companies and an enemy of union recognition. Her message in each of the cities she visited was, "the operators must organize to the last girl" if they were to gain an agreement similar to what was won in New England.[15]

On the Pacific Coast, in the South, and in the Midwest, O'Connor's organizing tour was followed by settlements in which the telephone workers won wage increases modeled after the New England agreement—and including union recognition.[16]

BACKGROUND OF THE BOSTON POLICE STRIKE

In 1919, the Boston police force numbered 1,544 officers and patrolmen. In a year of massive, militant strikes, the walkout by fewer than two thousand Boston policemen drew as much attention as the more extensive struggles of the nation's working class. As it had done with the other labor struggles of the period, the press rushed to characterize the desire of Boston's police to redress their grievances as part of a Bolshevik plot. The grievances were primarily a pay scale that lagged behind wartime inflation, exessively long working hours, and filthy, antiquated facilities.

In 1885 the predominantly Protestant Massachusetts legislature took control of the Boston police away from the city's first Irish mayor and created a police commission whose members would be appointed by the governor. In 1906 the commission was replaced by a single commissioner and the governor was given the authority to appoint the Boston police commissioner to a term of five years, as well as the power to remove him. The city of Boston remained responsible for the policemen's pay and working conditions, but, since they had no say in the management of the police, Boston politicians simply ignored the men's requests for any improvements.[17]

However, policemen's working conditions became intolerable. Inflation, which began during the war and continued after it, reduced their real income. In May 1919 the starting salary was fixed at $1,100 a year, reaching a maximum of $1,600. Between 1913 and May 1919 the only wage increase granted averaged between 14 and 22 percent, while the cost of living for the same period had risen 76 percent.[18]

The patrolmen worked an average of 80 hours per week, based on a three-shift system: day duty, 75 hours per week; night duty, 87 hours; and patrol duty, 90 hours. John Cadigan, one of the veterans of the Boston police strike, put it vividly:

> The day crew came in at 8:00 a.m. and worked until 6:00 p.m. At six o'clock a crew came in and worked the first half of the night until 1:00 a.m. The other shift was from 1:00 a.m. to 8:00 a.m. Once every two weeks, after a man

finished his tour of duty at 1 o'clock, he stayed and slept at the station house for the next seven hours, in case any extra policemen were needed. But he wasn't paid for it. That was one of the things we wanted to change. . . .

Nor was that all. "If a man had to testify in court about an arrest in the daytime, he went to district court the next day and hung around all day. He wasn't paid extra for that. If he were a green night man, forget about getting paid at all for going to court. . . ."[19]

In general, the pay and tour of duty of Boston policemen ranged from 25 cents an hour for an 83-hour week to 21 cents an hour for a 98-hour week. And this at a time when coal miners were asking for a thirty-hour week!

An investigation conducted in 1909 had substantiated the complaints about unsanitary conditions in the station houses. The report disclosed that there were too few toilets and bathtubs (in the most flagrant case there was one bathtub for 135 men), not enough beds and lockers, and all station houses were found to be infested with vermin, cockroaches, and rodents.[20] Nothing was done in the ten years since that report had been issued. The excuse was that the city of Boston did not have the necessary funds.[21]

BOSTON POLICEMEN'S UNION

For 13 years prior to 1919, the Boston police had an ineffective organization called the Boston Social Club as their sole means of adjusting grievances. This Club was arbitrarily abolished by Commissioner Edwin U. Curtis, a Protestant who disliked the predominately Irish-Catholic police force, and replaced the Club with a so-called "grievance committee," a nonentity that "asked for little and got less."[22]

In June 1919 the American Federation of Labor reversed its policy and started to grant charters to police unions. The police local in Knoxville, Tennessee became the first such group in the nation to affiliate with the AFL, and by September 1919 police forces in 37 cities had applied for and received charters from the AFL.[23] Boston's firefighters and library workers had also organized, and its city hall clerks had formed an AFL local. On August 9 the AFL's New England organizer Frank McCarthy, granted the Boston Social Club a union charter.[24]

Commissioner Curtis, a staunch Republican and ultraconservative, was not ready to tolerate any outside interference in the conduct of his duties. He immediately issued an edict forbidding any policeman to join any outside organizations—other than the nationally known war veterans' organizations. Unionization was specifically forbidden for city police, who were said to be "state officers," not employees.[25]

On August 15 the police, disregarding Curtis's order, gathered at Fay Hall in the South End and formed a union. Two days later, the Boston Central Labor Union held its largest meeting in a decade. "The mood was militant," writes Francis Russell in his history of the police strike.* "A delegate introduced a carefully prepared resolution denouncing Curtis's actions as ' a tyrannical assumption of autocratic authority . . . foreign to the principle of government under which we live'. . . . The delegate congratulated the police for their courage in asserting their rights, promised 'every atom of support that labor can bring to bear,' and bade a hearty welcome to the policemen's union to the ranks of organized labor."[26]

Commissioner Curtis was unmoved. He refused to meet with a committee of the new union, and late in August he suspended eight members of the committee and eleven other union officials. A trial was scheduled to determine if they were guilty of violating the commissioner's anti-union rule.

At this point it was clear to any observer that a police strike was inevitable if nothing was done to restrain Commissioner Curtis. Mayor Andrew J. Peters thereupon appointed a committee headed by James Storrow, the Boston reformer, to study the problem and find a compromise solution. The Storrow Committee, as it was called, proposed that "the Boston Policemen's Union should not affiliate or be connected with any labor organization, but should maintain its independence and maintain its organization."[27] The committee also called for an investigation of the existing wages, hours, and working conditions, and for the adoption of all recommended adjustments. Members of the Boston police force, said the committee should not be prevented from or discriminated against for joining the Boston Policemen's Union, and no member of the union "should be discriminated against because of any previous affiliation with the American Federation of Labor."[28] In other words, all suspended policemen were to be reinstated.

The proposals of the Storrow Committee were acceptable to the legal representatives of the police, but Commissioner Curtis refused to even consider them. He was supported in this stand by Governor Calvin Coolidge, who shared Curtis's Protestant antipathy toward the Boston police force. Of Boston's five papers, however, four dailies favored the compromise plan, including the reinstatement of suspended policemen. Only the *Transcript*

---

*Although Russell's study, sensationally entitled *A City in Terror,* contains some useful information on the background of the strike, once the strike begins its emphasis is on Bolshevik influence, rioting, pillaging, and rape, which, according to it, converted Boston into "a city in terror." But there is no documentation for these charges. Without citing a single source, Russell writes about smuggled Tsarist crown jewels being used to finance subversion. His indiscriminate use of the word "mob" shows a total unfamiliarity with the work of recent scholars on this subject, such as that of George Rudé.

supported Curtis's rejection of the Storrow Committee's proposals.[29]

THE STRIKE BEGINS

On September 8, the 19 union officials who had been suspended were found guilty of union activism, but instead of being summarily discharged they were again suspended. The policemen, however, were furious over the rejection of the Storrow Committee's proposals, and late that very evening a strike vote was taken by the aroused union members. By the overwhelming majority of 1,134 to 2, the police voted to strike. The strike date was set for the following evening, September 9, 1919.[30]

On September 9, at 5:45 p.m., 1,117 policemen left their posts. Four hundred and twenty-seven did not join the walkout. Of these, a number were either ill or on vacation.[31]

Governor Coolidge's initial reaction to the strike was to place at Curtis's disposal 100 of the 183 state-controlled Metropolitan Park police in the Boston area. They gathered immediately in the Chamber of Commerce building. They were told to hold themselves in readiness. They were also reminded that under Massachusetts law they could, when on duty, ask bystanders for help if needed. Anyone who refused to assist them was liable to a month's imprisonment or a $50 fine.[32]

But 58 of these "volunteers" refused to do Boston police street duty as scabs and were immediately suspended. A number of policemen from other Massachusetts towns and cities showed their solidarity by appearing at the strike headquarters.[33]

Throughout these developments, Commissioner Curtis kept assuring Governor Coolidge and Mayor Peters that every precaution had been taken to ensure the city's safety in the face of the strike, since he had many volunteers on reserve, among them approximately 250 Harvard students.[34]* But in reality, the city of Boston was without any police protection on the night of September 9 when the strike began, because Curtis had instructed the volunteer force to report the following morning.

"A CITY IN TERROR"

On the night of September 9 South Boston was the scene of a consider-

*A Harvard emergency committee of three acting deans and two seniors opened an all-night recruiting office for strikebreakers at University Hall. When one alumnus protested, the committee replied: "We want it understood that the Harvard students are not going into this matter merely for the sake of defeating the policemen. It is not as strike-breakers that the undergraduates are offering their services. They are enrolling solely to protect life and property." ("Harvard Men in the Boston Police Strike," *School and Society* 10 (Oct. 11, 1919): 425-26.)

able amount of rioting and looting. The next morning the first volunteer policemen reported to their stations and drew badges, revolvers, and nightsticks. Other citizens flocked to police headquarters for pistol permits, and several thousand were issued in one day. One group declared that what was now at stake was "whether any element, no matter what, shall assume control of the destinies not merely of our city, but inevitably, of the republic itself." To the nation's press, that "element" was the Bolsheviks.[35]

On the second day of the strike Mayor Peters asked for 3,000 additional troops. While the strike was brewing, Coolidge had avoided involvement and had hesitated to call out the State Guard until he was certain that public opinion had turned against the strikers because of the rioting and looting. Now he called up the 11th, 12th, and 15th Regiments, plus a machine-gun company. These guard companies converged on Boston from across Massachusetts. In South Boston, guardsmen fired on a crowd, killing three and wounding eight. "The firing," Adjutant General Sevens wrote happily in his report, "had a salutary effect; it cowed the mob."[36]

In truth, the greatest loss of life and bodily harm during the strike was caused by troops firing on citizens. But the picture that emerged was that the Boston "mob" had rioted, pillaged, and created "a city in terror." Yet Francis Russell, who stresses this in his account of the strike, concedes that "The life of the city went on much as usual." In fact, none of the schools closed.[37] Moreover, there is no evidence to prove that the two days of "rioting" produced more rapes and attacks on life than ordinarily occurred in a similar period, nor that property damage exceeded customary bounds. In the end, local merchants filed claims with the city clerk for property damages amounting to only $35,000, and the city of Boston settled all claims for $34,000.[38]

Nevertheless, such violence as did occur hurt the policemen's cause. Many policemen and their supporters felt that Governor Coolidge deliberately withheld the troops until violence was apparent. John Cadigan points out that "it was not the union's fault" that Coolidge waited three days before calling in the National Guard: "There were about 1,500 guardsmen, militia men, and volunteers stationed in the area. Now, that isn't leaving a city helpless." He concedes, however, that public opinion did turn against the policemen because of the rioting.[39]

Nevertheless, a study of the nation's press reveals that it was basically the fact that the police had unionized and gone on strike which guaranteed that their struggle would be viewed with deep hostility. On September 11 the *New York Times* carried an editorial demanding "simple justice" for the New York policemen who are underpaid in this period of high living costs." Yet in another column on the same page was an editorial headed "Disorder in Boston" that characterized the Boston police strike as "an army . . . which has revolted and deserted."[40]

Within a ten-day period—from September 10 through September 19— the *New York Times* carried seven major editorials on the strike, all of them revealing the paper's hostility toward the strikers. According to the *Times*, they were guilty of "a serious offense in the moral, if not the legal view." The police were "faithless and unworthy, guilty of treason."[41] That such editorial opinion reflected national and not merely sectional press reaction was confirmed by the *Literary Digest*, whose investigation of press opinion concluded that "virtually the entire press were agreed that the policemen had no right to strike."[42] It presented as a typical view the statement of the Grand Rapids *Herald*:

> As an abstract proposition, a "walk-out" in a police department is equivalent to a "walk-out" in the army. Is there any sane person who could presume to say that an "army" would be justified to "strike" for higher wages on the eve of a battle?[43]

The *Engineering News-Record* voiced a common opinion in the periodical press, liberal and conservative alike, when it declared: "If the country were to condone the strike, we should be on the verge of Bolshevism." The Philadelphia *Evening Public Ledger* felt that the nation had passed beyond the "verge." "Bolshevism in the United States," it cried, "is no longer a specter. Boston in chaos reveals its sinister substance." The Boston police strike was the American version of "the mad minority which overthrew Kerensky and ruined Russia."[44]

All over the country, newspapers, periodicals, and political figures denounced the strike in similar language, at the same time ignoring the fact that policemen's unions were established in such cities as Oklahoma City, Knoxville, Washington, D.C., Jersey City, Los Angeles, and Miami; Portland, Oregon; St. Paul, Minnesota; Lynn, Massachusetts; Vicksburg, Mississippi; and Topeka, Kansas. "It is a tremendous issue," wrote Massachusetts Senator Henry Cabot Lodge, "and if the American Federation of Labor succeeds in getting hold of the police in Boston it will go all over the country, and we shall be in measureable distance of Soviet government by labor unions." Elihu Root, Wall Street lawyer and former Secretary of War and State, declared that the strike "raises distinctly the question whether our system of government represented in the Constitution is to be abandoned or not." If the strike succeeded, it would mean "the end" of the American government. President Wilson added to the chorus by pointing to the strike as evidence of the "poison of unrest that is spreading to America from Europe."[45]

"We followed the flag and faced death in two wars. Won't you tell the people of Massachusetts in which war you served?" This question was asked Governor Coolidge in resolutions adopted at a mass meeting of members of the Boston Policemen's Union after they had been stigmatized by the Governor as traitors to their country when they struck for improved working conditions. The resolutions said in part:

> When we were honorably discharged from the United States army we were hailed as heroes and as saviors of our country. We returned to our duties on the police force of Boston.
>
> Now, though only a few months have passed, we are denounced as deserters, as traitors to our city and as violators of our oath of office.
>
> The first men to raise the cry were those who have always been opposed to giving to labor a living wage. It was taken up by newspapers, who cared little for the real facts. You finally added your word of condemnation. It had great weight, because you were governor of this commonwealth. . . .
>
> Among us are men who have gone against spitting machine guns single-handed, and captured them, volunteering for the job. Among us are men who have ridden with dispatches through shell fire so dense that four men fell and only the fifth got through.
>
> Not one man of us ever disgraced the flag or his service. It is bitter to come home and to be called deserters and traitors. We are the same men that were on the French front.
>
> Some of us fought in the Spanish war of 1898. Won't you tell the people of Massachusetts in which war you served?[46]

ROLE OF THE CENTRAL LABOR UNION

In the end, the key to victory or defeat for the Boston Policemen's Union was the degree of support it received from other AFL workers in the city. At the outset of the strike, prospects for wide and deep backing were bright. Several unions supported the police union's strike despite the fact that their members had suffered at the hands of the men in blue in their own struggles. Even though the tailors in 1913 and the garment workers in 1916 had been beaten and arrested by police, the 30,000 members of the United Garment Workers were fully behind the police strikers. The telephone operators also overlooked the fact that only recently police wagons had transported students from Harvard Yard to Boston to take over their switchboard positions. Mae Matthews, secretary of the telephone union, declared that "the girls will back up the police and will go out, if necessary, to help them win." Several other unions, including the firefighters and the streetcar operators, also expressed a willingness to engage in a general strike. Daniel Looney, president of the firemen's union, told reporters: "We are in the hands of the American Federation of Labor. It is for the Central Labor Union to take some action, and what labor demands of us we will deliver."[46]

Organized labor in Boston, especially the most militant unions—garment workers, carmen, firemen, telephone operators, and electrical linemen—waited for a signal from the Central Labor Union. At a CLU meeting on the second day of the strike, President O'Donnell polled the delegates of each local secretly on the question of a sympathy strike. Eighty percent of the delegates went on record in favor of striking at once. But O'Donnell and the executive committee, nearly all of whom were conservatives, decided to keep the results secret. Instead, they announced that the issue of a general strike would be decided at the next CLU meeting. While stalling for time in the hope that the strike would be over by then, the Central Labor Union leaders hypocritically announced that the body would continue "to work in conjunction with the Police Union, to the end that justice be given the members of the Police Union."[47]

At the same time, AFL President Gompers worked behind the scenes to prevent a general strike in Boston. Regretting now that the Federation had granted the police a charter, and frightened by the upsurge of labor militancy that had already expressed itself in the Seattle general strike, Gompers announced that he had appealed to the Boston Policemen's Union "to cooperate and return to their posts. . . ."[48]

Eighty-five percent of the firemen were reported to be in favor of a general strike. The figure reached 100 percent among the 30,000 members of the United Hebrew Trades, and the same percentage applied to the bartenders. But soon even these unions backed down, while several of the unions that had initially supported the police, such as the telephone operators and the streetcar operators, indicated unwillingness to engage in a sympathy strike.[49]

The Boston Central Labor Union, which represented over 100,000 workers in 1919, could still have turned the tide in the policemen's favor. But when the BCLU met, in the largest gathering in the organization's history, it was the conservative leadership that dominated the meeting. President O'Donnell informed the delegates that he and the executive committee had decided that "the time was not opportune for ordering a general strike." He reminded the delegates that "the eyes of the nation are upon this meeting today—for this and other reasons we are not to act in a manner that will give the prejudiced press and autocratic employers a chance to criticize us. . . . We don't intend to give anybody a chance to say we have not used good judgment, as has been said of the police." The delegates voted to accept the committee's recommendation. They were willing, they said, to give the police "their moral support"—but nothing more.[50]

END OF THE BOSTON POLICE STRIKE

The failure of the Boston Police Union's strike was now a virtual certainty. All of the strikers—some 1,100 men—were fired, and the rush of candidates for the new police force began. Soon the new replacements numbered 1,574—more than had been on the force when the strike began.[51]

Thus, after the Boston trade unions had withdrawn their support, Commissioner Curtis recruited an entirely new police force to replace the defeated strikers. The strikebreakers were hired from the ranks of unemployed war veterans. The United Garment Workers refused to make uniforms for the new policemen, so many recruits had to go on duty in civilian clothes.[52]

In December 1919 the Boston Policemen's Union became the Association of Former Police of the City of Boston.

The new policemen were granted a starting salary of $1,400 and a pension plan, and the initial costs of uniforms and equipment were paid for. These benefits were more than the striking police had requested. Moreover, the citizens of Boston collected approximately $572,000 to pay the volunteer police force—money enough to have granted every member of the old force approximately $300.[53]

In his study of the Boston police strike, Frederick Manuel Ross condemns Calvin Coolidge for his "irresponsibility." Nevertheless, Coolidge emerged from the strike situation as a politician of national stature. "No doubt it was the police strike of Boston that brought me into national prominence," he wrote later.[54] "That furnished the occasion and I took advantage of the opportunity."[55] When Gompers called on the strikers to end the walkout he wired Coolidge, urging that the strikers be reinstated pending the outcome of the Industrial Conference called by President Wilson. In reply to the second such request Coolidge issued the statement: "There is no right to strike against the public safety by anybody, anywhere, any time."[56] This statement swept the country. Not even President Wilson's denunciation of the Boston police strike as a "crime against civilization,"[57] made as deep an impression on the panic-stricken middle and upper classes.

Had the strike not occurred, Coolidge would have faced defeat at the polls. After the strike, he was reelected governor of Massachusetts by a plurality of 124,000 votes.[58]

In 1931, twelve years later, the Massachusetts state legislature authorized the reinstatement of the police strikers, but the then police commissioner refused to take any of them back. In any case, twelve years after the event, most of the men no longer expected to return to the force; they were asking only for something approaching vindication.[59]

During the streetcar strike of October 1919 in Knoxville, Tennessee (which we will discuss later), police of the city who were the first to affiliate with the AFL, were reported in the antilabor press to have "either stood idly by or actually assisted the strike sympathizers." The press charged that it was because the police "were unionized and detested KRL's [Knoxville Railway and Light Company's] strikebreaking efforts."[60]

Although the streetcar strike was broken, antiunion employers deluged City Hall with claims that union affiliation had caused police bias in favor of the strikers. Police Chief Ed M. Haynes promptly suspended several police officers for neglect of duty, but the employers demanded more punitive measures. Under tremendous pressure, the police were forced to meet on November 2 and voted 42 to 7 in favor of surrendering their union charter. To make sure that the police force remained nonunion, the City Commission in mid-November passed an ordinance prohibiting either the police or the firemen from belonging "to organizations having the power to order strikes. . . ."[61]

The news that Knoxville's policemen had renounced their AFL affiliation was hailed in Boston by Governor Coolidge. Coolidge exclaimed that "the citizens of Knoxville, including members of their police force, are to be congratulated that the issue so vital to their interests has been settled in a clear and decisive manner."[62]

The failure of the Boston police strike decided the fate of police unions throughout the nation almost to the present day.* After the defeat, police unions, when permitted, were purely local organizations and had no right to strike. In exchange for giving up their union charters, local officials in some places agreed to correct the policemen's grievances.[63]

---

*On August 3, 1918 the "world famous Bobbies," the police of London, went on strike and won union recognition after the soldiers made it clear they supported the strikers. In July 1919 the police union called another strike, but this time failed to hold its own against the government, and a bill prohibiting trade unionism in the police forces of England became law. (Gerald W. Reynolds and Anthony Judge, *The Night the Police Went on Strike*, [London, 1924]; R. and E. Fren and Michael Katunta, *Strikes: A Documentary History*, [London, 1971]: 169-71.)

CHAPTER 6

Streetcar Strikes

Of the 3,600 strikes in the period immediately following World War I the most spectacular were the Seattle general strike of February 1919, the Boston police strike, the nationwide steel walkout of September, and the general coal strike of November. But throughout the period a series of streetcar strikes gripped the United States at large and usually dominated the front pages of local newspapers. "Chicago Afoot," and "Pittsburgh Forced to Walk," were typical headlines in the press. One read: "East St. Louis Carmen Out. Strike Ties Up Traffic in 13 Nearby Cities and Towns."[1]

Skyrocketing increases in the cost of living during the war years were the underlying cause of most of the streetcar strikes. Robert H. Murray has estimated that by late 1919 the purchasing power of the 1913 dollar had fallen from 100 to 45.[2] Wholesale prices during and shortly after World War I increased about 170 percent above the prewar figure. Streetcar workers refused to accept the war as a cause of higher prices and lagging wages, blaming them instead on the greed of the transit corporations.

During the 1890's horse-drawn trolleys had given way to the new electric trolleys, and following the 1893-97 depression, urban streetcar companies were rapidly consolidated by merger in order to achieve more efficient operation. By 1900 many urban transit systems operated a combination of routes that included surface streetcars, elevated railroads, and subway trains. The urban transportation workforce was clearly stratified by skill and sexual differentiation. Pay scales reflected this stratification and ostensibly denoted skill level, seniority, and ability. Motorman and conductor jobs represented the highest skill levels, the most prestigious positions, and were therefore the best paid on the streetcar systems. Next were those of the clerks, cashiers, carbarn workers, and the car service workers who cleaned and maintained the equipment. The jobs to which women had been admitted before World War I were those of ticket sellers, cashiers, and car cleaners. The jobs of motorman and conductor were reserved for males and jealously safeguarded by a collective male egoism that extolled virility and physical stamina. Black workers, if employed at all, were confined to such menial jobs as sweepers and porters.[3]

But whether the workers were motormen or car cleaners, their wages, compared with most other industries, were deplorably low, their working hours were excessively long, and working conditions, especially concerning safety, deplorable.

The key union in the streetcar field, apart from a smattering of company unions, was the Amalgamated Association of Street and Electric Railway Employees of America. Organized in 1892, the Amalgamated affiliated with the AFL a year later. It barely survived its first few years, but began to make progress at the turn of the century. By 1916 the union had grown to a membership of 60,000, and after the United States entered the war the union expanded enormously.[4]

With their large memberships, the transit unions had considerable influence in central labor councils, which were used to mobilize assistance when needed. It is not surprising then that striking carmen were often joined by thousands of sympathizers who threw rocks, overturned cars, and beat strikebreakers. Streetcar strikes, unlike a number of other labor disputes, were highly visible and touched the lives of the entire city's population. The appearance of strikebreakers, protected by police or the armed forces at public expense, coupled with long-standing resentment over the corruption of state and local administrations by transit managements, as well as poor service, high fares, and outdated equipment, usually unleashed a torrent of hostility toward the companies and support for the transit workers.

In 1913 a reporter for the *International Socialist Review* commented: "A street railway strike must always be swift and furious, carried on among scenes of violence. Attempts to operate the cars of a struck service brings the hated scabs within close view of the strikers and their sympathizers, acting upon them as an insult and a slap in the face."[5] Yet for most of its early life, the Amalgamated Association was headed by William D. Mahon, a conservative labor leader who served on the executive committee of the National Civic Federation, and who strongly advocated voluntary arbitration of labor disputes in the street railway industry.[6] During World War I Mahon's message emphasized the importance of the work of streetcar employees in winning the war. He conceded that the rising cost of living and the unwillingness of companies to adjust wages accordingly caused discontent among the streetcar workers. "But no matter how justifiable this unrest may be," he insisted, "it must not influence us to acts that will compromise our integrity as an organization of workers that stands by its agreements and holds it obligations sacred."[7] This, however, did not keep Mahon and the General Executive Board of the Amalgamated Association from approving wartime strikes by its locals to prevent the hiring of women as conductorettes.*

Mahon was able to curtail most strikes of streetcar workers during the war, but when he insisted on continuing this policy after the armistice, he met with open resistance and opposition from the growing union membership. This was reflected in the wide-scale series of transit strikes after the war.

CHICAGO AND DENVER

In late July 1919, 15,000 Chicago public transportation workers struck, causing what *Survey* magazine called a "complete tie-up" of the elevated and surface trains there. The strikers defied their union leadership, including international president Mahon, who told the press that the strike was "illegal." Mahon came to Chicago to try to convince the men to accept a previously negotiated settlement, but was "howled down" by a crowd of 4,000 at the ratification meeting. The leadership therefore asked for a referendum on ending the strike. The back-to-work motion carried by only 186 votes among more than 12,000 cast. The surface train employees, who had sought a basic 8-hour day spread over no more than ten hours, a 6-day week, and no more than a 6-hour day on Sunday, were firmly opposed to the settlement. Under it, just 60 percent of these workers received the 8-hour day, and the working time was spread over as many as 14 hours. Neither the 6-day week nor 6-hour Sunday prevailed. Elevated train workers, whose votes had given the pact its margin of victory, did slightly better, with 70 percent gaining an 8-hour day spread over no more than 13 hours.[8]

In July 1918 over 1,000 employees of the Denver Tramway Company organized Local Union 746 of the national Amalgamated Association. For the next two years the local made fruitless attempts to obtain higher wages. In May 1920 the company announced a forthcoming wage cut, whereupon the union declared its intention to strike. Despite an injunction obtained by the company, the union decided to go ahead with the strike.[9]

---

*For a discussion of the conductorettes' issue during World War I, *see* Philip S. Foner, *History of the Labor Movement in the United States* 7 (New York, 1987): 201-13.

When the walkout began on July 12, the *Denver Post* immediately charged that it was caused by "foreign agitators," and accused the union rank and file of having listened "to the serpent tongue . . . of the IWW, the Soviets and other revolutionists."[10] The Tramway Company picked up the theme, and charged that immediately after the strike vote was taken a "revolutionary element" began pouring into Denver:

> It was the IWW. From every harvest field they came. From the mining districts, from faraway Montana . . . flocking to Denver like the vulture swarms toward the carrion. . . . From the south, from the north and east they came, gaunt men, narrow-eyed men, bearded men, treacherous men—all with a purpose. There was a strike. There was trouble brewing—and they would help in the spilling of blood.[11]

There was blood spilled in the strike, but it was not by Wobblies, proof of whose presence in Denver was never presented. Rather it was spilled by strikebreakers furnished by "Black Jerome," a notorious professional strikebreaker agency. On August 4 partial service was inaugurated on the streetcars, protected by the police and by American Legion volunteers. The cars were operated by armed motormen and conductors. On August 5 strikebreakers killed two strikers and injured 32 sympathizers. The following day, at the East Side Tramway barns, five strikers and sympathizers were killed and 25 injured when strikebreakers fired into a crowd.[12]

Martial law was declared, and U.S. troops were called in from Fort Logan, Kansas to break the strike. The commander of the federal troops refused to permit strikers to meet. Supported by the U.S. army, Frederick W. Hilde, general manager of the Denver Tramway Company, announced: "We will not deal with the union." The union offered to return and "have the cars running," if the company "will run the 'scabs' out of Denver." But the company insolently replied that all preference would be given "to strikebreakers employed to run the cars," and in the future, "streetcars will be manned by strikebreakers."[13]

Not a single strikebreaker was arrested, but seven members of the union's executive committee were convicted of contempt of court for having called the strike in the face of the court injunction. Each was sentenced to six months in prison.[14]

Local 746 suffered a severe defeat. The union was broken and did not reorganize until 1933. Anti-union publications cited the methods used in smashing the Denver streetcar union as a model for open-shop employers to follow.[15]

KNOXVILLE

In an August 1918 decision, the National War Labor Board awarded the employees of the Knoxville (Tennessee) Railway and Light Company (KRL) a wage increase from 36¢ to 46¢ an hour. When the contract between the company and its employees expired on September 1, 1919, Local 767 of the Amalgamated Association of Street and Electric Employees, representing 250 streetcar workers, requested wage hikes of 10¢ to 20¢ an hour. The company refused, and insisted that the demand be submitted to the National War Labor Board for arbitration. But the union pointed out that since the Board no longer functioned, the company had to give the answer directly to the union.[16]

On August 17, 1919 the streetcar workers in Nashville, Tennessee had struck the Nashville Railway and Light Company, and met with success. The strike was precipitated by the refusal of the company to deal with the union organized by the workers, and by August 21, confronted with a militant strike, the company capitulated and recognized the new local.[17]

The victory in Nashville was on the minds of the Knoxville streetcar workers when they voted to strike on October 17, 1919. Two days later the company placed a call for two hundred men, "soldiers preferred," in the Knoxville *Journal and Tribune*, and announced that it would resume limited service on October 21.[18]

Although Local 767 promised that the strikers would refrain from any acts of violence, the Knoxville police immediately went on 12-hour shifts, and Tennessee Adjutant General E.B. Sweeney and "a party of officers" arrived "to watch developments."[19]* Mayor E.W. Neal set up a meeting between the union and the company for October 21; the union showed up, but the company refused to send a representative. "We are too busy at this time to attend a conference with our former employees who saw fit to violate their obligations," KRL explained. The reference to the strikers as "former employees" clearly indicated that the company was determined to break the union and operate as an open shop. Indeed, at a meeting between the mayor and the company, held behind closed doors on October 24, KRL officials said bluntly they would not arbitrate or even discuss the dispute with the strikers' representatives.[20]

Meanwhile, the company kept placing strikebreakers on its payroll, most of them demobilized veterans unable to find work as a result of the

---

*According to James A. Burran, the race riot in Knoxville in August 1919 influenced the city to begin "girding itself for violence." ("Labor Conflict in Urban Appalachia: The Knoxville Streetcar Strike of 1919," *Tennessee Historical Quarterly* 38 [Spring 1979]: 68.)

postwar economic crisis. In local press advertisements, the company offered to re-employ striking motormen and conductors as nonunion men and at beginners' salary. It received no applications.[21]

On October 26 the strikers held a mass meeting to present the union's side of the dispute. One of the speakers, a Black preacher, described the workers as "slaves of capital," and defined "scabs" as the "lowest and most dangerous types of humanity in existence." The strongest demand to emerge from the meeting was that the company agree to arbitrate the wage question. As the Knoxville *Tribune and Journal* noted: "If one attended the meeting expecting to hear I.W.W. or Bolshevik doctrines, he was disappointed."[22]

That same morning, October 26, the company resumed full daytime operations with strikebreakers operating the streetcars. Roving bands of enraged strikers, strike sympathizers, and ordinary citizens attacked cars in the center of Knoxville. By the end of the day, cars were badly damaged, the word "scab" chalked over many of them, and a number of strikebreakers had suffered injuries severe enough to warrant hospitalization.[23] Most serious, in the eyes of the company and the city authorities, was that a number of policemen had either "stood idly by or actually assisted the strike sympathizers."[24] Knoxville, it will be recalled, was the city whose police force had been the first to affiliate with the AFL.

Reacting to the events in Knoxville, Adjutant General Sweeney ordered about 800 national guardsmen from the Fourth Tennessee Infantry into the city. They arrived before noon on October 27, but Governor Albert H. Roberts in Nashville felt this was not enough. Shortly after 9 p.m. on October 27, he sent an urgent telegram to Camp Gordon, Georgia: "Please entrain two infantry companys and one machine-gun company, total three hundred, with equipment for Knoxville, Tenn." Within hours, Major General E.M. Lewis and a contingent of federal troops left for Knoxville. On October 28 they arrived in Knoxville—the first of 2,000 troops brought to the city to break the strike.[25]

In the name of Tennessee's union workers, John O'Connor, president of the state federation of labor, wired Governor Roberts: "Will you allow armed forces of our state to support company's position? In the name of Justice, I ask you that you immediately withdraw these troops." Governor Roberts dismissed the plea. "The issue is clear," he announced. "Either you stand by the flag or you stand against it." "We are now facing the greatest crisis in the history of this republic," he thundered.[26]

Governor Roberts was wildly applauded by the press and other business groups, but the Knoxville Central Labor Council denounced his stand, and initiated plans for a general strike vote to be taken. The Council urged the city's 80,000 workers to vote in favor of a sympathetic walkout by October 30th. The police union and two other unions associated with essential services were excluded from the vote.[27]

Alarmed by the prospect of a general strike in solidarity with the streetcar strikers Governor Roberts appealed to the company to meet with the strikers' representatives. But KRL President James Harvey refused. "The time has passed for dealing with our former employees," he responded. But Governor Roberts remained in Knoxville, hoping to bring about a meeting between the company and the union.[28]

On October 31 state labor head O'Connor revealed that the area locals had voted overwhelmingly to stage a sympathetic walkout to begin the next day. But he went on to state that in view of the governor's efforts to settle the dispute, the strike would be held in abeyance. The general strike was never called. On November 1 the strike of 394,000 coal miners, members of the United Mine Workers, began. All attention in Knoxville now shifted to the walkout of the miners, and supporters of the streetcar strike found it increasingly difficult to be heard.[29]

By November 1 the Knoxville Railway and Light Company had resumed daytime service, and four days later it resumed its full streetcar schedule, including both day and night service. The strike had been broken.[30] Protests against the company continued, however. A group of 200 veterans paraded to denounce the company's policy of preferring ex-soldiers as strikebreakers. They carried banners proclaiming that "The Men Who Broke the Hindenburg Line Will Never Scab on American Workmen. Stay Off the Cars."[31] Although the union never officially admitted defeat, all strike activity was over by Christmas, 1919.[32]

KANSAS CITY

The streetcar strike that began in Kansas City on December 11, 1918 was the third in that city in sixteen months. The men struck first in August 1917 for recognition of the union. They struck again in March 1918 when they participated in a general strike to aid the laundry workers' strike,*

---

*In July 1917 laundry drivers in Kansas City formed a union that succeeded in gaining the membership of all the drivers when laundry employers refused to grant a wage increase in February 1918. The organization of laundry drivers encouraged laundresses to seek a wage increase of their own. By mid-February, all of the city's laundry workers had gone on strike. After five weeks of refusal by laundry employers to discuss the workers' demands for union recognition, increased wages, and enforcement of state legislation regulating laundress' hours and conditions of labor, the unions of Kansas City voted for a general strike to begin on March 27 in support of the laundry workers. The citywide strike lasted a full week, and has which began in July 1917 and reached a climax in February and March 1918. The third strike was the first involving wages. It was also the first to include women as well as men on the picket line, for in stark contrast to the situations in Cleveland and Detroit, the Amalgamated Association in Kansas City, Missouri welcomed conductorettes (as the women conductors were called) into the local, and insisted that the guaranteed minimum pay of the women be raised to equal that of the men.

At the conclusion of the second strike in August 1918, an agreement was signed by the Kansas City Railways Company and Division 7649 of the Amalgamated Association in which the union pledged not to call strikes until after wage differences were submitted to arbitration. In September 1918 the union submitted a request to the National War Labor Board for a cost of living increase. In the request it also called for the same rate of pay for women.

The company argued that it would only abide by a NWLB decision for a wage increase if the money for the wage increment could be obtained from a raise in customer fares. The case involved both the Amalgamated in Kansas City, Missouri and its sister city in Kansas.

After several hearings in September and October 1918, the NWLB determined on October 24 that a wage increase should be paid to the streetcar workers,* that women conductors should receive equal pay for equal work, and that the money for the increase should come from a raise in fares, the amount of the raise to be determined by the respective Missouri and Kansas state authorities.[33]

After the NWLB award, the streetcar workers remained at work, confident that the company would abide by the decision. The award was the same as that which was made in Detroit, Washington, Cleveland, Buffalo, and Chicago. These cities had only a five cent fare, yet had put the award into effect and were operating their cars successfully.[34]

But the Kansas City Railways Company took steps quickly against the

---

*The existing wages were: 1-year men, 30¢ an hour; 2-year men, 32¢ an hour; 3-year men, 34¢; 4-year men, 36¢; 5-year men, 38¢; maximum, 38¢. The wages allowed by the National War Labor Board per hour were: for the first three months, 43¢; second three months, 46¢; and after six months, 45¢; maximum 48¢. The wages applied equally to men and women.

---

been called the most important U.S. general strike of the war years. It involved nearly all sections of the city's working class, including streetcar workers. The general strike ended when laundry employers agreed to grant their workers the right to organize. (*Labor Herald,* Kansas City, Mo., February-April 1918; Alexander Bing, *War-Time Strikes and Their Adjustment,* [New York, 1921], p. 30; Maurine Weiner Greenwald, *Women, War and Work: The Impact of World War I on Women Workers in the United States,* [Westport, Conn., 1980], pp. 174-75.)

wage increase. Instead of submitting a request to the state public service commissions that regulated the twin cities' fares, the company took the position that the NWLB had directed it to raise the fares itself without interference by any municipality. The company sought an injunction against the municipal and state regulatory bodies from the federal courts for the districts of Kansas and Missouri. Once the courts denied the injunction, the company appealed the decision to the U.S. Supreme Court as a further delaying tactic.[35]

The *Labor Herald*, official organ of the Kansas City (Missouri) Central Labor Union charged that "sinister influences" were behind the refusal of the Kansas Railways Company to institute the NWLB award. J. Ogden Armour, Chicago meat magnate, it pointed out, was a majority stockholder of the Kansas City Railways Company, and was the real power behind company president Colonel Philip J. Kealy. Armour was joined by the "big four" of Kansas City: leading businessmen W.T. Kemper, R.A. Long, J.J. Heim, and Walter Dickey. The "big four," with several colleagues, controlled the Employers' Association, which had built up a fund of one million dollars specifically to combat workers' militancy and to carry through a vigorous antiunion policy, including opposition to union recognition and higher wages. Those employers who dissented from the dominant policy of the association suffered reprisals and other harassments.[36]

By early December 1918, nine weeks after the original award, the streetcar workers had not yet received any wage increase. On December 11, fed up with the company's stalling tactics, 2,675 streetcar men and 127 women conductors voted to strike at four o'clock the following morning. The Kansas City *Times* reported that "the conductorettes stood firmly by the men, and their ballots were cast for a strike, just as those of the men."[37] The next day only members of the Kansas City Employees' Association, a company union, remained at work.

The strike affected every car line in the twin Kansas Cities. The men also walked off at the power plant, and the interurban lines ran only to the city limits.[38]

During the rest of December 1918 and early January 1919 the Amalgamated tried repeatedly to negotiate with the Kansas City Railways Company. But from the start of the strike, the company, backed by the Employers' Association, rejected all efforts to end the dispute peacefully. At the very outset, KRC president Kealy declared that the company would "resume operations at the first moment possible after protection is provided by the city. But that protection must be adequate and guaranteed."[39]

Mayor Cargill immediately offered "completely adequate police protection for the operation of the cars."[40] Ten days later, without the slightest evidence of an emergency, the police were supplemented by the 7th Regiment of the National Guard, who were ordered into Kansas City by Governor Gardner. Armed with rifles, soldiers in automobiles followed streetcars and patrolled the car lines.[41]

The following advertisement began appearing in the press:

MEN WANTED

Street Railway Motormen and Conductors; Experienced Men Preferred. Those with no Previous Training Also Desired; Splendid Consideration Will Be Given to Former Employees of the Company; in accordance with the policy of the National Government we are glad to Employ Demobilized Soldiers, This is an Unusual Opportunity to Obtain Regular Runs at once, and steady permanent employment; Details will be given at the Employment Office, 2d Floor, 15th and Girard Ave., Kansas City, Mo.

THE KANSAS CITY RAILWAYS CO.[42]

The "details" informed the strikebreakers that they would receive 38 cents per hour in wages, and a bonus of $5 per day. Operating cars with strikebreakers, many of them ex-soldiers, and with police and National Guard protection, the company began slowly to attempt to resume operations.

However, the strikebreakers confiscated almost all of the company receipts, and raw motormen burned up motors and smashed cars in all parts of the city. About half of the company's cars were soon in the repair shops with nobody to repair them. Dozens of accidents occurred every day, several with loss of life. Union men and women and sympathizers patronized jitneys or walked to work. The company lost thousands of dollars each day, but, supported by the Employers' Association, it continued to refuse to meet with strikers' representatives even to discuss some solution to the dispute.[43]

As soon as this limited service had resumed, Kealy told a meeting of the Employers' Association that the "entire situation is progressing as satisfactorily as possible, and in accordance with the schedule mapped out." He added that "any one of our employees having a clean record may have his job back for the asking." He made it clear that all workers who continued membership in the union would be viewed as not having "clean records, and have no place in our organization."[44]

Refusing to be intimidated, male and female strikers continued to picket the car barns and lines. The strikers received benefits of $5 a week from the International in addition to funds provided by other locals of the Amalgamated and other unions for those who needed more money. Men and women strikers received equal strike funds. As one reporter noted: "Practically all conductorettes in the employ of the company wear union buttons and have proven enthusiastic in their determination to win the strike." Another observed: "It is difficult to find a picket line in which conductorettes are not serving as pickets with the conductors and motormen."[45]

The use of ex-soldiers as strikebreakers aroused widespread indignation in Kansas City, and the *Labor Herald* published a poem that summed up this indignation. Written by labor poet Thomas H. West and entitled, "Disgracing Their Uniforms," it was reprinted as a leaflet and widely distributed.

> *It was generally thought when our soldiers fought*
> *For the "freedom of the world,"*
> *They all realized why tyrants*
> *From their royal thrones were hurled.*
> *Yet right here in Kansas City*
> *As strike breakers—sad to say—*
> *We see soldiers running street cars*
> *In their uniforms today.*
>
> *These soldier "finks" are a disgrace*
> *To the uniforms they wear.*
> *Have they so soon forgotten*
> *What was fought for "over there"?*
> *These "wage reducing heroes"*
> *Should feel proud (?) of what they've done;*
> *Any soldier who is guilty*
> *Can be called a "Labor Hun."*[46]

On the Missouri side, police and National Guardsmen continued to protect the strikebreakers, while U.S. marshals under court order guarded the Kansas side of the urban railway network.[47] The company, fully assured of the support of city, state and national government, inserted full-page advertisements in the local newspapers, which carried headlines reading:

Public Officials Say Strike is Unwarranted. Protection Assured.
The Cars Must Run.
A Strike Against the Community
The Entire Community Owes a Debt of Gratitude to the Loyal Men and Women Who Are Giving It Streetcar Service
Union Leaders, Foreign and Local, continue to Deceive Men[48]

The reference to "Foreign" union leaders was to convey the impression that "outside agitators" were behind the strike. The Kansas City *Times* went further; its headlines read: "Foreigners In Disturbances," and the paper explained that "foreign-born workers are playing a leading role in strike violence."[49]

The company's advertisements were supplemented by full-page ads inserted by the Employers' Association, "empowered," said the ads "to act for the Business and Civic Interests of Kansas City." "Normal Street Car Service *Must* Be Resumed," was the headline on one of the Association's ads, which closed:

> The people of Kansas City recognize a debt of gratitude to those faithful workers who are now operating the cars. They must be protected in their right to work and the people will insist that the company retain them in their present position.
> We voice a unanimous civic demand when we say:
> *Normal street car service must be resumed.*[50]

To reply, the strikers distributed a series of bulletins giving their side of the case. They informed the public that because of "the power behind the throne" in the form of J. Ogden Armour and the Employers' Association, "all efforts at negotiating a settlement were a farce." Efforts by the union to settle the strike were "fruitless," and it should be obvious to the people of Kansas City that a conspiracy is under way

> to smash the streetcar union and use the car strike as a lever to deliver a body blow at trades unionism and all unions. The organized employers of the country are looking forward to the period of reconstruction and pre-war wages and it seems evident that Kansas City has been chosen as a storm center to try and break the power of the unions and have the workers at their mercy.[51]

"Who are the Bolsheviki of Kansas City?" asked one of the strikers' bulletins. "The capitalists who refuse to live up to the decision of the War Labor Board or the men who abide by them?"[52] Another bulletin was headed "Might Vs. Right," and was addressed "To Those Who Ride on Street Cars and Those Who Do not, But Believe that Right Should Triumph over Might." It declared in part:

> All of the people of Kansas City know of the law-defying, money-grabbing methods of this company. They know also of the defying of the state and city laws by this company.
> We, the members of the Street Car Union of Kansas City, are asking that you come over on our side and stand by us for one-half the time you have stood for

what the company has put over on you, and we will be back on the cars.
Amalgamated Association of Street and Railway Employes,
Good Division 764 of the Service for the People.[53]

The Amalgamated finally appealed to the National War Labor Board for an order confirming its original award and forcing the company to abide by it. On January 20, 1919, the fortieth day of the strike (making it already one of the longest streetcar strikes on record), the NWLB met in Washington to adjudicate the controversy. Although he had said publicly that he "wouldn't spend the car fare" to travel to Washington, Kealy was subpoenaed to appear.[53]

The union representatives pointed out at the hearing that only two companies in the United States had refused to obey the mandates of the War Labor Board—the Bethlehem Steel Company and the Kansas City Railways Company. In its decision on January 31, 1919, signed by William Howard Taft and Basil M. Manlon, joint chairmen, the Board observed that "the men . . . made the mistake of striking," but complimented them for their willingness to go back to work, leaving the issue to be settled by arbitration. On the other hand, the Board accused the company of having tried "to prejudice the community against the men" with its full-page advertisements. Moreover, it had failed to show good faith in its dealing with its workers. The Board concluded:

> The attitude of the company seems to have been, as far as we can observe, from the evidence, that it was content that the men had made the mistake of striking because it would enable them to defeat the union and to avoid the burden of increased wages.[54]

The National War Labor Board reaffirmed its award of a wage increase and ordered the company to pay it retroactively after reinstating the striking carmen and women. But it could do nothing to enforce its ruling, and the company continued to ignore it.[55]

The strikers on the Missouri side had been aroused by representatives of the Department of Labor who assured them that on his imminent return from Europe, where he had attended the peace conference at Versailles, President Wilson would stand behind the National War Labor Board and see to it that its decision was enforced. "President Wilson," John T. Smith of the Department of Labor told the strikers, "has not forgotten what organized labor stood for during the war, that it never faltered in its stand for win-the-war democracy and was loyal to the core."[56] Distrustful of promises, however, the Central Labor Council of the Missouri side sent C.B. Nelson, its secretary, and Ms. Sarah Green, president of the Kansas City

Women's Trade Union League and an indefatigable worker for the strikers, to Washington to meet with President Wilson on his return from Europe. They were to urge him to enforce the NWLB award and to make sure that the strikers received back pay and reinstatement.[57]

The Central Labor Union on the Kansas side, which represented approximately 22,000 men and women, came out for municipal ownership of the streetcar lines as the solution to the continuing crisis. A bill calling for municipal ownership had actually passed the lower house of the state legislature but was stalled in the state senate. In a telegram to Senator James F. Getty, the Central Labor Union asked him to work for the bill for municipal ownership of the street railway system.[58]

But the steps taken by the Central Labor Councils of the twin cities ended in failure. The delegation from the Council on the Missouri side were not allowed to meet with President Wilson, while the bill for municipal ownership, advocated by the Council on the Kansas side, died in the state senate. Meanwhile, the streetcar workers continued to withhold their labor. On March 7, 1919 the *Labor Herald* conceded that the strike had "settled down to an endurance test." In April a federal grand jury indicted six of the union leaders for having violated a federal injunction against interfering with the operation of the cars.[59]

A number of observers now declared that only a sympathetic general strike by the other trade unions of Kansas City could save the streetcar strike. In a letter to the *Labor Herald* appealing for such action, a veteran trade unionist wrote: "The streetcar strikers are fighting your battles and the battles of organized labor all over the world, and they must have the full support and encouragement that organized labor can give them. This is a new organization, but I do not know that I ever saw a body of 2,700 men and women more loyal, more steadfast, more thoroughly imbued with the true spirit of trade unionism."[60]

The trade unions of Kansas City were willing to continue financial support of the streetcar strikers and to denounce any trade unionist who rode the cars as "a traitor to his class,"[61] but they refused to entertain the idea of a general strike. C.B. Nelson assured the press that all reports predicting "a general strike of all union labor in Kansas City would be declared in sympathy with the streetcar men are totally false." "Organized labor," he continued, "stands squarely behind the men in this controversy and is ready to back them with every ounce of their moral and financial support—in short, whatever aid of this nature that is necessary for them to win. But a general strike is out of the question, and has been so decided by the trade unions."[62]*

With the law, money, commercial press, and employers behind it, the company won the Kansas City struggle. By May 1919 the strike had failed. During the six month struggle, 400 men and two women of the original 2,802 strikers had returned to work for the Kansas City Railways, while the other strikers sought employment elsewhere. Because so many women had participated in the strike, the Kansas City Railways Company refused to hire them as of February 1919. In July 1919 only 26 women, 23 of whom had been hired in October and had not gone on strike in December, were still working as conductorettes.[63]

The prolonged contest with its workers proved financially disastrous to the Kansas City Railways Company. In August 1919 President Kealy conceded that the company was "nigh unto death." By October 1920 the company had become insolvent and was placed in receivership. "The company resisted the union to the very end," observes Maurine Weiner Greenwald, "but its victory was a Pyrrhic one."[64]

The defeated strikers took some satisfaction from this outcome. They had played a role in the catastrophic decline of the company's revenue by convincing the public and returning soldiers not to ride streetcars, and to use jitneys instead. In other cities, streetcar companies were so financially weakened at the end of the war** that they usually suspended service when strikes occurred and made no effort to operate with strikebreakers. As a result, the strikes were short and frequently ended in victory for the union. But the Kansas City Railways Company owners adopted a different policy, and while they succeeded in destroying the union, they also drove the company into receivership.[65]

*The final outcome of the laundry workers' strike, in spite of the general strike called in their behalf, was probably a factor in the decision not to call a general strike in support of the streetcar workers. The laundry employers yielded after the general strike had lasted a week, and promised wage increases and support for the union's campaign to obtain enforcement of state statutes concerning women's hours and working conditions. But they subsequently refused to live up to their promises. As a result, the laundry workers' union declined. (Greenwald, p. 175.)

**"We have reached a crisis in our street railway business," wrote Dr. Delos I. Wilcox, chief of the Bureau of Franchises of the Public Service Commission of the First District of New York, and the nation's leading authority on street railway franchises. Everywhere in the United States, he argued, unbridled speculation, the competition of the automobile and jitneys had brought street railways to the edge of a crisis. (Kansas City *Star*, Feb. 4, 1919.)

CHAPTER 7

Strikes of Clothing and Textile Workers

In the printing trades 1919 witnessed the first in a series of protracted battles for the 44-hour week. Although the 1905-06 "eight-hour" strike of the International Typographical Union (ITU) had helped to establish the 48-hour week in commercial printing and the allied trades,[1] that did not mean that the 8-hour day actually prevailed. Instead, many employers gave the industry's traditional half-holiday on Saturday and tacked the lost time onto each of the other five working days.[2] As early as 1912 the International Brotherhood of Bookbinders had suggested the 44-hour week as a way to have both the Saturday half-holiday and the 8-hour day. Six years later, the ITU followed suit, asking for "eight hours the first five days" and a Saturday half-holiday. The employer-union International Joint Conference Council agreed on a 44-hour schedule at the then prevailing wage in April 1919 for commercial printing, but postponed implementation until May 1, 1922.[3]

Some unionists argued that the delay was unjustified and that the new working week could be put into effect immediately. Especially in New York City, bargaining centered on the goals of the 44-hour week and a pay raise, to take effect on October 1, 1919. When no agreement was reached, members of the ITU and the International Printing Pressmen and Assistants Union (IPPAU) prepared to strike. The international leadership of the two unions, however, responded by citing the earlier May 1 agreement. They advised arbitration and branded the strikes as illegal.[4] Nonetheless on October 1 as many as 10,000 IPPAU members were locked out as they were not in good standing with the International. Perhaps as many as 8,000 workers represented by the ITU's Local Six walked off their New York City jobs on October 1. Local Six deferred somewhat to the union's top leadership by voting to term their action a "vacation" rather than a strike. Dubbed the "vacationist movement," the conflict lasted almost until Thanksgiving. Although a few shops granted the 44-hour week almost immediately, most "vacationists" returned to their jobs under the old system.[5]

New York City's firefighters vigorously supported a Socialist-sponsored municipal resolution calling for the introduction of the "three-platoon" (that is, 8-hour) system in the firehouses. Cleveland witnessed a firefighters' strike over working hours as the main issue.[6] As we have seen, long hours constituted a major grievance of the Boston police and figured prominently in the pre-strike union organizing.[7]

Other struggles also advanced shorter hours as a rallying cry. In the Pacific Northwest the lumbermen in the AFL's International Union of Timberworkers (IUT) undertook an 8-hour-day organizing drive, concentrating on three camps in which the government-sponsored Loyal Legion of Loggers and Lumbermen had allowed the restoration of longer shifts. The IUT also attempted to extend the 8-hour system from the Northwest to forests throughout the nation. Orange pickers in parts of California unionized around demands for an 8-hour day at a half dollar per hour.[8] In Seattle, hotel maids chartered a union that emphasized a 6-day week. The Laundry Workers' Union there tried, with some success, to establish the 8-hour day.[9] In Kansas City, Black domestic workers, organized by the Women's Trade Union League in 1918 and 1919, won the 8-hour day and a 67 percent raise.[10]

There were also significant organizing campaigns around the shorter working day in the clothing and textile industries.

MEN'S CLOTHING WORKERS

The 1919 campaigns of the Amalgamated Clothing Workers (ACW) and the International Ladies' Garment Workers' Union (ILGWU) for a 44-hour week expressed a desire on the part of these unions to regulate seasonal joblessness, ease destructive competition, and stabilize a weakening industry.

Even before the war was over, the ACW moved to institute the 44-hour week. Its May 1918 convention vowed to establish that standard throughout the men's clothing industry, emulating a schedule already won by Toronto's clothing workers. On August 9, 1918 the union wrote to the Associated Boys' Clothing Manufacturers suggesting that the 44-hour system go into effect on December 1 and arguing that "Modern methods of production are steadily intensifying the prevailing speeding-up system, thereby undermining the health of the workers." It asked for a reply by

October 1.[11] Since the request came from the union's Children's Clothing Trades Division, it did not raise the issue of war production, but the answer, from the American Men's and Boy's Clothing Manufacturers' Association, impugned the ACW's loyalty and focussed on the need to make Army uniforms. The employers' association denied the existence of speedup and, significantly, offered to negotiate the demand for a 20 percent pay increase if the hours' issue were dropped.[12]

On October 28 the children's clothing workers struck to win their wage and hour demands and two weeks later the employers locked out workers in the other men's clothing trades. The ACW responded on November 11 by declaring a general strike throughout the New York City industry, specifically around the 44-hour demand. The struggle began just as the war was ending, and uniformed soldiers returning to the States addressed strike meetings, prompting irate manufacturers to wire their protests to the Secretary of War. The union was increasingly successful in posing the issue of working hours as a way "to enable industry to absorb...the returning soldiers and sailors." After eight weeks, the employers agreed to bargain on both wages and hours, but they then pressed for a series of vaguely worded changes in work rules and for harsh provisions against wildcat strikes. Despite appeals for settlement by financier Jacob Schiff, who stressed the common Jewish heritage of many of those on both sides of the dispute, the negotiations got nowhere.[13]

The impasse was broken by the January 7, 1919 agreement with Hart, Schaffner & Marx in Chicago, providing for the 44-hour week and an 8.75 percent pay increase. By demonstrating the practicability of the former demand, the settlement absolved the ACW leaders of the charge of being "visionaries and rainbow chasers."[14] Shortly thereafter, Felix Frankfurter, chairman of the War Labor Policies Board and long an advocate of shorter hours, invited the New York City manufacturers and the union to a conference to settle their dispute. The ACW and the Manufacturers' Association agreed to submit the dispute to Frankfurter and two others for arbitration. Before agreeing to do so, however, the union leaders received specific instructions from their membership: "No modification in the demand for shorter hours, and freedom of action for the officers to do the best they can in the demand for higher wages." On January 22 the arbitrators granted the shorter hours and deferred their decision on wages. After thirteen weeks on strike the 44-hour week became, in the words of the union, "a real and living fact."[15]

Within a month, employers' groups in Rochester, Chicago, Baltimore, Boston, Montreal, and Cincinnati had acceded, and by August 1919 large manufacturers in St. Paul, Buffalo, Syracuse, Louisville, and Milwaukee, as well as groups of employers in Philadelphia, Worcester, and St. Louis, had followed suit. By May 1920, through a combination of bargaining and further strikes, the ACW could boast of the establishment of the 44-hour standard "in all important clothing markets."

At the union's 1920 convention, the ACW's Executive Board was able to ask rhetorically: "Were we dreamers? Were we visionaries?" And they could answer:

> January 22, 1919 is the answer. We dreamed of the realization of the workers' rights, and the dream came true. We saw a vision of a better life for the toiling masses, and the vision had become a reality.[16]

With some justification, the ACW proclaimed the 44-hour victory one "for the entire labor movement."[17]

THE LADIES' GARMENT WORKERS

In the ILGWU the dress and waist workers were the first to demand the 44-hour week. They did so in the context of their general dissatisfaction with existing conditions in the industry. Although the protocol machinery in the ladies' garment industry had come to an end in 1916, a revised protocol had been framed for the dress and waist section of the industry, and it was due to expire December 31, 1918. This "model agreement" was supposed to eliminate the weaknesses of the previous "Protocol of Peace." Thus, the preferential union shop was specifically spelled out as one in which union members were to be preferred "in the hiring, employing, and retaining of help and in the distribution of work." Again, while the employers were free to hire and fire within this limitation, the workers were supposed to be "safeguarded against the oppressive exercise of this right by employers." New features included a carefully planned system for the determination of piece rates, and the appointment of a Board of Protocol Standards with power to inspect the shops, enforce standards, and make recommendations for changes.[18]

It was not long before the "model agreement" proved to be as meaningless to the dress and waist workers as the old protocol, which most of the industry had been forced to scrap. Even ILGWU President Benjamin Schlesinger, who had urged the continuation of the revised protocol for the dress and waist industry, conceded that the "arrangement did not always work to the satisfaction of the workers."[19] This was an understatement. Workers' grievances that should have been settled in a few minutes dragged on for months, and it often took a work stoppage, usually condemned by the union leadership, to resolve the difficulty. Moreover, during the war years many new workers had been brought into the industry. Since they were never organized by the union, they worked at wages and under conditions that undermined union standards. In a report of December 15, 1918 the director of the Joint Board of Sanitary Control stated flatly that the employers paid no attention to protocol provisions regarding sanitary conditions, and that only 18 percent of the 825 shops in the dress and waist industry were without defects: "The rest of them either had serious fire dangers or have dirty walls, dirty ceilings, dirty water closets, etc."[20]

Long before this, however, the manufacturers had stopped paying heed to the protocol provisions. In September 1916, a few months after the "model agreement" went into effect, the director of the Board of Protocol Standards charged that employers were using it at the expense of the workers. He called for strict enforcement of every phase of the agreement. The employers' association promptly rejected his recommendations. Although the agreement itself lingered on, for all practical purposes, it was dead.[21]

Two months before what was left of the protocol in the dress and waist industry was due to expire, the union presented a number of proposals to be embodied in a "new protocol." The demands reflected the spirit of the times: "an increase of 15 percent in wages to enable the workers to meet the present high cost of living" and a "reduction in the hours of work to 44 hours a week, so as to make employment in our industry more regular and continuous." Clearly, the dress and waist makers had been influenced by the victories gained by the men's clothing workers in establishing a 44-hour week. The proposal for a "new protocol" also included a demand for permission for a representative of the union to visit the shops once a month "in order to ascertain whether the standards established by the protocol are observed."[22]

The Dress and Waist Manufacturers' Association rejected all the demands, and the independent shops followed. The association announced that it would "resist the union's effort to enslave us, up to the limit of our ability" and called on New York City Mayor John F. Hylan to provide sufficient "police protection" to enable the employers to operate their shops without having "faithful workers" beaten up by "union goons."[23]

On January 20, 1919, in response to the union's strike order, 35,000 garment workers, the vast majority of them women, walked out of the dress and waist shops. The call read in part:

Sisters and Brothers: You are hereby requested to leave your employment as orderly and quietly as possible. Do not make any disturbance. Pack up your tools and everything that belongs to you promptly at 10 a.m. and leave your shops and join the ranks of the strikers. Avoid arguments and enter into no discussion with your employer or any of his representatives. If the employers refuse to permit you to use the elevators, walk down the stairs. Let the workers of each shop, headed by its Shop Chairman, march in an orderly manner to the meeting hall to which you are directed. All workers of open shops are required to go to the meeting hall as directed. Do not wait for any committee to take you down. Let this circular be your committee.[24]

It was clear from the outset that the police and private detectives would work for the employers, and that the women strikers were to be their special targets. Daily the police arrested women pickets and daily the magistrates fined them $5 each for "disorderly conduct" and sent those who could not pay the fines to the workhouse. On February 2, ten thousand women pickets kept a round-the-clock vigil at a large number of shops said to be operating with strikebreakers. They were told "to perform their task in an orderly manner" so that the police would "get no opportunity to assault or arrest" them, but scores of pickets were arrested nevertheless.[25]

During the dispute between the ILGWU and the Dress and Waist Manufacturers' Association that led to the 1919 strike, the employers' organization had accused "the present Revolutionary leadership" of the garment workers' union of seeking to raise the "red flag of Bolshevism" over the city. And during the strike itself, the Merchants' Association's request for additional "police protection" charged that the "spirit of Bolshevism" was so deeply ingrained in the women pickets that only the effective employment of police clubs could prevent it from destroying the city. This prompted ILGWU President Schlesinger to reply: "It would appear that the mere fact that a number of these girls were born in Russia and Italy is sufficient to hurl against them the epithet 'Bolshevism' and rob them of their right to a square deal and impartial treatment."[26]

On February 18 the dress and waist strikers were joined by 5,000 kimono and wrapper makers, and six days later by 7,000 children's dressmakers. Then, early in March, the white-goods workers declared a general strike. Like the dressmakers and waistmakers, all these strikers demanded the 44-hour week and a 15 percent wage increase. The bonnaz embroidery workers, however, won the 44-hour week by simply threatening to strike.[27]

On March 13 the key firms in the Dress and Waist Manufacturers' Association gave in, and on April 7 the entire industry capitulated. A new agreement was negotiated, incorporating the union's demands for a 44-hour week, an increase in wages, and the right of union representatives to observe working conditions. The agreement not only achieved the first 44-hour week in the industry, but also brought a final end to the protocol, which was abandoned in the settlement.[28]

The women ILGWU members had led the campaign for the 44-hour week, and the cloakmakers, 90 percent of whom were men, picked it up. The latter conducted general strikes for the 44-hour week, wage increases, and the introduction of week work instead of piece work beginning in New York on May 14, 1919, followed by Chicago, Boston, Baltimore, Los Angeles, Montreal, Toronto, Worcester, and San Francisco. On July 14, the ILGWU's official organ, *Justice*, was able to report that "the whole country was in the grip of cloak strikes."[29] Through these strikes, the cloakmakers gained both the 44-hour week and week work.

In the summer of 1919, a wave of strikes swept the other branches of the ladies' garment industry—corset workers, raincoat makers, and ladies' tailors. When they were over, almost the entire membership of the union had gained the 44-hour week.[30] The fever spread to other needle trades. Both with and without strikes, the capmakers won both the 44-hour week and a change from piecework to week work. The New York fur employers, who made tremendous profits after the importation of furs from Paris and London was cut off by the war, quickly agreed to a 44-hour week with a year round minimum wage scale for each class of work and a 40 percent increase in the minimums. Other fur centers quickly followed suit.

A few years earlier, notes Joel Seidman, "the needle trades had been notorious for excessively long hours; now they were among the leaders in American industry in introducing the short working week."[31]

THE TEXTILE WORKERS

Stimulated by wartime demand, new mills sprang up in the South during World War I, old mills ran day and night, wages rose, and profits soared. But when peace came, the southern textile industry faced an economic crisis. Immediately mill owners cut workers' wages. But to their surprise mill hands refused to abandon the small advances in their standard of living. When wage cuts were announced in 1919 thousands of workers joined the AFL's United Textile Workers.

During wartime expansion of industrial activity in the South, the United Textile Workers, which had been largely discredited in the North because of its strikebreaking roles in the Lawrence, Fall River, and other IWW textile strikes, moved into the South,* where its history was little known.

*See Philip S. Foner, *History of the Labor Movement in the United States* 4 (New York, 1965): 87-88, 337-40, 353-54.

By 1918 it had set up about forty locals, the largest of them in Columbus, Georgia. There, a long and bitter conflict took place, first against a lockout and then against the discharge of 25 union members after the lockout was withdrawn. It ended at last in a settlement negotiated by the War Labor Board. This included a change in the bonus system of payment to a straight wage, the reinstatement of the employees whose discharge had precipitated the strike, and the establishment of the right of the workers to report grievances through their shop committees. At the end of the struggle about 4,500 cotton mill workers in Columbus were affiliated with the United Textile Workers.[32]

A similar situation prevailed in North Carolina after the wage cuts of 1919. Speaking of the textile workers, the *Raleigh News and Observer* noted: "They are in deadly earnest, and almost religiously serious in their belief in the union."[33]

It is interesting to note that the Southern cotton mill workers who joined the UTW set up their unions on an industrial or plant basis rather than the craft form of organization traditionally followed by that union. Knowing little of the union's method of organization and operation, they chose the form that they believed would best serve their interests. However, they did not include Black workers in the industrial unions: in addition to the injustice of this course, it left the way open for disunity that the employers would use.[34]

At its November 1918 convention the United Textile Workers passed a resolution calling on textile mill owners to institute the 8-hour day. The resolution noted that "the principle of a maximum work day of eight hours" had been endorsed by President Wilson and "by the United States government." The union's propaganda "made full use of the official support for this goal."[35]

No clear strategy was developed by the UTW for the accomplishment of this goal. Instead of calling for a strike, the union urged the holding of conferences with mill agents to arrange for peaceful inauguration of the 8-hour day.[36] What UTW President John Golden overlooked was that the war had created a new spirit among hundreds of thousands of textile workers.

By the time the war was over, about half of UTW's 60,000 members were in the South.[37] On the appointed date for the transition to eight hours, February 3, 1919, many "spontaneous strikes" erupted in Southern cotton mills. With substantial support from local craft unions, well over 10,000 millhands in Columbus, Georgia; Horse Creek Valley, South Carolina; Chattanooga, Tennessee; and Sherman, Texas simultaneously left their jobs. Barely a third of the strikers in Columbus received UTW strike benefits, but the conflict there nevertheless lasted for more than two months before the workers were forced to return under the old schedules of more than ten hours daily. Shortly after their return, management granted a 55-hour week, as had several other Georgia mills and the major South Carolina factories.[38]

A strike for the 8-hour day in Macon, Georgia in August 1919 involved 2,000 operatives from five mills and resulted in the tragic deaths of two Black strikebreakers during an attack by white picketers. This incident, which exposed the Achilles heel of UTW organizing in the South—its failure to enlist Black workers—also signalled the defeat of the strike. In exchange for reemployment of the strikers and non-prosecution of those responsible for the picketline violence, the unionists agreed to return under the old system and "to give up all outside association." As a result, the UTW withdrew its organizer from Georgia.[39]

In North Carolina two 1919 summertime settlements in Charlotte and others in Concord and Kannapolis won the 55-hour week at 60 hours' pay for over 5,000 millhands. These reforms sparked a surge of organizing in Carolina Piedmont mills. By the fall, the UTW was claiming 40,000 members in North Carolina alone. However, little of this organization survived the depression of 1921-22, during which, as we shall see in our next volume, the UTW's capitulation to wage cuts helped speed the union's disintegration in the South.[40]

Late in January 1919 the *New York Times* reported that more than 120,000 workers in New England mills had joined the UTW campaign, including branches of the UTW, the International Loomfixers' Association, the International Sorters' Union and local Joint Textile Councils. Moreover, it reported, employers all over New England were eager to come to terms with the UTW, reducing the workweek in the mills to 48 hours—six days of eight hours each—with time-and-a-half for overtime.[41] In fact, UTW President John Golden was busy signing agreements with leading manufacturers everywhere in New England on the basis of a 48-hour week, including such major firms as the Amoskeag Manufacturing Company and Stark Mills of Manchester, New Hampshire, and the Hamlet Textile Company of Pawtucket, Rhode Island. The biggest of them all—the American Woolen Company of Lawrence, Massachusetts—was preparing to sign such an agreement and was ready to make the offer. Meanwhile, Golden traveled to Paterson, New Jersey, where, amid great publicity, he signed an agreement with the employers in that conflict-ridden silk mill city.[42]

It soon became public knowledge, however, that all of these agreements for a 48-hour week included a provision for reduction of wages by six hours' pay! In effect, both the workweek and the workers' paychecks were being reduced by six hours.[43]

THE AMALGAMATED TEXTILE WORKERS UNION AND THE LAWRENCE STRIKE

When the United Textile Workers initiated its campaign for the 8-hour day, only some 200 of the more than 32,000 mill operatives in Lawrence, Massachusetts belonged to the union; another 500 or 600 belonged to an independent union. In order to press the demand for a reduction of the work week from 54 to 48 hours, the support of unorganized workers, mostly immigrants, was solicited. They responded eagerly. Immigrant workers began to mobilize as meetings were held in Syrian, Italian, Russian, Franco-Belgian, Polish, Greek, and Lithuanian meeting halls.[44]

With the demand for wool way down after the war, the American Woolen Company and other Lawrence firms agreed to a shorter work week, but with a commensurate reduction in wages. When the non-English speaking workers learned that the agreement about to be signed by the American Woolen Company and other mill owners of Lawrence with the UTW would result in a 12.5 percent reduction in their already meager pay, they flatly rejected it. In spite of threats by UTW officers, a general committee composed of representatives of all the nationality groups demanded a 48-hour work week, with 54 hours pay—48/54 became the slogan of mill employees in Lawrence. At a mass meeting, the textile workers voted unanimously to strike if this demand was not met by January 31.* On February 3, after the mill owners had rejected the demand, practically all of the 32,000 mill hands walked out, shouting the strike slogan "48-54."[45]

Unwilling to lead a mass strike of immigrant workers over whom it could not maintain a controlling hand, the United Textile Workers washed its hands of the struggle in Lawrence.[46] In truth its place had already been taken by a new union.

The new union was the Amalgamated Textile Workers of America (ATWA). As its name indicated, it was modeled after the Amalgamated Clothing Workers of America (ACWA). It was the brainchild of the Dutchborn one-time clergyman, Reverend A. J. Muste. Muste convinced Sidney Hillman of the ACWA that the textile industry could be organized, but only through a militant industrial union that unlike the UTW would fight for the interests of all workers—skilled and unskilled, men and

*Only the Greek workers failed to endorse the strike call.

women, foreign-born and native-born—and would not collaborate with the employers against the interests of the underpaid, oppressed mill workers. But he also emphasized that the textile workers of New England were disillusioned with militant unionism because of their experiences with the IWW and could be brought into class-struggle unionism again only if it were combined with practical methodology. He insisted that if the mill workers knew of the new union's link with the Amalgamated Clothing Workers—a union that had succeeded in organizing the men's clothing industry while retaining a militant approach to trade union strategy and tactics—they would be ready to try again with the Amalgamated Textile Workers of America.[47]

Probably no other American union was as aware that the postwar years would bring huge major confrontations between labor and capital as was the Amalgamated Clothing Workers. The ACWA viewed the shorter workweek as a major "reconstruction measure" that would materially reduce postwar unemployment. Emboldened by the success of the New York City clothing workers in winning the 44-hour week—a victory that they viewed as the "first great victory" of American labor in the postwar period—the ACWA was anxious to exert leadership in the national movement for the 8-hour day. Believing firmly in the principle of labor solidarity, the Amalgamated was interested in aiding the organization of textile workers. The ACWA's entry into this field promised to bring additional resources in the form of money and trained organizers to the largely unorganized textile industry.[48]

When Muste and a group of fellow ministers came to Lawrence, along with a number of Amalgamated Clothing Workers' organizers, all assisted financially by the ACWA, they were able to sign up enough workers to provide the union a solid foundation. Then, late in January 1919, the Amalgamated Textile Workers presented its demands to the mill owners for a 48-hour week at 54 hours' pay. The mill owners rejected the demand, replying that they could not afford to pay for six hours' work time without any production. It was not possible, they continued, to operate the machines with two or three shifts because "a large proportion of the workers are women and children, and the labor laws of Massachusetts prohibit them from working at night. A reduction of 12½ percent of working hours means a reduction of 12½ percent of production, but the overhead expenses remain the same."

The Amalgamated Textile Workers replied that the companies had made enormous profits during the war and were paying high dividends to their stockholders. If the companies remained adamant, the workers had only one choice: to strike.[49]

And strike they did! Although the IWW was no longer a factor in Lawrence,* when nearly 32,000 mill hands struck on February 3 they showed that the strike methods developed in 1912 had not been forgotten.** Once more, round-the-clock picketing began immediately, with some strikers in the vanguard, carrying placards bearing the figures "54-48," and shouting the slogan, "Fifty-four hours' pay for forty-eight hours' work." The General Strike Committee was again organized along nationality lines, and meetings were held on the same basis. In at least two respects, however, the 1919 strike was different from that of 1912. For one, Reverend Muste and two ministers associated with the Amalgamated Textile Workers were members of the General Strike Committee. For another, aware of the headline in the *Lawrence Evening Tribune* reading "Strikers Will Send Away Their Children. Plan Repetition of Famous Incident of Strike Seven Years Ago," and fearing that there might be the same kind of unfavorable publicity as that which followed in 1912 when the police had brutally interfered with removal of the children, the Lawrence Child Welfare League promised to provide for the needs of any children suffering as a result of the strike so that none would have to be sent away.[50]***

Although the English-speaking workers, including the Irish and French-Canadians, broke the solidarity of the woolen workers and gradually drifted back into the mills, and were followed by some Greeks, Portuguese, and Turks, the main body of immigrant workers stood firm and united. "The Italians, Poles, Lithuanians, Russians, Ukranians, Syrians, Franco-Belgians, Germans, and Jewish [workers], numbering between fifteen and twenty thousand" were the backbone of the strike, "and there never was a serious break among them in the 16 long weeks of the strike," noted Harnell L. Rotzell shortly after the strike.[51]

As in 1912, the United Textile Workers played a strikebreaking role. UTW President Golden immediately denounced the action of the workers

---

*Although Melvyn Dubofsky demonstrates that the IWW did not abandon Lawrence after the 1912 strike, the organization did rapidly decline in the city as employers introduced a sophisticated spy system, sent work out of Lawrence to other cities, and applied effective blacklisting. (Melvyn Dubofsky, *We Shall Be All*, p. 257.)

**For a detailed discussion of the 1912 Lawrence strike, *see* Philip S. Foner, *History of the Labor Movement in the United States* 4 (New York, 1965): 306-50.

***Nevertheless, as in 1912, families sent their children to sympathizers in other cities, "smuggling them out of Lawrence in moving vans." (Rudolph J. Vecoli, "Anthony Capraro and the Lawrence Strike of 1919," in George E. Pozzetta, *"Pan E Lavoro: The Italian American Working Class* [Toronto, 1980], p. 13; *New York Call*, March 29, April 9, 1919; *Lawrence Telegram*, April 25, 1919.)

as an "outlaw strike" and praised the American Woolen Company for its readiness to grant the UTW's demand for a 48-hour week. If the Lawrence strikers really wanted to serve their own best interests, he said, they would accept the agreement worked out in the "original demands" of the UTW and repudiate the Amalgamated Textile Workers, which was misleading them in the interests of Bolshevik Russia.[52]

The Lawrence workers gave their answer to Golden's advice the very next day. The press reported that

> ...the strike of textile operatives to obtain fifty-four hours' pay for forty-eight hours' work grew today. It was estimated tonight by persons familiar with the situation that not more than 5,000 of the 30,000 workers were at their places. Fully sixty percent of the strikers are women, with the Italians and Polish nationalities most prominently represented among them, and they are already proving themselves to be worthy of the textile women who amazed the nation with their spirit and militancy in 1912.[53]

Nor was this an exaggeration. Already, arrests of strikers, most of them women, were becoming a daily occurrence. Typical headlines in the three Lawrence papers during the strike read: "Women Strikers Given Two Months. Stiff Fines Imposed on Women Pickets."[54]

February 7 saw the first fatality: a Polish striker, killed by the police. That same day the Massachusetts State Board of Arbitration announced that the manufacturers had offered 51 hours' pay for 48 hours of work. The strikers voted to adhere to their original demand; in their reply to the Massachusetts Board they noted the report in that day's press of a further increase in the cost of living.[55]

On February 24 the *New York Call*, the Socialist daily, carried a lengthy article on the Lawrence strike that concluded:

> Despite all the powers arrayed against them, the strikers are courageously keeping up the struggle, but there is a limit to their endurance, and that limit is the hungry cry of their little children. The suffering of the little ones is the weakest point in the armor of the workers as it is the strongest weapon that the bosses can wield.

With the limited resources of the workers depleted, Muste appealed to Sidney Hillman, president of the Amalgamated Clothing Workers, to further aid the strikers with money and organizers. After consulting with August Bellanca, an ACW vice-president, Hillman sent two organizers: Anthony Capraro and H.J. Budrenweiss. In the next two months nearly $100,000 was contributed in support of the Lawrence textile workers' fight, the greater part of it from members of the ACW.[56]

Originally an anarcho-syndicalist, Capraro was greatly influenced by the Bolshevik Revolution and deeply impressed by the writings of Lenin, whom he regarded as "the greatest of the living true Marxists," and he aligned himself with the Communists. "There is no question," writes his biographer, "that when he arrived in Lawrence in late February (1919), Capraro was a Communist—or Bolshevik, if you preferred."[57]

Entrusted with the disbursement of the Amalgamated's funds, Capraro immediately became an important member of the General Strike Committee and its executive committee, as well as chairman of the all-important finance committee. Although often in poor health, Capraro was tireless and efficient in his strike activity, raising funds, organizing relief, supervising picketing, speaking, and writing.[58]

One of the many problems the Strike Committee faced was that Lawrence mills were transferring new orders to other cities. With its multiplant operations, the American Woolen Company had a huge advantage in any battle with Lawrence workers.[59] To meet this problem, the Strike Committee came up with the idea of generating a sympathy strike in other textile centers. On April 11 the Strike Committee sent out circulars in a number of languages calling on mill employees to organize a general strike in support of the Lawrence workers.* The call, which was addressed "To All Textile Workers of America," urged:

> Arise then ye men and women of the mills of the loom and spinning frames. Be ready to stop work, strike in great numbers, battle all and everyone of you. Organize one big walkout and line up in battle array with the strikers of Lawrence and for a shorter work day and more pay, in order to live and enjoy the good things of life.
>
> Drudge no longer. Band together. Lend a hand to the Lawrence strikers, send in funds for the needy and for the inevitable big strike in the textile industry. Get ready for the time is ripe. One big Strike! One big union! One big victory![60]

The general strike movement ran into many problems and finally the

---

*A previous call for a sympathy strike by the textile workers in Lowell, Massachusetts ran into the hostility of most of Lowell's 10,000 Greek operatives. The UTW-controlled Lowell Textile Council, which represented many of the skilled workers, also opposed the movement. (Lawrence *Sun-American*, February 24, 1919; Lawrence *Evening Tribune*, March 3, 1919.) In January, federal agents had reported that Lowell's large Greek population was "thoroughly loyal" and that if there was any trouble in Lawrence, it would not spread to Lowell. (Report of F.W. Webb, January 18, 1919, RG 165, File . 10110-913, National Archives.)

Dan Georgakas, a student of Greek workers in the United States, questions the accuracy of these reports. He writes that "From 1900 to 1920, there was rarely one year in which Greek workers were not striking at one or another Lowell mill...." ("The Greeks of New England," *The Greek American*, Nov. 1, 1986, p. 10; letter of Dan Georgakas to present writer, Dec. 1, 1987).

Strike Committee in Lawrence abandoned attempts to spread the struggle, and concentrated its efforts on the difficulties that had to be overcome in the woolen city. A major problem was Police Commissioner Peter Carr, who worked in league with the millowners to break the strike. Carr called in reinforcements from neighboring cities and towns to supplement the antistrike activities of the local force. A ban was then placed on practically all strikers' actions, with special attention paid to the women, who were causing the police a great deal of trouble. "Women Can Not Parade," "Women Must Stay Distance from Mills," read the headlines. Thereupon, a delegation of women strikers appealed to Governor Calvin Coolidge for the appointment of an impartial investigating committee to determine if the reasonable demand of the strikers for shorter hours without a reduction in wages warranted the wholesale violation of their democratic rights:

> We protest, especially, first the denial of the permit to parade the streets in the interests of our efforts to prevent a reduction in our wages.
>
> Secondly, the denial of the permit to hold meetings in the common in the same cause and the autocratic activity of the mounted police who persist in riding their horses on the sidewalks and who, with threats of brandishing of clubs, ride around and among the strikers.
>
> Thirdly, if we are not to have the protection of the government of the state as we conduct a peaceful strike for what we consider a most modest demand, how can you expect our foreign-speaking fellow workers who are not citizens, to become American citizens? We have these many years worked at starvation wages. Indeed we were brought to Lawrence, many of us, to keep the wages of American workers down. The Commonwealth has profited by our labor, the labor of our husbands, and the labor of our children. In fact, our children have grown up and given themselves to the monotonous life of the mills rather than to the educational institutions of which the Commonwealth boasts. We ourselves have given to the great war husbands and sons, and were have been told that from these sacrifices, a new American spirit would emerge. We now look for a little of this new spirit in the United States.

Governor Coolidge refused to even meet with the delegation of women strikers. Instead, he had his secretary read them a statement indicating his unwillingness to interfere with the local authorities, who were doing their best under "difficult circumstances to uphold law and order." As for the "new spirit" that was to emerge from the war, "Silent Cal" waxed positively eloquent, for him, as he told the Lawrence women delegates: "The result which you will secure from the great war and from your residence in America will be exactly what you desire to make it."[61]

On March 7 Commissioner Carr announced that the strikers would "not be permitted to assemble on either public or private grounds." Muste denounced this order as absolutely unacceptable, and the following day even more pickets were on duty and more arrests were made. On March 18 the long-brewing conflict broke out into the open. The police, reinforced by contingents from nearby communities, repeatedly attacked strikers with their clubs, and when the men and women refused to disperse, they shot into the crowd. Several strikers were wounded, but so were several police as infuriated strikers and sympathizers fired back. Even strikers' meetings were attacked by the police. "A fight took place," one reporter wrote, "when Polish operatives who had been attending a meeting were attacked by the police as they came out of the hall. Clubs, stones and bottles were called into play, and the police beat a number of the operatives, including women, severely."[62]

On April 5, 1919 *Survey* carried an article on the Lawrence strike by John A. Fitch, considered the foremost industrial investigator in the United States, in which he characterized the strike as "an ordinary rebellion against excessively low wages."[63] But that was not what the local and national press were saying about the strike. According to them, the Lawrence strike was purely and simply "a political strike" in which "Socialist agitators who were advocating the destruction of property rights" were able to use thousands of "unruly, illiterate and excitable foreigners, not thoroughly in sympathy with our American system of government," in an effort to create "a Soviet Lawrence." Police Commissioner Carr justified his refusal to permit parades, public meetings, and even peaceful picketing by the strikers on what the press regarded as the "most reasonable and logical grounds." As Carr explained, "Lawrence is a city of 100,000 population and thirty-three different nationalities, most of them foreign. We feel this is a fertile field for the implanting of Bolshevist propaganda, and as American citizens, it is our duty to suppress it."

The Massachusetts Board of Conciliation endorsed Carr's analysis and his stand on the strikers' rights—or lack of them. Its own investigation, the Board reported, had convinced it that the strike had nothing to do with the issues of hours or wages, but was aimed at destroying "private property, was revolutionary in tendencies, and destructive to orderly government," with the ultimate objective of achieving a Bolshevist society.[64]

The United Textile Workers distributed these descriptions of the strike far and wide, and the AFL's Lawrence Central Union added to the barrage by blaming the strike on "a group of Bolshevik and IWW propagandists who had turned the heads of the foreign elements, especially the women."[65]

When Secretary of Labor Wilson characterized the strike as "a deliberate organized attempt at a social and political movement to establish soviet governments in the United States," the mill owners congratulated him for understanding that "the trouble in Lawrence" was not a conflict over wages but part of "the world wide revolution of the proletariat." Winthrop L. Marvin, speaking for the National Association of Wool Manufacturers, wrote to Secretary Wilson: "Manufacturers of the Lawrence district are in harmony with you and with leaders of organized labor in the vicinity that Bolshevist propaganda in Lawrence is the real cause of the continuing troubles there." In rejecting conciliation of the strike the mill owners declared: "There can be no arbitration between Americanism and Bolshevism."[66]

Most members of the Lawrence clergy echoed this interpretation of the strike in their Sunday sermons. Father James T. O'Reilly, pastor of St. Mary's Church, who had also been a leading foe of the IWW-led strike of 1912, was characterized by the General Strike Committee in 1919 as "the most persistent and bitter opponent of the strikers." The committee charged that he "has done more than any other single individual in Lawrence to try to discredit our cause and inflame the public mind against us by circulating false reports to the effect that we are a body of Bolshevists, anarchists, etc." Other Catholic priests shared O'Reilly's views, and Father Mariano Milanese, pastor of the Italian Church of the Holy Rosary, who had also opposed the 1912 strike, was openly accused of having been "paid by the woolen companies" to denounce the strike and strikers. "Not surprising," notes one student of the strike, "feelings against Father Milanese ran high. Windows in his church were broken, religious functions were boycotted, and even physical assaults took place."[67]

Given the forces arrayed against them, it was widely expected that the strikers would soon abandon the strike and return, defeated, to the mills. Indeed, the initial report of the Commissioners of Conciliation, appointed by the U.S. Department of Labor to mediate the strike, emphasized that the strike was "Bolshevik-inspired" and predicted that it would be "short-lived." Summarizing their discussions with the strike leaders, the Commissioners reported:

> We told them that we [sic] our judgment the strike was lost, that they had attempted to kick up a violent agitation such as obtained in Lawrence in 1912, that the State officials had organized so effectively and produced such a show that [sic] force that it was impossible for them to make any headway, that they would need at least $10,000 a week to carry on the strike and that they couldn't possibly do that...Surely the strike for 54 hours pay for 48 hours work will not succeed in Lawrence. The employers are as firm as a rock on that point and the City officials, and as far as we could find out the general public, are all in favor

of the mills opening up on a 48-hour week for 48-hours' pay.[68]

But although they continued to live on the verge of destitution, the strikers continued to struggle on—indeed, for almost four months. A General Relief Committee was formed; soup kitchens and food stations were established and tickets were issued to strikers for meals and provisions; medical care was provided for the ill and injured. Speakers at daily meetings exhorted the strikers in various languages to remain firm, and songs of resistance were sung with the "Internationale" opening and closing the meetings. *Victory Bulletins* were published to provide news. *Bulletin* No. 8 reported: "Sunday was another *May Day*. We visited our comrades of other nationalities, talked with them, sang with them. National lines are disappearing. We are making our Union one solid international organization." So successful was the inter-ethnic collaboration among about fifteen ethnic groups, with diverse languages, customs, and temperaments, that Muste commented: "If the League of Nations has been realized nowhere else, it has been realized in Lawrence. Fifteen nationalities are represented on the strike committee and are working together harmoniously." An example of this harmonious relationship was the joint activity of Samuel Bramhall, chairman, and Imre Kaplan, secretary, of the General Strike Committee. Bramhall was an Englishman, a long-time socialist and anticlerical, and president of the Lawrence carpenters' union. Kaplan, a twenty-seven-year-old Russian Jew, was a delegate of the Mulespinners' Union and outspoken revolutionary. Like many of the strike leaders, they were not "outside troublemakers," as was charged by enemies of the strike. They, like the other strike leaders, "came from the rank-and-file of mill workers and local labor."[69]

Having failed by all other means to break the strike, the employers and their agents tried a new strategy: force and violence! On April 27, 1919 the *Lawrence Leader* cited the example of Bisbee and other western cities where citizens had herded Wobblies and other labor militants into freight cars and shipped them out, abandoning them in the desert with the threat of death if they returned. The newspaper asked in bold type: "WHERE ARE THE VIGILANTES?" On April 30 City Marshall O'Brien announced that police protection had been withdrawn from the strike leaders in Lawrence. On May 3, the *Lawrence Telegram* commented that if the authorities did not take steps against the radicals, "the common people of America will, even if they have to form mobs to do so." On May 5, a Liberty Loan speaker urged "the use of the lamp post for foreign-speaking strikers."[70]

These threats were not confined to words. At two o'clock in the morning of May 6 a gang of masked men broke into Anthony Capraro's room in the Hotel Needham, kidnapped him and Nathan Kleinman, an Amalgamated Clothing organizer from New York, and ordered them out at gunpoint and into a car. They were then taken to the outskirts of Lawrence, beaten, and told to leave town and stay out if they wanted to remain alive. Capraro, brutally beaten and threatened with lynching, managed to escape his assailants. He also managed to have a photograph taken of his bloodied body prior to receiving medical attention, a photograph that was widely published.* While still recovering from his injuries, Capraro returned to Lawrence on May 18 to a hero's welcome. In his speech Capraro said: "I am back to tell you, Comrades, that I am not a hero, but a mere victim of the capitalistic system we are all fighting."[71]

Instead of intimidating the strikers and stimulating back-to-work sentiment, the murderous attack on Capraro and Kleinman had the opposite effect. After visiting Lawrence, August Bellanca wrote that the "villanous act," rather than intimidating the workers, had "electrified them all, men and women, Italians, Syrians, Germans, Lithuanians, French, Irish, Armenians, and disposed them to the greatest, the most noble sacrifices." A.J. Muste commented: "These brutal tactics instead of breaking the strike have only welded more firmly together the various race elements and imbued them with revolutionary ardor." The attack also stimulated an outpouring of financial contributions; a thousand Italians visited Capraro and pooling their pennies and nickels, presented him with a gift to express their appreciation and affection. The General Strike Committee paid tribute to Capraro with a resolution in his honor which said in part:

> ...we shall treasure your friendship as one of the priceless byproducts of our struggle which gives us hope that a cooperative commonwealth will come in which men shall no more be brutalized by the competitive struggle for bread.[72]

It is clear from these statements that the scope of the Lawrence strike had gone beyond the issue of "48-54" and had expanded into what Muste, Capraro, and their colleagues called a "struggle for industrial democracy to prepare the day when the workers of the world shall own and control their own industries." Federal agents who covered strikers' meetings reported speakers telling workers not to worry about the press calling

*Kleinman was left on the road to Lowell, which city he finally reached battered and bloody. (Lawrence *Evening Tribune*, May 6-7, 1919.) Three months earlier, Paterson officials had deported Kleinman from that city, where he was aiding striking textile workers. (New York *Call*, Feb. 9, 1919.)

them Bolsheviks because "Bolsheviki is all right. Bolsheviki government is all right." This was especially true of meetings of Russian and Lithuanian workers, who were most influenced by the Bolshevik Revolution. According to the reports of federal agents, the Russian workers organized an 80-member Bolshevik club. These sentiments were not confined to the Russians. The first issue of the Amalgamated Textile Workers' newspaper printed the "Declaration of the Soviet Republic of Bavaria."[73]

As the strike entered its fourth month, the endurance of the strikers appeared to be reaching the breaking point. For several weeks in May the strike fund was depleted, ending regular relief. Nevertheless, an effort to reopen the Everett Mill on May 19 failed, with only a handful of the former 1500 employees reporting for work. The very next day the mill owners announced that a 15 percent increase in wages would go into effect June 2 and that there would be no discrimination against strikers. That last point had blocked any progress toward a strike settlement, for the strikers made it clear that they would never end the walkout unless the General Strike Committee obtained an absolute guarantee that all strikers would be taken back without discrimination. Faced with the workers' militancy, the mill owners agreed to this final condition at separate meetings held at each of the mill sites.[74]

At a huge mass meeting the workers voted unanimously to accept the recommendation of the General Strike Committee that the strike be declared at an end. The *New York Times* of May 23, 1919 carried the following from its reporter in Lawrence:

> The final strike meeting was held last night in Lexington Hall. So great was the crowd that tried to enter the hall that the strike leaders were forced to order all of their followers to the streets about the building and then addressed them from the windows of the hall. The assembled workers unanimously endorsed the work accomplished by the strike leaders.

Muste put it more eloquently:

> Thus, amid the gay shouting and singing of thousands of men, women, and little children, the weary struggle came to a glorious end. AND NO SENTIMENT WON SUCH LONG AND WILD APPLAUSE FROM THAT IMMENSE MULTITUDE AS THE APPEAL TO STICK TO THE AMALGAMATED TEXTILE WORKERS OF AMERICA, THEIR OWN ONE BIG UNION, BORN OUT OF THE AGONY OF THEIR STRUGGLE!

"The victory of Lawrence," A.J. Muste declared further, "was not due to the 'intellectuals' who aided them. Rather, it was due to the determination, the sacrifices and the ideals of the workers themselves. It is the spirit of solidarity and cooperation which wins in labor struggles."[75]

After 107 days, Lawrence workers had scored one of the first significant triumphs of the postwar labor movement. As David Joseph Goldberg points out: "The granting of a wage increase was a clear victory for the workers. Most importantly, the mills had been forced to meet with representatives of the Strike Committee. Lawrence workers had accomplished what many neutral observers had considered impossible—they had won a strike for higher wages that had begun at a time of great unemployment."[76] To this one must add that the Lawrence workers had triumphed in the face of an unprecedentedly well-orchestrated and vicious Red Scare!

THE AMALGAMATED TEXTILE WORKERS OF AMERICA TAKES SHAPE

For men like Capraro, Muste, and others, as well as for many of the strikers, the victory in Lawrence was not the end of the struggle but "the first step in the creation of the One Big Union in the textile industry—and beyond that the workers' commonwealth."[77] When the Lawrence General Strike Committee had voted to affiliate with the Amalgamated Textile Workers of America, it also endorsed the draft of a constitution for the new union that defined its purpose as follows:

> Our ultimate aim is, by whatever method of proletarian action may be most effective, to help achieve the abolition of capitalism and the system of wage slavery, and to establish the ownership and control of industry by the workers for the workers.[78]

A call for a convention formally to found an independent textile workers' union went out to the textile centers that had recently experienced or were still engaged in strikes. The call was signed by Joseph Corti of West Hoboken, H.J. Rubenstein and G. Artoni of Paterson, Louis Boches and A.J. Muste of Lawrence, and Matthew Pluhar of Passaic. It read in part: "In recent weeks there has arisen in various textile centers such as Paterson, Passaic, Hoboken, and Lawrence a spontaneous protest against the so-called "leaders" of the textile workers, because the policy of these leaders has resulted in dividing the workers instead of uniting them upon a strong program.... The workers themselves in these various centers, as well as in other places, have realized that they have a common cause to defend, and have been communicating with each other with a view to getting together and laying the foundation for a united and powerful organization for the textile industry."[79]

The first convention of the Amalgamated Textile Workers' Union of

America was held in New York City, April 12 and 13, 1919, while the Lawrence strike was still in progress. Under the patronage of the Amalgamated Clothing Workers, 75 delegates from various textile centers assembled at the Labor Temple at 14th Street and Second Avenue. With Muste in the chair, the convention adopted the preamble of the Amalgamated Clothing Workers' constitution as its own. Based on the Marxist doctrine of class struggle, it called for organization of labor according to principles of industrial unionism and for education of the workers in preparation for the time when they would assume control of the system of production. The radical spirit of the convention was also expressed in its resolutions, which supported the "proletarian dictatorships" in Russia, Hungary, and Bavaria, and praised the Soviet form of government as "the only existing form of government" that guaranteed "to the working class its full rights of representation...and the full social value of its production." The resolutions also extended greetings to Soviet Russia, Hungary, and Bavaria, and hailed "Long live the Soviets!" They demanded the immediate withdrawal of U.S. troops from Russia, and protested the incarceration of political and industrial prisoners in the United States. In its "Call to Organize," the convention invited "our fellow workers in the textile industry to join with us in organizing a class conscious, industrial union which shall be organized and controlled by the rank and file of the workers themselves."[80]

With a loan of $5,000 from the Amalgamated Clothing Workers, the ATWA set up its headquarters in New York City with Muste as general secretary and Capraro, after he recovered from the beating, as editor of its organs the *New Textile Worker* and *Il Tessitore Libro*. Capraro envisaged the merger of the ACW and ATWU to form "one Big Industrial Union of the Textile and Clothing Workers," which would unite labor "from the weaving of the cloth to the sewing of the garment."[81] Evidently this vision was shared by many in the ACW, for at its 1920 convention, the union voted for unity with the ATWU.[82]

But the merger never took place. One reason was that Sidney Hillman, president of the ACW, feared domination of the clothing union by the militant, radical, immigrant textile workers. Another reason was that these militant workers, particularly in Lawrence, influenced by former Wobbly Ben Legere, were beginning to believe that the ACW was "not sufficiently revolutionary."[83]*

*Because he disagreed with this view, Capraro resigned his position in the union in late February 1920. (Rudolph J. Vecoli, "Anthony Capraro and the Lawrence Strike of 1919," in George E. Pozzetta, editor, *Pane E. Lavoro: The Italian American Working Class* [Toronto 1980], pp. 18-19.)

While ideological disputes began to emerge in the infant ATWU, the union spread rapidly through the milltowns of the New England states, New Jersey, New York, and Pennsylvania. Some union organizers were English-speaking intellectuals like Robert W. Dunn and Paul Blanshard*, but with more numerous foreign-language organizers and their literature the new textile union was especially successful in attracting immigrant workers.[84]

The 1919 Lawrence strike helped to publicize the Amalgamated Textile Workers as an alternative to the "8-hour day with less pay" strategy of the United Textile Workers. In Paterson, hatband weavers, ribbon weavers, and broadsilk workers broke with the latter union over its cautious bargaining in a February 3, 1919 strike of as many as 27,000 workers seeking the 44-hour week in mills where not even the 8-hour day had as yet been obtained. The UTW and the mill owners, jointly negotiating with the War Labor Board,** agreed to a schedule of five 8½-hour days with the prospect of adding a 5½-hour Saturday shift. In July the hatband weavers struck without UTW authorization to win the 44-hour standard. After hundreds were expelled by the UTW and after the local ribbon weavers lost their AFL charter, the Associated Silk Weavers was formed to unite the two specialized trades.[85]

More importantly, the broad-silk weavers and dyers in Paterson responded to UTW hesitancy by taking up the call of the Amalgamated Textile Workers for "One Big Industrial Union for the Textile Industry" and for the 44-hour week. However, Amalgamated agitation in Paterson started very slowly. Before July 10 the union's organizers could not even find a hall in which to meet and had to limit their activities to issuing two brief leaflets. (One concentrated on the need for industrial organization, and the other denounced long hours of work). Finally, on July 10 the ATW managed to hold a meeting at the Sons of Italy hall. Two of its convenors were arrested after speeches which again stressed the length of the working day. The charges against them and against two others seized the following day when the police raided the ATW offices were: "attempt by speech or writing, printing or in any other way whatsoever, to incite or

---

*Both Dunn and Blanshard were Socialists. Dunn, however, was soon to become a Communist and director of the Labor Research Association. Dunn had opposed U.S. entrance into World War I. After the war he concentrated on studying labor problems. He was in Lawrence during the 1919 strike and wrote an article, "At Lawrence—Preparing the Workers for the Next World." (*Young Democracy*, vol. 1, April 15, 1919, pp. 32-38.)

**After the war the National War Labor Board accepted only cases that were jointly submitted by labor and management.

abet, promote or encourage hostility or opposition to the government of the United States or of the state of New Jersey."[86] It was a typical example of American justice in the era of the Red Scare.

After this unpromising start, the Amalgamated Textile Workers rapidly organized silk workers in Paterson and led a massive strike for the 44-hour week among the broad-silk operatives, and a smaller one among skilled dyers, who worked especially long hours. By August, the 44-hour standard was established in the Paterson silk industry.

In July 1919 the United Textile Workers had claimed 8,500 members in Paterson. A year later, its local there disbanded.[87] The Amalgamated Textile Workers meanwhile grew quickly, drawing on the desire for shorter hours not only in Paterson, but also in Passaic, where it led a successful hours strike of 10,000 workers. Addressing the Amalgamated Clothing Workers' 1920 convention as an honored guest, Muste could boast also of shorter-hour victories in Allentown, Pennsylvania, in the Hudson River valley, among 12,000 knit fabric workers in New York City, and in Chicago. After just a year's existence, his union was able to claim 50,000 members and to take credit for igniting a campaign that brought the 48-hour week, and sometimes shorter workweeks, to 250,000 workers.[88]

CHAPTER 8

Strikes of Coal Miners and Steel Workers

BACKGROUND OF THE MINERS' STRIKE

On November 1, 1919, rank and file miners, who had suffered through postwar depression and war-related inflation, walked off their jobs. The coal strike of 1919 was the first nationwide strike in the industry since the days of John Mitchell. Central Competitive Field (District 5—Western Pennsylvania, Ohio, Indiana, and Illinois) was completely closed. In the established outlying districts of Central Pennslyvania, in Kansas, Missouri, Montana, Washington, Wyoming and the Tri-state Southwest, the strike was overwhelmingly effective. However, the strike was only marginally successful in the less well organized areas, and nationwide 30 percent of the coal tonnage still reached the market.[1]

The roots of the miners' strike go back to the Washington Agreement of October 1917 between the federal government, acting through the War Fuel Administration, the mine owners and the miners' union to insure production of enough coal to win the war. The contract was scheduled to go into effect April 1, 1918 and to extend to the end of the war, but for a period not to exceed two years. The Washington Agreement stipulated that, in return for wage increases, the miners would not go on strike for the duration of the war. A penalty clause provided for the automatic collection, by the operator, of $1 for each day a miner was guilty of striking in violation of the agreement. This clause provoked a bitter debate at the United Mine Workers' 1918 convention, but the officers urged its acceptance because of the wage increase that was included. They also insisted that it was necessary for the good name of the organization, and they prevailed.

Because consumer prices rose rapidly during 1918 and remained high in 1919, the wage increase was soon dissipated by the mounting cost of living. In June 1919, the War Fuel Administration, the agency through which the government had become a party to the Washington Agreement, went out of existence. The miners' resentment of the agreement grew rapidly after the armistice in November 1918, as the miners felt that they should no longer be bound by the provisions of the Washington Agreement. On the other hand, the union officials were inclined to accept the ruling that the war was not yet officially ended. On August 1, 1919, the union's official publication said editorially:

> It is true that actual fighting between the United States and the Allied nations on the one hand and the central powers on the other hand ceased with the signing of the Armistice, but the fact is that we are still in a state of war with the central powers and will remain so until the war is officially terminated....

In the summer of 1919, the smoldering discontent of the miners erupted in a rash of wildcat strikes. The strikers were fined and the fines were deducted from their pay when the operators enforced the penalty in accordance with the Washington Agreement. Infuriated, the miners struck again, this time against their officials as well as the operators. Union officials admitted that in District 12, Illinois, 25,000 miners were out, while the insurgent leaders claimed at least three times that number.[2]

Although the insurgents were expelled and their locals suspended, when the UMW convention assembled in Cleveland in September 1919, their view prevailed. The convention's resolutions called for a labor party, among other things, for the investigation of possible alliances with the railway unions and for the nationalization of the mines under the control of workers and technical personnel. The convention also authorized a strike for November 1, 1919 if the operators did not grant a six-hour day and five-day week (down from six eight-hour days), the abolition of double shifts on coal mined for commercial use, a 60 percent wage increase and other reforms.[3]

The authority to manage the strike fell to John L. Lewis, the acting president of the UMW. "President Lewis has picked up all the demands of the radicals whose champion he now appears to be," reported the *Literary Digest*. "One is led to believe, however, that Lewis has not assumed this role but rather that it was thrust upon him."[4]

In 1910 Lewis had become president of the UMW local in Panama, Illinois. He resigned the local post a year later to become special organizer for Gompers, and he was succeeded as local union president by his brother Thomas, even though the latter was also the manager of the coal mine that employed the union members.

Although from 1911 to 1918, Lewis never ran for office in the UMW his rise to power was phenomenal. In June 1915, UMW president John P. White appointed him union statistician. A year later he was appointed business manager of the *United Mine Workers' Journal*, a powerful position from which he was able to influence the coal miners. A short time later, White resigned as UMW president to join the War Fuel Administration, and was succeeded by Frank J. Hayes, "an amiable, ineffectual dipsomaniac" who had no heart for the routine work connected with the job of chief executive. Hayes appointed Lewis as vice-president, but with the president continuously intoxicated, Lewis took over the union completely. He consciously sought to project an image of militancy before the rank and file, while maintaining an appearance of responsibility in the eyes of business, government and conservative trade union leaders.[5]

The wage-hour package over which nearly 400,000 miners ultimately fought was considered "impossible" by Labor Secretary William B. Wilson on the ground that it would "put the miners out of line with the other workers of the country." Indeed, the 60 percent wage increase and the eighteen-hour reduction in the workweek were condemned as unreasonable by most of the press. Gradually, however, the logic of the union's position began to win popular backing.[6]

Coal mining, probably more than any other U. S. industry, was plagued by overproduction, mismanagement and seasonal unemployment.[7] "Frequently," declared the Lancaster (Pa.) *Examiner*, "the operator closes the mines entirely; at other times they work them at half-time only; yet the miner cannot leave the fields for other employment, for he does not know when the mines will open again. One week it may be operating while the next it may be shut down entirely....The whole contention of the miners for their shorter working-day is that they will be employed regularly rather than intermittently."[8] In 1918, despite war orders, an average of 63 working days were lost in the mines; in 1919, this figure rose to 115, with no more than 29 of these attributable to strikes.[9]

President Wilson reacted to the miners' demands by reactivating the Fuel Administration which had ceased functioning in the spring.[10] The Administration brought operators and the union together, but was unable to obtain union agreement to its proposal that the strike order be rescinded, that work continue under the old terms after the November 1 expiration of the contract, and that the 48-hour week be held inviolable.[11] Negotiations among the two parties and Labor Secretary Wilson held between October 21 and 24 similarly foundered. All Wilson accomplished was to lay plans for a future meeting of the miners and operators to which the operators outside the Central Competitive Field would also be invited.[12]

ROLE OF THE FEDERAL GOVERNMENT

On October 25, the government openly took the side of the operators when President Wilson, in a statement prepared by his aides, insisted that "the war itself was still a fact," and that therefore the contracts agreed to in October 1917 were still in effect. He also declared that "the mine workers' projected strike is not only unjustifiable, but unlawful...wrong, morally and legally."[13] Headlines in a press overwhelmingly opposed to the strike fairly shrieked: "STRIKE A CRIME—WILSON."[14] Attorney General A. Mitchell Palmer, planner of the soon to be launched Palmer Raids against alleged radicals, echoed Wilson:

> The facts present a situation which challenges the supremacy of law, and every resource of Government will be brought to bear to prevent the national disaster which would inevitably result from the cessation of the mining operations.[15]

The executive branch accepted the central argument of the employers, holding that the strike should be treated as a conspiracy to restrict the production of fuel during wartime and should be prosecuted under the Lever Act, which prohibited strikes until after the membership of the union had been polled. Congress was "deluged with telegrams from businesses, American Legion posts, the National Security League and the American Defense Society, pleading for action to prevent a 'Bolshevik revolution' in the coal industry."[16] Delegations of mine owners also visited Washington. Their chief spokesperson, T. T. Brewster, maintained that Lenin and Trotsky had directly ordered the strike.[17]*

On October 29, with Lewis resisting pressure from Gompers to delay, the UMW announced that it would not rescind the strike order. President Wilson's secretary, Joseph Tumulty, then further hardened the administration's line by writing that the miners, by walking out, would "go to war with the government."[18] Two days later, the Fuel Administration was suddenly reactivated and Palmer secured from Federal District Judge A. B. Anderson a temporary injunction against the strike. It required that the union officials refrain from dispatching messages to carry out the strike and also refrain from any activities in pursuance of the strike, including the paying of benefits to striking miners. The order set November 8 for a full hearing.[19]

On November 1, Lewis nominally complied with the injunction by not

*Brewster stopped making the charge when Lewis demanded proof.

directly abetting the walkout, but 394,000 "leaderless" miners began their strike without any discouragement from union officials. Federal troops quickly showed massive force and, in the words of one study of the strike, "became tin-hatted commuters on the coal barons' business." Federal agents further moved against the UMW by acting as labor spies and by tapping Lewis's telephone.[20]

With an election looming and with Palmer a presidential contender, the Democrats did not wish to alienate the labor vote completely. Neither, however, did they relish being blamed for the rise in coal prices which the mine owners were certain to institute in the wake of any settlement favorable to the miners. Attorney General Palmer also saw the political potential of being antiradical and insisted that the strike was revolutionary in its intent.[21] Through Gompers, Palmer, who was far more active in confronting the strike than the ailing President Wilson, offered to delay court action and to convene an arbitration panel empowered to make a retroactive settlement if the UMW could prove its moderation by cancelling the walkout. However, Lewis could hardly disregard his membership's directive to strike and especially could not accept an arbitration agreement which was based on the mine owners' contention that a "state of war" did still exist and which promised lengthy delays. Nor would Lewis have relished acquiescing to a settlement engineered by Gompers.[22]

ANTI-STRIKE INJUNCTION

On November 7, the government's stance toughened. After convening a conference of the governors of coal-producing states, Palmer ordered an end to the strike, although with no effect.[23] The following day, Judge Anderson again ordered the men back to work. He gave Lewis and 85 other UMW officials until November 11 to cancel the order to strike. "It was," according to a recent study, "the most sweeping injunction issued against a major union since the Pullman boycott of 1894."[24] "About all you can do under this injunction," said a union organizer at the time, "is to go by night to your room, lock the door and pray in a whisper that the miners will win."[25]

At an emergency session, the AFL Executive Council denounced the injunction as "so autocratic as to stagger the human mind," and asked all members of the labor movement to support the striking miners. The AFL pledged to back the UMW's resistance to the injunction, but Lewis, who saw no possibility of a sympathy strike by the AFL, chose to capitulate. He made no attempt to resist the injunction, held no referendum, and did not even announce the terms under which the miners should go back to work.[26] After a seventeen-hour executive committee session, the UMW leadership called off the strike early on November 11, just meeting Anderson's deadline.[27]

But the cancellation of the strike produced no results in the coal fields. The miners stayed out, leading the *Iron Age* to declare: "Now there is no longer doubt of the imminent danger which the progress of Bolshevism carries to American industry."[28] The Wilson administration, amidst industrial shortages of coal, looked for a new solution. The initiative came from Labor Secretary Wilson, who calculated from price indices that to achieve parity with 1914 wage rates, miners would need a 31.6 percent pay boost. The Labor Secretary hoped to negotiate a settlement based on such an increase.

Lewis, silent on Wilson's contention that the six-hour day was "impossible," agreed to bargain on the basis of the proposed wage package, but the operators then balked, refusing to consider a pay increase of over 20%. At this point, the administration split, with Palmer and others arguing, ostensibly in defense of consumer interests, against the Labor Secretary's proposals and for a settlement somewhat less liberal than the mine owners themselves had appeared willing to grant. According to the attorney general, and to the operators who quickly embraced this position, no more than a 14 percent pay increase could be justified. By December, negotiations had again broken down completely. Ironically, as the strike continued and further shortages loomed, the Fuel Administration introduced a six-hour day in some plants to save coal.[29]

LEWIS CALLS OFF THE STRIKE

On December 3, Anderson cited Lewis and 83 others for contempt. Lewis, William Green, the UMW secretary-treasurer, and two other officials were compelled to post $10,000 bonds and were apprised that prosecution was impending under the Sherman Act as well as the Lever Act. The government offered 100,000 troops to defend the reopened mines. President Wilson then called Lewis and Green to Washington and on December 6 offered a 14 percent pay increase and arbitration. After three days, Lewis and his associates decided "to submit to the inevitable" and asked that the miners return to work under the terms set by the government. Lewis had made his position clear two days earlier when, repeating a statement he had made when accepting the first back-to-work order issued in November by Judge Anderson, he had said: "I will not fight my government, the greatest government on earth."[30]

President Wilson hailed Lewis's action, writing directly to the UMW

President: "Your action in response to my statement urging the striking miners to return to work has gratified me very deeply indeed. It is the action of a patriotic citizen and prescience."[31]

The UMW officials had been instructed in Cleveland not to accept any proposition without reporting back to a reconvened convention. In January 1920, Lewis called the delegates together again. Instead of considering proposals for ending the strike, the reconvened convention was presented with the settlement already agreed to by the officials. Lewis explained: "It has been found quite impossible to follow the rigid and inflexible policy laid down by the Cleveland convention. We have been forced to adjust ourselves to a changed situation not contemplated or considered when the original plan and policies were adopted."[32] The convention was asked to approve of the actions taken by the officers. In the debate that followed, a delegate protested:

> I do not see what this convention was convened for unless it was to try to smooth matters over and take all the blame off the backs of the officers who did not carry out the instructions of the Cleveland convention. If we are going to have officials at the head of our organization, let us have officials who will stay with us on strike first, last and all the time, and when we call a strike that they cannot call it off without our sanction.[33]

Lewis argued that he had agreed to the government's proposal "for purposes of expediency, to insure the material welfare of our people and protect the interest of the public weal of our country." Indicating that the miners' demands would be acted upon favorably by Wilson's commission, Lewis declared, "As far as my judgment goes, I think we have a commission whose ability and integrity is beyond reproach."[34]

Immediately after Lewis and Green spoke in defense of the officials' actions, a motion was made to close debate. It was carried despite the fact that many delegates protested. But, exhausted by the strike, the delegates voted to accept the accord by the vote of 1,639 to 231.[35]

It was December 14 before production returned to even two-thirds of the normal rate, but by December 29, when the operators agreed to arbitration, almost all of the men were back in the pits. The final settlement came three months later on March 10, 1920 when the United States Bituminous Coal Commission awarded wage increases of 31 percent to tonnage miners and 20 percent to day workers, which amounted to an average increase to all miners of 27 percent. However, the demand for a five-day week and six-hour day was ignored. There was no change in the hours of work.[36]

Lewis's handling of the 1919 strike has prompted sharp debate. "Like a pusillanimous poltroon," wrote one critic, "he betrayed the rank and file, obeyed the injunction and cowered behind the skirts of 'Americanism'."[37] Many miners were especially outraged, as this statement indicates, by his "greatest-government-on-earth" remark, made at the time of federal repression of both the coal and steel strikes. John Walker, the Illinois UMW leader, who was one of Mother Jones's closest friends, told her that Lewis's "surrendering and bowing in abject submission, allowing the men to be driven into the mines like cattle, without a fight at all...makes decent mine workers, who understand what it means, blush for shame."[38]

Melvyn Dubofsky and Warren Van Tine, recent Lewis biographers, argue that the UMW's leader "did what...circumstances and the realities of power demanded" in ending the strike.[39]* But the failure to press for sympathy strikes by AFL unions, the failure to make strong alliances with the steel strikers, and the failure to extend the strike to the anthracite fields all weakened the strike. So, too, did the virtual dropping of the 30-hour week demand. With that gone, the strike was changed from a conflict over the right to leisure—and health and safety—and the workers' ability to plan for an end to unemployment and to rationalize an ailing industry to a struggle that was only interpreted in terms of wages and consumer prices for coal. William Green justified the UMW officers' retreat with the statement: "Public sentiment, the most powerful factor in the decision of decisions, was crystallized against us, and there wasn't anything to do except to bow to the inevitable and show courage and wisdom enough to meet the crisis in the light of intelligence, rather than in the light of feeling."[40] In abandoning the 30-hour week demand, Lewis and his associates contributed substantially to this outcome.

BACKGROUND OF THE STEEL STRIKE

The 1919 steel strike was the pivotal industrial conflict in the postwar period. Involving hundreds of thousands of workers in a key industry, led by left-wing industrial unionists, uniting the skilled and unskilled, and expressing the rising expectations of the postwar labor force, the steel strike summed up many of the trends of the prior decade. It also repre-

---

*In a later biographical essay on John L. Lewis, Dubofsky and Van Tine insist that Lewis had no choice but to call off the strike, but also claim that he succeeded in "skillfully managing the 1919 coal strike." ("John L. Lewis and the Triumph of Mass-Production Unionism," in Melvyn Dubofsky and Warren Van Tine, *Labor Leaders in America* [Urbana and Chicago, Illinois, 1987], pp. 189, 190.) But in *Industrialism and the American Worker, 1865-1920*, Dubofsky wrote that even after Lewis called off the strike, "rank-and-file miners proved recalcitrant, and they later voted that their union seek the nationalization of the nation's coal mines." (Arlington Heights, Illinois, [1975], p. 128.)

sented a new high in redbaiting, in both public and private repression of the labor movement, and in the failure of its official leadership. In general, the steel strike was recognized as a major turning point in the organization of mass production industries by participants on both sides.[41]

As in the textile and clothing industries, the drive to organize the steel industry began while the war was still raging. Some two million workers joined labor unions during the war, but the gains in the iron and steel industry were minimal. Such gains as were made were primarily the result of the policies of the War Labor Board that protected union members. They were not the result of the organizational policies of the Amalgamated Association of Iron and Steel Workers, the AFL union which had jurisdiction over the iron and steel industry, but did nothing to organize it.[42]

Increased demand for steel products, a sharply reduced labor supply, and the national government's concern to keep the industry operating during wartime encouraged progressive elements within the labor movement, led by William Z. Foster and Chicago Federation of Labor President John Fitzpatrick, both fresh from organizing victories in the Chicago stockyards, to make an effort to organize steel in 1918. Steel workers, eager to organize, were displaying widespread discontent and unrest for which there were good reasons.

Most of the immigrant workers in the steel mills were of rural background, born and reared on tenant farms in Austria-Hungary, Greece, Italy, or Poland, where life was hard. America offered something better. The new life usually began in a boarding-house, where the new worker shared a bed with another worker and often reliquished his place to a man returning from an alternate shift. Work in the mill was unremittingly hard, dirty, and not infrequently dangerous. There was no sick leave or workmen's compensation. The work day was twelve hours long, the work week six or seven days. When shifts were changed, half the men worked 24 hours at a stretch, while the other half spent most of their 24 hour holiday sleeping the sleep of the exhausted. To be sure, saloons and ethnic clubs provided off-the-job recreation for the steel workers, but many were simply too exhausted to enjoy these facilities.*

*For a picture of life of the immigrant steel workers, *see* Matthew S. Magda, *Monessen: Industrial Boomtown and Steel Community, 1898-1980*, Harrisburg, Pa., 1985. In 1920, Monessen, which lies along the Monongahela River south of Pittsburgh, had a population of 18,000 and its mills and factories employed some 6000 persons, "primarily...semiskilled and unskilled steelworkers who manufactured the city's main products of tin plate, fence, tubes, nails and wires." (p.9.) Most of the inhabitants of Monessen were immigrants. Magda's book consists of interviews, conducted in 1981 and 1982, with 16 long-time residents of Monessen, and includes a section on the 1919 steel strike.

The Interchurch World Movement* found that half of the employees in the iron and steel manufacturing plants worked a twelve-hour day, and that that percentage had increased during the decade preceding 1919. The steel worker's average workweek was 68.7 hours—over twelve more than the hours in any other industry. Double shifts each fortnight meant twenty-four consecutive hours of labor. The twelve-hour day deprived the worker of any time "for family, for town, for church, or for self-schooling, for any of the activities that begin to make full citizenship...let alone the energy even for recreation...."[43]

Wages rose considerably by the end of World War I, but the cost of living had increased as well, thus wiping out most of the gains in terms of real income. According to the IWM *Report*, the earnings of unskilled steel workers in 1918 and 1919 were still below the subsistence level and substantially below the "minimum comfort level" (the level of "animal well-being"). Thus, a large proportion of the unskilled and semi-skilled iron and steel workers took home "wages which, statistics indicate, were actually inadequate to maintain an American standard of living."[44] Moreover, when the steel workers in Pittsburgh mills were working a 12-hour day and often as much as an 84-hour week, their counterparts in England were working only 54.7 hours per week.[45]

Nearly a decade previously Elbert H. Gary had established the sprawling company town and named it for himself. Its creator was U.S. Steel, and it was created not as a haven for immigrants, Blacks, Hispanics, or even Anglo-Saxon Protestants, but as a money-making venture. Gary existed because U.S. Steel wanted a good location to produce steel where it could control the political, economic, and social climate. For U.S. Steel stockholders, Gary was indeed a "magic city." But for those drawn to Gary in search of work, the city proved to be a center for poor housing, ill-health, poverty and racism. U.S. Steel's urban planners did not even bother to plan for the army of semiskilled and unskilled workers who operated the mills. A shantytown and an industrial slum resulted.[46]

The majority of steel workers lived in two or three-room tenement apartments that faced onto a court. "In the courtyards...were...open unsanitary drains, and...the community pump which furnished water to a half a dozen or more families....A large proportion of the families were obliged to depend on dilapidated wooden closets in the yard which were

---

*The Interchurch World Movement was established in 1919 by leading Protestant clergymen to study and propose "the solution of the definite social and industrial problems of the new day of readjustment and reconstruction." (Philip C. Ensley, "The Interchurch World Movement and the Steel Strike of 1919," Labor History 13 [Spring, 1972]: 218).

used by many others and were in bad sanitary condition."[47]

The steel workers expressed their opposition not only to long hours and low wages, but also to the lack of collective bargaining and the absence of democracy in the shops, often expressed in the foremen's autocratic rule. Too exhausted to eat or spend time with their families when they returned home after thirteen or fourteen hours in the mill, the men risked losing their jobs if they even suggested any reduction in hours.[48]

ROLE OF FOSTER AND FITZPATRICK

William Z. Foster's general proposal, conceived in April 1918, for a national steel organizing drive quickly won the assent of the Chicago Federation of Labor, and at least lukewarm support from the Amalgamated Association of Iron, Steel and Tin Workers, the AFL union which had jurisdiction over the industry but which had been reduced to a bare skeleton of an organization.[49] At the June 1918 AFL convention, Foster and the CFL pressed for a conference on steel organizing and succeeded in holding three large meetings on the subject. A feeling of optimism prevailed. Labor reformer John Fitch asked rhetorically in June, "If an industry so completely nonunion may become organized under the new conception of human rights as formulated in Washington, what may not be possible?"[50] Fitzpatrick shared Fitch's enthusiasm when he predicted optimistically: "We are going to socialize the basic industries of the United States. This is the beginning of the fight. We are going to have representatives on the board of directors of the Steel Corporation. President Wilson has promised that, in effect, in his program for the placing of industry on a better basis."[51] Foster did not share this glowing view of Wilsonian ideals. He saw a victory in steel as a prelude to the speedy organization of five to ten million workers. As he pointed out in testimony before the investigating panel of the Interchurch World Movement:

> We have to organize everyone around the plant. The advantage of organizing the steel industry, so far as trade unionism is concerned, is a tremendous thing. If this campaign is a success and the steel industry organized, it simply means that the trade union movement in this country is established.[52]

*The Senate Committee on Education and Labor investigated labor conditions in the steel industry during the strike, and in its brief report, published late in 1919, it agreed with the Interchurch Report regarding long hours of work. However, it incorrectly concluded that the "question of wages is not involved in the controversy." (*Senate Report No. 289,* 66th Congress, 1st Session, p. 10.) As the IWM Report noted, "many strikers who looked blank at the mention of 'Bolshevism,' and who knew little even of the A.F. of L., insisted on talking a great deal about wages to this Commission's investigators and to the Senate Committee." (Interchurch World Movement, *Report on the Steel Strike of 1919* [New York, 1920], pp. 98-99.)

A NATIONAL COMMITTEE

In the summer of 1918, Foster and Fitzpatrick asked the AFL to lead a national drive to organize the iron and steel workers. On August 1, the AFL established the National Committee for Organizing Iron and Steel Workers, a federation of twenty-four unions representing crafts and trades in the industry. Thus the scope and importance of organizing steel led to modifications of the traditional, autonomous craft-union structure. The twenty-four cooperating unions in the industry agreed to pool their resources and to centralize direction in the National Committee. Unfortunately, as events were soon to demonstrate, the twenty-four unions had not granted the National Committee real authority, for each union was mainly out to get "more numbers for each...separate organization."[53] Disunity became a problem from the very outset and continued thereafter.

Gompers presided over the Chicago Conference and nominally over the National Committee for Organizing Iron and Steel Workers. But he showed little inclination to aid in organizing work and virtually none to raise funds for the effort—displaying from the beginning only moderate support of the National Committee, a policy he continued throughout the crisis. Fitzpatrick as temporary chairman, and Foster as secretary-treasurer, led the campaign. However, the Chicago Conference rejected the specifics of Foster's plan for a six-week wartime organizing "blitz" in steel and funded the movement with $2,400 rather than the $500,000 Foster requested. Fitzpatrick and Foster had hoped to conduct a nationwide organizing drive, but the funds allocated were insufficient for such an undertaking. They therefore decided to initiate local organizing drives in Gary and Pittsburgh in the winter and spring of 1918-19.[54]

The U.S. Steel Corporation controlled 145 plants and produced about half of the nation's steel. The smaller, so-called independent companies looked to U.S. Steel to lead the fight against the organizing drive, and particularly to Elbert H. Gary, head of the corporation, whose labor policy was based entirely on the "open shop" doctrine.* The officers of U.S. Steel decided to break the organizing campaign in the Monongahela Valley. Five plants of U.S. Steel were located in this valley,** and government leaders in the towns along the Monongahela River, with the excep-

---

*Although E.H. Gary repeatedly insisted that the organizing campaign was seeking "Soviets, and the forcible distribution of property," he put main emphasis on the demand for "the closed shop." (Foster Rhea Dulles, *Labor in America* [New York, 1949], p. 235.)

**These were: National Tube Works in McKeesport, the Clairton Works in Pittsburgh, and three plants of the Carnegie Company in Braddock—the Homestead Works, the Duquesne Works and the J. Edgar Thompson Works.

tion of Braddock and Rankin, supported the steel industry's determination to crush the organizing drive. Some of these officials were employed as management personnel of the steel corporation, while others were connected with the business community that supported the corporation's labor policy. Most of the police chiefs in the Monongahela Valley and in the small towns around Pittsburgh had been placed in their positions by the steel industry.[56]

Iron Age and the *Iron Trade Review*, the steel industry journals, notified their readers that the steel companies were unconcerned about the organizing campaign. However, the latter were already systematically establishing a vast espionage network throughout the steel areas, and workers who "talked union" were reported by private detectives and fired.[57]

By far the greatest obstacle to organizing was the persistent denial of free speech to unionists, especially by the local governments in steel towns. Even though there was no reason to fear any violence, civic officials, particularly in Western Pennslyvania, denied permits for the National Committee to hold meetings. The mayor of Duquesne, who was the brother of a tin company president, proclaimed with pride that in his town, "Jesus Christ himself could not speak...for the AFL."[58] McKeesport's city council resisted the organizers' legal and lobbying efforts to obtain permits to hold meetings. The situation was similar in Monessen, Donora, Homestead, Clairton, Braddock and elsewhere. Where local authorities made no effort to prevent organizers from holding meetings, the County Board of Health would usurp the powers of local burgesses and close the meeting halls on the ground that they were a health hazard because of the flu epidemic. When meetings were held over the objections of the authorities, the names of the men who entered the halls were taken down by steel company superintendents, and the next morning these men were fired. As late as the middle of February 1919, Foster was complaining that the "free speech deadlock still persists."[59]

THE STEEL ORGANIZING DRIVE

Nevertheless, the steel organizing drive gathered force. In executing what historian Philip Taft has called "one of the great organizing feats in American labor history,"[60] the drive's tactical leadership was consistently brilliant. Beginning in the Chicago-Gary area, the National Committee built outward from an initial round of local successes to Ohio, Colorado and West Virginia. By early 1919, agitation started in the Pittsburgh region, where the opposition was fiercest. The National Committee's approach in all steel centers was to hold large public rallies at which union organizers addressed crowds of workers before distributing membership cards. "The idea," William Z. Foster pointed out, "was to make a hurricane drive simultaneously in all steel centers that would catch the workers' imagination and sweep them into the union *en masse*."[61]

In most centers this technique proved effective. Bert Evey, an organizer for the AFL, reported enlisting five hundred new steel workers in one plant in Canton, Ohio in a single week.[62]

Steel companies immediately announced plans to remain open and made arrangements to protect strikebreakers. They hired additional private guards, and stowed weapons, food, and other supplies inside the mills, and in general turned their plants into armed camps. Meanwhile, city officials in nearly all steel centers immediately began to restrict the right of free speech and the right to assemble. A notable exception was Canton, Ohio where Mayor Poorman merely urged the public to obey the law and that they not gather in crowds. However, Governor James Cox of Ohio made it clear that the state would not tolerate mass picketing.[63]

The National Committee was able to utilize the wartime protections of the right to organize, and it applied the idealistic rhetoric that accompanied the war effort to labor at home, making, as David Brody has observed, "the democratic line its own."[64] Among immigrants, unionism and the resistance to the "Hun-like" management were presented as symbols of patriotism and Americanism. The union's case was put forth in the immigrants' languages through foreign-language bulletins and the speeches of over two dozen multilingual organizers. The National Committee approved Foster's strategy of sending as many organizers as were available into the steel producing towns along the Monongahela River. These organizers were called the "Flying Squadron."[65]

The tactical skill of the steel organizers was most evident in the campaign for free speech in Western Pennslyvania. Presenting its grievances in postwar terms, the National Committee charged that "despite its indispensable services to the government,...the AFL is treated as an outlaw." Foster and others defied the bans on free speech in a series of illegal street meetings, first in Monessen and then in Donora, McKeesport, Homestead, Rankin, Clairton and elsewhere. A "flying squadron" of chosen organizers, led by Jack Beaghen of the Pittsburgh Bricklayers' Union, ignored death threats and suffered frequent arrests to restore civil liberties in city after city. Free speech was seized rather than won. As late as August 20, 1919, Mother Jones, then nearing her ninetieth birthday, asked in a speech in Homestead whether the town "belongs to Kaiser Gary or Uncle Sam." She was arrested for her question and then briefly released from jail to dissuade an angry crowd bent on freeing her.[66] Within a week, however, another woman supporter, Fannie Sellins, was brutally murdered.

A long-time organizer of miners, Fannie Sellins had been lent to the National Committee by the United Mine Workers. Before she was killed, she organized three huge U.S. Steel mills and two independent company plants. "...she was killed," declared *Steelabor* in September 1985, "because she organized thousands of steelworkers. She took the initiative and in the midst of terror went out to her work." Fannie Sellins was murdered outside the mill yard of the Allegheny Steel Company in West Natoma, where she was organizing the workers. On August 26 when she approached the company yards, she saw gunmen of the notorious Coal & Iron Police who wore the badges of Allegheny County deputy sheriffs, beating Joseph Starzelski, an old worker, with their guns. When she begged the gunmen to stop, a company official knocked her down. She tried to drag herself to the gate of a friend's home nearby. The *New Majority*, organ of the Chicago Federation of Labor, took up the tragic story:

> "Kill the---!" shouted the gunmen.
> An auto truck hurried to the scene. The body of the old miner [Starzelski] was thrown in. Mrs. Sellins was dragged by the heels to the back of the truck and a deputy took a cudgel and crushed her skull before the eyes of a throng of men, women and children who stood powerless before the armed men.[67]

Foster later wrote: "The guilty men were named in the newspapers and from a hundred platforms. Yet not one was ever punished for the crime."[68]

The two labor martyrs were buried in the Union Cemetery overlooking the Allegheny River. An ornate monument carries the inscription: "In Memory of FANNIE SELLINS and JOE STARZELSKI killed by the enemies of Organized Labor...." On August 26, 1938, the anniversary of her tragic death, a monument was erected to Fannie Sellins by District 5, United Mine Workers of America, with this tribute:

> *Faithful ever to the cause of Labor,*
> *All of us deeply regret the fate you met.*
> *Nobly you fought the fight against greed and gain.*
> *Never flinching with your efforts when the bullets came.*
> *Immortal to miners shall ever be thy name.*
> *Embellished to their hearts the sacrifice you made.*[69]

That the National Committee could enroll 100,000 unionists by June 1919 testified to more than brilliant tactics and individual heroism. Several factors favored organization. One Italian helper put it succinctly after completing a 24-hour double shift and being told that steel workers made "pretty good money." He replied, "To hell with money! No one can live." The words of Mother Jones spoke for many unskilled, immigrant workers whose annual wages did not reach the poverty line despite long shifts:

> If Gary wants to work twelve hours a day, let him go in the blooming mill and work. What we want is a little leisure, time for music, playgrounds, a decent home, books and the things that make life worth while.[70]

Although they joined the organizing campaign more hesitantly, the skilled American-born workers, many of them veterans of union defeats, joined in a second wave after the immigrants. On the average the skilled men worked shorter hours than the unskilled, but few of them totalled less than 60 hours a week. Grievances over speedup, arbitrary promotion policies and lack of power on the shop floor also acted as a stimulus to the skilled workers and gave them common cause with the semi-skilled operatives. The less skilled workers ultimately proved the most loyal to the strike, but all groups shared what David Brody has called "the terrible sense of betrayal" produced by a peace that brought with it none of the reforms they had hoped would follow. Layoffs early in 1919 only served to heighten the feeling of disillusionment and gave added force to the arguments for shorter hours and sharing the work.[71]

The conduct of the steel companies themselves also made a great contribution to the success of the organizing drive. Indeed, the Interchurch World Movement investigators later declared that "the Finance Committee of U.S. Steel" was "the principal organizer of the strike." Repression, in the form of the firings of union leaders, and the refusal to bargain strengthened the workers' resistance. The corporate use of power and influence over local officials and clergy provoked free speech fights, which the unions often turned into organizing tools, and by its very heavy-handedness, divided the immigrant workers from the pro-company community leaders. As David Saposs wrote shortly after the strike: "For almost the first time, the immigrant workers dared to defy the dominant element, the old leaders and newspapers, and followed the National Committee."[72]

In such a situation, rank-and-file commitment to militant unionism grew so fast that it changed the plans of the union strategists. Local leaders, for example, began to preach of the possibility of the six-hour day, although the National Committee had no such plans. On May 25, 1919, when 683 local union representatives met in Pittsburgh, they had to be reminded that only the international unions could call strikes. The delegates mandated the National Committee to quickly "enter into negotiations with the various steel companies."

FRUITLESS NEGOTIATIONS

The Amalgamated Association of Iron, Steel and Tin Workers had already written to Elbert Gary, requesting a meeting between the representatives of the U. S. Steel Corporation and the union. On May 20, 1919, Gary responded: "As you know, we do not confer, negotiate with, or combat labor unions as such. We stand for the open shop, which permits a man to engage in the different lines of employment whether he belongs to a labor union or not. We think this attitude secures the best results to the employees generally and to the employers." This reply did not prevent the National Committee from writing to Gary on June 20, asking that he meet with a negotiating committee. No reply came, and three weeks later, Foster warned: "Some action must be taken...men are in a state of great unrest...great strikes are threatening."[73]

After nine more days of waiting, the National Committee, although reluctant to move until 60 percent of the industry was unionized, authorized a strike vote if the companies did not grant the demands of the union committees. A nationwide vote to stop work if the industry refused, taken during July and August, resulted in a show of support from 98% of those who voted. The ballot had been printed in six foreign languages and English.[74]

Twelve demands were to form a basis for bargaining. Union recognition and the rehiring of fired activists headed the list. Below these were demands for an eight-hour day, one day's rest in seven, the elimination of the twenty-four hour shift, wage increases "sufficient to guarantee an American standard of living," double pay for overtime after eight hours and for holiday and Sunday work, a check-off system for collecting union dues, the principle of seniority to apply in any reduction of the work force, and the abolition of company unions.[75]

The immediate issue of the strike, however, was whether or not the steel corporation would meet with union representatives and recognize collective bargaining. When the National Committee submitted a request for a meeting to Gary on August 25, he refused, repeating his statement that although the members of his corporation did not combat labor unions, they did not discuss business with them. He also repeated that the corporation traditionally stood for the open shop. In a letter to the presidents of the subsidiaries of the U. S. Steel Corporation, Gary stated that his reasons for declining to meet with the committee were that it did not represent the workers, and that "a conference with these men would have been treated by them as a recognition of the 'closed shop' method of employment. The principle of the 'open shop'" he added, "is vital to the greatest industrial progress and prosperity."[76]

Gompers, still the nominal head of the National Committee, asked President Wilson to bring Gary to the bargaining table, assuring the administration that the unions only wanted a conference and would negotiate on the demands. At this time, Fitzpatrick was still sure that Wilson "would never allow a great struggle to develop between the steelworkers and their employers."[77]

Although Gompers reported that Wilson felt that Gary's intransigence was out of place, the president made no public move. After two visits, Wilson's emissary, Bernard Baruch, failed to persuade Gary to bargain. The steel leader remained fixed in the view that "if this country should become generally unionized, it would mean the commencement of industrial decay." President Wilson ultimately followed Baruch's advice not to push Gary any further.[78]

The United Mine Workers issued a statement comparing the federal government's opposition to the miners' strike with "Gary's autocratic attitude":

> It seems remarkable to the miners, that the government should feel called upon to use such extraordinary powers when dealing with workers while the same government finds itself powerless in any way to coerce such great aggregations of capital as represented by Mr. Gary.
>
> Instead of publicly rebuking Mr. Gary for refusing to confer with the men in his employ, the government honored him by placing him on the public committee in the industrial conference....
>
> Now the question is whether Gary owns America or one hundred and ten million people own it. This is the question, you are up against, "Who owns this nation, one hundred and ten million people or one Gary?[79]

In his study of the 1919 steel strike, David Brody cites the difference between the federal government's attitude towards Gary and the steel workers as explaining how industry gained and labor lost after the war. When Gary refused a governmental request to discuss the issues involved in the conflict, President Wilson suffered his rebuke in the silence.[80] In his autobiography Gompers points out that he was unable to secure even a response to a letter to Gary, his erstwhile ally in the National Civic Federation, during the course of the steel strike. Thus his assurance to workers that his policy of seeking acceptance from corporate leaders would bring concrete results for them, once again proved to be an illusion.[81]

THE STEEL STRIKE BEGINS

The National Committee met in Pittsburgh on September 10 and set September 22 as the strike date. Labor officials learned on September 10th that Wilson had requested Gompers to postpone the impending steel strike until after the White House Industrial Conference, scheduled to convene on October 6. Gompers was only too willing to comply. By early September, he had become convinced that the strike against the steel industry would face enormous obstacles. He had learned that employer groups supporting the developing "open shop" movement had agreed that U. S. Steel should make a test case of the pending strike, and that they would render the company all necessary assistance to break the strike. Moreover, Gompers was plainly worried about what the "over-enthusiasm of the unorganized or lately organized" might produce in the way of militant action. "I have never yet run away from or been unduly apprehensive of any situation occurring in the labor movement," he wrote to Michael Tighe, the conservative president of the Amalgamated Association of Iron, Steel and Tin Workers, "but I have not failed to understand that 'discretion is the better part of valor.'"[82]

Gompers therefore urged compliance with President Wilson's request, and the heads of seven participating unions expressed their agreement with him. But Fitzpatrick and Foster, as well as the bulk of the local unions involved, were convinced that any delay would lead to demoralization and to weak wildcat strikes. They adhered to the order: "STOP WORK SEPTEMBER 22." Just before the strike date, Gompers left the leadership of the National Committee, leaving Fitzpatrick as its head. On September 13, Foster wrote to all AFL unions, informing them of the strike scheduled to begin on September 22 and adding:

> This strike will be one of the largest in the history of this country. Upon its outcome will depend, to a great extent, the future of all organized labor in America. If it is won, it will mean that the fight of every trade union is made easier, the backbone of the opposition to organization will have been broken. But if it is lost, the opposition to trade unionism will be strengthened. Every labor hater in the country will be encouraged to fight his employes and to destroy their unions. In the steel strike Organized Labor is facing one of the most important situations it has ever had to contend with.[83]

At the same time, Gary received a wire from J.P. Morgan, for whom he operated U. S. Steel:

> Heartiest congratulations on your stand for the open shop, with which I am as you know, absolutely in accord. I believe American principles of liberty are

involved and must win out if we all stand firm.[84]

Few union leaders and fewer executives envisioned a strike of large proportions. Foster was virtually alone in appreciating that group loyalty among the immigrants could generate a mass strike with only a minority of the workers actually enrolled in unions. On September 22 as many as 275,000 workers struck. The strike peaked early the next week at about 365,000. Plants in Chicago, Wheeling, Johnstown, Lackawanna, Cleveland, Youngstown, and in Pueblo, Colorado virtually shut down. In the Pittsburgh area, the walkout was totally effective in Monessen and Donora and somewhat less so in Homestead, Braddock and Bethlehem. It largely failed in Duquesne and in some Pittsburgh Mills. In Gary, Indiana about 85% of the 18,000 work force went out. Particularly involved were the immigrant workers, whom Foster described as "bold, militant and tenacious." According to David Saposs, the strike was nothing less than an "immigrant rebellion" in which "hunkies"—the term which loosely and derisively described steelworking Romanians, Bulgarians, Hungarians, Greeks, Italians and other Southern and Eastern Europeans—fought for nothing less than elementary human dignity.[85]

THE VICIOUS ANTI-STRIKE OFFENSIVE

In the face of so unexpectedly strong a strike, the steel corporations mounted a fierce counterattack. As David Brody observed: "The hard-won fruits of the free speech fight were immediately cancelled."[86]

On the first day of the strike, state constables relentlessly harassed the strikers who picketed the mills. Mounted constables rode down pickets who gathered at the mill entrances. Company guards killed a child, a young mother and several men in Newcastle. In Duquesne Mayor Crawford met with merchants and property owners and urged them to demand cash and the payment of rent a month in advance, and to eject from their homes anyone who was on strike.[87]

After brief rioting in Gary, precipitated by the importation of strikebreakers in early October, the repression grew worse. In McKeesport, no more than six strikers were permitted to gather even in their own headquarters. Meetings were banned outright in Monessen, Duquesne and Farrell, and severely limited in Pittsburgh, Braddock and Homestead. In a few cities, most notably Wheeling, West Virginia, labor did command sufficient political power to have its own men deputized to keep order, but in the key Pennsylvania centers the strikers faced hostile local police, a state constabulary dubbed "Cossacks" by the Slavic immigrants, and company guards.[88]

Strikers were not allowed to meet with each other. Mounted constables with clubs swinging rode down groups of men as they gathered on the sidewalks to talk. Many arrests were made. In the magistrates' courts, defendants were denied the right to an attorney and were summarily sentenced to thirty days in jail. Mobs also victimized strikers, at one point kidnapping Foster and forcing him to leave Johnstown. As many as twenty-two steelworkers and their supporters were killed during the conflict. Labor spies reported on union activities and attempted to sow ethnic and racial discord and to foster disillusionment among the strikers. Epithets of "hunky" were hurled at the immigrant strikers, who were also accused of being disloyal to the United States. Non-strikers were supplied with "I Am Loyal" buttons.[89]

The corporations at first labored under a twin disadvantage. As long as the twelve-hour day and Gary's refusal to bargain constituted the main strike issues, public opinion would not support the steel trust. The solution they hit upon was likewise twofold: the use of anti-immigrant and anti-radical propaganda to change the perception of the strike. The sermon of Father P. Molyneux, a Catholic priest in Braddock, for example, became a widely circulated anti-strike pamphlet, commended by Pennslyvania's governor. Part of it read:

> This strike is not being brought about by intelligent or English-speaking workmen but by men who have no interest in the community, are not an element of our community....But you can't reason with these people. Don't reason with them...knock them down.[90]

As the strike progressed, the press, with almost total unanimity, portrayed the strikers as "foreign born" and "aliens."[91] During the early weeks of the strike, more than thirty full-page advertisements appeared in Pittsburgh papers emphasizing this theme and associating the strike with destructive radicalism. According to one such advertisement, the strike had "no good American reason" and was "not between workers and employers, but between revolutionists and America."[92]

Even the rhymes of the popular sentimental poet, Edgar Guest, drove the nativist, anti-radical themes home in a factory magazine:

> *Said Dan McGann to a foreign man who*
> *worked at the selfsame bench,*
> *"Let me tell you this, and for emphasis,*
> *he flourished a monkey wrench,*
> *"Don't talk to me of this bourjoissee, don't*
> *open your mouth to speak*

> *Of your socialists or your anarchists,*
> *don't mention the bolshevik,*
> *For I've had enough of this foreign stuff,*
> *I'm sick as a man can be*
> *Of the speech of hate, and I'm telling*
> *you straight, that this is the land for me.*"[93]

Although the mass strike was remarkably free of any violence initiated by the workers, headlines and editorials featured lurid accounts of bomb plots and incipient revolution. The *New York Times* warned against "the foreign element...steeped in the doctrines of class struggle...ignorant and easily misled."[94] —in short, the dumb "Hunky."[97]

THE STRIKE IN GARY

The strike situation in Gary, Indiana provides a picture of the forces arrayed against the steel workers. Although the strike was "notably non-violent," Gary mayor William F. Hodges prohibited parades and open-air meetings, and the strikers were limited to a total of fifty pickets.[95] Mayor Hodges and the city council, composed in part of steel company officials, fully supported the steel industry's position during the strike. The Gary police department served as an effective anti-strike force throughout the crisis. Moreover, they were supplemented by the Loyal American League, composed primarily of Gary businessmen, professionals, and others "from the city's WASP establishment."[96] When the steel workers went out on September 22, the League condemned the strike as "led by radicals who have no respect for American institutions, and who are followed largely by foreigners who do not know or care what American institutions are." Several hundred League members were deputized by Mayor Hodges, "providing official sanction for vigilante violence against the striking steel workers."[97]

On October 4 the first violence broke out in Gary when a group of pickets got into a fist fight with some strikebreakers on a stalled streetcar. Within a day, Mayor Hodges asked Indiana Governor James J. Goodrich to send the state militia to Gary to maintain law and order. On October 6, 2,000 steel workers, led by 200 veterans in army uniform, marched through the streets of Gary in defiance of the militia and the city's anti-parade ordinance. Mayor Hodges promptly requested that Governor Goodrich send more militiamen, but since no other militia units were at hand, the governor requested that federal troops be sent to Gary. That same day, some 1,500 army regulars, commanded by Major General Leonard

Wood, arrived from Chicago's Fort Sheridan. As a contemporary observer noted: "Gary took on the appearance of a city of occupation, with machine gun squads at all strategic points between the mills and the city and company patrols scattered throughout the city."[98] General Wood declared martial law, further restricted strike meetings, prohibited all picketing, and started arresting strike leaders and pickets. At the same time, the military began raids on Gary socialists and radicals, arresting leaders and seizing radical literature. In an interview, General Wood justified these actions by asserting that Gary was "a hot bed of anarchy," and that "the influence of the Reds on workingmen is a real and a great danger to the United States right now."[99]

"The military restrictions simply destroyed the strike [in Gary]," concludes Raymond Mohl. "In imposing martial law, General Wood prohibited picketing and parading, restricted free speech and union meetings, and clamped censorship on strike news in the newspapers, thus making it difficult for the union to maintain the strike's momentum." The soldiers, housed in steel corporation property, arrested over 300 men in Gary on charges "ranging from picketing and intimidation of scabs to distributing or possessing radical literature."[100]

General Wood, whose 1920 presidential candidacy was being promoted by a group of leading businessmen headed by U.S. Steel's Elbert H. Gary, was determined to strengthen his anti-labor and anti-Red reputation. Thus he wrote to Gary in December, 1919: "If we can wake up the real American element among labor, we can get rid of the very dangerous, agitating class that is now at the bottom of most of these acute disturbances."[101] Gary was enthusiastic over Wood's success in painting the steel strike with radicalism. "The country, and particularly our people, owe you a debt of gratitude," he wrote Wood.[102]

Colonel W.S. Mapes, Wood's second-in-command, told the press that evidence gathered by the military and intelligence officers "show conclusively that the steel strike in Gary was fostered by Reds and Revolutionists in the hope of plunging the entire country in a nationwide revolt against the United States government...." Later, Mapes told the press: "We have conclusive evidence that the strike is in the hands of the Reds and we can prove it." The evidence was never revealed, and later the Department of Justice admitted that there was none. "But," as Raymond Mohl observes "the damage to the strike had been done."[103]

Damage was also done to the Gary strike and elsewhere by a number of other forces. The basic policy of the steel industry was to avoid any public discussion of the strike issues—wages, hours, collective bargaining, etc.

Instead, the industry sought, and largely succeeded, to make radicalism and Bolshevism the only issue. The steel companies ran full-page newspaper advertisements that attacked the strike as un-American, and charged that the foreign workers were planning to turn the steel mills into soviets. Industry propaganda concentrated on strike leader William Z. Foster and the revolutionary tract *Syndicalism* that he had written in 1915 shortly after he left the IWW. The industry reprinted and supplied copies of *Syndicalism* to newspapers, government officials, police authorities, and vigilante groups.[104] The press played a large part in promoting anti-strike propaganda all over the nation; editors called the strike a "foreign-inspired" walkout with the aim of establishing a "Bolshevistic" regime in the United States. As the Report of the Interchurch World Movement noted: "A stranger...reading the newspapers during the strike...must have concluded that the strike represented a serious outbreak of Bolshevism red hot from Russia."[105]

Corporate strikebreaking was another problem that faced the strikers. Inland Steel in Chicago recruited Mexicans as strikebreakers. Most mills were operating with Negro workers, the majority brought North to break the strike. Foster paid tribute to a Black preacher who had forfeited a contribution of $2,500 from the steel corporations by urging the Black workers in his congregation to support the strike. But Foster conceded that such efforts were futile: "Race prejudice has everything to do with it. It lies at the bottom....The white man has enslaved them, and they don't feel confident in the trade union....in the steel strike he lined up with the bosses." Roger Baldwin, who had worked in the steel mills and interviewed many of the Black workers reported that most were in favor of the union but "complained of union discrimination against the Negro (and) felt that they owed nothing to white men who had so long ignored and oppressed them." According to the Interchurch Commission of Inquiry into the Steel Strike, "the greater number of Negroes who flowed into the Chicago and Pittsburgh plants were conscious of strikebreaking. For this attitude, the steel strikers rightly blamed American organized labor....Through many an experience Negroes came to believe that the only way they could break into a unionized industry was through strikebreaking."[106]

The strike also suffered from conflict between foreign-born strikers and American-born workers which the steel companies did much to arouse. A major weakness also was the organizing scheme adopted by the National Committee for Organizing the Iron and Steel Workers, a method imposed upon it by the leadership of the AFL. The scheme called for a uniform initiation fee for all workers, collected by the Committee's team of organizers. But all workers would be transferred subsequently to the craft unions which the AFL recognized as having jurisdiction over their jobs.* The Amalgamated Association of Iron and Steel Workers received half of the new recruits. "The prospect of joining the Amalgamated," Robert Asher points out, "could hardly have appeared encouraging to steel workers with an intimate knowledge of the union's historical record.** And workers who were enthusiastic about the idea of a single union for all steel workers were disappointed when they were ordered to join the craft unions."[107]

Added to all this was the poor cooperation the strike received from the AFL leadership. Gompers, who had opposed going ahead with the walkout, justified continued support of the strike on the ground that otherwise "the IWW's and Bolsheviks would have taken control of the strike and the dangers to the welfare of the country would have been enormous." The AFL president staked his hopes on pressuring Gary at the White House Industrial Conference, which began on October 6. The meeting, it will be recalled, brought together representatives of labor, industry and the public. Baruch, eyeing a possible detente between Gary and Gompers, persuaded Wilson to add the former as a "public" spokesperson. Gompers introduced a resolution calling for immediate arbitration of the steel strike by the Conference. It called on the Conference to create a committee of six men—two each from labor, industry and the public—to whom would be submitted "the existing differences between the workers and employers in the steel industry." The committee would be empowered to adjudicate and settle the strike, while the strikers were to be reinstated and return to work pending the committee's findings. In support of his resolution, Gompers again raised the danger that if the strike ended in a complete defeat, the existing labor leadership might be overthrown and replaced by the IWW and the Bolsheviki. But Gary refused to yield. "I am of the fixed

*David Montgomery argues that the National Committee to Organize Iron and Steel Workers, including William Z. Foster, "saw themselves in combat not only with the Steel Trust, but also with two foes within the immigrant communities, whom they called the 'clan leaders' (middle-class nationalists) and the 'intellectuals' (revolutionaries)." Therefore, at their organization meetings "they deliberately avoided discussion from the floor, kept the proceedings brief, and tried to whip up enthusiasm for the union." Organization of industrial unions did not take place "from the bottom up" in this "setting of ethnic suspicions." ("Immigrants, Industrial Unions, and Social Reconstruction in the United States, 1916-1923," *Labour/Le Travail* 13 [Spring 1984]: 112). Montgomery says not a word about the opposition of 35 craft unions in iron and steel, and Gompers, to any idea of industrial unions in steel, and their vetoing of any move in that direction.
**For a picture of this sorry historical record, *see* Philip S. Foner, *History of the Labor Movement in the United States* 3 (New York, 1964): 78-83, 83-86, 190-92.

opinion that the pending strike against the steel industry of this country," he declared in his first and only comment before the Conference, "should not be arbitrated or compromised, nor any action taken by the Conference which bears upon the subject."[108]

Thus Gary flatly refused arbitration and Gompers could not force him into a discussion of the issues. The Conference did not press Gary on the steel situation, and Gompers walked out of the meeting in protest. All he accomplished, however, was that in the public's perception the mantle of intransigence passed from Gary to the AFL.[109]

More importantly, the AFL contributed little to the support of the strike. Most of the men financed the strike from their own savings. The twenty-four participating unions pledged a strike fund of $100,000 but raised only $46,000. All other AFL unions added just $272,000, nearly one-third of which came from the ILGWU and the Furriers. The Amalgamated Clothing Workers, who were outside the AFL, were more generous than any union in it, giving $100,000. Even if all funds had been directly distributed, only $1.15 would have gone to each striker during the course of the fifteen-week strike. Moreover, the participating AFL unions often subordinated support of the strike to their narrow craft interests. The Amalgamated Association sent its members who were under contract back to work during the walkout and, despite the fact that it gained half the new recruits generated by the steel drive, contributed little in the way of money or organizers. The Operating Engineers broke with the strike leadership over jurisdictional matters. Solidarity actions by the railway unions were too little and too late to compensate for the AFL's disunity and inaction.[110]

END OF THE STEEL STRIKE

By November 24, with the strike deteriorating, the National Committee concluded that arbitration was its lone hope for even partial success. Fitzpatrick therefore sought intervention by the Interchurch World Movement. The IWM accepted his overture, although it insisted on acting not as an arbitrator, but as a mediator, facilitating a "new deal" in the industry. On December 5, after a cordial meeting with the churchmen, Gary refused mediation. He insisted that the aims of the strike were "the closed shop, soviets and the forcible distribution of property," and, without allowing the IWM to present its mediation plan, he concluded that there was "absolutely no issue" to discuss.[111]

On December 13, 1919, the day on which the National Committee resolved to fight "to the last ditch," the number of strikers dipped below the 100,000 mark. Although the leaders voted to continue, the strikers were weakening rapidly. On January 8, 1920, the strike was officially called off. The announcement stated:

> The steel corporations, with the active assistance of the press, the courts, the federal troops, state police and many public officials, have denied steel workers their rights of free speech, free assemblage, and the right to organize, and by this arbitrary and ruthless misuse of power have brought about a condition which compelled the National Committee...to vote today that the active strike phase is now at an end.

The Committee managed a last act of defiance and bravado, announcing: "A vigorous campaign of education and reorganization will be immediately begun and will not cease until industrial justice has been achieved in the steel industry."[112]

FOSTER EVALUATES THE STRIKE

Immediately after the strike, William Z. Foster sat down and wrote his book, *The Great Steel Strike and Its Lessons*, in which he drew the lessons of the struggle for the entire working class. Foster declared that even though the vicious terrorism unleashed by the steel barons and by the police and the troops succeeded in crushing the strike, both the organizational campaign and the strike's direction marked a great advance in trade union tactics. But that was not enough, for

> ...it represented only a fraction of the power the unions should and could have thrown into the fight. The organization of the steel industry should have been a special order of business for the whole labor movement. But, unfortunately, it was not. The big men of Labor could not be sufficiently awakened to the supreme importance to induce them to give the movement the abundant moral and financial backing so essential to its success. Official pessimism, bred of thirty years of trade union failure in the steel industry, hung like a millstone about the neck for the movement in all its states."[113]

The failure to follow through on the original organizing plan envisioned by Foster was, for him, a "monumental blunder" on the part of the participating unions. The number of organizers and the amount of funds provided could not possibly do the job required. This fact soon became apparent to all and spread pessimism in the ranks. "Had it [organized labor] but stirred a little," Foster wrote, "the steelworkers would have won their battle, despite all the Steel Trust could do to prevent it."[114]

Several years after the steel strike, Foster wrote that the defeat was "a tremendous disaster" not merely because it destroyed the steel unions, but because it thwarted a "much greater plan." Had the strike been a success,

Foster would have proposed "the formation of a great organization committee with branches in the big industries, to sweep the masses into the unions."[115] In this way, he planned to transform the AFL into a federation of industrial as well as craft unions, embracing the majority of the American working class.[116]*

A major lesson Foster drew from the experience of the steel strike related to the success of the tactic of the Steel Trust in pitting Black workers against white workers. He wrote:

> For the tense situation existing the unions are themselves in no small part to blame. Many of them sharply draw the color line, thus feeding the flames of race hatred. This discriminatory practice is in direct conflict with the fundamental which demands that all the workers be organized, without regard to sex, race, creed, politics or nationality. It injures Labor's cause greatly. Company agents harp upon it continually, to prevent Negroes from joining even the organizations willing to take them in. This was the case in the steel campaign-....Such a condition cannot be allowed to persist. But to relieve it the unions will have to meet the issue honestly and broad-mindedly. They must open their ranks to Negroes, make an earnest effort to organize them, and then give them a square deal when they do join. Nothing short of this will accomplish the desired result.[117]

Essentially, Foster drove home the point that only industrial unionism, based on nationwide, simultaneous organization in all plants, companies, and areas, and on the organization of unskilled and semiskilled, as well as skilled workers, Black and white, could do the necessary job of organizing steelworkers in the United States and lead them in militant struggles for their needs and interests.

On November 4, 1919, as the steel strike was on the verge of collapse, the citizens of Lackawanna, New York, site of the Lackawanna Iron and Steel Company, elected John H. Gibbons, a pro-Socialist, pro-labor candidate as Mayor. Gibbons defeated John Toomey, the incumbent, who had brazenly aided the steel company with a most vicious anti-labor, red-baiting campaign during the strike in which several workers had been fatally wounded, including a decorated war veteran. Toomey ran for reelection with the support of the steel firm, but workers and small businessmen alike rallied to vote for the Socialist candidate as their way of

---

*In *The Roots of Communism*, Theodore Draper, a professional anti-Communist, sees this perspective as a sinister plot on Foster's part to dominate the entire labor movement. After the defeat of the steel strike, Draper writes, "Foster's dream of taking over the whole A.F. of L. was shattered." (New York, 1957, pp. 186-87.) Thus the desire to launch a much-needed drive to organize the unorganized in the mass production industries becomes, in Draper's paranoid outlook, a secret plot to take over the whole labor movement.

showing their hatred of the Mayor's strikebreaking role. The election of a pro-labor Mayor reinvigorated the strike in Lackawanna. In January, after the National Committee called off the Great Steel Strike, Lackawanna steel workers voted to stay out, and they remained on strike for another six months.[118] This action was kept in mind by William Z. Foster when he wrote in *The Great Steel Strike and Its Lessons* that the steel strike was not a "lost" struggle.[119]

History has demonstrated the correctness of Foster's evaluation. In 1923, the twelve-hour day was abolished in the steel industry.* The Interchurch Investigation laid the groundwork for the LaFollette Senate Committee of 1936; the limitations of the National Committee for the Organization of the Steel Industry were carefully studied by the Steel Workers Organizing Committee, CIO; and the failure in 1919 was a incontrovertible lesson that the organization of the mass production industries required industrial unionism to be successful. In 1936 a successful campaign to organize the steel industry materialized.

In the immediate sense, however, the defeat of the steel strike was an important factor in the open shop drive of the postwar era. Most industrialists viewed the strike as the beginning of a larger struggle. As the *Iron Age* put it: "The struggle between the open and closed shop, between law and anarchy, between syndicalism and the republic, has started." And as Allen M. Wakstein points out:

> The steel strike of 1919 was the largest national strike since the anthracite coal strike of 1902. The latter had been used as a springboard for the open-shop drive of the earlier period; the steel strike now served somewhat the same purpose in reviving it. Gary made the open shop a public issue, and various periodicals lent their media to spreading the idea. That the strike had occurred in steel is also of importance, since many other industries tended to follow the labor policy of the steel corporation.[120]

---

*The action was hastened by the publication of the *Report* of the IWM which aroused widespread public hostility to the steel industry and led to President Warren G. Harding's intervention to abolish the twelve-hour day. (Samuel H. Adams, *Incredible Era: The Life and Times of Warren G. Harding*, [Boston, 1939]: 267-69, 369-71, 388-89; Ensley, p. 229.)

CHAPTER 9

The Open Shop Drive, 1919-1920

OPEN SHOP ASSOCIATIONS

When the government ended its support of unionism after World War I, employers who had reluctantly yielded to federal pressure to recognize unions were now ready to throw the principle of collective bargaining overboard. The December 11, 1919 *Manufacturer's Record* announced the formation of open shop associations in various parts of the country "to contest radical labor unions."[1] Texas was cited as a prime example, with a group of open shop associations already in full operation.

Among the first of these was the Open Shop Association of San Antonio, organized in May 1919. It was incorporated by the state on June 20 and represented all the employing interests of the city except the retail merchants, who were not asked to join. It had only one purpose: to replace the closed or union shop with the open shop.[2]*

The Open Shop Association of Jefferson County, including the city of Beaumont, Texas, was chartered by the state on October 10, 1919. In its application for a charter, the employers indicated that they were seeking it "for an educational undertaking, to wit, for the purpose of collecting and disseminating information to the public showing the advantages of the open shop to the public in the manufacture, sale and distribution of goods, wares and merchandise." Granted a charter, the association grew in size from 400 members in October to over 1,200 in December 1919. About 90 percent of the employers in Beaumont were affiliated with the association.[3]

In November 1919 the Dallas Chamber of Commerce voted almost

---

*A closed shop meant that only union members could be hired, while in a union shop, a non-union worker could be hired, but he or she had to join the union within a specified time. In an open shop, a worker could be employed whether or not he or she belonged to a union, and union rules did not apply. In practice, open shops usually employed only non-union workers.

unanimously "to instruct the directors of the Chamber of Commerce to declare Dallas an open-shop city and to establish an open shop association." Unlike San Antonio and Beaumont, where the associations were formed by independent employers, the organization in Dallas was sponsored by the Chamber of Commerce and became a department in it.[4]

By the end of 1919 open shop associations were functioning in Toledo, Ohio; High Point and Louisville, Kentucky; Miami, Florida; San Diego, California; Indianapolis, Indiana, and Minneapolis, Minnesota.[5] The Industrial Association of San Francisco led the way on the Pacific Coast by developing a complete plan of action for introducing the open shop. Its essential features were a full-fledged attack on the closed shop in the building trades, including a pledge by the contractors to employ a designated number of nonunion men. Material dealers refused to supply materials to contractors who did not adopt the open shop. The entire industry was policed by the Industrial Association to see that wages and hours of work agreed upon by the Association were actually put into effect.

The Industrial Association of San Francisco adopted the so-called "Ten Commandments," which became a model for associations in other cities. Among the "Commandments" were: (1) Employ working men and women without any regard to their affiliation or nonaffiliation with labor organizations; (2) Base the pay of such employees upon their individual skill, ability and industry; pay employees as high wages as existing conditions will permit; (7) Recognize the right of employees to submit any and all complaints and wage questions to their employers, either individually, collectively, or by committee; (8) Deny the right of outside parties to interfere in matters arising between employer and employee; (10) Endorse and support every organization, whether of capital or labor, standing for the rights of American citizens.[6] Not included in the public "Ten Commandments" was a secret agreement that required employers to cease doing business with all businessmen who signed union agreements.[7]

This plan, was copied in Los Angeles in most of its details, and it was brought to San Diego not long afterwards by two representatives of the Los Angeles Merchants' and Manufacturers' Association.[8] Led by the San Diego Labor Council, the unions struck back, and many members refused to work unless union conditions were upheld and the products bore the union label. On July 1, 1921, the Manufacturers' and Employers' Association called a general lockout and demanded that the unions accept the open shop and wages determined solely by the employers. The lockout dragged on through the summer months of 1921 and ended with a victory for the employers. The Building Trades Council was broken up, and many of the unions in San Diego were almost destroyed.[9]

In August 1920 the Associated Industries of Washington compiled a list of 78 cities in which "commercial and industrial organizations have taken steps which definitely aligned them with the open shop movement...."[10] By October 1 of that year, it was reported that there were 168 cities and towns operating on an open shop basis. The following month there were said to be 489 "purely open shop associations functioning actively," and this list excluded those associations that had "other interests than the open shop," or Chambers of Commerce, boards of trade, merchants' associations, or other business, trade or civic organizations "which have signed or subscribed to open shop principles."* The total number reported to be actively promoting the open shop was put at 540 in 240 cities of 44 states.[11] Of 68 cities in the United States with over 100,000 population, all but seven were included in this list, and of 210 leading manufacturing cities 130 were associated with the open shop movement. While it is true that of the 240 cities listed 76 had under 25,000 people, a strong open shop movement did exist in the large industrial centers.[12]

THE "AMERICAN PLAN"

In explaining the establishment of these open shop associations, the Citizens' Alliance of Duluth claimed that both during the war and after it had ended "businessmen were confronted with a situation where it was necessary for them either to close their doors or put their plants on the open shop basis."[13] Specific reference was made to "the demands of the unions for increases in wages and shortening of hours," but the major complaint was against the closed shop. By requiring every worker to belong to a union, it was contended, unions gained monopolistic power that inhibited the freedom of individuals. This was labelled "un-American." The open shop was the "American Plan."[14] Addressing the National Association of Manufacturers in May 1920 on "The Open Shop and Democracy," Gus W. Dyer declared: "You can hardly conceive of a more un-American, a more anti-American institution than the closed shop."[15]

The term "American Plan" to describe the open shop was adopted as early as March 1919 by the Associated Industries of Seattle, formed—it will be recalled—after the general strike in that city. It sought to defend the open shop "against Bolshevism," "foreigners," and "European radical-

---

*In July 1920, by an overwhelming vote—1,700 in favor to 2 against—the membership of the Chamber of Commerce of the United States adopted a platform on industrial relations which declared for the open shop in all of American industry. (Tampa *Morning Tribune*, July 31, 1920.)

ism." The "American Plan" slogan was officially adopted to describe the open shop at a 1921 conference in Chicago of 22 state manufacturers' associations.[16]

OPEN SHOP PROPAGANDA

To the advocates of the open shop, the terms "closed shop" and "unionism" were synonymous. Once a union was recognized, the argument went, it was inevitable that the closed shop would certainly follow.[17] And unionism not only produced a closed shop; it also inevitably led to strikes. As William H. Barr, one of the most aggressive of the open shop advocates, put it: "Labor unionism is, as you well know, synonymous with strikes...."[18] The declaration of several open shop organizations specifically stated that they had been formed to oppose all strikes, and especially sympathy strikes.[19]

The open shop would end this danger. Once the "monopolistic power of arrogant, selfish labor leaders is curtailed," strikes would be avoided. There would be other benefits as well. With no union contracts, an employer would be free to hire anyone he chose, basing his decision on ability alone. Workers would also be free to bargain individually with their employers, rather than through an "outside" party who neither understood nor was concerned about the local situation. Then, too, the open shop would enable the worker to work as fast and as long as he desired. This would benefit both the employer and the worker.[20]

The patriotic theme dominated all of the literature of the open shop movement. The open shop was described as "the synonym of American independence," reflecting "the spirit in the Declaration of Independence"; "a perfect manifestation of the American spirit"; "the spirit of the Constitution"—in short, "pure Americanism." Open shop associations adopted the word "Americanism" as their label; the organization in Indianapolis had as its emblem a bald eagle perched on a shield, bearing the words "American Plan Product—INDEPENDENT SHOP."[21] Allen M. Wakstein points out:

> Though the concern over Bolshevism and radicals had diminished, the patriotic energies of the public remained focused on unions, and attention toward the closed shop, and support for the open shop, grew.[22]

Employers knew how to take advantage of the patriotic theme to remove unionism from their shops and factories.

According to its advocates the open shop was not only patriotic but it was the key to a community's prosperity. If a community did not want to see its industries close their doors and establish themselves in open shop cities, it had to replace the closed shop with the open shop. Moreover, the open shop was "the magnet that draws new industries." A community was destined to decline if it did not go along with the open shop trend. The open shoppers pointed to the example of the Goodrich Tire and Rubber Company. It had recently completed a $10 million plant in Los Angeles, employing thousands of workers. The president of the company announced that, after careful consideration of other locations on the Pacific Coast, the company had chosen Los Angeles because it was "open shop."[23]

Dallas boasted that through the activities of the Open Shop Association of its Chamber of Commerce, the city had gained "inestimable value." It was proud of the fact that "leading magazines and newspapers in New York and scores of other cities have requested and chronicled the gratifying results of our open shop accomplishments." The Chamber of Commerce concluded from its own experience and that of other open shop cities that "the greatest inducement any city can offer for the location of new industries is stable, open shop working conditions."[24]

Open shop associations printed and distributed pamphlets and other literature to employers urging them to join the movement and spelling out its benefits. In September 1920 the Indianapolis organization was reported to have "distributed during the past year 1,500,000 pieces of literature devoted to this [open shop] cause."[25] Literature in favor of the open shop was also distributed to newspapers, magazines, and other publications throughout the country. In many cities the press gave full support to the open shop campaign. The closed shop was routinely classified as "un-American," and the newspapers attempted to demonstrate the high prosperity of American cities that had adopted the open shop. Editorials regularly hit at closed and union shops and hailed the open shop as marking the "dawn of a new day of freedom for the American working man." "The greatest menace today to the perpetuation of the free institutions of the United States," went a typical editorial, "is to be found in the destructive propaganda, aims and practices of the American Federation of Labor, which represents less than 3 percent of the country's entire population."[26]

OPEN SHOP PRACTICES

Richard B. Lovett, president of the Florida Federation of Labor, responded to the repeated assertions that the closed shop was "un-American" by pointing out that the manufacturers had "remained home [during World War I] and piled up profits." Indeed, if anything was "un-

American," he went on, it was the tactics used by open shop associations in forcing businessmen to join.[27] Thus, the Cigar Manufacturers' Association of Tampa, reorganized in January 1920 to maintain the open shop, required each member to post a bond of not less than $500 nor more than $10,000, which was automatically forfeited if the member violated the rules and by-laws of the organization. On March 16 agreements were reached between the association and each of the three box producers in Tampa under which the cigarmakers pledged to purchase the complete output of each box factory through a purchasing agent, who would coordinate box orders for association members and decide to whom boxes would be sold. Nonmembers were then informed that they could not purchase boxes until they joined the open shop association.

Several manufacturers who were not members filed for an injunction against the association, alleging a "combination in restraint of trade." But Judge Robles found no grounds for granting an injunction, and he dismissed the case with the comment that the box manufacturers could sell to whomever they pleased; all of their output could go to the open shop association if they so desired. But after a year of investigation the Federal Trade Commission found the open shop association guilty of a "combination in restraint of trade," and, on May 22, 1920, issued a cease-and-desist order. But the same newspapers that featured articles and editorials on the "un-American" closed shop and other practices of trade unions either ignored the FTC finding or buried it in their back pages.[28]

The St. Paul [Minn.] Citizens' Alliance was another open shop association that used economic pressure against employers who refused to join the open shop campaign. The Alliance instituted a boycott against a firm of plumbing contractors because it refused to place an "open shop" show card in its window. The plumbing firm applied for an injunction to prevent the Alliance's boycott, but the court upheld the organization in its right to enforce the boycott. In this instance, the Federal Trade Commission did not investigate.[29]

The Employers' Association of Detroit took a full-page advertisement in a local newspaper, advising businessmen how they could aid the open shop drive. It contained several examples of the "un-American" use of economic pressure. It read:

> The Open Shop made Detroit a great industrial center.
> Detroit needs the Open Shop if she is to continue to advance.
> What can Mr. Average Citizen do to promote the welfare of Detroit and incidentally of his fellows, his family, and himself?

The answer is a simple one:

Property owners specify the Open Shop and employ only local contractors who are fighting for progress.

Purchasers of goods buy only from Open Shop producers.

If you need printing, see an Open Shop printer.

Manufacturers buy patterns and castings from open pattern shops and foundries.

Think Open Shop!

Talk Open Shop!

Yes, and vote for those who support the Open Shop.[30]

THE NATIONAL FEDERATION OF OPEN SHOP ASSOCIATIONS

By the fall of 1920 the open shop movement had reached into nearly every state. Most of the highly industrialized centers had one or more organizations supporting the open shop. In New York State alone there were at least 500 active open shop associations; Massachusetts had 18 associations in eight cities; Connecticut had 20 in 13 cities; and Illinois had 46, with 21 of them in Chicago. There was already a regional federation formed—the Southwestern Open Shop Association—consisting of associations in Texas, Arkansas, Oklahoma and Louisiana. Many open shop advocates now insisted that the time had come for a national federation of open shop associations.[31]

An attempt to form such a federation by Andrew J. Allen, secretary of the Associated Employers of Indianapolis, failed. But in 1920 the American Employers' Open Shop Association, with headquarters in Chicago, did come into existence. Hastily organized, it was essentially an effort to use the open shop drive "to cash in on the anti-union sentiment of the day." It promised all manufacturers who paid an initiation fee of $50 and yearly dues of $25 that they would obtain "a great deal" in the way of assistance in enabling them "to run their shop as they see fit, and not be dictated to by some unscrupulous delegate of some union." Thus:

(1) Should you be threatened with a labor controversy or strike, you can immediately get in touch with us and we will handle the situation for you.

(2) Should you want an under-cover man on the inside among your employees, we will also furnish you such a man, and you will receive a daily report on what is going on.

(3) In the event of trouble, we will replace any men that may strike against you.

(4) We establish welfare clubs in your plant from which you derive a lot of benefit; and all manufacturers are alive to this issue.[32]

In the fall of 1920 the National Association of Manufacturers announced that it had established an Open Shop Department. The NAM, as we saw in a previous volume,* had a long tradition of opposing labor unions. It had been associated with the earlier open shop movement from 1903 to 1909. The great strike wave of 1919 so frightened the association's Board of Directors that it asked James A. Emery, the NAM's legal counsel and a long-time foe of unionism, for his suggestions as to how best to meet the tremendous upsurge in labor militancy. On February 12, 1920 Emery recommended that the NAM undertake once more to promote the open shop "in a special and systematic manner." He continued:

> It is not enough to offer the open shop as an employer's right or panacea. It must be a popular theory of shop practice to be embraced as the only one which assures the protection of the public interest in the economic and political issues involved. This purpose requires more than abstract argument upon the principles involved. It must be overwhelmingly demonstrated by facts and figures that the open shop condition secures a larger return to the worker, a lower cost to the consumer and a greater opportunity for American production to enlarge its facilities, better its service, expand its competition with other nations and bring a larger measure of the convenience, comforts and luxuries of life within the reach of the average man by immensely multiplying our capacity for the production and diffusing of its benefits among our people.[33]

To accomplish this goal, Emery recommended that the NAM set up an organization which, among other functions, would "systematically stimulate open shop organizations who are in their turn to be helped by every form of educational assistance that can promote their growth and firm adhesion to open shop principles."[34]

On October 1, 1920 the NAM's Open Shop Committee recommended that the association establish an Open Shop Department "for the purpose of promoting the recognition and observance of open shop principles in American industry and a better understanding of such principles on the part of employers, employees and the general public." One of its purposes would be to encourage and foster local movements. This would be accomplished by collecting, compiling, and disseminating information, data, and discussions regarding the open shop "and its essential relation to our national ideals and institutions and to industrial stability, productivity and national program," and by

> ...initiating, encouraging and fostering local movements for the mainte-

*See Philip S. Foner, *History of the Labor Movement in the United States* 3 (New York, 1964):36-42.

nance and extension of open shop operation or the spread of open shop principles...[and] by cooperation with different bodies, national or local, devoted to
these ends.[35]

The Open Shop Department of the National Association of Manufacturers launched a vigorous campaign to aid existing local open shop associations, to assist in the formation of new ones, and to disseminate
propaganda on a national scale. Thus, the open shop movement that had
begun early in 1919 as a reaction to the upsurge of postwar labor militancy
in numerous local communities had, by the fall of 1920, assumed national
proportions.[36]

THE REAL OBJECTIVE

A referendum submitted by open shop associations read:

> I am—in favor of the open shop in which there is no discrimination against
> union or non-union employees; and where the right to work, wages and terms
> of employment depend primarily upon individual merit and personal choice
> and not upon membership or non-membership in any organization.

According to this, open shop associations publicly asserted the right of
workers to belong to unions if they so chose. Frank Waterhouse, the first
president of Associated Industries, the open shop organization of Seattle's
businessmen, was quite specific on this point:

> Understand, the Associated Industries of Seattle is by no means opposed to
> trade or labor unionism or to organized labor; but it is unalterably opposed to
> the closed shop, which system means that a working man cannot seek a job
> unless he belongs to some particular union, and an employer cannot employ
> him. We are for the open shop, the fair, square American plan of industry,
> which permits the union man, as well as a non-union man, to find a job.

Nevertheless, in practice, the open shop associations made it clear that
their reason for existence was to oppose and eliminate trade unions from
American industry. In addressing a membership meeting of the Oklahoma
City Chamber of Commerce, the president of the Tulsa Open Shop Association urged those in attendance "to go after the unions" and destroy
them.[37]

So common were such calls from leaders of open shop associations that
John E. Edgerton, president of the NAM, criticized not only the associations for opposing the hiring of any union members but also those employers who hired only non-unionists. He claimed that such actions violated
the open shop principle that no person "should be refused employment in
any way or discriminated against on account of non-membership in any

labor organization." However, the NAM itself did nothing to inhibit any actions along these lines by its members. In fact, the association supported the employment of only non-unionists in such industries as coal mining, where even a few unionists could prove to be "troublesome." Moreover, it refused to take a position against "yellow dog" contracts which, in essence, excluded all unionists from work.[38]

In denying the legitimacy of the regular functions of the trade unions and in demonstrating an unwillingness to bargain with union representatives, the open shop associations rendered meaningless the right of labor to organize. From the enormous body of literature published by open shop associations, one thing emerges clearly: the open shop drive sought to destroy unions and obliterate them from the U.S. industrial scene. Where it could not achieve this goal, it sought "to remold them in the employers' image of what they should be."[39]

Not all employers' associations joined the open shop movement; some preferred to deal with trade unions. This was especially true in situations wherein the unions held strategic positions or where, because of the competitive nature of the business, it was to the employers' advantage to deal with them. In this category were the Stove Founders' National Defense Association, numerous building trades associations, and several railroads.[40]

Some public officials, too, refused to endorse the open shop campaign. Asked by the Worcester (Mass.) Metal Trades' Association to support the drive against the closed shop, Governor George P. Hunt, the progressive chief executive of Arizona, accused the association of being "one of those organizations incapable of realizing that your community is reaping all the benefits of organized labor without sharing any of the responsibility." Hunt accused the antiunion employers of advancing justifications for the open shop which "are not only misleading but anarchistic."[41]*

THE STRUGGLE IN TAMPA

Probably the most bitter battle over the open shop occurred in Tampa's cigar industry. Involved in the battle were the Cigar Manufacturers' Association (which was organized specifically to maintain the open shop and which demanded that its members enforce the open shop principle) and the Joint Advisory Board of the Cigar Makers' International Union (CMIU)

*For the unusual role Governor Hunt played in Arizona in labor disputes, see Philip S. Foner, *History of the Labor Movement in the United States* 6 (New York, 1983): 17-24, and Alan V. Johnson, "Governor G.W.P. Hunt and Organized Labor," unpublished M.A. thesis, University of Arizona, 1964, pp. 70-95.

locals 336, 462, 464, 474, and 500 in Tampa. Although wage negotiations took place between individual manufacturers and their own workers and were usually settled without strikes, union leaders in each factory shop, known as shop collectors, were active in recruiting members to the CMIU. In December 1919 the manufacturers' association decided to halt union activity in the factories and all union shop collectors were discharged, blacklisted, and refused employment by other association members. In January 1920, after attempts to negotiate with the manufacturers failed, each local held a referendum in which a majority approved a motion to strike if the collectors were not reinstated. The CMIU executive board also authorized strike action if the dispute was not resolved.

Efforts by the Joint Advisory Board to persuade the manufacturers' association to arbitrate the issue failed, and on April 12, 1920 the Board presented their demands to the Association as a strike ultimatum. The JAB asked that the shop collectors be reinstated and that all new employees be required to join the union. Clearly, a union shop was the main objective.[42]

On the same day (April 12) José Muñiz, secretary of the JAB, called on the members of the employers' association to reinstate all union members who had been fired and blacklisted "with the same duties as they had when discharged." He also requested a union shop agreement that would require that all new employees become members of the CMIU, and that the shop collectors be permitted to collect union dues and verify union membership of all new employees. The manufacturers rejected the demands and announced that as members of the Cigar Manufacturers' Association they would operate only open shops and would forbid any "labor union or association" to represent any employees.[43]

On April 14, 6,400 cigar workers from 27 of the largest shops—representing 95 percent of Tampa's cigar workers—walked off the job. Two days later the manufacturers adopted new rules for the industry, reducing wages, increasing working hours, and announcing their intention to hire anyone, whether or not he or she was a union member, and that all terms and conditions of employment would be put into effect without consulting the union. The companies belonging to the Association then announced that their shops would be closed the following day, and would not reopen until the workers agreed to the new rules.[44]

When United States Commissioner of Conciliation Joseph R. Buchanan offered to mediate the conflict, he was informed by the manufacturers that "the principle of open shop cannot be arbitrated." The Association announced publicly in advertisements in the *Tampa Morning Tribune* that it would have "open shops or no shops at all."[45]

In pursuit of that objective, the Cigar Manufacturers' Association continued the lockout for more than two and one-half months. On July 6 it announced that factories would reopen July 8 for all workers who wished to return under open shop conditions and the new rules. "The principle of open shop shall be maintained in each department of the factories of all members of the association....," the CMA resolved.[46] The Joint Advisory Board turned down the manufacturers' invitation to return to work, but ordered its members not to congregate around the factories and not to interfere with anyone who wanted to work. José Muñiz, JAB secretary, warned that violence would not be tolerated and that proper punishment would be handed out to any member who tried to prevent workers from going back to work.[47] If Muñiz hoped that this policy would soften the employers opposition to the union, he was soon proved wrong.

However, the attempt to reopen the factories failed, and in full-page advertisements in the *Tampa Morning Tribune* the association charged that "Public Sentiment" in Tampa was behind the open shop citing the stand taken by the Kiwanis Club and the Rotary. Both organizations had unanimously voted in favor of the open shop and had condemned the "unlawful and cowardly practices" of the union in preventing cigarworkers, through "intimidation," from returning to work.[48] In still another full-page ad in the *Tribune*, the Association charged that the strike was called by "radicals" who dominated the Joint Advisory Board and whose "sole purpose" was "GAINING CONTROL OF TAMPA'S CIGAR INDUSTRY."[49]

At the same time, with the assistance of the *Tampa Morning Tribune*,* the Association sought to show that the strike was defeated, and that

---

*Throughout the strike, the *Tampa Morning Tribune* and the *Tampa Sunday Tribune* gave full support to the open shop campaign. Editorials denounced the closed shop as "un-American," and articles pictured "the higher prosperity" of American cities that had adopted the open shop. The paper predicted that "it will be but a short while before it will be a recognized policy of all progressive cities and communities...." Indeed, "the nationwide movement" for the open shop already embraced forty cities, while "others are demanding it," all of which marked the "dawn of a new day of freedom for the American working man." As for the strike itself, the *Tribune* saw it only as a coup by "professional agitators who have kept fifteen thousand industrious, but unsophisticated cigar makers out of employment...." (*Tampa Morning Tribune*, June 24, Aug. 1, 15, 23, 1920.)

As might be expected, the *Tampa Morning Tribune* was in favor of unlimited violation of the constitutional rights of strikers and other radical workers. "We must not allow any sentimental considerations for free speech to blind us to the imminent peril of allowing treason and anarchy to be preached in our streets," it editorialized in April 1919, and concluded "We have been far too lenient in the past. We should tighten the reins in the future." (April 21, 27, 1919, and quoted in Gary R. Mormino and George E. Pozzetta, *The Immigrant World of Ybor City: Italians and Their Latin Neighbors in Tampa, 1815-1985* [Urbana and Chicago, Illinois, 1987] p. 159.)

Italians, described as "the backbone of the strike" and "always the last to return to work, were reporting to the factories for employment."[50] These reports had no real foundation since the great majority of cigar workers who had walked off their jobs in April had not returned. But with the Cigar Manufacturers' Association refusing to negotiate or to go to arbitration,[51] thousands of Tampa workers were forced to leave the city, many of them going to Cuba for jobs, making it easier for the manufacturers to employ hundreds of strikebreakers.[52]

George W. Perkins, president of the CMIU, had endorsed the workers' walkout, declaring that "there never was a more righteous and determined strike." Perkins assured the Tampa unionists that the International would continue to help the strikers morally and financially.[53] This assurance helps explain the fact that when the JAB held a referendum on October 14, after six long months on strike, to determine whether the strike should be continued, the strikers voted in the affirmative.[54]

Unfortunately, a large number of nonunionists had been thrown out of work by the Association's lockout. Financial support for striking union members was assured by the national strike fund of the CMIU, the treasuries of the Tampa locals, and regular financial contributions from locals and unionists in other cities. (New York members of the CMIU also conducted sympathetic strikes against Tampa companies with factories in that city.) But there was no support for nonmembers who had been thrown out of work. This seriously weakened the JAB's ability to maintain the strike.[55] In an appeal to Mayor H.C. Gordon, written in Spanish and signed "Los Padres de cien Familias" (The Fathers of 100 families), nonmembers described the sufferings of their families, especially the children, and stated they desired to return to work, "but not at the cost of being termed strikebreakers." They urged Mayor Gordon to call a meeting of both sides to settle the strike. In his reply the Mayor said that since "the manufacturers have distinctly stated that they are not open to any outside interference from anyone," nothing could be done, and the nonmembers would have to continue to suffer unless they were willing to return to work immediately.[56]

Maintaining that the strike had been over since the factories reopened in July, the Association ignored all attempts to settle the walkout. So the day-to-day battle of the cigar makers continued until February 4, 1921 when the union workers finally surrendered to the open shop and the new rules of the employers. In a referendum, over 2,500 of 3,557 who voted (about half the number that originally voted the strike measure) favored returning to work.[57] The strikers declared that "the strike is not lost and the return to work is but a temporary measure" caused not by a weakening of the workers' morale but by a lack of funds to continue."[58] But CMIU president Perkins admitted the defeat while paying tribute to the Tampa strikers who had conducted the most "determined and prolonged strike and walkout" in the union's long history.[59] It was also one of the most expensive, since CMIU paid out more than $1,000,000 in strike benefits and locals from all over the United States, Canada, Cuba, and Puerto Rico sent thousands of additional dollars to help support the strike.[60]

Since there was no negotiated settlement with the manufacturers' association, each worker had to apply for employment at the shop in which he was employed before the strike, but with no guarantee of reemployment. In all cases workers had to accept the open shop and the rules set by the manufacturers.[61] They were hardly ready to join in the "Congratulations" voiced by the *Tampa Morning Tribune* in its editorial rejoicing at "the victory of the employers" or to echo its declaration that the end of the strike was a "cause for handshaking."[62] "The fact that the association's factories no longer permitted readers* most clearly revealed the new balance of power," Gary R. Mormino and George E. Pozzetta point out.[63]

In an ironic twist of events the Federal Trade Commission, after more than a year of investigation, found the Cigar Manufacturers' Association guilty of a "combination in restraint" of trade and issued a cease and desist order. But the Commission's order of May 22, 1922, came too late to revive union strength in Tampa. Not only the cigar manufacturers, but all business interests in Tampa hailed the decisive defeat of the union shop in the city. It was not until the New Deal period of the 1930's that the union shop returned to Tampa.[64]

RESULTS OF THE OPEN SHOP DRIVE

Similar situations prevailed in many other parts of the United States. Although it was by no means the only factor, the open shop movement contributed to the curtailment of the number and effectiveness of trade unions.[65] The 1.5 million decline in union membership from 1920 to 1923 is clear evidence of this fact. The increase during the same period of one million workers in employee representation plans hardly compensated for the loss. These plans were, in practice, little more than company unions that left the workers under total employer domination.[66]

*The *lectores* (readers) were paid from contributions by the workers to read aloud during the workday—from the daily press, from classics of literature, as well as from socialist and labor sources. (See Jesus Colon, *A Puerto Rican in New York*, [New York, 1961, 1982], pp. ix, 11-12.)

Some unions, like Steam Fitters Local 665 of Buffalo, New York, with 180 members, capitulated peacefully and "renounced the closed shop as leading to the reduction of output."[67] But in many communities, the unions surrendered to the open shop only after bitter strikes. In nearly all cases, workers had to apply for reemployment and had to accept the open shop and the rules framed by the employers. They lost the closed or union shop, which they felt to be their only defense against reduction in wages, lengthening of hours, and worsening of working conditions. As a result of the open shop drive, in many industries the concept of the union shop was not to return until it was guaranteed by federal legislation during the New Deal period of the 1930's.

There was a tragically ironic aspect to the open shop drive. Although the AFL had been a major participant in the antiradical Red Scare campaign, the open shop employer organizations, which played a leading role in generating the hysteria of 1919-1920, were determined to limit the growth of organized labor, regardless of whether it was radical or conservative. Consequently, as Gompers sadly noted, no distinction was made between a "patriotic, constructive organization...and an organization of anarchists and bolshevists."[68] The result was that during this period the open shop movement expanded, union membership and influence declined rapidly, and the Red Scare was used increasingly as a weapon to curtail and limit the development of organized labor.

CHAPTER 10

Strikes and Black-White Relationships

In a number of important strikes of 1919, the racial discrimination practiced by organized labor bore bitter fruit. How serious the problem was is illustrated in the important story of the attempt to organize the meatpacking industry of Chicago.

Meatpacking was the major industry in Chicago during World War I as regards employment of Black migrants from the South. "A Negro could always get a job in the stockyards," a railroad porter later recalled, "They could go to the stockyards any day of the week and get a job."[1] As early as 1916 5,000 Blacks were reported to be working in Chicago's stockyards. At one large firm the number of Black employes increased from 311 in January 1916 to 3,069 two years later. By 1918, between ten and twelve thousand Black men and women traveled daily to the stockyards.[2]

In 1910 only 357 Black men worked in the Chicago stockyards, and 37 more in blast furnaces, rolling mills, and iron foundries. Only 46 Black women worked in factories of any kind.[3]

In our previous volume we described the organizing campaign that took place during World War I in the stockyards, and we saw how the Stockyard Labor Council, a consortium of thirteen craft unions formed by the Chicago Federation of Labor, won an agreement with the packers, arbitrated by Federal Judge Samuel B. Altschuler.* The award handed down in March 1918 increased unskilled minimum hourly wages from 27½ cents to 32 cents and provided a basic 8-hour day with 10 hours pay and premiums for overtime. An appendix to the award declared that "There shall be no discrimination against any employe or prospective employe because of race, color or nationality."[4] Phil Bart notes that the "inclusion of this appendix was of his-

---

*Philip S. Foner, *History of the Labor Movement in the United States* 7 (New York, 1987): 235-36.

toric importance for a trade union at that time." But he adds: "although in practice there still remained a gulf between word and deed."[5]

It was the first union victory, and union membership soared. By November 1918 62,857 packinghouse workers nationwide belonged to the Amalgamated Meat Cutters and Butcher Workmen, twice the total recorded in January of that year.[6]

With Altschuler's award due to expire in 1919, leaders of the Stockyards Labor Council, headed by William Z. Foster, Jack Johnstone, Joe Manley, Bill Herrin, and Sam Hammersmark,* sought a new agreement that would include recognition of the union as bargaining agent for the packinghouse workers. The packers refused, and offered only to renew the existing agreement. Although the Stockyards Labor Council opposed renewal, the leadership of the Amalgamated Meat Cutters and Butcher Workmen rejected the idea of a strike and agreed to extend the existing agreement. The Stockyards Labor Council reluctantly acquiesced.[7]

THE STOCKYARDS LABOR COUNCIL CAMPAIGN

The Council, however, determined to win union recognition, mounted a massive organizing drive. Union workers refused to work with non-union men, and throughout June and July 1919, spontaneous walkouts in departments not "one hundred percent" union, interrupted production.** The wildcat strikes brought the issue of Black-white relations among stockyard workers to the fore.[8]

The Stockyards Labor Council concentrated its energies on special efforts to organize Black workers. Viewing racial division as the greatest threat to the campaign for union recognition, the Council stepped up efforts to convince Black workers that they were welcome in the union, recognizing at the same time that efforts were needed to break down the hostility of white workers. Jack Johnstone, who had replaced William Z. Foster as secretary of the Council (after Foster turned his energies to the steel campaign) was the leader of this move. Marches and demonstrations were arranged, uniting the people of both white and Black communities.[9] William M. Tuttle describes one march:

*The campaign to organize the packing industry had been headed by William Z. Foster, who was joined by the others mentioned above. Later they all joined the Communist Party and held leading positions in the organization. (Phil Bart, *Working Class Unity: The Role of Communists in the Chicago Federation of Labor, 1919-1923* [New York, 1975] p. 8).

**The campaign to organize inside the packinghouses violated the Altschuler agreement, which prohibited "advocating for and against unionism on the premises." Both sides, however, frequently violated this clause.

Black and white workers paraded through the black belt on Sunday, July 6, and congregated in a playground near the yards. Brass bands led the way, and marchers waved miniature American flags and carried placards, on one of which was printed, "The bosses think because we are of different colors and nationalities that we should fight each other. We are going to fool them and fight for a common cause—a square deal for all." Union leaders delivered speeches....[10]

The parade was underway when members of the Amalgamated's Local 651 (known as the "colored" local because most Black workers gravitated toward it even though nominally they could join any of the forty locals organized by the Stockyards Labor Council) gathered at the local's State Street office before setting out for the parade and rally. Two miles away, a group of white packinghouse unionists prepared to march to the mass meeting. The two groups—one Black, the other white—had intended to merge and march the final ten blocks together along State Street through the heart of Black Chicago. But Police officials warned that racial tensions were too high to risk a joint march. Threatened with revocation of their permit, union leaders agreed to abandon their plans to have white and Black unionists demonstrate their solidarity. The Chicago Federation of Labor charged that the packers had pressured the police into the ruling. Noting that the demonstration and rally were designed largely to "interest the colored workers at the yards in the benefits of organization," the Stockyards Labor Council reluctantly and bitterly agreed to the segregated parade.[11]

Three Blacks and four white workers addressed the 3,000 union members who gathered in the playground at the western edge of the "Black Belt."

"It does my heart good," cried out Jack Johnstone, "to see such a checkerboard crowd. You are all standing shoulder to shoulder to shoulder, as men, regardless of whether your face is white or Black." John Kikulski, speaking in Polish, urged his countrymen "to abandon their prejudices and cooperate with their Black co-workers." C. Ford, a Black organizer, used an analogy to drive home the point that fighting between Black and white could only result in continual battle and mutual degradation. Thus he warned both Black and white packinghouse workers that if they continued to wrestle with each other they would have to remain on the ground; if a wrestler fails to stay down with his opponent, "he'll get up and you got to throw him down again."

T. Arnold Hill of the Chicago Urban League reminded the audience that Black-white relations were a two-way street. Thus, while implying that he supported the union, he warned that "if he and his colleagues were expected to advise the colored workers to join the union, they expected the union men themselves to be fair toward their [Black] workers."[12]

Stockyard Labor Council organizers were hopeful that the demonstration, despite the enforced segregated parade, would show graphically that the union stood for Black-white unity, and that onlookers of the parade through the ghetto would obtain a clear picture of the union's concern for and fellowship with Black workers. At the same time, white participants would recognize that Black workers could be organized, that there was Black community support for the union, and that whites should therefore reject Samuel Gompers' repeated slander that Blacks were a "scab race."[13]*

Whether or not the Council's hopes went beyond what was possible at that time in Chicago, the fact is that the march and rally did take place; that Black and white workers did mingle in an interracial meeting; that two Black organizers and an influential leader of the Urban League did speak. "The Stockyard Council," concludes James Richard Grossman, "had succeeded in making unionization a meaningful proposition to many Black workers, and was continuing to present its case to thousands of others."[14]

This was soon demonstrated in the growth of enthusiasm for the union among Black stockyard workers. "In the mornings," went a report in New Majority (organ of the Chicago Federation of Labor) "at 7:30 we find applicants waiting to be signed up (in Local 651) and every night until 9 and 10:30 a steady stream of humanity rolls in and out of the office."[15] Soon an "elevated train committee" of Black union members was handing out union literature to laborers at transfer points between the stockyards and the south side of the ghetto.[16] By July, Local 651's per capita payments to the International indicated 2,213 members, including 160 women, were in good standing. A larger number of Black members had joined but their dues were not paid in consistently.[17] Unfortunately, strikebreaking continued despite this development, and some white workers openly repeated Gompers' slanderous charge, "with exceptions."[18]

THE CHICAGO RACE RIOT

Even more unfortunate, in late July 1919 the ugly Chicago race riot erupted. From July 27 until July 31 Blacks and whites battled in the streets, and occasional attacks continued for another week. By August 8 twenty-three Blacks and fifteen whites lay dead, and at least 537 other Chicagoans had suffered injuries. Fifty-one percent of the clashes had taken place in the stockyards district.[19]

*See Philip S. Foner, *History of the Labor Movement in the United States* 3 (New York, 1955): 233-44.

The Chicago Federation of Labor acknowledged that attempts were being made "to blame the race riots on labor, saying that labor is probably the cause of the riots. When as a matter of fact, labor has done everything in the stockyards and held out its hand to the Negro and established organizations and invited the Negro into the white man's unions."* The Federation statement put it bluntly:

> The profiteering meat packers of Chicago are responsible for the race riots that have disgraced the city.

Referring to the mass meeting and demonstration held on July 6 "at which white and black workers were to parade together throughout the stockyards district and gather to hear speakers in a public playground," the statement noted:

> On the last day before this event the packers called upon the police and said they had information that the [N]egroes were arming to assault the whites and they wanted the parade permit revoked—at least they wanted the [N]egroes and whites to march separately.
> Is not their purpose clear?
> They succeeded in having the whites and [N]egroes separated into two parades, instead of letting them march together. This was done, but the marchers in the two parades merged into one audience at the playground to hear the speakers. And there they fraternized peacefully and cordially—united workers.

"Organized labor has no quarrel with the colored worker," the Federation insisted. "Workers, white and black, are fighting the same battle." In fact, "the only thing that saved the city from becoming a shambles [during the riot] was organized labor."

> It stands to the credit of the union workers of Chicago that neither black nor white union men participated in the rioting, despite the lying accounts published daily by the kept press, bought body and soul by the advertisements of the packers and other crooks of big business.[20]

What actually did cause the bloodiest riot during the "Red Summer" of 1919? The *Chicago Defender*, the city's Black weekly and no friend of the AFL, answered that the riot was mainly the result of problems involving housing, and that racial conflict among Chicago's workers were not

---

*Phil Bart comments: "It had to plumb the depths of white chauvinism to come up with a generalization of 'white man's unions' and particularly in an industry where over 20 percent of the workers were Black." p. 11.

significant factors "because most of the laborers of our group have become unionized, thus doing away with the occasion for friction along those lines."* The Chicago Commission on Race Relations did not agree with this estimate of the extent of Black union membership, but did agree with the *Defender's* dismissal of industrial issues as a cause of the riot.[21]

But others differed, insisting that the riot had arisen out of conditions involving the workplace. Both William H. Tuttle, Jr. and James Richard Grossman, in their studies of the Chicago riot, conclude that labor issues were major contributors to the riot.[22]

Whatever part it may have played in the riot, unionism itself was a victim of the terrible event. For the friction created between Black and white workers in the poisoned social atmosphere enabled the employers to further exploit racism to split the union.[23]

Packinghouse firms moved quickly to turn the riot to their advantage. In a conference with the commander of the militia and the chief of police, the employers proclaimed they would protect Blacks from hostile whites if they returned to work on August 4. Excluded from the conference, union leaders charged that the packers would be doing what they had wanted all along, namely, to bring in thousands of non-union Black workers under the protection of the state militia. This was "a tactic well known to Chicago's labor movement," the Chicago Federation of Labor charged. If the packers went through with their plan, threatened the Stockyards Labor Council, it would call a strike until the situation had cooled sufficiently for Black workers to return to the stockyards without the militia's protection.[24]

When Black workers returned for work on August 7, under the guard of the police and militia, white unionists promptly walked out and later that day, announced a mass meeting to call a strike for the closed shop, which would exclude non-union Blacks.[25] But the officials of the Amalgamated Meat Cutters and Butcher Workmen opposed a strike on the ground that it would violate the Altschuler agreement, so the Stockyards Labor Council did not extend the one-day walkout. However, the Council broke with the Amalgamated over the issue and over the Council's charge that the Amalgamated was impeding efforts to organize Blacks. Accordingly, on its own the Council renewed its efforts to organize Black workers.[26]

---

*In an editorial addressed to AFL President Gompers entitled, "Come Now, Lord Gompers!" the *Chicago Defender* declared bitterly: "THERE IS NO COLOR LINE IN THE HANDIWORK OF LABOR AND THERE SHOULD BE NONE IN THE COUNCILS OF LABOR." (*Chicago Defender*, Feb. 23, 1918; Bart, pp. 10-11. Capitals in original.)

ORGANIZING EFFORTS CONTINUE

But it now proved to be an almost impossible task. With the militia withdrawn, Black workers were literally afraid they would be attacked by whites, some of whom now viewed all Black workers as scabs. Local 651 petitioned the mayor of Chicago the week after the riot to provide its members with protection "to the end that we can reach our places of work and not be menaced or intimidated by any group of people who are seeking our employment by trying to place the entire race in a discreditable light."[27]

Just at this time the Chicago Federation of Labor charged that the packers "subsidized Negro politicians and Negro preachers and sent them out among the colored men and women to induce them not to join unions."[28] Black organizer Charles Dixon agreed, and he added editors to the list of the packers' agents.[29]

These Black agents of the packers flooded the ghetto with propaganda picturing white union men as the aggressors in the riot, declaring that employers, not the unions, offered assistance in the emergency and that "Armour, Swift sent truck loads of meat" into the ghetto, "otherwise some of the people would have starved."[30] The result of the packers' campaign to turn Black workers against the union were reflected in the records of Local 651. This Black local's per capita payments to the Amalgamated declined sharply toward the end of 1919, and by December had dipped to $200, indicating only 800 paid-up members. Five months later, only half of these remained. Local 213, also made up largely of Black workers, made payments in only two of the first five months of 1920.[31] In August 1920 District Council Nine of the Amalgamated, comprising the Chicago region, declared that the proportion of organized Black workers was "insignificant—not exceeding 15 percent at any time." It blamed the dismal figures on the "unconcern and often resentful attitude" of Black workers—without, of course, mentioning that they might have had good reason to resent racist policies and practices. Many Black union members charged that although they were welcomed into the Amalgamated Meat Cutters and Butcher Workmen, the union was primarily interested in the welfare of the white members.[32]

By December 1921, membership in Local 651 stood at 112, with only 49 in good standing![33]

Explaining the failure of the five-year organizing campaign by the Amalgamated and the Stockyards Labor Council to attract and retain Black members, Urban League official T. Arnold Hill, noted for his general support of the trade unions, wrote that even though most union leaders in packinghouse were sincere in their efforts to combat racism, they found a "general attitude on the part of Negroes that the trade union movement is not earnestly seeking to get Negroes to join it."[34] Unfortunately, even progressive white labor leaders put the blame for this belief on the Black workers. They did not really understand that such actions as the appointment of Black organizers, the establishment of Locals 651 and 213 to allow Black unionists to control their affairs, and some special attention paid to grievances of Black workers could not overcome the influence of racism still prevalent in the union among white rank-and-file members, leaders, and even the union's official organs.[35]

Black leaders resented the fact that the *New Majority*, organ of the Chicago Federation of Labor, consistently printed racist anecdotes, usually in dialect, and never capitalized the word "Negro." They especially resented the fact that the paper mentioned Black workers only when they were perceived as a threat to a unionization campaign such as the drives to organize packinghouse and steel.*

It was all because of the anti-union influence exerted by the Black community, argued leaders of the Chicago Federation, in explaining the reasons for the decline in Black union membership. "Every effort," declared two of them, "has been made to organize the colored workers in the Stockyard and elsewhere and offered the same chance as the white man or woman, but the Negroes were guided by their ministers and the Y.M.C.A., who were under the influence of the packers and big interests."[36]

In fact, a few Black ministers in Chicago, such as Lacey Kirk Williams of Oliver Baptist Church and John Thomas of Ebenezer Baptist Church, were pro-union and allowed union representatives to speak to their congregations and even preach a "sermon regarding the benefits of unionization." But most Black ministers agreed with Archibald J. Carey, AME Bishop, that "the interest of my people lies with the wealth of the nation and with the class of white people who control it." Many of Chicago's Black churches received funds from the packers and aided them in recruiting nonunion Black workers.

Similarly, the Wabash Avenue YMCA, an all-Black branch established in 1913, worked closely with packinghouse firms and other Chicago industrialists to mold Black migrants from the South into a "loyal, tractable, efficient labor" force.

---

*James Richard Grossman, "A Dream Deferred: Black Migration to Chicago, 1916-1921," unpublished Ph.D. dissertation, University of California, Berkeley, 1982, pp. 303-04, 336-37, 341-42, from which, unless otherwise indicated, are drawn the details of the events in Chicago.

BLACK LABOR AND UNIONS

As the past history and current evidence of relations between organized labor and the Black workers demonstrate, putting the blame on the Black workers was a simplistic and racist evaluation. But even more ignorant of the history of Black workers was John Fitzpatrick, president of the Chicago Federation of Labor, who, despite his efforts to organize Black workers into Chicago's unions without racial discrimination, described the packers as pitting one group of workers against another to defeat efforts at unionization, "until they got down to,—well, the very lowest." This was the Black migrant from the South whom Fitzpatrick described as "hopeless" so far as possibilities of organizing were concerned.[37] "The Southern Negro," Fitzpatrick lamented, "is different. We figure that his slavery days ended at about the time he came here to work in the Packing houses."[38]

However, as we have demonstrated clearly in previous volumes, many Southern Negroes had belonged to unions in the South and had engaged in militant struggles for higher wages, shorter hours, better working conditions, and union recognition. In New Orleans, Black longshoremen had begun organizing as far back as 1872 and in another major strike in 1907. In many southern cities and towns Black carpenters, bricklayers, and painters belonged to craft unions, and during the first decade of the twentieth century in the Birmingham, Alabama district, at least 8,000 Black workers belonged to trade unions, mainly the United Mine Workers.[39]

Rural Black southern workers also had a trade union tradition. Over 60,000 of them joined the Knights of Labor in the 1800's. Although the Colored Farmers' Alliance may or may not have reached a membership of one million—as it claimed—and was not exactly a labor union, it did call a strike of cotton pickers in 1891.[40] In a sense, the Progressive Farmers and Household Union of America, the organization of sharecroppers whose existence and activities led to the bloody riot near Elaine, Arkansas in 1919, was a continuation of the legacy from the experiences of Colored Farmers' Alliance in the 1890's.[41]

Approximately 17,000 Black workers had belonged to the Brotherhood of Timber Workers, which organized in 1910 and conducted a series of bitter strikes between 1912 and 1914. Many of these workers also joined the Industrial Workers of the World after the Brotherhood affiliated with the IWW in 1912.[42] It is significant, in light of Fitzpatrick's derogatory comment on the southern Negro and trade unionism, that the May 1919 report of the Southern Pine Association on Negro migrants from the South in Chicago, noted: "A surprising number of these Negroes have at some time in the past been employed in the saw mills and woods in the Southern States." Not a small number of them, it added, had once belonged to the Brotherhood of Timber Workers and then to the IWW.[43]

BOGALUSA SOLIDARITY

The tradition of Black-white labor unity even in the deep South, exemplified in the Brotherhood of Timber Workers and carried on after it affiliated with the IWW, is illustrated in 1919 in Bogalusa, Louisiana. Bogalusa then boasted the largest lumber mill in the world, the Great Southern Lumber Company. Although Great Southern had made enormous profits during the war, in 1919 its workers, both Black and white, still earned less than 30 cents an hour. Not only were wages low but hours were long, housing conditions were wretched, and safety virtually nonexistent.[44]

Even the mill owners admitted among themselves that "persecutions, brow-beating and bulldozing by petit officers, who profit by arrests, is the cause of dissatisfaction among Negro labor in various localities."[45]

In May 1919 two AF of L unions, the United Brotherhood of Carpenters and Joiners of America and the International Timber Workers Union, began organizing the workers of the Great Southern Lumber Company. The AFL was successful in organizing a sawyers' and filers' union (which was taken over by the Carpenters) a regular Carpenters' local and timberworkers' union. The three unions organized a Central Trades Assembly, with the head of the Carpenters' union, Lum Williams, as president, and began a campaign to organize the lumber workers of the area, including Blacks.[46]

The organizing drive brought results. The 1919 Labor Day parade was participated in by 1200 Bogalusa workers, and Great Southern was so impressed that 17 days later the company announced a ten percent wage increase, bringing mill wages up from 30 cents to between 33 and 35 cents an hour.[47]

Shortly after the Labor Day celebration the union approached Great Southern officials and asked for formal recognition. The company responded by laying off many workers in a lockout, and ordered the proprietors of the local stores, whom they dominated, to announce that credit "would no longer be extended to those workers who remained in the union."[48]

The workers answered with the first strike in Bogalusa's history. Great Southern immediately brought in Black workers from New Orleans by the carload to fill the strikers' positions. "Many of these workers," notes a student of the strike, "refused to stay and returned to New Orleans when they found that they were being used as strikebreakers."[49]

Great Southern now launched a huge campaign accusing the union of being integrated, and called for mob violence against the "[n----r] loving union." Black workers were actually organized in a segregated local. The drive to organize them in this local had been spearheaded by Sol Dacus, now the Black president of the Negro local.[50]*

The effort of the union to organize both Black and white workers, even if in separate locals, led Great Southern to sponsor the formation of a Self Preservation and Loyalty League (SPLL) in Bogalusa, consisting of company supervisors, some war veterans, and local business and professional men. SPLL members were deputized as sheriffs; they harassed the union members and pillaged Dacus's house on several occasions. The *Enterprise American*, the local paper controlled by Great Southern, reported on November 20, 1919:

> According to reports from various citizens who knew, Sol Dacus, the Negro for whom the special policemen of the Law and Order Committee had a warrant, was considered a "bad" Negro. He was president of the Colored Timberworkers Local No. 116, and is charged with being very active with agitating the Negroes.[51]

The SPLL delivered a message to Dacus's house informing him that he was no longer wanted in Bogalusa and warning him to leave town immediately. Fearing for his life, Dacus fled to the swamps for a day, but returned on November 22, 1919 to consult with L.E. Williams, the white president of the Central Trades Assembly. They met at Williams' garage, which was also used as headquarters for the Trades Assembly. Three other white unionists were there, along with Williams, to protect Dacus from the vigilantes.

Hearing of Dacus's return, the SPLL sent 20 armed men to Williams' garage with orders to get rid of the Black "agitator" for good. When the gunfire ceased, Dacus and three of the white union men, including Wil-

---

*Although Black lumber workers in Bogalusa were compelled to accept segregated unions in the hope of overcoming Great Southern's vicious racist propaganda, in other parts of the South Black workers did not always accept "Jim Crow" unionism. Excluded from the all-white union at the Oscar Daniels shipyard in Tampa, Florida, Blacks were offered a "Negro union," but refused. "They demanded equal rights, with an open door for themselves." When this demand was rejected, Black workers helped break a strike at the shipyard in April 1919 by refusing to honor the white union's walkout. (Wayne Flint, "Florida Labor and Political Radicalism," *Labor History* 9 [Winter 1969]: 86.

liams, lay dead, and a fourth died shortly after.* The members of the SPLL who participated in the attack were brought to trial but were quickly acquitted. The jury declared it was unable to determine who of the 20 SPLL members actually shot the union men, so it acquitted all of them.[52]

The Messenger, Black socialist weekly edited by A. Philip Randolph and Chandler Owen, devoted a special front page editorial in tribute to the white workers who had forged such splendid unity with Black workers in Bogalusa:

> All hail to the white workers of Bogalusa! Your are learning! You are on the road.
>
> Your enemy is the Southern white employing class, not the Negroes. Your only weapon is the solidarity of the working class, Black and white.[53]

Unfortunately, the tragic events of November 22, 1919 doomed the union organizing effort, and from 1919 to 1933 when a new union drive got under way led by the International Brotherhood of Paper Makers, Great Southern totally dominated the Bogalusa labor scene as "fear prevented them [the workers] from organizing."[54]

Strikebreaking was a major issue discussed at the 1919 convention of the National Urban League. In the belief that Black workers would benefit more by joining unions than by serving the interests of the employers, the Urban League established a Department of Industrial Relations to facilitate "the organization and assistance of Negro mechanics." But the problem could not be solved merely by resolutions in favor of unionism. What was required was a determination on the part of the white unions, and especially the American Federation of Labor, to end the racist exclusion of Black workers.[55]

---

*Over the years, accounts have differed as to whether Dacus was present when the vigilantes attacked, or whether he escaped. See Art Shields, *On The Battle-Lines, 1919-1939*, (N.Y., 1986) pp. 177-185; Philip Foner, *Organized Labor and the Black worker 1619-1981*, (N.Y., 1982) p. 150n.

CHAPTER 11

The AFL and the Black Worker, 1919-1920

THE MESSENGER, NATIONAL BROTHERHOOD OF WORKERS, AND THE IWW

In the spring of 1919, *The Messenger* welcomed the formation of the National Brotherhood of Workers of America (NBWA). Delegates from twelve states and the District of Columbia, representing unions of carpenters, riveters, blacksmiths, caulkers, electricians, engravers, painters, longshoremen, janitors, jewelry workers, railroad firemen and other railroad workers, plasterers, molders, hod carriers, plumbers, porters and waiters attended the founding session. T. J. Free and R. T. Sims, two radical Black unionists (Sims was an early member of the IWW), were elected president and vice-president, respectively, and resolutions were adopted urging the organization of "every Negro worker into industrial labor or trade unions in all skilled or unskilled occupations"; condemning "the unjust and inexcusable discrimination against Negro workers by the organized white labor unions," and calling upon Blacks, wherever possible, to "enter the unions side by side with their white brothers; but in the event of discrimination, we urge that the Negroes, in any place, shall organize their own unions to exact justice from both the employer and the white labor unions."[1]

The initial strength of the NBWA came from Black workers employed in the shipyards and on the docks of Newport News, Norfolk, and Portsmouth, Virginia. The fact that many of these workers maintained their affiliation with AFL locals gave the Brotherhood substantial influence in the councils of the Virginia Federation of Labor. Shortly after its establishment, the new labor body was powerful enough to influence the selection of the president of the state federation and to obtain representation on its executive board. Moreover, these militant Black unionists were able to exercise an important influence at AFL national conventions.[2]

By the time the AFL met in convention in 1919, a new spirit of militancy had emerged in the Negro community, reflected in what was called the "New Negro" movement. Many Black workers were rejecting Booker T. Washington's solution to discriminatory practices and to whites-only unionism: an alliance with the employers against organized labor. Instead, they chose to organize outside of the AFL and the Railroad Brotherhoods. The result was a rise of independent Black unionists and a growth of radical, pro-IWW influence among Black workers.[3] According to *The Messenger*, for example, the future of Black workers lay, not with the AFL, but rather with the IWW.

The Messenger hailed the IWW as "the only labor union that has never, in theory or practice, since its beginning twelve years ago, barred the workers of any race or nation from its membership." According to *The Messenger*, the IWW also deserved Black support because it dealt chiefly with the unskilled workers, and most Black workers were unskilled. Another important point in its favor for the largely disfranchised Negro was the fact that it advocated direct action. With the ballot box closed to them, the only way Blacks had of advancing themselves was through industrial action. Unlike nearly all other labor bodies, the IWW favored industrial over craft unionism. Industrial unionism was not only alone in having the ability to include the vast majority of Black workers, but it was also the only effective labor instrument for class struggle. Time and again in the past, strikes had failed because the craft unions did not support each other and actually acted as strikebreakers against sister craft unions. The IWW's brand of unionism, *The Messenger* insisted, eliminated this fatal flaw by unifying all workers in the struggle against the employers.[4]

At the same time that they were urging Black workers to join the IWW, Randolph and Owen also favored the formation of an independent Black labor movement. They maintained that the postwar militancy of the Negro, as reflected in the new spirit of self-assertion and fighting back during the "Red Summer," indicated that the time was "ripe for a great mass movement among Negroes," which should take the form of labor unions, farmer protective unions, cooperative business and socialism."[5]

THE 1919 AFL CONVENTION

The spirit of militancy among Black workers, the move to establish independent Black unions, and the growing appeal of the IWW for the Black workers were all reflected at the postwar conventions of the AFL. On the eve of its 1919 convention in Atlantic City, New Jersey, the Negro Workers' Advisory Committee, representing every Black fraternal, welfare, religious and labor organization in Chicago, wired the AFL urging the removal of all restrictions against Black workers by its affiliated unions and warning that unless this were done, Black workers would move in increasing numbers into the IWW.[6] The convention itself had a larger number of Black delegates—twenty-three delegates from federal and local unions across the country—than had ever before been present at the annual assembly. (In fact, the convention just prior to this one had less than one-third of that number.)[7] Seated at one table in the convention hall, the Black delegates told reporters of their disappointment over the fact that the AFL's methods had failed to achieve greater organization of Negro workers, and of their determination to fight hard to force the affiliated unions "to loosen up and give the Black man of the South a chance to organize." Several complained bitterly that Black members of the AFL were denied the rights and benefits enjoyed by the whites.[8]

The convention also witnessed a sharp confrontation between the protesting Black unionists and the AFL officials. One resolution sought the services of two Black organizers for the Southern District of Alabama. Another asked that a Black organizer be appointed in every state where one was needed, particularly in the South, and where white organizers had had trouble recruiting Black workers. It also urged that a laboring man, preferably Black, be appointed from each craft where separate Black organizations existed to represent the Black workers in any business.[9]

A third resolution protested the refusal of the International Union of Metal Trades to issue a charter to Black craftsmen, and boldly requested that the convention declare Black unionists entitled to any charter according to their trade. Still another concerned a complaint by organized Black freight handlers, express and station employees, that the Brotherhood of Railway Clerks, under whose jurisdiction they operated, gave them little or no assistance in bargaining with the railroads over wages and grievances. The sponsors of this resolution asked the AFL to organize the freight handlers for their mutual protection and benefit, and to help them form a grievance committee to secure a working agreement with the railroads.[10]

The fifth and final resolution called upon the convention to either grant an application to a representative group of Black unionists for an International Union of Organized Colored Labor, or exert its influence over the international unions having jurisdiction over Black workers to compel them to charter Black labor bodies, thereby assuming responsibility for their welfare. Fourteen Black delegates, representing federal and local unions from a variety of trades, signed this last resolution.[11]

The Committee on Organization, to which the resolutions were referred, refused to endorse the demand for an international charter for Black workers on the ground that it would violate the jurisdictional rights of several unions affiliated with the AFL. Passing over the other four resolutions without comment, the committee went on to maintain strenuously that many international unions within the AFL admitted Black members and granted them full protection of their rights and interests. In the case of member bodies that did not accept Black members, the committee recommended organizing the workers affected under direct charters from the Executive Council. "We further recommend," it continued, "that the Executive Council give particular attention to the organization of colored workers everywhere and assign organizers for that purpose whenever possible." The committee concluded by listing sixteen prominent AFL affiliates that admitted Black workers.[12]*

The chairman of the committee, Frank Duffy, then asked the delegates if any other unions represented at the convention admitted Black workers. At that point, John Lacey, a Black union leader from Norfolk, Virginia, rose and appealed to the convention to extend a hand of welcome to Black workers. "If you can take in immigrants who cannot speak the English language," he asked, "why can't you take in the Negro, who has been loyal to you from Washington to the battlefields of France?" Lacey assured the delegates that he was not asking for social equality for the Negro: "We ask for the same chance to earn bread for our families at the same salary our white brothers are getting...equal rights the same as you have to earn bread for your families."[13]

Lacey's emotional plea broke the dam the Committee on Organization had constructed against Black militancy. In an unprecedented demonstration for Black-white unity, forty heads of international and national unions rose, one after another, to proclaim that their organizations would welcome Black workers into their ranks. Mollie Friedman of the ILGWU declared that her union had six thousand Black women in its membership and was proud of them. A delegate from the Meat Cutters and Butcher Workmen also voiced pride in the large Black membership employed in the meatpacking plants and boasted that his organization had five Black organizers at work in the field. Even a Southern white delegate from the Brotherhood of Railway and Steamship Clerks spoke up for equality of Black and white labor.[14] At the end of the speeches, the convention unanimously adopted the report of

*The unions listed were the United Mine Workers, the Mine, Mill and Smelter workers, the Longshoremen, the Carpenters, the Textile Workers, the Seamen, the Cigarmakers, the Teamsters, the Plasterers, the Bricklayers, the Maintenance of Way Employees, the Laundry Workers, the Cooks and Waiters, the Tailors, the Brewery Workers and the Upholsterers.

the Committee on Organization, which, although rejecting the requests for an international charter for Black workers and ignoring the other four resolutions introduced by Black delegates, did call for special emphasis on organizing Black members within the AFL.[15]

A NEW ERA FOR THE BLACK WORKER?

The AFL convention was said to have heralded a new era in labor relations. Not since the abolition of chattel slavery, declared the New York *Age*, a Black weekly, had so important a step been taken toward the industrial freedom of the race: "If carried out toward its logical conclusion, it should mean the loosening of the shackles that have encouraged peonage and industrial dependency of all kinds."[16] The *New York Times* predicted that "all over the country, the Negro worker will have, as he has not had hitherto, a chance to enter all of the skilled, and therefore better-paid trades, and in them to be judged on his merits." "There is promise," the *Times* declared enthusiastically, "in the fact that this change is to be thorough—that there are not to be white and Black unions in inevitable rivalry and probable hostility."[17] According to the New York *World*, the convention had wiped out "the part of the color-line which most impeded the progress of the Black race."[18] The Boston *Guardian*, a militant Black weekly, declared that the federation's action "opens the gateway to real American life for the first time within the last half century."[19] Eugene K. Jones, executive secretary of the National Urban League, hailed the "farsightedness" shown by the federation: "The American Federation of Labor has sensed the absolute necessity for organizing Negro workingmen along with white workingmen in order to face capital with a solid front in working out the serious problems of the new era."[20] The NAACP reported to its members that "the Negro was invited into full and equal privileges of organized labor. It is now his business to accept this invitation." It urged Blacks "to follow it up and go a hundred strong to the next meeting of the Federation." Both the National Urban League and the NAACP emphasized that there was now no need for an independent Black labor movement or for Blacks to join the IWW.[21]

Gompers adjudged such an approach to be just what was needed to make the AFL's stand a reality: "The action of the convention removes every class of race distinction from the [organized labor] movement. It should mark an era in the struggle of the Negro for equality of rights, as well as an advance in the history of political and economic liberty of America." He noted: "In the past it has been difficult to organize the colored man. Now, he shows a desire to be organized and we meet him more than half-way."[22] Typically, Gompers blamed the Black workers, not the AFL affiliates, for the small number of Negroes in his federation."

W. E. B. Du Bois, on the other hand, was not easily swept off his feet by the AFL convention's declarations. Well acquainted with the difference between nonexclusion on paper and Black membership in actuality, Du Bois cautioned in *The Crisis* that the convention might not have marked the beginning of a "square deal" from the AFL for the Black worker—it might mean a great deal or it might mean nothing:

> It will only mean a great deal provided that in every locality throughout this country, the colored men and women come together and demand of the various labor locals recognition of Negro workingmen. It means that in Washington, there ought to be stationed men who are big enough to see the importance of this decision on the part of organized labor, who will see that the internationals change their constitutions so as to admit Negro men; and see that the internationals and the Executive Council pass on the final word to the locals in regard to this matter. Because, after all, it is not entirely a local question as to whether a man will or will not be admitted when he is qualified. The internationals only decide as to policy, as to constitutional rights. Putting into execution is a matter of local concern.[23]

Du Bois, of course, touched on the key issue in the relationship between organized labor and the Black worker since the days of Reconstruction: To what extent did the state and local unions of even those sixteen national affiliates originally listed as nondiscriminating accept Black members, and how many of those and other local unions would change their practices in the light of the action taken at Atlantic City? To what lengths were the national officials, who had been so eloquent at the convention, willing to go to persuade their locals and members to open their doors to Black workers? To Du Bois, history suggested that the answer in post-World War I America would be the same as it had been in post-Civil War America.

In fact, the report adopted unanimously by the convention did not call for full membership for Black workers. Where national or international affiliates would not accept Blacks, those in the occupations involved would be organized into separate federal and local labor unions chartered by the Executive Council. As John D. Finney, Jr. points out: "The Committee, in recommending that the Executive Council pursue the organization of Negroes everywhere and appoint organizers for that purpose whenever possible, was in reality suggesting a renewed drive towards separate rather than integrated organization of Negroes."[24] The federal and local labor bodies organized by the Executive Council before 1919 had already proved to be incapable of protecting their Black members.

THE 1920 AFL CONVENTION

Events soon demonstrated that the AFL was no more open to Black workers than it had been before the 1919 convention. The federation was able to boast of a phenomenal growth in membership when it met in convention in Montreal in 1920. Its overall membership stood at a little over 4 million, nearly twice the number reported in 1916.[25] The number of Black members in 1920 was not announced, but it could not have exceeded by more than a few thousand the 60,000 generously estimated in 1916, and nearly all of the new Black members were in separate local and federal unions.[26]

The truth is that the number of AFL affiliates that denied admittance to Black workers by constitutional provision or ritual had risen between 1910 and 1920 from eight to eleven. During those ten years, four new affiliates that specifically barred Blacks had joined the AFL: the Brotherhood of Railway Carmen, the Order of Sleeping Car Conductors, the National Organization of Masters, Mates and Pilots of North America, and the Rail Mail Associates. One affiliate, the Brotherhood of Maintenance of Way Employees, had voted at its 1917 convention to admit Blacks in allied or auxiliary lodges, which were placed under the control of its systems division. This removed it from the list of affiliates that specifically barred Black members.[27]*

Clearly, any expectations that the great migration of Black workers from the South would be able to open the doors of the AFL and the railroad brotherhoods had proved only a dream. It is hardly surprising, then, that the Black unionists who had raised the issue of Negro membership in Atlantic City a year earlier returned the following year angrier than ever and more determined to press their claims. Early in the proceedings, a group of delegates from federal locals of the Railway Coach Cleaners initiated the battle by demanding that the Brotherhood of Railway Carmen, which had jurisdiction over the coach cleaners, either drop its color ban or allow the coach cleaners to acquire an international charter of their own. Other Black federal unions requested immediate AFL action on the refusal

---

*In addition to the railroad brotherhoods, eight unions unaffiliated with the AFL limited their memberships to white workers in 1920 through their constitutions or rituals. These were the Brotherhood of Dining Car Conductors, the Order of Railway Expressmen, the American Federation of Express Workers, the American Federation of Railroad Workers, the Brotherhood of Railroad Station Employees, the Train Dispatchers, the Railroad Yard Masters of America and the Neptune Association.

of the machinists, the boilermakers and the blacksmiths to admit Blacks. They also insisted that the federation either use every means possible to have the words "white only" removed from the Brotherhood of Railway Clerks' constitution, or else force the clerks to relinquish their jurisdiction over the freight handlers—mostly Black and organized into separate federal unions—and permit them to establish their own national body.[28]

For the first time, the Black delegates had stopped talking in generalities and had hit directly at the AFL leadership's refusal to do anything about the racial restrictions of its affiliates. The far-reaching resolutions were once again referred to the Committee on Organization.

In its report, the committee said that the boilermakers and the machinists had "nothing in their constitutions prohibiting the admission of colored men of trade,"[29] and that the blacksmiths had actually issued charters to Black workers in the trade and also had no law denying them admission. This was an evasion, for it was well known that the boilermakers and the machinists accomplished the exclusion of Blacks through their rituals. The blacksmiths admitted chartered Negro unions, but they were auxiliary locals that had no voice in the affairs of the blacksmiths and existed only to prevent the Black workers from organizing independently. Since the AFL leadership had sanctioned and even counseled such methods of exclusion, or accepting Blacks with second-class status, the report of the Committee on Organization was an outrageous insult to the Negro delegation.[30]

The committee acknowledged that the railway carmen barred Blacks from membership by constitutional provision, but it reported having received assurances from the president of that union that he would ask his organization, at its next convention, to admit Black coach cleaners or, failing that, to surrender all claims to jurisdiction over that class of work. In view of these assurances, the committee declared, it could "only recommend that the carmen eliminate all references to the admission of Black workmen from its regulations." At the same time, the Committee on Organization said it could not approve the coach cleaners' request to form an international of their own. "The American Federation of Labor," it stated, "does not organize workers of any trade or calling along racial lines." The committee conveniently overlooked the existence of the United Hebrew Trades, an AFL affiliate that had been successful in promoting the interests of Jewish workers. It rejected the plea of the freight handlers with the customary observation that the AFL could not interfere with the autonomy of its affiliated national and international unions. To Black workers unable to join AFL member bodies, the committee held out the possibility of obtaining membership in the separate unions chartered by the Executive Council. Thus far, and no farther, the

Committee on Organization was willing to go.[31]

The report sparked another debate, and this time it did not end in the unanimous approval of the committee's recommendations. Robert Buford, a Black delegate from Richmond, Virginia, who had originally submitted the freight handlers' proposal, pointed out that the refusal to take any action on the railway clerks' written exclusion of Blacks, in open violation of the AFL's national charter, proved the hypocrisy of the federation's contention that it did not discriminate against Negroes. He complained that the freight handlers, forced to contribute toward the expenses of the railway clerks' officials, who were supposed to handle their grievances, were not even given representation in the national union, and he insisted that the clerks be compelled to remove the provision barring Blacks from their bylaws. If the federation refused to do this, it should give the freight handlers a charter of their own "that would enable them to have their own committee to handle their grievances."[32]

A spirited debate followed between Frank Duffy, chairman of the Committee on Organization, and delegate Buford. Duffy called the freight handlers' resolution illegal because it asked the convention to decide who was or was not eligible for admission as an AFL affiliate, an authority that the national and international unions alone possessed. All the AFL could do if affiliates refused to remove their prohibitions against Negroes was provide Black workers with a charter. "What kind of charter?" asked Buford. "As freight handlers," Duffy replied. That was exactly what the freight handlers, who opposed separate organization outside the international union, wanted to avoid. "We don't want to be separated," Buford said vehemently. "We want the same kind of charters [as the whites]."[33]

While the AFL leadership sat squirming on the platform, one white delegate after another arose to challenge the federation's drawing of the color line. A motion was made and seconded to amend the Committee on Organization's report with the recommendation that the convention formally request the railway clerks to delete the term, "white only" from their constitution. Over the opposition of the representatives of the clerks, the original recommendation of the Committee on Organization was rejected and the amendment passed.[34]

Thus, for the first time since 1891, when AFL delegates had endorsed Gompers' efforts to force the machinists to abandon their exclusion of Blacks, an AFL convention recommended that affiliated unions—in this case, the railway clerks and the railway carmen—remove racial restrictions from their membership provisions.

Other resolutions were also introduced by Black delegates at the 1920 convention. These requested more effective representation of the interests of Black federal and local unions; the launching of a program to increase Negro membership in the AFL; the mounting of a campaign of education among both white and Black workers to convince them of the necessity of bringing workers into the ranks of organized labor regardless of race, nationality or color, and the appointment of a Black worker to a position in AFL headquarters in Washington to express the aspirations of the Negro working class to the federation. But only an emasculated version of the program to increase Black membership was adopted. It simply called for the appointment of Black organizers "where necessary," and referred the matter to the Executive Council for action if the funds of the federation permitted it.[35]

In the excitement produced by the unusual action of the delegates in requesting an affiliated organization to remove the color ban from its constitution, little attention was paid to the rejection of the other resolutions introduced by the Black delegates. Newspaper reporters covering the convention placed all their emphasis on the rejection of the Committee on Organization's report and the request that the railway clerks delete the term, "white only" from their constitution. They stressed the militancy of the Black delegates. Men like David E. Grange, agent of the marine cooks and stewards in New York; Charles A. Sumner of the sterotypers and electrotypers; O. A. Anderson of the International Longshoremen's Association; D. D. Alesandre of the hod carriers and common laborers, and Cornelius Foley of the journeymen barbers, as well as Buford, were widely applauded in the Black press for speaking up boldly "for full industrial equality for the Negro workers."[36] The Black delegates vehemently protested the repeated use of the word, "n----r" by O. D. Gorham, delegate of the Order of Railroad Telegraphers, and they bluntly denounced as "taxation without representation" the AFL's practice of shunting Black members into federal and local unions that received no protection from the international affiliates, but who were assessed to pay the salaries of union business agents. Finally, they put it squarely to the delegates to say, once and for all, if they stood for the equality of all workers. "Do not pussyfoot," David E. Grange shouted. "Stand for democracy the American Federation is supposed to stand for. It did not offend the dignity of any man to send the Negro into the firing lines in France."[37]

ANOTHER NEW ERA FOR THE BLACK WORKER?

The rejection of the Committee on Organization's report by the 1920 convention was generally regarded as the most significant AFL action up to that time on the issue of Black labor. *Justice*, the official organ of the International Ladies' Garment Workers' Union, heaped praise upon the convention "for removing a degrading clause pertaining to Negroes."[38] The Amalgamated Clothing Workers was not at the time affiliated with the federation, but its journal, *Advance*, hailed the news that "the American Federation of Labor was finally compelled to proclaim the identity of interests of the white and colored workers" and predicted that a new era was opening for the Black workers.[39]

Such predictions usually proved to be illusionary, and this one was no exception. For one thing, the rare progressive resolutions on Black workers adopted at AFL conventions seldom influenced the course of events on the state and local levels. A good example was the events in Texas after the 1920 AFL convention. Black helpers of the Texas and Pacific Railway shops, who had been kept out of the Boilermakers' Union, were organized into Local 562 of the Firemen and Oilers. The boilermakers vented their anger by ordering foremen not to hire any Black helpers. In desperation, the Black workers appealed for justice to the 1920 convention of the State Federation of Labor. In one of the most moving documents in labor history, they pleaded:

> We have been as loyal as the times demanded and our conditions would allow. We have bought Liberty Bonds, War Savings Stamps, and War Saving Certificates. We have contributed to the Red Cross, the War Work Activities, and whatever was for the advancement of the Nation and its people in the great struggle for the liberation of humanity. We have suffered with all others during the periods when the people of the country were called upon to deny themselves of the many comforts of and necessities of life. Most of our "boys" have made the Supreme Sacrifice. We have helped the boys Over There. What more can we do? All of this and more we have done for the cause of the Nation and Democracy.
>
> Tell us, please, if it is the purpose of the Organized Labor Movement to organize the colored helpers so as to discriminate against them and force them out of the jobs which they have held and are holding, and make scabs of them.
>
> We ask you, the State Federation of Labor of Texas, for assistance. We ask that we may but receive justice. Even-handed justice. We ask no more than a chance to work as we have always been known to do. Gentlemen, we implore you to assist us in seeing that we get justice. We ask no more! See that we get nothing less.

The plea was referred to the executive committee and promptly buried.[40]

CHAPTER 12

The IWW in the Postwar Years

In September 1917, as we have seen in our previous volume, secret agents of the Department of Justice raided and occupied the offices of the Industrial Workers of the World all over the United States. On the basis of thousands of seized documents, prosecutions against IWW members were begun in Illinois, California, and Kansas. In Chicago alone, over 100 Wobblies were arrested, jailed, and tried in the federal court. Their conviction was a foregone conclusion and as expected, the jury found 93 of them guilty of violating the Federal Espionage Act. Judge Kenesaw Mountain Landis imposed heavy fines and prison sentences, as drastic, in a number of cases, as 20 years in a federal penitentiary and $30,000 in fines.

After the Chicago codefendants were found guilty, the government's battle against the IWW shifted to trials in Sacramento, California, and Wichita, Kansas.

THE SACRAMENTO TRIAL

On December 17, 1917 an explosion occurred in the official residence of the governor of California in Sacramento. Little damage resulted, and although the identity of the men who had planted the bomb was not known, Sacramento's chief of police Ira Concoran blamed the IWW.[1] The police chief could give no justification for his belief, but then William Hood, an IWW member, was accidentally discovered trying to ship several sticks of dynamite by express. He planned to use them on a mining trip, he claimed. Hood was arrested for illegal shipment of explosives, and George F. Voetter, who was with him in the express office, was also arrested.[2]

On the basis of the prevailing anti-IWW hysteria of the time, arrests were made throughout California. On January 19, 1918 the police rounded up 53 men in and around the IWW hall in Sacramento, supposedly for questioning in the dynamite case.[3] Don S. Rathkin, special agent of the Department of Justice, let it be known that there was insufficient evidence to hold any of the arrested men and that he would not undertake, "in behalf of his department, to make further investigation and to order the men held pending results."[4] But the city commissioners of Sacramento rejected this viewpoint, and the 53 men already arrested continued to be held in jail. In fact, Governor Stephens, the sheriff, and the chief of police all sent a protest to Washington denouncing agent Rathkin's attitude.[5]

Early in February 1918 the federal grand jury in Sacramento indicted 54 male and one female Wobbly (Theodora Pollock). The male prisoners were thrown into a common cell 21 feet square. Some had to remain standing while others reclined. One of the prisoners described the food as consisting of "two ounces of mush in the morning, less than two ounces of bread, and at night three fetid little smelts and less than two ounces of potatoes, with 'coffee' twice." The prisoners claimed that they gave their own money to the guards to buy food, but then the purchases were placed just beyond their reach to tantalize them.[6]

Five prisoners died before the trial opened on December 13, 1918. A number of those originally arrested were freed, but 46 were indicted on four counts. They had been charged originally with conspiring to oppress employers throughout the United States, but the indictments were changed to the same ones that had been used to convict the IWW members in the Chicago cases. The first count charged interference with the government's war activities by means of strikes accompanied by acts of violence. The second, third, and fourth counts charged conspiracy to intimidate persons not to fulfill contracts and to refuse to register for military service. The defendants were also charged with causing insubordination in the military and naval forces, and with using the mails to cheat and defraud employers.[7]

All attempts to prepare a defense for the prisoners were frustrated. Several members of the defense committee were arrested; its secretary was arrested 15 times in four months, and the Wobbly directly in charge of defense work was arrested and held incommunicado for eight months. All mail coming into and going out of prison was censored.[8]

After their comrades in Chicago had been convicted and sentenced to long prison terms, most of the prisoners in California became convinced that the existing hysterical climate would render an ordinary legal defense useless. They decided on a method which they believed might rally support from the working class and win them an early release after they had been convicted and sentenced: 43 of the 46 defendants decided to offer no defense. Mortimer Downing, spokesman for the "Silent Defenders," explained:

> We decided upon the silent defense because we despair of justice for the working men being achieved through the courts. The Mooney case, the Frank Little incident, the Bisbee cases,* the Chicago trials, these have convinced us of the uselessness of legal defense. We are tried in a prejudiced community. Some of our men have been held incommunicado. They have been prevented by United States agents from mailing courteous appeals to the court. Some of them have been confined, untried, for a year. These conditions are intolerable, and this "silence strike" is to preserve the self-respect of ourselves as members of organized labor.[9]

It has been argued that the California defendants committed a "fatal error" in following this type of defense, or lack of it. The prosecution, it has been noted, did not claim that these men had committed any overt acts, but contended merely that they had conspired to commit such acts. Accordingly Hyman Weintraub maintains, "the defendants, by acting in concert on a silent defense, by being tried *en masse*, lent credence to the prosecution's story that all the defendants were tied together in an attempt to sabotage the government. By their unanimous silence, they helped to convict themselves."[10] There is some validity in this analysis. Although the distinction between acting and conspiring to act meant little in the existing anti-IWW hysteria, it is true that the task of the prosecution was made easier by the fact that there was no effort to contradict its evidence by those defendants who chose the silent defense. Moreover, the court was able to allow the introduction of evidence antedating the period in which the alleged conspiracy took place, as long as testimony was also introduced to show that the conspiracy existed during the time the so-called offense was committed. Letters and pamphlets going back to the beginning of the IWW in 1905 were allowed as evidence on the ground that they would show the existence of a conspiracy.[11]

On January 16, after only 70 minutes of deliberation, the jury returned a verdict finding the 46 defendants guilty as charged. On the average, less than two minutes were spent in considering the guilt of each defendant. Judge Frank H. Rudkin asked the prisoners if they had anything to say. After having sat silently for almost a month and a half, a number of the defendants decided to speak out. Frank Esmund, weak and ill after ten months in jail, said:

*The Mooney, Frank Little, and Bisbee episodes are discussed in Foner, *History of the Labor Movement in the United States*, volume 7.

I am not asking for mercy. I'll take neither mercy nor pity from you or any other representative of this government!...I want to go on record for myself and the organization as saying that we, the outcasts, have been framed up, clubbed, beaten, slugged, martyred and murdered. Is it any wonder that I do not consider myself bound by your procedure when this court and its proceedings are a disgrace to the United States? You have done more than any IWW could possibly do to drag your Stars and Stripes through the mire.[12]

Mortimer Downing, speaking "to get a few things off our chests," defended the philosophy of the IWW:

The IWW has taught and will continue to teach that the worker on the job shall tell the boss when and where he shall work, how long, for what wages and under what conditions. It will continue to teach that gradually the worker will get more and more power until finally he will take over the industries.[13]

The next day, the defendants were sentenced. Theodora Pollock was fined $100, and the other two defendants who were represented by counsel were sentenced to two months each in jail. The remaining 43 received prison sentences ranging from one to ten years, which were upheld by the state Supreme Court.[14]

THE WICHITA TRIAL

On November 17, 1917 Fred Robertson, United States attorney for Kansas, working closely with oil company detectives, arranged for federal agents to seize IWW literature and letters at the union halls of the Oil Field Workers' Industrial Union No. 450 in Augusta, Kansas and Drumwright, Oklahoma. More then 40 Wobblies were arrested.[15] Caroline A. Lowe, attorney for the IWW, charged that the Wobblies were arrested on "John Doe" warrants issued in Butler County, Kansas, "at the suggestion of agents of the Carter Oil Company, the Sinclair Oil Company, Gypsy Oil Company and other oil companies doing business in this section of the country."[16] Thirty-two Wobblies were eventually selected for trial. Robertson conceded privately that he did not "have a strong case...but we are going to give them a run for their money...."[17] This consisted largely of releases to the press intended to further enflame the atmosphere against the men scheduled for trial. At regularly scheduled press conferences Robertson told reporters that "many members of the IWW consider the strike situation in Seattle to be a product of the general strike seed sown by the IWW in 1917, when Seattle was the hot bed of IWW draft resisters." The government, he continued, would "show numerous exchanges of ideas between the Pacific Slope IWW and sixty Bolsheviki who embarked from Seattle with the IWW propaganda mission to Petrograd," and "scores of interviews, promises and exhortations along with encouragements for the Bolsheviki had been collected." Robertson quoted from a document that he claimed was issued by the IWW and which contained the statement: "But we realize we must call a general strike for more than the city of Seattle." The implication was that the IWW was responsible for the Seattle general strike.[18]

Based on material furnished by Robertson, the *Kansas City* (Kansas) *Star* of March 19, 1919 presented the nature of testimony that would be offered by the prosecution. Documents would be shown to the jury decorated with emblems of the black cat and wooden shoe, which were described as "the official emblems of the IWW" and signified sabotage, "the chief weapon of the IWW in their plan to overthrow the present organization of things, politically and industrially in the United States." The documents had been seized during a raid by government agents of IWW headquarters in the Kansas oil fields, and included letterheads of the Agricultural Workers' Organization and Oil Workers' Union No. 400, which was "the branch of the order to which the members belong who are now on trial in Wichita." "As a body," the *Star* observed, "the general strike is the weapon of the IWW at all times. But for the individual members always and everywhere, the black cat and the wooden shoe—sabotage— are 'he chief weapons." What does this mean? the paper asked. It answered that it meant that the harvest wheat and oil production of Kansas were "doomed by the scab-cat"—the "IWW term for the black cat," unless the men on trial were found guilty and put away.

Knowing that if these men were imprisoned all problems with the IWW would not necessarily cease, mayors, city attorneys, and police chiefs from more than twenty towns in the Kansas wheat belt met on May 2, 1919 at Hutchinson, Kansas and issued the warning that IWW members "will find Western Kansas unhealthy this summer." A major point stressed was that the Wobblies "demand higher than standard wages, and the scale of their demands keeps pace with the advance in prices as the season progresses."[19]

A Wichita grand jury returned an indictment against 25 Wobblies in March 1918, charging the men with conspiracy, but the defense succeeded in having the indictment quashed twice. The government then obtained an indictment that was upheld in the courts. But the trial was delayed when the National Civil Liberties Bureau brought a complaint to the Justice Department about intolerable conditions for the prisoners in the Sedgwick County jail in Wichita, conditions so terrible that Stephen Shurin, one of the defendants, cut his throat from ear to ear in a fit of depression over continued imprisonment in those circumstances. After considerable pressure, Judge Pollock ordered an investigation of the Sedgwick County jail and found it unfit for prisoners.[20]*

The indictment contained five counts. The Wobblies were charged with entering into a conspiracy to violate, hinder and delay:

1. The general declaration of war with Germany.
2. The proclamations and regulations of the President of the United States governing the conduct, treatment and disposition of alien enemies.
3. The act of Congress to increase the military establishment of the United States.
4. The act to increase the signal corps of the army and to purchase, manufacture, repair, maintain and operate airships.
5. The act of Congress to provide for the national security by encouraging the production, conserving the supply and continuing the distribution of food supplies.
6. The general laws of the United States.[21]

The first four counts were similar to the charges against the Chicago and Sacramento defendants. The fifth count was new. It added to the charge of conspiracy to violate the Espionage Act a violation of the Lever Act, a law relating to the distribution of food and fuel products. Thus the defendants were charged with conspiracy to limit the production and transportation of petroleum and farm products.

The indictment listed no specific instance of such interference with the production of food or fuel, but it did cite "The Harvest War Song" by Pat Brennan in the IWW's *Little Red Song Book*, which contains the words, "Up goes machine" if John Farmer did not meet the Wobblies demands "on wages."

The trial began in Wichita on December 1, 1918. As expected, a major portion of the prosecution's case was presented through seized IWW literature and letters. As in the indictment, the prosecution drew attention to songs in the *Little Red Song Book* that suggested sabotage of farmers' machinery: "If Farmer John don't please us/ His machine will visit Jesus."

After a week of testimony and cross examination, the prosecution rested. The defendants then voted not to present any evidence. The reasons were never explained, but it seems that they believed, particularly

---

*For a description of the terrible conditions in the jail, *see* Earl B. White, "The Wichita Indictments and Trial of the [IWW], 1917-1919, and the Aftermath," Ph.D. dissertation, University of Colorado at Boulder, 1980.

after Chicago and Sacramento, that their cause was hopeless and that "the funds were exhausted and we could not put on a defense in this case properly."[22]

The jury deliberated for 20 hours and found all 27 defendants guilty. Twenty-six were sentenced to terms ranging from one to nine years. One, who had joined the IWW by mistake, received a sentence of one day.[23] On December 19, 1918 the Wobblies boarded a special interurban car and, singing their favorite songs from the *Little Red Song Book*, rode to the Leavenworth penitentiary. The Kansas City *Journal* hailed the verdict on its front page:

> Americanism triumphant!
> Long live Americanism!
> Anarchists outlawed forever!
> The welcome on Uncle Sam's doormat eternally erased for all IWW![24]

In his study of the Wichita case, Earl Bruce White points out: "The Wichita prosecution is different from other I.W.W. cases because it was the only successful federal prosecution specifically directed against the I.W.W.'s concept of industrial unionism. The defendants were in the midst of an organizing campaign in the Mid-Continental Oil Field when they were arrested...." After the Wichita convictions, the state obtained a permanent injunction prohibiting the Agricultural Workers Industrial Union No. 400 (AWIU) and the Oil Workers Industrial Union No. 450 (OWIU) from operating in the state.[25]

CENTRALIA

By mid-1919 the condition of the IWW was desperate. Legal battles had left it financially destitute, most of its leadership imprisoned, and its organizing campaigns were faltering. Then, in November 1919, a tragic event occurred in Centralia, Washington that further weakened the organization.

In the fall of 1916 a committee of Centralia townspeople had forcibly escorted a group of IWW members to the county line and warned them never to return.[26] Undaunted, the IWW opened another hall in Centralia in the spring of 1918. During a Red Cross parade on April 30, 1918, the hall was raided by a group of businessmen, and the building in which it was located was almost demolished. Some captured Wobblies were taken out of town in trucks, beaten, dumped into a ditch and again warned never to return.[27]

In June 1919 a group of businessmen, in broad daylight, raided a newsstand operated by a blind vendor named Tom Lassiter, because he sold the

Seattle Union Record and the IWW *Industrial Worker*. When Lassiter continued his operation, a group of vigilantes seized him at his stand, drove him out of town, dumped him into a ditch at the county line, and warned him never to return. The *Seattle Union Record* protested against this treatment, but no one was ever prosecuted.[28]

Following Lassiter's forcible deportation, G. F. Russell, secretary of the Washington Employers' Association and president of a local lumber company, called a group of businessmen together at the Chamber of Commerce. At this meeting the Citizens' Protective League was formed, and F. B. Hubbard, president of the Eastern Railway and Lumber Company, was selected to lead the organization. Its declared purpose was to deal with the IWW.[29]

When the IWW opened another hall in Centralia in September 1919, the Citizens' Protective League decided to take action. The League met on the night of October 20 with the stated and published objective of getting rid of the Wobblies. Its leader was reported to have become "highly incensed" when the Centralia chief of police told him that "there was no law under which he could drive the organization out of the city," and that the IWW "had a right to remain in Centralia." The league's response was that it would take "direct action" to get rid of the IWW, and it was assured by the same chief of police that "he did not believe any jury would be obtained that would find those taking part in a raid on the IWW hall guilty of violating the law."[30]

When a trade union representative refused to serve on the League's committee to oust the IWW, a secret committee was appointed composed of employers, businessmen, and American Legion officials.[31] The line of march of the American Legion's Armistice Day parade was then announced: it was to pass twice by the IWW Hall. The IWW expected a raid, and Mrs. J. G. McAllister, who owned the hotel in which the IWW hall was located, appealed to the police for protection of her property. In addition, Elmer Smith, the IWW attorney, travelled to Olympia to seek protection from the governor. But neither of them obtained satisfaction. The chief of police told Mrs. McAllister that there were not enough police in Centralia to stop the marchers if they intended to raid the hall. The governor refused even to see Smith.[32]

Smith told the Wobblies that they had a legal right to defend their lives and property, with force if necessary, if they could not secure protection from the law enforcement authorities.[33] In an effort to ward off violence the IWW distributed copies of a circular in Centralia that read:

To the Citizens of Centralia
We Must Appeal!
To the law-abiding citizens of Centralia and to the working class in general.
We beg of you to read and carefully consider the following:
The profiteering class of Centralia have of late been waving the flag of our
country in an endeavor to incite the lawless element of our city to raid our hall
and club us out of town. For this purpose, they have inspired editorials in the
Hub, falsely and viciously attacking the IWW, hoping to gain public approval
for such revolting criminality. Those profiteers are holding numerous secret
meetings to that end, and covertly inciting returned servicemen to do their bidding.[34]

The Centralia *Hub* called repeatedly for the use of whatever force was
necessary to oust the IWW from the city, openly charging that the Wobblies were worse than the Germans.[35] But the local AFL Trades Council
tried to prevent the inevitable attack on the IWW hall. Vice-President William Dunning informed Warren O. Grimm, the new commander of the
American Legion, that the labor unions strongly disapproved of the law-
lessness being planned, but the protest had no effect.[36]

Anticipating a raid and believing they had a right to defend their property, the Wobblies prepared to do so. Britt Smith, secretary of the local
IWW, Wesley Everest, Ray Becker, James McInerny, and other Wobblies
were gathered in the hall. Loren Roberts, Bert Bland, and Ole Hanson
were stationed in Seminary Hall to the east. O. C. Bland and John Lamb
were in the Arnold Hotel, and "John Doe" Davis was in the Avalon Hotel
on the opposite side of the street.

The Armistice Day parade began at about two o'clock in the afternoon
with the Centralia Legionnaires leading the march. They walked up Tower
Street past the IWW hall. About a block north of the hall, at Third Street,
the marchers halted, turned, and marched back. As they passed by the
IWW hall for the second time, some of them broke ranks and charged
toward the door of the hall. The entire Centralia platoon then broke formation and surged toward the door. They kicked in the door, shattered the
windows, and eagerly sought to crowd into the hall.

Rifle and revolver shots rang out from inside the hall, from Seminary
Hall, and from the Avalon and Arnold Hotels. Grimm, who had been leading the parade, was shot in the abdomen and staggered into the street
where he died. Arthur McElfresh, shot in the head, died almost immediately. Cen Casagranda was fatally wounded as he tried to flee. Several
other paraders suffered minor wounds.

The enraged Legionnaires rushed into the hall, wrecked it, and dragged several IWWers out of the large unused ice box at the rear of the hall. One of the Wobblies, Wesley Everest, an ex-serviceman, escaped and fled down an alley, firing his Colt .45 at his pursuers as he went. Everest reached the Sookunchuck River, which he tried to ford, but he found it too deep and its current too swift. He returned to its bank, and as he waited there, Dave Hubbard, nephew of F. B. Hubbard, rushed toward him and ordered him to drop his revolver and give himself up. Everest shouted that he would surrender to an officer of the law but not to the mob. He ordered Hubbard to stay where he was. Hubbard charged and Everest fired, killing Hubbard instantly. His revolver empty, Everest was seized by the mob; his teeth were knocked out and he was dragged to the Centralia jail. In front of the jail, the Legionnaires tied a rope around his neck and threatened to lynch him. "You haven't got the guts to lynch a man in the daylight," Everest said through his bloody lips, defying the mob.[37]

At eight o'clock that night, the lights of Centralia went out for about 15 minutes. During this brief period of darkness the handful of guards at the city jail surrendered Everest to a small mob. "Tell the boys I died for my class," Everest said as the men dragged him from his cell.[38]

The lynchers threw Everest into a car, drove to a railroad trestle over the Chehalis River, and as the car sped to the selected spot some of the lynchers castrated him. At the trestle, they hanged him, illuminating their work with automobile headlights. Before he died, the lynchers pulled the body back up, and after tying a longer rope to his neck, dropped him over again. Then they riddled the swaying body with rifle bullets.

The following morning someone cut the rope and Everest's body fell into the Chehalis River. County Coroner David Livingstone, who was president of the Citizens' Protective League, led a posse to remove the body before Everest's friends could rescue the corpse and bury it. They dumped the mutilated body on the floor of the jail where the other Wobbly prisoners could see it. It lay there for two days. On November 15 the deputies gave four imprisoned Wobblies shovels, took them to a field on the outskirts of town, and forced them to dig a grave into which Everest's body was flung.[39]

The coroner's report, presented by Livingstone, remains a classic of its kind. Everest, the coroner declared, had broken out of jail, fled to the river, tied the knot around his neck and jumped off the trestle. Failing to kill himself, he had climbed back up, replaced the rope with a longer one, and jumped again. He then shot himself several times, and finally, after cutting the rope, he drowned in the river.[40]

Everest's lynching was defended as "the rough and ready practice of the old-time vigilance committee. But it was justice."[41] Ralph Chaplin's poem on Wesley Everest put it quite differently:

> *Torn and defiant as a wind-lashed reed,*
> *Wounded he faced you as he stood at bay;*
> *You dared not lynch him in the light of day,*
> *But on your dungeon stones you let him bleed,*
> *Night came...and you, black vigilante of greed....*
> *Like human wolves, seized hard upon your prey,*
> *Tortured and killed...and silently slunk away*
> *Without one qualm of horror at the deed.*
> *Once...long ago...do you remember how*
> *You hailed Him king for soldiers to deride—*
> *You placed a scroll above his bleeding brow*
> *And spat upon Him, scourged Him, crucified....*
> *A rebel unto Caesar—then as now,*
> *Alone, thorn-crowned, a spear wound in his side.*[42]

Mobs gathered outside the city jail, threatening to lynch the Wobbly prisoners, cursing, blaring auto horns, flashing lights into the darkened jail windows, throwing missiles through the windows and pushing loaded guns through the bars. The terror continued for nine consecutive nights. In the cold November nights, there were neither mattresses nor blankets for the prisoners. It is hardly surprising that in this hellish environment, Loren Roberts, a youngster of nineteen, was found insane.[43]

Meanwhile, Legionnaire posses searched the countryside for Wobblies who might have been in Centralia on Armistice Day and escaped. In their haste the posses picked up anyone who looked suspicious. A posse shot and killed John Haney, who turned out to be a posse member looking for Wobblies. The Portland *Oregonian* reported at first that Haney had been "slain in a skirmish with IWW suspects," but when the truth emerged, it was buried in an inside page and called an unfortunate accident. The legal authorities made no inquiry into Haney's death, and not even his 20-year-old son would call for one. "I don't blame you fellows," he was reported as saying in the Centralia *Chronicle*, "Don't think I do for a minute. It's tough to lose dad, but you fellows did your duty."[44]

Placards were mounted in shop windows throughout the area carrying the message:

Have you any information of the whereabouts of an IWW?
Any person or persons having information, no matter of how
little importance, concerning the whereabouts of a member of
the IWW or any information whatever concerning

the outrage on Armistice Day will confer a favor on the city
officials if they will call at once at the city hall and give
whatever data they have to the chief of police.
All information will be treated strictly confidential. Office open
at 8:30. Come at once.[45]

All but one of the Wobblies who had participated in the defense of the
IWW hall were captured. But across the state more than a thousand Wobblies were arrested, not to be tried for participating in the Centralia riot
but under the newly enacted criminal syndicalist law.*[46]

The Centralia *Chronicle* made it clear that is was not necessary to have
been involved in the tragedy on Armistice Day to be summarily dealt with:
"To even sympathize with the perpetrators of the tragedy is proof evident
that the sympathizer is a traitor to his country."

County prosecuting attorneys were called into session by state Attorney
General C. C. Thompson and were advised "to rush IWW cases through
the courts as rapidly as possible, to try defendants *en masse* in order to
save taxpayers' money and to insure the maximum number of convictions." They were also urged to make certain that only "courageous and
patriotic" jurors were chosen to hear the cases.[47]

With very few exceptions, and those mainly in the radical and labor
press, newspapers all over the United States reported that armed members
of the IWW had deliberately fired into a Legionnaires' parade, killing four
marchers. "It was not murder," went one report. "It was an attack on the
American government. It was monumentally worse than either of these
crimes....It is rebellion....It is treason....It was an attack on American
sentiment, American honor, American traditions of right and wrong;
American ideals of freedom, democracy and fair dealing."[48] Even "Big

---

*A "Criminal Syndicalism Bill" was introduced into the 1917 legislative session in the state
of Washington and passed both the House and Senate. The bill made it a felony to practice
"criminal syndicalism," which was defined as advocating crime, sabotage, or other unlawful
methods of terrorism as a means of accomplishing industrial or political reform. But the
passage of the bill outraged the labor movement in Washington, which viewed it as an
attempt to destroy trade unions under the guise of attacking the IWW. Opponents of the bill
flooded Governor Lister's office with their complaints and he was forced to veto the bill. In
his veto message, the governor expressed concern over the bill's effect on loyal dissenters
and said that he could only support a bill that would insure their safety. Two years later in the
1919 legislative session another "criminal syndicalism" bill was passed, and this time the
governor signed it. (Patrick Renshaw, "The IWW and the Red Scare, 1917-1924," *Journal
of Contemporary History* 3 [1968]: 63-72; Dorothy N. Schmidt, "Sedition and Criminal Syndicalism in the Senate of Washington, 1917-1919," MA thesis, University of Washington
[1949], pp. 13-36; *Seattle Times*, Feb. 24, 27, March 17, 1917.)

Bill" Haywood, who was out on bail in the Chicago trial, was fooled by the reports and was quoted as saying that the IWW did not condone murder and that the Wobblies involved, if guilty, should be punished to the limit.[49]

A reflection of the prevalent hysteria was the arrest of the editor, the president, and the secretary of the board of directors of the *Seattle Union Record* and the shutting down of its press, on the ground that it had published an unpatriotic editorial that violated the Espionage Act. The editorial read:

DON'T SHOOT IN THE DARK
Violence begets violence
Anarchy calls forth anarchy

That is the answer to the Centralia outrage. And the reason for it is found in the constant stream of laudation in the kept press of un-American, illegal and violent physical attacks upon the person of those that disagree with the powers that be.

The rioting which culminated in the death of three or four returned ex-servicemen in Centralia last night was the result of a long series of illegal acts by the men themselves—acts which no paper in the state was American enough to criticize except the *Union Record*....[50]*

The *Union Record* continued to publish on a rented press. In a noon "extra" edition on November 14, 1919 it reported that in the coroner's inquest over the death of the four Legionnaires, Dr. Frank Buford, one of the marchers in the Armistice Day parade, had testified that the Wobblies had fired only after the marchers had launched their attack upon the hall. Moreover, because of this and other similar testimony, "the coroner's jury...has failed to fix the blame for the shooting."[51] The *Union Record* also published the indictment of his fellow Legionnaires delivered by Commander Edward F. Bassett of the Silver Bow Post in Butte, Montana, who said:

The IWW in Centralia who fired upon the men that were attempting to raid the IWW headquarters there were fully justified in their act. Mob rule in this country must be stopped, and when mobs attack the home of a millionaire,

*When the case of Harry Ault, editor of the *Seattle Union Record* (charged with violating the Sedition Act) came to court in January 1920, the charges against him were dismissed for lack of evidence. (Seattle *Union Record*, Jan. 23, 1920.) Since Ault was a champion of a Farmer-Labor Party and endorsed the party's candidates in the Seattle municipal election, many in Seattle believed that "the real reason for the seizure of the paper was to suppress the political rights of labor." (Hamilton Cravens, "The Emergence of the Farmer-Labor Party in Washington Politics, 1919-20," *Pacific Northwest Quarterly* 57 [Oct., 1966]: 152.)

or of a laborer, or of the IWW, it is not only the right but the duty of the occupants to resist with every means within their power. If the officers of the law cannot stop these raids, perhaps the resistance of the raided may have that effect.[52]

But the *Seattle Times* called on the government to ignore such views. "There is but one effective answer to the methods employed by the IWW," it counselled. "TERRORIZE THE AMERICAN BOLSHEVIKI!"[53]

Eleven IWW members were indicted by the grand jury and charged with the murder of Warren O. Grimm; those not accused of the actual shooting were indicted on a charge of conspiracy to kill. Among the eleven was Elmer Smith, singled out because he had advised the Wobblies of their rights.[54]*

THE TRIAL

Since the Lewis County Bar Association had voted that none of its members should defend the Wobblies, the defendants had a difficult time obtaining local counsel. They finally had to call upon George Vanderveer, the long-time IWW lawyer, who came to Washington from Chicago just a few days before the trial.[55]

The defense sought a change of venue and the trial was moved to Montesano in Grays Harbor County, a town of some 2,000 in which organized labor had little influence. Vanderveer asked for a second change of venue to Olympia or Tacoma, but Judge John M. Wilson rejected his plea. This was hardly surprising since Judge Wilson had delivered a eulogy for the slain Legionnaires and had denounced the IWW.[56]

As his life was repeatedly threatened in Montesano, Vanderveer and his staff had to stay at a hotel in Aberdeen and travel some 20 miles each day to the scene of the trial. The trial itself, which opened on January 25, 1920, was marked by some astonishing irregularities. Some 50 Legionnaires attended, in uniform, occupying the front of the courtroom. They were paid $4 a day to attend, from a fund of $11,750 raised by the Legion among the employers—mostly lumber companies. The jurors later claimed in sworn affidavits that they had interpreted the presence of so many uniformed Legionnaires as a deliberate plan to intimidate them.[57]

*The other defendants included Eugene Barnett, a coal miner and member of both the IWW and the United Mine Workers. (He was directly charged with the murder of Grimm). There were also Ray Becker, James McInerney, Bert Bland, Loren Roberts, O. C. Bland, Bert Faulkner and John Lamb, all loggers; Britt Smith, IWW secretary; and Mike Sheehan, who was 64 amd a long time union activist. Faulkner was also an ex-serviceman. Ole Hanson and "John Doe" Davis escaped and were not found; Tom Morgan, who was in the hall, unarmed, turned state's evidence and was not indicted.

In addition, there was the presence of a troop of federal soldiers on the courthouse lawn. Vanderveer angrily protested their presence and demanded that Judge Wilson order their immediate removal, but the judge, although at first angry because he had not been consulted, accepted the prosecution's explanation that the troops were needed to protect the court and the jurors if the IWW descended on the town to free the prisoners. So the troops remained encamped on the courthouse lawn for the duration of the trial.[58]

The case for the defendants was based on the argument that they had killed the Legionnaires in self-defense; they had defended their hall, as they were legally entitled to do. They had had every reason to fear violence from the Legion parade since the businessmen of Centralia and the Legion let it be known that they were conspiring to drive the Wobblies out of town and wreck their hall. The Wobblies had made efforts to secure police protection, and they had acted in self-defense only when attacked.

The prosecution maintained that the IWW had deliberately fired upon unsuspecting and peaceful marchers, and that the IWW had planned the attack for days in advance of the parade. Since the Wobblies had conspired to attack the Legionnaires, they were severally guilty of murder. The fact that Grimm's body was found in the middle of the street was the reason the Wobblies were charged with his murder. Thus the prosecution could argue that the defendants shot at the marchers in the street and were not simply protecting themselves and their property. If the defendants had been charged with the murder of the others slain in the Armistice Day attack, whose bodies were found immediately in front of the IWW hall, it might have been easier for the IWW lawyer to prove that the shooting was in self-defense, especially since Judge Wilson refused to permit the introduction of evidence of self-defense unless the defense could prove an overt act on Grimm's part.[59]

On the eve of and during the trial, a circular was distributed which insisted that "it is the duty of every juror, as an American citizen, to cast his ballot for conviction and maximum punishment and thus sever a few heads of a many-headed monster that is eating at the heart and vitals of the nation Centralia's Armistice Day victims fought to save. For a juror not to cast his ballot would be as traitorous an act as the Armistice Day massacre itself."[60] Judge Wilson's conduct of the trial practically guaranteed that the jurors would respond in the manner called for in the leaflet. He refused to permit introduction of evidence of a businessmen's conspiracy to oust the IWW from Centralia or of plans to attack the hall, insisting that such evidence would only be permitted if it demonstrated that Grimm had actively participated in the conspiracy or in the raid upon the hall before the shooting began. When two witnesses testified that Grimm did attack the hall, they were arrested for perjury as they left the stand. Although the two were never prosecuted, the arrests intimidated other potential defense witnesses.[61]

In his instructions to the jury, Judge Wilson ruled that the IWW had no legal ground for pleading self-defense, even if the Legionnaires had attacked first. He therefore advised the jury that it had to bring in verdicts of guilty either of murder in the first degree or murder in the second degree. A verdict acquitting the defendants might be entertained, but Wilson indicated that this was virtually impossible.[62]

After 20 hours the jury found two of the defendants—Barnett and Lamb—guilty only of third degree murder; Sheehan and Elmer Smith, not guilty; Loren Roberts, insane at the time of the shooting; and the other defendants, guilty of murder in the second degree. Judge Wilson held this verdict to be inadmissible and sent the jury back. Two hours later, it returned and this time found Barnett and Lamb guilty of second degree murder along with the other defendants; the jury again acquitted Sheehan and Smith and again found Roberts insane. With this second verdict the jurors submitted a petition to the court, which they all signed, and which read: "We the undersigned jurors respectfully petition the court to extend leniency to the defendants whose names appear on the attached verdict."[63]

Wilson ignored the recommendation for leniency and sentenced all the convicted Wobblies to the maximum sentence allowed under Washington law—25 to 50 years in prison![64] For all practical purposes this was condemnation to life imprisonment.

An "unofficial jury," composed of six labor men representing AFL unions in the Northwest, sat through the trial and reported its own verdict. The labor jury held that the defendants were "not guilty," that there had been a "conspiracy by the business interests of Centralia...that the hall was unlawfully raided," and that "the defendants did not get a fair trial."[65]

Vanderveer appealed the decision to the Washington Supreme Court. In his appeal Vanderveer noted: "A more senseless verdict is inconceivable. The function of a verdict is to decide the issues. The verdict decides nothing. Did the defendants conspire, or did they not? Yes, for otherwise they should have been acquitted. No, for otherwise they should have been convicted of murder in the first degree...." On April 14, 1920, in an amazingly short time, the Supreme Court upheld the verdict and sustained all of Judge Wilson's rulings.[66]

THE AFTERMATH

Their immediate available legal remedies exhausted, the Centralia prisoners were transferred to the state penitentiary at Walla Walla and began to serve time in June 1921. Meanwhile, individuals and organizations had already begun to take up the cause of the prisoners. Leading the drive to free the men were the Centralia Publicity Committee of the IWW and the American Civil Liberties Union. From its Chicago and Seattle offices, the General Defense Committee of the IWW launched a vast propaganda campaign picturing the prisoners as victims of the "lumber trust" that controlled the state of Washington.

Labor and religious leaders in Seattle formed the Centralia Liberation Committee and held mass meetings and demonstrations in several parts of the state, at which speakers from various parts of the country called for the governor of Washington to pardon the prisoners.[67]

Although one governor after another refused, the campaign did bring some results. Most of the jurors signed affidavits admitting that they had believed the defendants to be innocent, and that they had agreed to the final verdict of guilty because of the hysteria that prevailed, and to protect themselves, and because some of the members of the jury had been in favor of hanging the defendants regardless of the evidence. Although some of the jurors worked tirelessly along with other interested persons for the release of the imprisoned men, their efforts were in vain.[68]

James McInerney was the first prisoner to be "released." He died in the prison hospital on August 13, 1930. Seven days later, on August 20, 1930, Loren Roberts became the first of the Centralia prisoners to be officially released. He was the defendant who had been adjudged guilty but criminally insane at the time of the shooting. A sanity hearing was granted, and Roberts was released in his own custody.[69]

In 1931, the tenth anniversary of the Centralia imprisonment, the statutory minimum term was fulfilled. The parole board began formal deliberations on freeing the prisoners. One after another the Centralia prisoners were released until in June 1933 only Ray Becker was left in prison. He refused, however, to accept a parole, declaring to the penitentiary parole board in mid-1933:

> To hell with a parole. I want a full and complete pardon, or nothing at all. I never was guilty of this crime. I was found guilty by a capitalist jury, and when the State of Washington saw fit to try me, an innocent man, and charge me with the crime of murder and find me guilty of the same, they can only readjust the matter, as far as I

am concerned, by granting me a full and unconditional pardon.[70]

The plea was denied and Becker remained in prison. In 1936 the International Woodworkers of America, a progressive industrial union, established a Free Becker Committee to work for his freedom. After much maneuvering, on September 20, 1939 Governor Clarence D. Martin signed a decree commuting Becker's sentence to the time served—18 years and three months. Although not a full pardon, it was enough to satisfy Becker.[71]

As Becker left prison another political prisoner in California—Tom Mooney—also was released from a living death in prison. Both had been innocent and had paid a high price for their activity on behalf of American workers. California's Governor, New Dealer Culbert Olson, released Mooney with an elaborate apology, something Governor Martin refused to offer Becker.[72]

INTERNAL DISSENSION IN THE IWW

At the same time that the IWW was reeling under the avalanche of massive repression, it was further weakened by a series of internal crises, which hastened its decline.

One of the first postwar controversies in the IWW revolved around the demands of the Philadelphia branch of the Marine Transport Workers (MTW), a leading IWW industrial union, that action be taken to protect that union's job control on the docks. Organized as a local in 1913,* the Philadelphia branch of the MTW had by 1916 grown to a membership of 3,000 and had gained job control on the waterfront, operating a virtual closed shop. During the war the United States Shipping Adjustment Board had even recognized the MTW as the bargaining agent for the Philadelphia longshoremen.[73]**

After the war the Philadelphia branch raised its initiation fee to $15 in order to keep its job control in the face of discharged workers and ex-servicemen drifting onto the docks looking for work. The action of the Philadelphia branch violated two basic IWW tenets: first, the principle of the universal transfer of the union card. A card from one port was sup-

---

*For the early history of the Philadelphia branch of the Marine Transport Workers, see Philip S. Foner, *History of the Labor Movement* 4 [New York, 1965]: 35-40.
**This did not prevent the federal government from indicting and trying Benjamin Harrison Fletcher, the Black leader of the Marine Transport Workers and an organizer of major importance of the Philadelphia branch, on the charge of violating the Espionage Act. Fletcher was found guilty with others at the Chicago trial and sentenced to twenty years in prison and $10,000 fine.

posed to be good at all ports, but the higher initiation fee meant workers from other docks had to pay again to work in Philadelphia, and the fee applied to non-Wobblies as well as IWW members. Secondly, it violated the tradition of opposition to high initiation fees. Indeed, both the 1919 and 1920 IWW conventions had reaffirmed the constitutional provision that the initiation fee for entrance into any part of the organization should be no higher than $2.00.[74]

Then, in August 1920 another issue emerged when the Philadelphia group was accused by other IWWers of loading munitions for the White Russian General Wrangel, who was receiving Allied help in the civil war against the Bolsheviks. This alleged breach of international labor solidarity was enough to cause the IWW General Executive Board to suspend the Philadelphia branch. However, it was reinstated in October after protesting that its members were innocent and that the suspensions had come without a proper hearing.[75]

Hardly had the Philadelphia group been cleared of charges and its suspension lifted than the issue of high initiation fees reappeared. Disdaining the IWW's reaffirmation of its $2.00 limit, the Philadelphia branch not only refused to withdraw the $15.00 initiation fee but actually raised it to $25.00. This caused the Marine Transport Workers, the parent industrial union, to accuse the Philadelphia branch of being "a craft union within the IWW" and to note: "We always made it our duty to assail the fakers of the craft unions for charging prohibitive initiation fees, and here one of our own branches is practicing the very same thing."[76]

Other groups in the IWW now began openly to criticize the General Executive Board for shirking its duty to force the Philadelphia branch to live up to the constitution.[77] On December 1, 1920 the GEB again suspended the Philadelphia branch, this time for charging an unconstitutional initiation fee. Although the branch had its defenders,[78] delegates to the May 1921 convention of the IWW voted to uphold the GEB in expelling the branch. For the third time in as many years the convention voted to retain the $2.00 initiation fee throughout all sections of the IWW.[79]

Once again the action taken against Philadelphia was soon reversed and the branch was quietly reinstated in October 1921. The IWW had other problems to deal with, and the "Philadelphia situation" flickered and died out in the face of these problems.[80] Moreover, during the summer of 1921 the IWW made a number of gains on both coasts as a result of the unity between sailors and longshoremen.* In the glow of the successes of the

*Discussed in our next volume.

Marine Transport Workers' Industrial Union, the Wobblies were ready to overlook the ideological errors of the Philadelphia branch.[81]

Meanwhile, other developments were causing discussion and creating differences within the IWW. A major factor concerned the approach to the defense of Wobblies found guilty of violating the Espionage Act in the various federal and state trials, which we will discuss further.

Once the Chicago federal trial was over, the Wobblies who were British subjects tried to invoke their British citizenship in order to mitigate the punitive sentences levied by Judge Kenesaw Mountain Landis. But these efforts failed[82] amid much discussion of whether it was in accord with IWW principles to seek individual or small-group redress, or all stand together in solidarity regardless of the outcome. The British appeals were effectively subverted by English consular agents in the United States. In addition, the Anglo-Wobblies were harassed by American and British agents. In the end, they had to serve out their sentences and were then deported to England and Australia.[83]

"BIG BILL" HAYWOOD

When the appeal on behalf of the defendants in the Chicago trial was filed with the Circuit Court of Appeals, Haywood and his co-defendants were released from prison on bond—July 28, 1919. With the war over, there was some hope that the Appellate Court would reverse the convictions, but its decision affirmed the sentences, eliminating only the fines.[84]

Another appeal was taken to the United States Supreme Court, while the defendants continued free on bail. Haywood still served as secretary of the General Defense Committee and succeeded in raising substantial sums for the committee.[85] However, he learned that there was little chance of a reversal by the Supreme Court and that he faced the prospect of returning to Leavenworth with a 20-year sentence. As he wrote later: "I learned that President Harding* was interviewed by Meyer London, Socialist Congressman from the State of New York, [who] was told by the president that the IWW members would be pardoned with the exception of Haywood, whom they were going to hold.[86]

While the appeals were pending, the IWW received a lengthy letter from the Communist International in Moscow. It outlined the principles held in common by the IWW and the Communists and described how the Soviet state of workers and peasants was constructed. To Haywood, this

---

*Warren Gamaliel Harding (1865-1923) was elected President in the election of 1920, running on the Republican ticket. His administration was notorious for corruption in what came to be known as the "Harding scandals."

letter represented "a momentous circumstance in my somewhat eventful life." He told Ralph Chaplin: "Here is what we have been dreaming about; here is the IWW all feathered out." He explained later: "While it was addressed to the IWW as an organization, I felt, as I knew many other members did, that it was a tribute to ourselves, as each had helped to build this class-conscious movement."[87]

In 1920, while still awaiting the outcome of his appeal to the Supreme Court, Haywood joined the Communist Party of the United States. Meanwhile, he was advised by friends that he should not return to prison, where his usefulness to the working class would be cut off. He was fifty-two years old, and he came to the conclusion that if he lived in the Soviet Union he could still do important work for the movement to which he had devoted his life. In the spring of 1921 he obtained passage out of New York, along with George Andreytchine and Vladimir Lossief, two other Wobblies; he ended up in the Soviet Union, arriving in Moscow in May 1921.

By failing to surrender to the federal authorities after the Supreme Court declined on April 11, 1921 to review the Chicago trial, Haywood and eight of his codefendants forfeited $80,000 in bail. When Haywood offered to return from the Soviet Union if the forfeited bail money would be returneu to those who had posted it, the government refused.[88]*

There has been a great deal of disagreement over the impact on the IWW of Haywood's flight. Some historians have argued that after an initial wave of indignation within the organization, the membership soon settled into an attempt to "forget him."[89] Others insist that Haywood's action "left the IWW financially shattered and lacking in experienced, competent leadership," and that it intensified opposition among Wobblies to the Soviet Union, the Third International (Comintern), and the U.S. Communist movement.[90] Another effect was to strengthen the position of those in the IWW who had opposed legal defense activities.

POLITICAL PRISONERS

When World War I ended, agitation for the release of all political prisoners began. The demands for amnesty included not only members of the IWW, but Socialists and other dissidents, as well as conscientious objec-

---

*Haywood did not abandon work on behalf of U.S. workers during his years in the Soviet Union. In 1925 he suggested the formation of a comprehensive defense organization for political prisoners in the United States. Out of this suggestion emerged the International Labor Defense. (*Daily Worker*, June 2, 16, 29, 30, and July 6, 13, 14, 18, 1925; Sasha Small, *Ten Years of Labor Defense* [New York, 1935] pp. 6-9.)

tors to military service who had been imprisoned during the war. Amnesty committees were organized in a number of cities, and the General Defense Committee of the IWW and the National Executive Committee of the Socialist Party launched campaigns for the release of all political prisoners. In addition, the Workers Defense Union, headed by Elizabeth Gurley Flynn, played a leading role in the defense of men and women caught in the federal and state Red raids. In a letter of March 25, 1919, Elizabeth Gurley Flynn wrote: "There are nearly two thousand political prisoners in the United States to-day. Many of them are well-known and well-beloved, others are obscure and almost forgotten. We must speak and act at once and in a determined manner for all those who pay with their freedom for their devotion to their class." She declared that "some 250 organizations" were affiliated with the Workers Defense Union, "representing approximately 800,000 workers and radicals in the New York district...."[91]

When President Wilson visited Seattle during his campaign for the League of Nations in September 1919, "thousands...wearing hatbands with streamers, 'Release Political Prisoners' lined the streets through which the president passed." Among them were members of the IWW.[92]

But many Wobblies felt that the defense activities weakened the organization precisely when it needed strengthening. "Defense submerged organization," wrote Art Shields, in explaining this attitude. "Through the rank and file of the IWW is a sullen, half-suppressed resentment against any defense program that interferes with organization work. The new society is not built through propaganda in the courts but 'out in the works where the blueprints are.'"[93]

Wobblies opposed to the defense activities argued that the only legitimate work for the IWW was "economic." By engaging in "political" activities, such as electoral politics or litigation in the "capitalist courts," the IWW was wasting its time and resources, diverting them from the primary task of industrial organizing, and playing into the hands of the "bosses" who controlled the state apparatus, including the courts.[94] As one opponent of legal defense activities put it, the capitalists "like to have the IWW exhaust its financial resources and waste its energies on legal defense without any results great enough so you might notice them. They like all this because they know that if only they can induce the IWW to adhere to this policy long enough, then the organization through exhaustion in all directions, will lose its effectiveness as an instrument in the hands of the workers to gain better conditions and to put the capitalists to work."[95]

Supporters of the legal defense activities of the IWW, however, argued that it had been because of the Wobblies' "ability to defend all the victims of the Class War that we have inspired the workers with confidence and have given them the courage necessary to carry on the fight." "It might be fine reading for students of history 200 years after the revolution," another defender of legal defense activities declared, "to come across the pages telling of how the IWW let thousands go to the gallows and prisons by spurning legal defense in capitalist courts, but many have been saved by legal defense in those courts, and as long as there is a possibility of saving more we will keep on with legal defense." One would hate to stay in prison, he continued, until the spirit shown by the opponents of legal defense developed "enough power to tear down the walls and tie knots in the steel bars. Hell will be frozen over pretty well by that time, to say the least."

To the purists within the ranks of the IWW, the only legitimate activity for the organization was "economic" activity, while "political" activity was regarded not only as useless but as a betrayal of the purposes of the union. For those holding these views the capitalist industrial and political system could be overthrown only through organizing workers into industrial unions and preparing them to operate the industrial society after the capitalist industrial and political system had crumbled under the impact of the general strike. (Indeed, a sizeable segment of the membership had a somewhat mystical faith in the efficacy of an IWW-led general strike to force an amnesty for all Wobbly prisoners.) "Isn't it clear by this time," asked one Wobbly, "that we spend time, energy and money upon lawyers and court procedure...[we are] diverting same...away from agitating, organizing and taking action in industry...."[96]

Internal dissension developed further over the manner in which IWW political prisoners gained their freedom. To demonstrate solidarity and loyalty to the class struggle, several Wobblies in Leavenworth federal prison decided not to apply for individual clemency but to demand a general amnesty. Those who, like Ralph Chaplin, accepted individual clemency were regarded as traitors to the working class. Most Wobblies in prison pledged "not to accept individual paroles, but to demand that we all be released together, or we will do our complete terms." Later, however, as the IWW became increasingly weaker, Wobblies left prison however they could, with paroles or with pardons.[97]

As a Christmas gesture, President Harding commuted the sentence of Eugene V. Debs, the grand old man of American socialism, late in 1921. At the same time the Administration offered pardons to a number of alien Wobblies in Leavenworth on the condition that they accept immediate deportation. Twelve accepted.[98]

THE IWW AND THE INTERNATIONAL COMMUNIST MOVEMENT

IWW's attitude toward political action emerged in bold relief over the question of its relations with the Soviet Union. On January 24, 1919 a call went out from Moscow to all revolutionary workers' movements and proletarian groups to send representatives to the First Congress of the Third International (Comintern).* The IWW was included because, as the invitation noted, in the "epoch of the disintegration and collapse of the entire capitalist world system...the task of the proletariat now is to seize state power immediately," and to that end, according to the invitation,

> ...it is necessary to form a bloc with those elements in the revolutionary workers' movement who, although they did not formally belong to socialist parties, now stand by and large for the proletarian dictatorship in the form of Soviet power. Chief among those are the syndicalist elements in the workers' movement.[99]

On August 14, 1919 IWW's General Executive Board voted unanimously to "provide for the representation of the IWW as a constituent member of the Third International." The resolution read:

> Whereas, the Soviet Republic of Russia, in the call for the organization of the Third International, included the IWW as one of the bodies eligible to such new international; and
>
> Whereas, the IWW is the only revolutionary organization in the United States whose program is absolutely scientific and uncompromising, and is the logical American unit of the Third International; and
>
> Whereas, the proletarian revolution is world-wide and not national or local in its scope;
>
> Therefore, the time has come for the IWW to assume its proper place as the American unit of the Workers' Red International, and to establish closer relations with groups of the same or similar principles in every country, such as the Communists of Russia, Hungary, Bavaria, etc., the Spartacus of Germany, the Syndicalists of France, Italy and Great Britain and other countries, and the industrial unionists of Canada and Australia.
>
> Resolved that the IWW shall create a Committee on International Relations, which shall at once establish and maintain correspondence and fraternal relations with each aforesaid revolutionary group throughout the world and shall provide for the representation of the IWW as a constituent member of the Third International.[100]

---

*Other groups in the United States invited were the left elements in the American Socialist Party (in particular, the group representing Debs and the League for Socialist Propaganda), the Workers' International Industrial Union (a Socialist Labor Party adjunct), and the Socialist Workers' Party of America. ("Invitation to the First Congress of the Communist International," in *The Communist International, 1919-1943: Documents, selected and edited by Jane Degras, [London 1956] 1 (1919-1922): 1-5.)*

No one, however, went to the Congress of the Third International from the IWW, but this was not because of any ideological differences. Rather, it was because of the difficulties facing the organization at home and the problems of travel.[101]

In January 1920 Zinoviev, the president of the Executive Committee of the Third International, sent a long letter to the IWW in which he extended the "hand of brotherhood" and urged it to

> ...take the initiative in trying to establish a basis for the uniting in one organization of all unions which have a class-conscious, revolutionary character, of all workers who accept the class struggle such as the WIIU [Workers' International Industrial Union of the Socialist Labor Party], the One Big Union [of Canada], and certain insurgent unions in the AFL.[102]

The letter took note of the IWW's opposition to "the State in general," and declared: "We, Communists also want to abolish the State." However, it insisted that, temporarily, "a State, the Dictatorship of the Proletariat," was necessary in order to "destroy the capitalist state, break up capitalist resistance and confiscate capitalist property in order to turn it over to the WHOLE WORKING CLASS IN COMMON." Once this was accomplished, and all class divisions were done away with, the letter continued, "the PROLETARIAN DICTATORSHIP, THE STATE AUTOMATICALLY DISAPPEARS, to make way for an industrial administrative body which will be something like the General Executive Board of the IWW."

Zinoviev's letter also referred to the IWW's aversion to "politics" and "political action," but went on to argue that the Wobblies used the word "politics" in too narrow a sense. Quoting Marx, the letter noted his statement that "EVERY CLASS STRUGGLE IS A POLITICAL STRUGGLE. That is to say, every struggle of the workers against the capitalists is a struggle of the workers for the POLITICAL power—the State power."

The letter called for two organizations—the union and the party: the former with an industrial task, the latter with an overall administrative task:

> The special and particular business of the IWW is to train the workers for the seizure and management of industry. The special function of the Communist political party is to train the workers for the capture of political power, and the administration of the Proletarian dictatorship. All workers should at the same time be members of the revolutionary industrial movement of their industry, and of the political party which advocates Communism.

Published in full in *Solidarity* on August 14, 1920, the letter was accompanied by an editorial urging all members and readers to study it, "and we invite and urge the fullest discussion and comment upon it in these columns from all members of the IWW and from readers." But on August 28, even before the debate on affiliation with the Third International began, *Solidarity* headlined the news that a "Special Referendum had been called by the GEB on whether to affiliate with the Third International." The referendum called for a vote on three propositions: (1) endorsing the Third International "without reservation"; (2) not endorsing the Third International "officially," and to notify it that the IWW was "in favor of an Economic Industrial International," (3) endorsing the Third International "with reservations as follows: That we take no part in parliamentary action whatever, and reserve the right to develop our own tactics according to conditions prevailing in America."

Significantly, the GEB itself had voted on each of the three propositions before sending them out, and by a majority of five to two opposed endorsing the Third International "without reservation;" the other two propositions were adopted by majorities. Moreover, the Board took two other actions to assure that affiliation with the Third International would be defeated. On the same day that it authorized the referendum, it also specifically banned further distribution of the pro-Bolshevik pamphlet published in 1918, *The Red Dawn: The Bolsheviki and the IWW*, by Harrison George, a prominent Wobbly. (Haywood wrote later that this action reflected "the opposition which had developed in the IWW against the state character of the Soviets.")[103] Then the GEB issued an advisory bulletin that seemed to advise all members to vote against affiliation with the Third International. For example, it urged that the referendum on the Third International should be "thoroughly discussed," and cautioned: "Beware, as an attempt will be made to stampede the IWW into parliamentary channels!"[104]

This position was quickly endorsed by the *Industrial Worker*, which came out unequivocally against affiliation in an editorial entitled "We Oppose Political Affiliation." It declared: "We refuse to permit the IWW to become the tail of the kite of a political organization, so far as we can use our effort to prevent it."[105] Two weeks later, in the same issue that carried the text of the affiliation referendum, the *Industrial Worker* carried a two-line editorial that stated bluntly: "Why not affiliation with the Salvation Army? That, too, is an international body."[106]

The deadline for voting was November 30, 1920, and shortly thereafter the General Executive Board declared that all of the propositions regarding the Third International had been defeated. The reported vote was:

	Yes	No
First proposition	602	1,658
Second proposition	913	1,113
Third proposition	994	1,111[107]

Thus, in a very small vote, the IWW refused to have anything to do with the Third International.

Another opportunity for the IWW to join with the international Communist movement arose in 1921. The 1921 IWW convention upheld a decision of the General Executive Board to reject cooperation with American Communist groups,* but the convention, over the strenuous objections of the most anti-Communist Wobblies, agreed to send George Williams as IWW delegate to the convention of the Red International of Labor Unions (RILU)** to be held later that year in Moscow. Williams was instructed to stand firm on all issues dividing syndicalists from Bolsheviks.[108]

Prior to the Moscow Congress, Williams met in Berlin with syndicalists from various countries and helped draw up a syndicalist manifesto, which called for an "independent economic international." The term "independent" was intended to mean politically independent of the policies of the Communist International.[109]

At the RILU Congress, which opened in Moscow on July 1, 1921, the syndicalists were in a minority and were voted down on these issues. Over the objections of Williams and other syndicalists, a "Resolution on Questions of Tactics" was approved by the Congress, which included:

> The IWW, an independent organization in America, is too weak to take the place of the old labor unions. The IWW have a purely anarchistic prejudice against politics and political action, being divided into supporters and opponents of such a cardinal question as proletarian dictatorship.... Therefore, the question of creating revolutionary cells and groups inside the American Federation of Labor is of vital importance. There is no other way by which one could gain the working mass in America than to lead a systematic struggle within the unions.[110]

*In the fall of 1920, the United Communist Party (Communist and Labor) suggested to the IWW that representatives of the executive boards of each should meet privately and decide on terms of cooperation. The terms proposed by the Communists included the statement "that the IWW cease misleading the workers with the teaching that the revolution can be achieved by industrial organization in the shops and factories and the direct seizure of industry, without first overwhelming the capitalist state and establishing the Proletarian Dictatorship of the Soviets." The IWW General Executive Board rejected the proposals and cooperation with the Communists. (*Solidarity*, Oct. 30, 1920; *Industrial Worker*, Nov. 13, 1920).

**The organization was also known as the Red Trade Union International (RTUI), the Red International of Trade Unions (RITU), and the Profitern.

As might be expected, Williams reported to the IWW's General Executive Board that his experiences at the Congress were "a great disappointment to me, and a great lesson." He charged that "the Congress was dominated by the Communist Party," and that the "political faction (the Communists) did not want an economic international in fact but in name only...that a real international of revolutionary industrial unions would become such a powerful organization and of such world-wide influence in the revolutionary field that the political organizations would have to surrender their present dominant position." Consequently, the "tacticians in the Communist International...are making every effort to control such an organization and keep it in the embryo stage." Williams concluded: "I am convinced that a truly economic international of revolutionary industrial unions cannot exist with headquarters in Moscow without being dominated by the Communist International. It is a physical impossibility."[111]

Several other IWWers were in Moscow at the time, and eight of them, including Haywood, cabled the IWW's General Executive Board that Williams' report was "fabricated and prejudiced." This protest was dismissed because the signers were "all Communists," but William Z. Foster, who was a correspondent for the Federated Press at the Congress, described Williams' report as "highly biased." He noted that the Congress had "elected a broad Executive Council, made up of four delegates from Soviet Russia, two each for all organizations from the large countries, and one each for the small movements."[112]

Calling "affiliation...with this so-called international not only undesirable, but absolutely impossible," the IWW's General Executive Board voted against affiliation with the Red International of Labor Unions. Six reasons were listed, but the most important was the sixth, which read: "Even if it were permitted [by the IWW constitution] to associate our activities with any political group, the IWW would find it impossible to cooperate with the Communist Party of America."[113]

In short, it all boiled down to anti-Communism. In his study, *The Decline of the IWW*, John S. Gambs points out that anti-Communism was a vital factor in the decline of the Industrial Workers of the World.[114]

Although the IWW had declined drastically in the early 1920's, we shall see in our succeeding volumes that it still was able to conduct militant struggles in San Pedro, California in 1923, in Colorado coal mines in 1927, in Boulder Canyon, Nevada in 1931, and in Yakima Valley, Washington in 1933. Moreover, while some of the Wobbly leaders turned to the Right, and some went into business to "make money," most of them stayed on the Left, and many, like Haywood, Elizabeth Gurley Flynn,

Charles Ashley, and others, found new areas of engagement in the Communist movement and in union activities it inspired.* As Len De Caux points out, all the Wobblies who continued on the Left "formed a living link with the Old IWW and the radicalism that marked the rise of the CIO in the mid-thirties."[115]

---

*Ralph Chaplin, who wrote the historic union song, "Solidarity Forever" became a vigorous anti-Communist and degenerated into a publicity agent for Dave Beck, the despotic, reactionary leader of the Teamsters' Union.

Similarly, Morris Sigman, ex-organizer for the IWW, became president of the ILGWU in 1923 and speedily demonstrated how to function as a despotic union leader, allying himself, "with employers, the police, and even with gangsters" to regain control of the union. (Stanley Nadel, "Reds Versus Pinks: A Civil War in the International Ladies Garment Union," *New York History* 66 [January 1985]:56, 71.)

CHAPTER 13

The Split in the Socialist Party and the Formation of the Communist Party

NATURE AND IDEOLOGY OF THE LEFT WING

The initial effect of American intervention in World War I was to strengthen the Socialist Party. Although some of its most prominent leaders—John Spargo, William English Walling, Upton Sinclair and Algernon Simons—broke with the party and supported the war effort, the party membership remained firm in opposition to the war, and the votes for Socialist candidates actually increased. The party won 34 percent of the vote in Chicago's 1917 municipal election, 35 percent in Toledo, and only slightly smaller percentages in other industrial cities. In the New York City mayoralty race, Morris Hillquit received 150,000 votes—22 percent of the total. While nationally, the Socialists elected few candidates to office, ten Socialists were elected to the New York state legislature.[1]*

Although the government persecution of the Socialist Party under the Espionage and Sedition acts did weaken the party in certain parts of the country, the number of dues-paying members rose from 70,853 in July

*Traditional scholarship holds that the strength of the Socialist Party peaked in 1912 and then entered an irreversible decline. These scholars, including David A. Shannon and Daniel Bell, maintain that the Socialist anti-war position provoked governmental repression which destroyed or severely weakened the party.

James Weinstein disputes this view, maintaining that the party did not decline after 1912 and actually grew in strength during the war. The decline of the party, he argues, did not take place until the postwar period when factionalism split it apart. Weinstein, however, fails to see the influence of the conservative ideology of Socialist leaders like Victor Berger and Morris Hillquit in the decline of the party.

See David A. Shannon, *The Socialist Party of America: A History*, (New York, 1935); Ira Kipnis, *The American Socialist Movement, 1897-1912*, (New York, 1952); James Weinstein, *The Decline of Socialism in America, 1912-1925*, New York, 1967.

1917 to 101,571 in March 1918. By August 1918, it had declined to 83,000, but a year later, in July 1919, it was up again, this time to 104,000.[2]

Most of the Socialist Party's increased membership came from the new immigrants. At a joint meeting of the state secretaries from New Jersey, New York, Maryland, Connecticut, and Wisconsin, large increases in membership were reported for most of the foreign language federations of the party. The Finnish, Lettish, Italian and Lithuanian federations all showed increases, while the Russian Language Federation reported that by August 1918, it had five times the membership it had had in April 1917.[3]

By the middle of 1919, the foreign language federations, which had constituted only 12 percent of the Socialist Party in 1912, contained about 53 percent of the total membership.[4] Meanwhile, the old English-speaking locals were either declining in membership or standing still. Clearly, the nature and composition of the Socialist Party had undergone a process of change during the war.[5]

There had always been a left wing in the Socialist Party, but the growth of the language federations and the inspiration of the Bolshevik Revolution in Russia combined to enhance greatly the power and zeal of the Left. The foreign language federations served as the network for discussions of a left outlook within the party. They also provided the financial support and political encouragement for English-speaking left-wingers who became the spokespersons for this trend.[6]

With the triumph of the Bolshevik Revolution, the prestige, zeal and membership of the left wing mushroomed. It organized its own caucuses, membership rolls, financial systems, propaganda organs and theoretical magazines. Throughout the summer of 1918, left-wing Socialists were consolidating their strength in Boston, New York, Cleveland and Chicago. These men and women were determined to revitalize the Socialist Party. While they were spurred on by the Bolshevik Revolution, it was the situation in the Socialist Party itself which intensified their demand for changes. In Boston on November 16, 1918, the Socialist Propaganda League began publication of a new left-wing biweekly newspaper, the *Revolutionary Age*. Later, the journal was moved to New York, and placed under the editorship of Louis C. Fraina. It was in the *Revolutionary Age* that Lenin's *Letter to American Workers* first appeared.[7]

The *Class Struggle* was also established in New York, edited by Fraina, Louis Boudin and Ludwig Lore. In its initial statement, the left-wing journal emphasized that for the first time in America a Marxism worthy of the name was possible:

The general mental unpreparedness which wrecked the Second International was particularly marked in this country. An opportunist leadership with limited mental outlook has kept the large masses of Socialists in this country in utter ignorance of the deeper currents of thought in the International Socialist movement. At the same time it discouraged all independent thinking, thereby destroying whatever chance there was of the movement in this country muddling through independently to some of the modes of thought indispensible to the modern Socialist movement, and preventing any serious and independent consideration of American problems. As a result there is practically no independent Socialist thought in this country, and the Socialist ideas elaborated abroad usually reach us only as soulless and meaningless formulae and often as mere reflexes of old-world radical and nationalistic sympathies, animosities and struggles.[8]

In an article published in *Class Struggle* in February 1918, the left wing declared:

As a preliminary, let us integrate the revolutionary elements in the party. *An organization for the revolutionary conquest of the party by the party!* The American Socialist Party needs a definite organized, vocal left wing, a unified expression of revolutionary socialism in theory and practice.[9]

The left-wing groups regarded themselves as the descendants of the left wing that had been in evidence in the Socialist Party since its formation in 1901, but they believed that the war had raised issues that demanded new socialist tactics.[10] The collapse of the Second International, the failure of many Socialist leaders to live up to the St. Louis Manifesto, and the Bolshevik Revolution—all combined to necessitate a new formulation of the left wing's position. Previously, the main emphasis of the left wing had been on industrial unionism and the general strike as a means by which the workers could seize the major industries of the United States. However, in line with Leninist doctrine, the new left wing believed that the aim of the workers should be to seize the machinery of government itself.[11] "The source of revolutionary practice," said the *Revolutionary Age*, "is not the theory of yesterday, but the experience of the revolution in Russia."[12]

The aim of the new left-wing group was to convert the Socialist Party to a new revolutionary philosophy and to use the existing party machinery to achieve this goal. This would be accomplished at an emergency national convention where the Left, working as a tightly knit organization, would eliminate all the reform planks from the Socialist Party's official program and replace them with a true revolutionary policy.[13]

We must clear the party of the bureaucrats, the reactionaries and the traitors by simply voting them out of their jobs and offices....It is our duty in this day of the world to make the party real red, instead of pink, as it is accused of being."[14]

In August 1918, reformists and left-wingers had combined forces at a joint meeting and placed the Socialist Party firmly on record as being "in accord" with Soviet Russia. The manifesto emerging from the meeting read:

The Socialist Party of America declares itself in accord with Revolutionary Russia and urges our government and our people to co-operate with it and to assist it to the end that democratic forces of the world may be victorious and autocracy and imperialism banished forever.[15]

In January 1919, the Socialist Party's National Executive Committee referred to the Bolshevik Revolution as "by far the greatest achievement in the establishment of working class government in the history of the world," and added that it "should receive the encouragement and support of the workers in all countries."* Above all, Allied troops should be withdrawn from Russia "in the name of democracy, in the interest of world peace, in the interest of the Russian workers, and in the name of international decency and fair play."[16]

To all this was added the issue as to which of the international socialist groups it would adhere. Should the party follow Victor Berger's advice and cooperate with the "patriotic" socialists of the Second International who had met in Bern, Switzerland in February 1919, or should it throw in its lot with the "revolutionary" socialists who had met in Moscow early in March at the founding convention of the Third International (generally known as the Communist International or the Comintern)?[17]

The call for the first convention of the Third International had been sent in January 1919 to thirty-nine different workers' groups. Four American groups had been invited: the Socialist Labor Party, the "Left-Wing Elements of the Socialist Party," the IWW and the Workers' International Industrial Union. No delegates actually arrived at the March convention from the United States. Boris Reinstein, who represented the Socialist Labor Party, had been living in Russia for a number of years. Another representative was S. J. Rutgers, living in Holland.[18]

*The platform of the Oakland (California) Socialist Party, adopted in January 1919, contained the following tribute to the Bolshevik Revolution: "The spectre of Socialism that has been haunting the world of capitalism since the beginning of the Nineteenth Century has now burst the bounds of mere theory and has become a living, constructive reality. Out of the East, in darkest Russia, the light has broken through the autocratic clouds of oppression and wrong and taken full possession of industry and politics." (Oakland *World*, Jan. 31, 1919.)

In its Manifesto issued on February 8, 1919, the left-wing section of the Socialist Party had unconditionally supported the Third International and had urged the Socialist Party to join it. The Manifesto was circulated among socialist branches throughout the country. It called, among other things, for the "abolition of all social reform planks" in the party platform and declared that "the party must teach, propagate and agitate exclusively for the overthrow of Capitalism and the establishment of Socialism through the dictatorship of the proletariat. The "Left-Wing Program" of the New York Socialists became the rallying point for left-wingers in the Socialist Party, and local after local endorsed the manifesto during 1919.[19]

VICTORY OF THE LEFT WING

"We of the Left Wing declare that we repudiate 'Moderate Socialism' and all its bourgeois affiliations," wrote John Reed in April, 1919, "whose activities, however sincerely meant, are nevertheless directed toward patching up the capitalist system and avoiding the Socialist Revolution." By the time this appeared, the left wing was in control of Local Boston, and the locals of Seattle, Cleveland, Rochester, and Philadelphia were either completely left-oriented or turning to the left. In New York, the locals in the Bronx, Brooklyn, and Queens had already affiliated with the Left Wing Section.[20]

The national referendum elections of the Socialist Party for positions on the National Executive Committee, held by mail in March 1919, gave big majorities to all left-wing candidates. The left wing won twelve of fifteen seats, and in the contest for international secretary, left-wing candidate Kate Richards O'Hare received 13,262 votes to 4,775 for SP stalwart Morris Hillquit, while left-winger John Reed got 17,235 votes for the second international post to 4,871 for Socialist ex-Congressman Victor Berger. Charles E. Ruthenberg and Alfred Wagenknecht, leaders of the left wing, also won posts on the new National Executive by large majorities.[21]

In short, the election of a new National Executive Committee found left-wingers in control of twelve of the fifteen seats, thus demonstrating, as one student points out, "a popular movement within the party nationally toward the left."[22]

THE PURGE

When the Old Guard that was in control of the Socialist Party refused to make the figures of the election public, it became known as the "suppressed referendum." A left-winger, L. E. Katterfield, who was in the national office, was finally able to disclose the tally. The results of the election revealed clearly that the left wing was far in the majority nationally and should normally have been in control of the Socialist Party.[23]

However, the Old Guard was unwilling to abide by the election results. As early as January 1919, the New York *Call* carried letters suggesting that the leftists be purged. By May, this sentiment had mounted considerably among the party's right-wingers. In articles in the *Call* and in the pamphlet, *The Immediate Issue*, Hillquit argued that it would be "futile to preach reconciliation and union." He suggested that the left wing separate: "Better a hundred times to have two numerically small socialist organizations, each homogeneous and harmonious within itself, than to have one big party torn by dissensions and squabbles, an impotent colossus on feet of clay. The time for action is near. Let us clear the decks."[24] It was a clear warning to the left wing that if they would not leave voluntarily, they would be expelled from the party. The fact that they had elected a majority of the National Executive Committee and represented the vast majority of the Party members did not matter.[25]

When the National Executive Committee met in Chicago on May 28, the Old Guard leadership who still controlled the NEC decided to act. When it assembled, the old NEC was faced with the situation that had developed in New York. The New York state committee had revoked the charter of seven of the state's language federations. The Russian, Lettish, Lithuanian, Ukranian, Hungarian, Polish, and South Slavic organizations were suspended because of their affiliation with the N.Y. Left-Wing Section. The expelled language federations of the state of New York now asked the NEC for full reinstatement and demanded further that the NEC "discipline" the New York state organization.[26]

It was practically certain that the NEC would side with the New York state committee on this issue. By a vote of eight to two, the NEC went even further. It suspended the seven national federations whose branches had been involved in the dispute with the New York state committee. Those members of the federations who were not in agreement with left wing organizations would be welcomed back into the regular branches and locals of the Socialist Party.[27]

The NEC also revoked the charter of the Michigan state organization when it amended its constitution to include the following: "Any member, local or Branch of a Local, advocating legislative reforms or supporting organizations formed for the purpose of advocating such reforms, shall be expelled from the Socialist Party." Although this unqualified rejection of social and parliamentary reforms was both anti-Marxist and anti-Leninist, the abrupt expulsion of the whole state organization with its 6,000 members was shocking.[28]

The NEC then voided the elections for the new National Executive Committee in which the left wing had triumphed overwhelmingly. The excuse was that there had been irregularities. A new committee would be elected at the special emergency convention scheduled to meet in Chicago on August 30, 1919.[29]

By these actions, the NEC had expelled 30,000 members, the great bulk of whom were members of foreign-language federations. It had declared open warfare against the left wing and made it clear that it was not prepared to tolerate serious opposition, even if this policy risked the virtual dissolution of the party.[30]

Meanwhile, in an attempt to insure that the party's convention would be dominated by those who accepted the leadership's ideology, it continued to purge the Socialist Party of left-wing elements. When Massachusetts socialists, at a convention held early in June, vented their anger at the NEC's voiding of the elections by deciding to send two representatives to the national conference of the left wing scheduled to be held in New York, the NEC voted by telegram to revoke the state party's charter and to reorganize it.[31] In New York, the state secretary, Walter M. Cook, set about revoking the charters of left-wing locals. "I have no doubt," he wrote on June 2, "but what the state of New York will be rid of this gang...before the 1st of August, and beginning with that month I expect to make a very vigorous drive for increased activity in the party."[32] In their determination to keep control of the party, the Old Guard leaders refused to send out for voting purposes a referendum that had been initiated by Local Cuyahoga County (Cleveland), Ohio, which called for the immediate reversal of the NEC's decision to expel the language federations and the Michigan Socialist Party.[33]

THE LEFT-WING CONFERENCE

As the trend of events became clear, Locals Boston and Cleveland and the left-wing section of New York issued a call for a national conference of the left wing to be held on June 21.[34] Ninety-four delegates from twenty states attended the conference. Most of them were from the four states of Michigan, Massachusetts, Ohio and New York, and from the expelled language federations. Among those present were John Reed, editor of the *New York Communist*, and other leaders of the Greater New York locals of the Socialist Party; Louis C. Fraina, writer and publicist; Charles E. Ruthenberg, Cleveland organizer and editor of the *Socialist News*; Alfred Wagenknecht, Socialist Party state secretary of Ohio; Rose Pastor Stokes;

Irish-born James Larkin, the youthful William Weinstone and Oakley Johnson, the latter being part of the delegation of the expelled Michigan socialists.* Besides these English-speaking socialists, there were the heads of the foreign language federations, such as Alexander Stoklitsky, head of the powerful Russian Federation, J. G. Stilson of the Lithuanian Federation, D. Elbaum of the Polish Federation and Charles (Karl) James of the Latvian Federation.[35]

The conference became the scene of a heated debate over the situation in the Socialist Party and how to cope with it. About one-third of the delegates were of the opinion that it was useless to continue trying to capture the Socialist Party machinery. Led principally by the Michigan and foreign language federation groups, these delegates insisted on withdrawing from the Socialist Party and calling a convention in Chicago on September 1 to form a new party—the Communist Party of America.

The majority of the left wing, led by Reed and Ruthenberg, were either American or spoke English; they argued in favor of continuing the struggle against opportunism in the party and of leaving the question of the party's future until the emergency convention scheduled for August 30 in Chicago. They expressed the view that only if the left wing failed to win over a majority at the convention should the majority group of the left wing organize a separate Communist Party.[36]

Speaking on the resolution that the left wing "sever all relations with the Socialist Party, and that we begin immediately the organization of the Communist Party," Ruthenberg declared:

> I believe personally that the proposition contained in that resolution would be the best way in the world to hamper the Left Wing movement in the organization of a virile Communist Party in the future....We have won the fight within the Socialist Party, and now some comrades come here and ask me to scuttle the ship and run away when we have won a victory. We only need to press that victory in order to take hold of the existing order. [Applause.]....We carried on a fight through the machinery of the party organization. We have won in a referendum....If we now step out of the organization—and remember there is in the heart of most members...some feeling of loyalty to the organization...the Socialist Party, which they have sacrificed for, for so many years, is something they don't want to easily let go of, and if we take this step and ask them to go

---

*The *New York Communist* began publishing on April 19, 1919 at which time the *Revolutionary Age* had been publishing for several months as the official organ of Local Boston. John Reed and others had tried to have the *Revolutionary Age* transferred to New York, but at this time Fraina (the editor) refused. The *New York Communist* was published only until the National Conference of the Left Wing established headquarters in New York City with *The Revolutionary Age* as its official organ.

outside the organization, we are not going to carry with us as many members of that party—those who even are in sympathy with our purpose and our manifesto and our program—than if we continue to fight through the two short months that still lie before the National Convention....

Although the minority criticized Ruthenberg, Reed and others who still believed that the Socialist Party could be captured or, for that matter, was worth capturing, the majority hoped that by staying in the party they could win the support of wavering elements in various sympathetic locals. But the minority, made up of 31 delegates or one-third of the conference, viewed this as opportunism, and decided to have nothing further to do with the convention.[37]

The conference continued for four days, approving the Left-Wing Manifesto which accused Hillquit and company of basing the Party program upon the petty bourgeoisie and the skilled aristocracy of labor; of failing to support industrial unionism and the workers' economic struggles; of supporting the discredited Second International, and of generally carrying on a policy of reform which led, "not to socialism, but to the perpetuation of capitalism."

The Left-Wing Manifesto called for full support of industrial unionism, support of the Russian Revolution, affiliation to the Communist International, and a program aimed at the abolition of the capitalist system and its replacement by socialism.

The conference elected a governing council of nine and combined the *Communist* with the *Revolutionary Age*. It also discussed the strategy to be adopted in order to gain control of the Chicago convention.[38]

THE PURGE CONTINUES

While the minority delegates insisted on withdrawing from the Socialist Party and went ahead with plans for a national convention to form a Communist Party, Reed, Ruthenberg, Wagenknecht and Isaac E. Ferguson—representing the majority—met in Cleveland on July 26 and declared that they had received a majority of the votes cast for the NEC and were therefore the rightful executive committee. The group demanded that Adolph Germer, the party's national secretary, hand over the national office to them.[39]

Germer and the Old Guard not only refused, but they kept a close watch on the national office in Chicago, fearing that the left wing might attempt to seize control of the party machinery, or at least of its records. Germer informed Hillquit that he had been staying in the national office at night, expecting the leftists to "try some rough stuff."[40]

Meanwhile, the "purge" of the party ranks continued. In August, the Ohio Socialist Party was expelled for left-wing affiliation, and several minor party organizations were also expelled. It is estimated that by the end of July, 1919, the number of expelled members had grown to almost 70,000, or two-thirds of the party membership.[41]

Enraged by the expulsion policy and the "undemocratic" procedures followed by the NEC, the Finnish-American Socialists, whose numerical strength in the party was at that point greater than ever, demanded that the Old Guard leadership step down. Twenty-five Finnish socialist branches sent protests to national headquarters, demanding reinstatement of the expelled federations and state party organizations.[42]

Not only did the Finnish-American Socialists fail in their attempt, but the party's press began a barrage against the left wing and predicted a split at the forthcoming convention. The *Call* declared that the left wing deserved to be expelled, labeling the idea of importing Russian revolutionary methods to America as "utopian" and comparing it with the attempts of supporters of Robert Owen and Charles Fourier to establish socialist colonies in the United States in the 1830's and 1840's. "Lessons can be learned from other countries, to be sure," argued the *Call*, "but policies cannot be copied everywhere." It was better, it went on, that the party be rid of those ridiculous enough to suppose that Bolshevism would succeed in the United States.[43]

THE CHICAGO SOCIALIST PARTY CONVENTION

Despite all this, right up to the opening of the Socialist Party's national emergency convention in Chicago on August 30, the majority group of the left wing continued to believe that they could capture the party machinery. It soon became evident that this was wishful thinking. From the very beginning of the convention, the Old Guard had control of affairs, insisting that the credentials of all delegates be cleared at the Socialist Party's national office before they would be allowed to be seated.

On August 29, the evening preceding the national convention, left-wing delegates met and unanimously agreed that the left wing should initially meet with the Socialist Party rather than bolt immediately to form a new organization. The caucus agreed that left-wingers would withdraw from the convention unless several conditions were met, including seating the new National Executive Committee, withdrawal of expulsions and suspensions, seating of contested delegations, and adherence to the Third International.[44]

When the convention opened on Sunday, September 31 at Machinists'

Hall in Chicago Adolph Germer ordered nearly all left-wingers present, to leave the hall. When the delegates protested that they held credentials, Germer demanded that they produce white admission cards, which none had. Germer then declared, "I shall ask you in a comradely way to leave the hall." John Reed challenged Germer, at which point Germer issued the "fateful order which broke the Socialist party."

"All right, officers, clear the hall!" Germer shouted. Many of the delegates held onto their seats as several uniformed and plainclothes officers of the Chicago police, already on the premises, forcibly ejected the left wing from the Socialist Party. Delegates were swept toward the doors and, one by one, broken loose from their chairs and moved out of the convention hall.[45]

To the left wing, the arrival of the police was evidence that the Old Guard was more ready to ally itself with "bourgeois" law-enforcement agents than with revolutionaries. Indeed, as soon as the convention resumed, a bitter dispute arose over this issue and even some moderate Socialists criticized the old Guard for having called in the police.[46] Above the tumult Ludwig E. Katterfield, left-wing leader from Kansas, was heard to say to Germer: "This will make ten thousand members for us!" Anita Whitney of California announced that Germer's "police tactics" had converted her to a new party of the left.[47]

Having excluded the left-wingers, the emergency convention of the Socialist Party pieced together a number of resolutions, a majority and minority report on international relations and a manifesto—all radical-sounding. The resolutions included denunciation of the military occupation of Ireland and a demand for self-determination for the Irish Republic; condemnation of pogroms against the Jews, along with noting the absence of such programs in either Communist Soviet Russia or Communist Hungary; a call for a one-day strike on October 8, 1919 to free Tom Mooney; a warning against the intensification of U. S. imperialism and a protest against intervention in Mexico; and an endorsement of industrial unionism and the establishment of a labor department in the party for the preparation of literature and more active work among the labor unions.

The majority report on international relations repudiated the Second International, the Bern Conference and all socialist parties that formed coalition governments with bourgeois parties. It called for the reconstruction of a Socialist International that included the Communist Parties of Germany and Russia and all other parties which accepted the principle of the class struggle. Even this did not seem radical enough, and a minority report was later adopted by referendum calling for immediate affiliation with the Third International. By a vote of 3,475 to 1,444, the referendum called upon the Socialist Party to apply for membership in the Third International.[48]

Noting that the SP manifesto endorsed Russian Bolshevism and declared "solidarity with the workers of Russia in establishing their Soviet republic," the New York *Sun* asked: "Why, then...did they expel the Left-Wing of their party?"[49] The answer was that with the expulsion of the left-wingers, the Old Guard no longer had to worry about any pressure to fulfill the radical program outlined in the manifesto.

The leadership made an attempt to exude confidence as it assured the membership that the party had survived "the terrorists within and the reaction without" and would emerge "stronger than ever after the cleansing."[50] Victor Berger openly rejoiced at the departure of a "lot of anarchists" from the ranks of the Socialist Party.[51] The fact was, however, that little remained of the old Socialist Party and that its membership after the 1919 split was hardly more than 20,000![52] As even a critic of the left has admitted, "The Right Wing had saved its hold on the party name and machinery, but had lost two-thirds of its membership."[53]

THE C.L.P. AND THE C.P.

On the afternoon of the second day of the Socialist convention, after standing in an anteroom as observers to the right-wing steamroller on the convention floor, over eighty leftists gave up any hope of entering the Socialist convention on equitable terms and met downstairs. One by one additional delegates defected from the Socialist meeting upstairs and joined the radicals below.

On September 3 these left-wing delegates moved to the IWW hall and proceeded to write a constitution, platform, and program for the newly-created Communist Labor Party of the United States of America. The Communist Labor Party declared itself in harmony with the principles of the Third International, and, following the national left-wing manifesto, pointed out that the major struggle was to be in the industrial arena; elections were of propaganda value since it was not believed that gains could be made through existing political institutions. Industrial unionism, as practiced by the IWW, was the proper form of labor organization. The phrase "direct action" appeared frequently in the party's official document, and it was specifically noted that it was "not associated with terrorism, violence, or by any other perverted meaning...but by it is meant such united action by the workers on the job which they made use in forcing concessions from the employing class directly, without the use of the capitalist state."[54]

Meanwhile, the minority of the left wing, which had given up all hope of capturing the Socialist Party some weeks before, was meeting a few blocks away at the inaugural convention of the Communist Party of America. On the first day of the Communist Party convention, the Chicago Anarchist Squad burst into the hall and arrested a delegate.[55]

The Communist Labor Party had 92 delegates at its convention. It issued no figures as to membership, but it was estimated that it represented about 10,000 members, most of whom were American-born. The Communist Party convention, on the other hand, was attended by 128 regular and fraternal delegates and claimed a membership of 58,000, mostly members of the foreign language federations. Alfred Wagenknecht was elected first secretary of the Communist Labor Party and Charles E. Ruthenberg first secretary of the Communist Party.[56]

Attempts were made to bring the conventions of the Communist Labor Party and Communist Party together, but they were unsuccessful. The English-speaking Communists did not wish to be lost in an organization dominated by European-oriented federations. The Communist Party was largely a federation of language units, while the Communist Labor Party made such language groups subordinate to the local organizations. The participants at the Communist Labor Party convention demanded that they must be accepted collectively into the Communist Party, but this proposal was rejected. The CP delegates insisted on individual acceptance, arguing that the Communist Labor Party contained a number of individuals who had joined its convention "because of personal grievances against the old party officialdom or against the Left Wing officialdom."[57]

Although the two Communist parties continued to work independently of each other, there were actually few ideological differences between them. Both denounced imperialism as the manifestation of monopoly capitalism, and both spoke of the need to abolish the capitalist system of industrial production and to create an industrial republic in which all industrial production would be socialized. Both parties resolved at their conventions to join the Communist International, and both determined to have nothing to do with immediate, partial political demands. The Communist Labor Party declared that its platform "can contain only one demand: the establishment of the Dictatorship of the Proletariat." The Communist Party asserted that its parliamentary representatives would neither "introduce or support reform measures."[58]

The program of the Communist Labor Party declared that its locals and branches were to "organize shop branches, to conduct Communist propaganda and organization in the shops and factories, and to encourage the workers to organize in One Big Union." The party would also "propagandize industrial unionism and industrial union organization, pointing out their revolutionary nature and possibilities." Indeed, it was to make "the great industrial battles its major campaigns, to show the value of the strike as a political weapon."[59]

The Communist Party likewise declared that it would "make the great industrial struggles of the working class its major campaigns, in order to develop an understanding of the strikes in relation to the overthrow of capitalism." It would "participate in mass strikes, not only to achieve the immediate purposes of the strike, but to develop the revolutionary implications of the mass strike." The Communist Party called for "mass action," which was "industrial in its origin," but acquired "political character...in the form of general political strikes and demonstrations," and for "councils of workers" to "be organized in the shops as circumstances allow, for the purpose of carrying on the industrial union struggle within the old unions."

> The Communist Party must engage actively in the struggle to revolutionize the trade unions.
>
> As against the trade unionism of the American Federation of Labor, the Communist Party propagandizes industrial unionism and industrial union organization, emphasizing their revolutionary implications....[60]

Both communist parties summoned the workers to organize on the job. Both, moreover, emphasized dual unionism. The Communist Labor Party called for the formation of "One Big Union" as a rival to the AFL, and the Communist Party considered it to be "a major task...to agitate for the construction of a general industrial union organization embracing the IWW, WIIU, independent and secession unions, militant unions of the AFL and the unorganized workers on the basis of the revolutionary class struggle."[61]*

There is no evidence that any Black delegates participated in the founding of either the Communist Labor Party or the Communist Party.** The

---

*In his brief mention of the founding of the Communist Party in 1919, David Montgomery comments on the labor program, but does not indicate the dual union outlook of both the Communist and Communist Labor Party at their founding. (*The Fall of the House of Labor: The Workplace, the State, and American Labor Activism, 1865-1925* [New York, 1987], p. 426.)

**Participation of Black socialists in the early Communist movement will be discussed in our next volume.

platform of the Communist Labor Party was silent on the Negro question, but the Communist Party did include a paragraph on it which read:

> In close connection with the unskilled worker is the problem of the Negro worker. The Negro problem is a political and economic problem. The racial expression of the Negro is simply the expression of his economic bondage and oppression, each intensifying the other. This complicates the Negro problem, but does not alter its proletarian character. The Communist Party will carry on agitation among the Negro workers to unite them with all class-conscious workers.[62]

While this statement did acknowledge that the racial factor made some difference, it still viewed the Negro question as simply one aspect of the broader labor question. Moreover, the paragraph provoked no discussion. Indeed, in a detailed report published in *The Liberator* on the three conventions in Chicago—Socialist, Communist Labor, and Communist—Max Eastman never once mentioned a discussion of the Negro question at any of the gatherings.

Nor did Eastman once mention a discussion of the woman question at either the conventions of the two Communist parties. The platforms of both the Communist and Communist Labor Parties were silent on women's equality.[63]

The truth is that throughout the spring, summer, and fall of 1919, as the split in the Socialist Party reached its climax, little attention was paid to the woman question in either the left or right-wing Socialist or the then early Communist circles. Actually, the editorial, "What's To Become of Women?" in the April 30, 1919 issue of the left-wing *Ohio Socialist* constituted the only discussion of this issue in the radical press during the period. It was prompted by a reader who asked the paper what would become of women "under Bolshevism." The editorial responded with the reply that "what is woman going to do with man under Bolshevism is a more pertinent question." According to the publication, under a social system where political and economic rights were equal, as they were under Bolshevism, "man may well fear some reprisals and revenges upon him for the age-long persecution and humiliation of woman. Having equal rights with man, and since the war, being in all probability in the majority, what is to prevent them from 'getting even' for the mountain of humiliation man has heaped upon them? It's a serious question. They will have the power. Will they use it?"[64]

COMMUNIST PARTIES FORCED UNDERGROUND

Writing of the Red Scare which was in full swing when both the Communist Labor Party and the Communist Party were formed, Robert K. Murray notes: "Virtually every local Communist in the nation was affected, practically every leader of the movement, national or local, was put under arrest."[65] Many members of the CLP and CP were the targets of brutal vigilante attacks. The California state convention of the Communist Labor Party in November 1919 was followed by mob action against the local Oakland headquarters and the offices of the Oakland *World*, both of which were sacked by a group of war veterans who burned a large amount of literature, official records, and furniture. Although the Oakland police had been alerted in advance and urged to provide protection, not a single police officer was present during the time of the riot.[66] Bay Area leaders of the Communist Labor Party, including Anita Whitney, were arrested on charges of criminal syndicalism after the Communist Labor Party state convention.[67]*

Federal agents indicted eighty-five members of the Communist Party in Chicago on charges of conspiracy to overthrow the government by force. Thirty-eight leaders of the Communist Labor Party were prosecuted for singing "The Red Flag" at the convention in Chicago and for declaring solidarity with the Soviet Union. As we have seen, on January 2, 1920, federal agents rounded up more than 4,000 suspected radicals, most of them believed to be Communists, covering thirty-three major cities in twenty-three states. It is estimated that more than 50,000 members dropped out of both Communist parties during this reign of terror. By 1920, the membership of the Communist Labor Party and the Communist Party had dropped from an estimated 70,000 to 16,000.[68]

Their very existence threatened, the Communist Labor Party and the Communist Party were forced underground. Still, they did not cease their activities. The *Voice of Labor*, the CLP's official organ, and the *Communist*, the CP's official organ, continued to publish, as did papers issued by the language federations. More than fifty publications, twenty-five in New York City alone, continued to express the views of the two Communist parties in the face of violence and threats of violence, as well as government prosecution.[69]

A UNIFIED COMMUNIST PARTY

Previously the opponents of unity in the Communist movement had

*Three—John Weiler, John Taylor, and Anita Whitney—were convicted.

insisted that the CLP join the CP as individuals, or at best, as locals. They now raised a new obstacle, arguing that the predominantly American-born CLP leaders and members would lack sympathy for and understanding of the foreign-born workers who predominated in the Communist Party and would even seek to destroy the language federations once the two parties were united.[70]

Eventually, however, a large section of the CP broke with the opponents of unity and, with Ruthenberg at their head, joined up with the Communist Labor Party. At the same time, groups separated from several of the language federations, and the majority of the Jewish Federation disaffiliated from the CP and joined the Communist Labor Party. In May 1920 a unity convention was held in Bridgman, Michigan, at which the United Communist Party of America was formed. Ruthenberg was elected executive secretary, and the Central Executive Committee was made up of five members from the CP and five from the CLP. The United Communist Party included most of the members of the two former parties.

The new party denied the desirability of reform within capitalist society, set as its goal the dictatorship of the proletariat, pledged allegiance to the Comintern and called on its members to work among Black workers with the aim of uniting them with all class-conscious workers. It also opposed Communists working within the AFL, thereby guaranteeing their isolation from the labor movement.[71]

The creation of a single party turned out to be only an uneasy truce. In mid-July of 1920, a group broke away from the United Communist Party. A convention of the Communist Party and the Communist Party of America took place in May 1921 in Woodstock, New York. The convention established the new Communist Party of America. Ruthenberg became executive secretary of the CPA and a ten-member National Executive Committee was elected, with five representatives from each party. It was decided to locate the party headquarters in New York City.[72]

An important step in developing a unified, effective Communist Party was taken with the establishment of the American Labor Alliance in July 1921. With the active support of the Communist Party, within a month the Alliance began to charter locals for a new organization. At the same time, the Workers Council, which had been formed in May 1921 by socialists who had been carrying on left-wing propaganda within the Socialist Party, also began work to create a new organization. Thus, the underground Communist Party, the American Labor Alliance and the Workers Council all worked to unite militant forces into a new legal party.[73]

An organizing convention met from December 23-26, 1921 in New

York City. Participating were 150 delegates from the American Labor Alliance, the Workers Council and affiliated organizations. Three fraternal delegates were also present from the Proletarian Party, which had been organized by the Michigan left-wingers.

Over the opposition of only the Proletarian Party delegates, who demanded that their own organization be chosen, the convention announced the formation of a legal party—the Workers' Party of America—with an Executive Committee of seventeen members, and with Ruthenberg as executive secretary. The *Worker* was chosen as the party's official organ.[74]

The first article in the constitution of the Workers' Party stated that its purpose was "to educate and organize the working class for the abolition of capitalism through the establishment of a Workers Republic." Its program stated: "The Workers' Party will centralize and direct the struggle of the laboring masses against the powerfully centralized opposition of their exploiters. It will courageously defend the workers and wage an aggressive struggle for the abolition of capitalism."

The program also vigorously endorsed the Russian Revolution which, it said, had ushered in a new period—"the era of Workers' Republic." It demanded recognition of the Soviet government by the United States. It also called upon all workers to join the unions of their trade, to form minority groups of left-wing workers within the unions, to work for fighting programs in the organizations and to depose the reactionary union leadership. The program condemned dual unionism and all ideas of destroying the old craft unions. It supported the amalgamation of the trade unions into industrial organizations.*

Under the heading of "The Race Problem," the Workers' Party pledged to "support the Negroes in their struggle for liberation" and for full equality, and to "destroy altogether the barriers of race prejudice" in the unions.[75] The recognition of this special responsibility marked an important step forward.

Although the Workers' Party was considered the "legal" party in the sense that it would be agitating for legal recognition as a party, the Communist Party of America was retained as the alternative "underground" organization, should the former be suppressed. It must be remembered that the efforts at unity of the two main Communist groups since 1919 were complicated by the constant federal and state attacks on the radicals

---

*This outlook was greatly influenced by the publication of V. I. Lenin's famous *Left-Wing Communism: An Infantile Disorder* and by the formation of the Trade Union Educational League. Both will be discussed in the next volume.

and the foreign-born—especially the Communists. This continued practically unabated.

In August 1922, the Communist Party of America held a convention in Bridgman, Michigan to discuss the question of ending the "underground" party. After the majority group had voted against liquidation and the convention was about to disperse, FBI agents and agents from the state of Michigan raided the gathering. Seventeen delegates were arrested and charged with violating a Michigan law against criminal syndicalism.[76]

Despite these developments, the move to establish a unified, legal Communist Party continued. In April 1923, the Workers' Party and the Communist Party of America were consolidated into the Workers' Party of America, thus bringing all Communist groups under one roof.

The Communist Party and the Communist Labor Party, both formed in 1919 and both affiliated with the Communist International, emerged in 1922-1923 from clandestine activity and persecution as the Workers' Party. In 1922, it had 12,394 members, and by 1923 the number reached more than 20,000.[77] More than half of its membership was foreign-born.[78] Although small, it was an influential force in Finnish, Slavic and Jewish fraternal organizations, and, as we shall see in our next volume, in the unions of garment workers, coal miners, machinists and other groups of workers.

CHAPTER 14

Political Action, 1918-1920

In his work, *A Theory of the Labor Movement*, published in 1928, in which he provided justification for the ideology of the AFL in the era of Gompersism, Selig Perlman advanced the thesis that the AFL survived "mainly because it knew how to resist the lure of politics."[1] In resisting this "lure," the AFL developed the doctrine called "voluntarism" in which the leadership of the AFL rejected the state as a means of achieving trade union goals, and, in some cases, adopted even an extreme anti-state position. It was a philosophy in which the AFL leadership encouraged workers (mainly white skilled male labor) to improve their lot by developing the only source of power that counted—trade union formation. It was a philosophy which allowed the AFL reluctantly and mainly rhetorically to endorse legislation for female workers on the basis of their "weakness," at the same time as it rejected social legislation in favor of collective bargaining. Opposing action in support of social insurance, Gompers explained:

> Sore and sad as I am by the illness, the killing, the maiming of so many of my fellow workers, I would rather see that go on for years and years, minimized and mitigated by the organized labor movement, than give up one jot of freedom of the workers to strive and struggle for their own emancipation through their own efforts.[2]

The AFL's de-emphasis on politics increased during the war. While

*For a defense of the AFL's doctrine of "voluntarism," *see* William English Walling, *American Labor and American Democracy*, vol. I, (New York, 1926), and George Higgins, *Voluntarism in Organized Labor in the United States, 1930-1940*, (Washington, D.C., 1944). For an incisive critique of the doctrine, *see* Michael Rogin,[3] "Voluntarism: The Political Functions of an Antipolitical Doctrine," *Industrial and Labor Relations Review* 15 (July 1962): 521-35.

World War I brought AFL leaders into participation in government to an extent never before achieved, it also increased their participation with management. "To Federation leaders," notes Michael Rogin,[3] "the war experience taught the value not of government action but of union cooperation with industry....Their aggravated anxiety to win a place as the partners of industry made the Federation leaders even more opposed to state interference (in labor-capital relations) than they had been before the war."

And they were definitely more opposed to independent political action.

FORCES FOR INDEPENDENT POLITICAL ACTION

On June 9, 1916, Samuel Gompers sent a packet of articles explaining the AFL's stand on political action to John Fitzpatrick, president of the Chicago Federation of Labor and an outspoken proponent of independent political action. The articles contained Gompers' political philosophy: first, avoid involvement in partisan politics and follow a policy of "reward your friends and punish your enemies" on the major party tickets; second, refrain from independent political action at all costs, and third, subordinate political to economic action. "I am sure," Gompers wrote, "that with a fair reading and understanding of these documents, you will be in a position to meet any opponent or adverse critic of the trade union movement and justify upon every ground the fundamental work and principles, struggles, achievements and ideals of the American Federation of Labor."[4]

Shortly after receiving this letter, Fitzpatrick intensified his activity for the formation of a labor party. By 1919, he had achieved the establishment of such a party, first in Chicago, and then in Illinois, and had even aided ' ı the formation of a labor party on a national scale.[5]

Several factors contributed to this, such as the clear hostility to organized labor, and the growing confidence of reactionaries—reflected especially in the "Open Shop" campaign—frightened a number of union leaders who had relied up to then on the AFL's traditional political policies, and convinced them that a new political movement was essential to safeguard the labor movement.[6]

A specific reason for this feeling was the increasing use of injunctions. Usually injunctions prohibited such activities as picketing, threatening, soliciting employees to join the strike, "addressing to any...employees words imparting hatred, criticism, censure, scorn, disgust, humiliation or annoyance because of their employment by the complainant," and "distributing handbills, cards, or other printed matter among employees."[7] "It is folly," wrote John P. Frey, editor of the *International Molders' Journal*, "to spend $50,000 or $100,000 in a strike...when a decision of the Judge can overthrow all that strikers are able to accomplish."[8]

As the use of injunctions increased during the strike wave of 1919, labor's anger mounted. "Government by injunction will increase the growth of Bolshevism," warned the *Columbia Labor News*.[9] One of the ten items in Labor's "Bill of Rights" was "Government by Injunction": It read:

> Government by injunction has grown out of the perversion of the injunction process. By the misuse of that process workers have been forbidden to do those things which they have a natural and constitutional right to do.
>
> The injunction as now used is a revolutionary measure which substitutes government by judicial discretion or bias for government by law. It substitutes a trial by one man, a judge, in his discretion, for a trial by jury. This abuse of the injunction process undermines and destroys the very foundations of our free institutions.[10]

Writing in *Survey*, John Fitch noted that the "Taff Vale case [in Great Britain] led to the formation of the British Labour Party, the election of labor representatives to Parliament, and the passage of the trades disputes action which protected the unions from attacks in the courts." Labor in the United States had believed that the Clayton Anti-Trust Act would do the same, Fitch wrote, but the continuing repression of the right to strike by the courts proved that they were wrong. Was it not time for American labor to follow their British trade union brothers and move towards the formation of a labor party?[11]

Actually, the success of the British Labour Party stimulated the movement for the labor party in the United States. In 1918 the British Labour Party increased its representation in Parliament from 39 to 59 seats.[12]

The Bolshevik Revolution strengthened the movement for a labor party. To those who sought a new political movement for U.S. workers, the Russian Revolution symbolized the results labor could obtain by determined and united strength. Although John Fitzpatrick made it clear that the labor party movement, as he saw it, did not seek the overthrow the existing capitalist system, he insisted that it could learn much from the Bolshevik Revolution. Fitzpatrick expressed the hope "that the day was only near when the workers would be able to concentrate their efforts and do a job such as Russia has done."[13]

The labor party movement got under way before the Armistice. The first attempt was made at Bridgeport, Connecticut, in September 1918, during the machinists' strike against the award of the National War Labor Board. President Wilson's use of executive power to force the arms and munitions workers back to work induced the strikers to enter politics. On

September 6, the Bridgeport workers established the American Labor Party "as an instrument of industrial emancipation," and adopted a platform similar to the British Labour Party's manifesto, *Labour and the New Social Order*.[14]

Before the year was out, agitation for independent political action by labor had spread to 45 cities across the nation. "This labor...thing...is breaking out in many places," Frank P. Walsh, the former chairman of the War Labor Board, wrote at the end of 1918. "The home of it is the Chicago Federation of Labor, the most intelligent and honest radical group in the country."[15]

THE CHICAGO PROGRAM

The Chicago Federation of Labor was a traditional stronghold of labor insurgency; it had tried to form a labor party in 1905, 1906, 1908, and again in 1910, and it had continually campaigned for municipal ownership of public resources and utilities. The sponsorship of successful wartime drives in meatpacking and the needle trades established the Chicago Federation as the most vigorous city central of the AFL in 1919. Under president John Fitzpatrick and his associates, Edward Nockels, Duncan MacDonald, and John C. Walker, Chicago and Illinois were the hub of the labor party effort.[16]

Barely a month after the Armistice, the Chicago Federation declared: "The time is ripe...a new day has dawned...an opportunity that comes but once in a lifetime is presented." The Chicago trade unionists exclaimed: "Labor in Chicago and labor in all other centers of America will join with their brothers and sisters of other lands under the slogan: 'ALL POWER TO THE WORKERS! THE HOUR OF THE PEOPLE HAS COME.'"[17]

The Chicago Federation then called on workers to support the movement for a mass labor party and presented what came to be called the "Chicago Program." Part of it was *Labor's Fourteen Points*, published by the Chicago Federation of Labor on November 17, 1918. Named in obvious imitation of President Wilson's program, it provided a platform for independent political action. Labor, it pointed out, wished to increase its voice in society and to counterbalance "private interests or bureaucratic agents of government." It could do this only by achieving its rights to organize and bargain collectively, to work an eight-hour day for a minimum wage, and to expect equal treatment for men and women in industry and government. Labor demanded equal representation in all departments of government, especially those involved in demobilization and reconstruction, representation at the peace conference, a larger voice in determining the methods, policies, and programs of public education, and a League of Workers as a supplement to the League of Nations to guarantee disarmament and to maintain or work toward open diplomacy and peace.

Labor's Fourteen Points called upon the government to abolish unemployment through public works projects during depression periods; to lower the cost of living by controlling "profiteering" in all phases of production and distribution; to extend soldiers' and sailors' insurance, including accident and illness insurance, to all citizens; to expedite the payment of the war debt by taxing inheritance incomes and land values, and to restore free speech, free assemblage and the free press. Finally, it called upon the government to nationalize and develop the nation's natural resources and provide for public ownership of public utilities, and, significantly, the "democratic management" of industry and commerce.[18]

THE COOK COUNTY LABOR PARTY

The Cook County Labor Party was organized on December 29, 1918, and less than a month later, it nominated John Fitzpatrick for mayor of Chicago. Fitzpatrick ran on a platform which was "organized to establish genuine democracy in all public affairs" by breaking "the power of rapacious public utility corporations, greedy big business interests and reactionary newspapers which now dominate our civic life." "Big Business" was held responsible for high gas bills, exorbitant elevated and surface car transportation charges, an anti-labor school board, anti-strike police department and courts, high taxes for the poor, and the distortions of truth in the Chicago daily papers. To correct these inequities the party demanded municipal ownership and operation of all public utilities, democracy in the public education system, full recognition of Union Labor in all departments of City Government, shorter hours for city workers, abolition of the contract system in public projects, and the neutrality of the police in industrial disputes. It called upon the municipality to clear the slums and inaugurate public housing projects, and to improve sanitation by electrifying steam railways in order to eliminate dust, by regularizing garbage collection, and by building playgrounds and forest preserves. The city should also readjust the tax system to place a greater burden on the wealthy. Home rule for Chicago was also demanded, "so that the people of this city may settle their local problems and manage their local government without outside interference." The initiative, referendum and recall were to be instituted as a final check upon the government.

Fitzpatrick pledged to conduct a vigorous campaign, to uphold the general goals of the party and to accept no contributions from "business men, or those who have personal ambitions" which he maintained were "nothing else but...blood money ground out of the lives of the toilers."

The Cook County Labor Party concentrated exclusively on gaining labor support. It conducted its activities mainly through local unions, and speakers appeared before as many meetings as possible to explain the party program. Fitzpatrick addressed a meeting of 5,000 members of the Amalgamated Clothing Workers, received the personal endorsement of Sidney Hillman and accepted a $500 donation to his campaign fund. Before a meeting of 8,000 workers, Frank Walsh similarly endorsed Fitzpatrick's candidacy.[19]

Although concentrating on the unions, the labor party leaders made a special appeal to the returning veterans. A resolution was adopted by the party to select a committee of soldiers, sailors, and workingmen "to deal with the problems of the returned soldiers and sailors, and to promote their cooperation with the workers of Chicago for the advancement of political and industrial democracy at home."[20]

The *Labor Herald* of Kansas City, Missouri reported that the "trade unionists of Chicago are enthusiastic over the new party and declare that they will win the election. The old line politicians are worried over the action of the workers in getting into the political arena and will do their utmost to defeat the ticket."[21]

Although the Cook County Labor Party campaigned vigorously, Fitzpatrick received only 55,990 votes, or 8 percent of the total, compared with the 37% received by the victorious Republicans. The Labor Party explained its low vote by insisting that it was cheated at the polls, that it received unfair treatment at the hands of the Chicago press and that it had encountered hostility from local unions that refused to break with traditional AFL political policies. However, it did point out that the Labor Party had replaced the Socialists as the third party in Chicago, and Fitzpatrick concluded that the party "has established itself on the map. It has come to stay."[22]

During the first week of December, 1918 a resolution was adopted at the convention of the Illinois Federation of Labor to form an "Independent Labor Party for the State of Illinois."[23] A referendum of the affiliated unions on the resolution showed 341 organizations in favor and 38 against. Of individual votes recorded, 22,722 were for and 2,561 against.[24]

In April 1919, at a state convention, the Labor Party of Illinois was formed. It adopted *Labor's Fourteen Points* as its platform, and in addition passed a resolution expressing its desire "to place on record a statement of appreciation of the great service rendered to the cause of labor by the

Socialist movement by its campaign of education carried on so vigorously and at such noble sacrifice, and we urgently invite all Socialists who see larger hope for the workers through the plans of the Labor Party to come into this party and become fellow-workers with us."[25]

THE AMERICAN LABOR PARTY

On January 11, 1919, the joint reconstruction committees of the Central Labor bodies of Greater New York called a convention of trade union representatives for the purpose of organizing a Labor Party. There were 884 delegates present representing the Central Federated Union, the Central Labor Union of Brooklyn, the Women's Trade Union League and the United Hebrew Trades, as well as delegates from 152 local and 41 international unions. The convention organized the American Labor Party of Greater New York.[26]

The new party's program was similar in many respects to that of the British Labour Party. Besides demanding a restoration of free speech, it called for the "democratic control of industry and commerce, by those who work by hand and brain, and the elimination of autocratic domination of the forces of production either by selfish private interests or bureaucratic agents of government, the equitable sharing of the proceeds among all who participate in any capacity and only among these...."[27]

The constitution of the American Labor Party of New York provided "that no candidate of the Labor Party shall accept endorsement of either the Democratic or the Republican parties nor of any other parties that stand for private ownership of public utilities; nor shall the Labor Party endorse any candidates of the above-mentioned parties." This, one observer noted, allowed "an endorsement of its candidates by the Socialist Party and *vice versa*."[28]

Labor parties appeared elsewhere, and by mid-1919, there were statewide organizations in Indiana, Pennsylvania, Kansas, Iowa, Idaho, Ohio, Michigan, Kentucky, California, and Montana, as well as the two main centers of independent political action, Illinois and New York. Twenty-three states had labor parties in 1920, with particularly strong ones in New York, Pennslyvania and Indiana. The movement gained the backing of the brewery workers, cigarmakers, bricklayers, carpenters, painters, molders, bakers, quarry workers, glass workers, machinists with a membership of 331,000, men's and women's clothing workers with a quarter of a million members, the United Mine Workers with 400,000 members, and the sixteen unions comprising the Railroad Brotherhoods of America, with 1.65 million members. In fact, the labor party movement was substantial enough to prompt Wisconsin's Progressive Senator Robert M. La Follette to seriously consider the party's presidential nomination in 1920.[29]

THE COMMITTEE OF FORTY-EIGHT

The move for a national labor party began as early as January 1919 with the formation of the Committee of Forty-Eight, composed of Eastern liberals and businessmen and promoted by the *New Republic*.[30] The plan was to organize a "political movement like the British Labour Party," to "keep in constant touch" with local labor parties "lining up" trade unionists and men outside of organized labor, single taxers, Bull Moosers, Nonpartisan Leaguers, and the like, and then merge "into one effective political instrument" when the time was ripe.[28]

To that end, the Committee of Forty-Eight recruited about a quarter of a million members in 1919 (although only 10,000 were "active"), distributed almost a million pieces of propaganda and set up organizations in more than a dozen states, with headquarters in Chicago.[31] It adopted a three-point platform that called for the restoration of all civil liberties, a single tax, "public ownership and democratic management of the means of transportation and communication, mines, finance, and all monopolies and natural resources."[32]

The Committee of Forty-Eight believed that political action through a labor party which could unite organized labor and its allies was a real possibility. In fact, a survey by the *New York Times* in December 1919 revealed that an alliance between organized labor, middle-class professionals, and farmers "was the talk of the people generally throughout the Middle West."[33]

THE NON-PARTISAN LEAGUE

The most important of these potential allies was the Non-Partisan League, created by Socialists in North Dakota who realized that the exploitation of the state's farmers by grain dealers, banks, and railroads had enraged innumerable life-long Republicans. The remedy envisaged by Arthur C. Townley and Arthur Le Sueur was to enter the Republican primaries with a disciplined organization of farmers and workers. The key to their approach was local meetings at which everyone who paid a dollar could help select one of their number for NPL endorsement in the primaries, a platform calling for state-owned banks, grain elevators and other marketing agencies, to which candidates were pledged, and a disciplined caucus of elected members.[34]

In the 1917 legislature, 72 of the 97 Republicans and 15 of the Democrats were in the NPL caucus. The 1919 session, where the NPL controlled both houses as well as Governor Lynn Frazier, created a state bank, grain elevators, hail insurance, workmen's compensation, income and inheritance taxes, home buyers' assistance, restrictions on injunctions in strikes, and the country's best mine safety law.[35]

The successes of the Non-Partisan League of North Dakota had an important effect on farmers in other areas. The League organizations gradually began to spread to all the neighboring states. In 1917, the National Non-Partisan League was founded, setting itself the task of uniting the efforts of all the local League organizations. By the end of 1918, the national organization had 188, 365 members. By 1920, it had reached 235,000.[36]

In 1917, in one of his speeches, Townley said: "The farmers control 35 percent of the vote of this country; labor controls about 27 percent; a combination of these two elements would make itself felt throughout the nation." In a number of the League's rural constituencies, the idea of a new party which would unite farmers and workers was opposed. Instead, they favored continuing to rely on controlling the primaries. But others, especially the labor sections of the League, believed they would benefit from a new party. They moved toward independent political action, convinced that the time was ripe for it.[37]

A NATIONAL LABOR PARTY

In the summer of 1919, the Committee of Forty-Eight, led by Herbert Croly, Amos Pinchot and Dudley Field Malone, issued a call summoning "from all parts of the country the leaders of its liberal thought and its forward-looking citizens to meet in conference." It was hoped that "from this assemblage of hitherto scattered forces for Americanism will come a flexible statement of principles and methods that will permit effective cooperation with organized labor and agricultural workers in the task of social reconstruction."[38] What actually did come from the meeting was a national labor party.

Late in November 1919, 1,200 delegates representing trade unions and labor party organizations, as well as non-labor groups such as single-taxers, farmers and intellectuals met in Chicago.[39] The labor delegates were men who advocated industrial organization, the nationalization of industry and comprehensive social insurance. A chief demand was that labor not be limited to bargaining with the existing system, but should rather control all future social change. "Labor will rule and the world will be free," they insisted.[40] As they saw it, thirty years of non-partisan political policy of the AFL had been thirty years of failure and had demonstrated that "we cannot deliver to the Democrats; we cannot deliver to the Republicans, and we cannot deliver to the Socialists. Now we have a right to see if we can deliver to ourselves." To John Fitzpatrick the conference was an opportunity for labor that "comes but once in a lifetime...to become a political force on its own account and for the benefit of the working people and their families."[41]

The unions present at the conference included the Amalgamated Clothing Workers, the International Ladies' Garment Workers, fur workers, brewery workers, quarry workers, glass workers, bakers, painters, miners, machinists, cigarmakers, printers and tailors, and the state federations of Pennsylvania, Illinois, Indiana, Missouri, Kansas and Wisconsin. Labor parties represented were those recently established in Illinois, Minnesota, New York, Ohio, South Dakota and Kansas. All of the unions represented had expressed admiration for the British Labour Party, and most had passed convention resolutions in the past two years labeling the AFL political program "a miserable failure" and urging independent political action on the part of "hand and brain workers."[42]

The National Constituent Convention of the national Labor Party opened in Chicago on November 22. Max Hayes of the International Typographical Union and John H. Walker and Frank Esper of the United Mine Workers were chosen chairman, vice-chairman and secretary, respectively, of the convention.[43]

"Labor," the convention declared, "is the primary and just basis of political responsibility and power. It is not merely the right but the duty of workers of hand and brain to become a party." The convention voted to participate in the coming presidential elections, deferring the nomination of candidates until 1920. The name of the new organization was to be the Labor Party of the United States.* Its object was to organize all brain and hand workers in support of the principle of political, social and industrial democracy.[44]

Although the convention deferred presidential nominations and the adoption of a platform until 1920, it did adopt a Declaration of Principles which emphasized many of the same points as the Chicago Federation of Labor platform, but was even more advanced than that document. For example, it affirmed the need to nationalize the basic industries, transport

---

*Until the summer of 1920, when it adopted the name Farmer-Labor Party, it variously called itself American Labor Party, U.S. Labor Party, and National Labor Party. (Stanley Shapiro, "'Hand and Brain': The Farmer-Labor Party of 1920," *Labor History* 26 [Summer 1985]: 413*n*.)

and the entire basic system. It also called for the democratization of the American political system by revising the Constitution, granting the people the right to legislative initiative and the right to recall elected Congressmen and substantially reducing the power of the Supreme Court, including the abrogation of its right to declare laws unconstitutional. Among specific demands of particular interest to labor were the demand for wages sufficient to enable workers to maintain themselves in good health and comfort; the abolition of unemployment through the further reduction of the hours of labor and through government activity during times of industrial depression, and the establishment of health, old age and maternity insurance and workmen's compensation throughout the country.[45]

Aside from the platforms of the Socialist and Communist Parties, the Declaration of Principles of the national Labor Party was clearly one of the most advanced documents of the period. The *Boston Herald* called it "Bolshevik" in principle, but the newspaper drew comfort from the fact that "radical as some of these declarations were, the convention voted down resolutions calling for the establishment of a *Soviet* government in the United States, and recommending the abolition of the Supreme Court."[46]

As for the formation of the national Labor Party itself, the Nashville *Tennessean* observed:

> There is no reason why we should become excited over this movement. It is a symptom of the industrial unrest from which we are rapidly passing. The ideals which animate its sponsors will be dead within a year, and with the return of prewar prosperity there will be no cause for the body's existence.[47]

But the Socialist *Cleveland Citizen* disagreed. "Those who assembled at Chicago burned their bridges behind them," it insisted, "and inaugurated a campaign that will not end until the Labor Party is in complete control of the machinery of government and incorporates its principles into the laws of the land."[48] The *New Majority*, official organ of the Chicago Labor Party and adopted by the convention as the official organ of the National Labor Party, also declared:

> It may not elect a President in 1920. This looks like a Republican year. But with the Democrats out of the way it should organize in four years so effectively that it can capture the Government of the United States for the workers of factory and farm in 1924, by the peaceful process of storming the ballot-box. It should send a few members to Congress at the coming election. It should capture state and local governments in many localities within the next two years.[49]

"The workers are through with the old parties," *New Majority* boldly asserted. The Republican Party had always been "the party of hateful, merciless exploitation of the wage-earners, both organized and unorganized," while the Democratic Party, within the last few years, "has shown how far it will go to grind its heel into the face of the workers when the bosses of big business crack the whip." The result was inevitable:

> Labor, organized and unorganized, labor of the farm as well as of the shop, has leapt to the fray for political war to the death with the crooks who rule this country by subsidizing its two old political parties in order that they may maintain their iron rule of industry and commerce from which they gorge themselves with profits that they can not spend, consigning the workers to poverty.[50]

THE FARMER-LABOR PARTY

Immediately after its founding convention, the national Labor Party launched a campaign to publicize its existence and its Declaration of Principles. Its appeals met with response among workers and farmers. New labor parties emerged in Iowa, Nebraska and Wyoming. In Minnesota, with the support of the State Federation of Labor, a Labor's Non-Partisan League was founded to become a sort of urban branch of the Farmers Non-Partisan League. Minnesota was the ideal setting for a farmer-labor alliance. Minneapolis was the site of the hated grain exchange, of flour milling and farm machinery; St. Paul and Duluth were manufacturing and shipping centers. The Mesabi iron range was peopled with militant miners from Finland, Croatia, Italy and the Ukraine as well as native-born Americans. Even the countryside was spotted with railroad junctions and meat-packing towns. Here the "Farmer-Labor Party" slogan found supporters among leading figures in the National Non-Partisan League who were not satisfied to rely only on dominating the primaries of the major parties.[51]

Early in 1920, the National Labor Party began making preparations for its second convention. It hoped to achieve unity with a number of radical farmers' organizations and to proclaim the formation of a Farmer-Labor Party.

The second Labor Party convention opened on July 11, 1920 in Chicago. In his keynote address, Fitzpatrick upbraided those who should have been the natural allies of labor in the new party movement but were not prepared to break with the existing major parties. He predicted that they would soon see the wisdom of independent political action. When that happened, he went on, nothing would be able to "prevent the present renderers of useful service in America [from] taking the reins out of the hands" of the men and women who controlled the national and international financial structures. What was involved in the new party movement, Fitzpatrick insisted, was a simple case of "men, women and children" against "greed, gold and avarice."

But unity did not come easily. The Committee of Forty-Eight was holding its own convention in Chicago at precisely the same time, and there was considerable sentiment there for the formation of a farmer-labor party. When it became clear that some of the committee's leaders were against this, the rank-and-file delegates made their feelings clear by joining the convention of the Labor Party.

Once they were at the Labor Party's convention, the Committee of Forty-Eight delegates clashed with the labor delegates over the party's Declaration of Principles. They objected to the demand for the nationalization of the basic industries. For the sake of preserving unity, Labor Party representatives agreed to concessions. While endorsing public ownership of the major industries like railroads (with an especially vigorous endorsement of the Plumb plan), coal mines, hydroelectric power plants, grain elevators, and telegraph and telephone, the party platform did not include a general demand for the nationalization of the basic industries. Having achieved this, the delegates from the Committee of Forty-eight ceased their opposition.

However, most of the delegates from the Non-Partisan League withdrew, led by Governor Frazier of North Dakota, after the convention went on record for the nationalization of unused land.[52]

A number of delegates also left when the convention decided to keep "hands off" the Prohibition issue. Prohibition had been instituted on January 16, 1920 with the ratification of the Eighteenth Amendment barring the "manufacture, sale or transportation of intoxicating liquors...." At a meeting in opposition to the proposed amendment, held in New York City's Madison Square Garden on May 24, 1919, Federated Union President Edward I. Hannah urged workers "to go first to the Republicans and Democrats for a redress of their grievances against the [Prohibition] Amendment." If "the traditional parties" refused to help, he urged, "then turn to an American Labor Party." But when the Labor Party also refused its aid, the "wet" delegates left in anger.[53]*

---

*Many unions were bitterly opposed to Prohibition, especially those whose very existence was threatened by it. There was even a strong movement for a general strike in a number of cities and states if beer was prohibited, but Gompers and other AFL leaders opposed it. (For a discussion of this issue, *see* Nuala McGann Drechsler, "Organized Labor and the Eighteenth Amendment," Labor History 8 [Fall 1967]: 280-99.)

Despite these withdrawals, the convention proceeded to organize the Farmer-Labor Party of the United States. It adopted a platform and nominated candidates for the forthcoming presidential election. Even with the concession to the Committee of Forty-Eight, the Farmer-Labor Party platform was an advanced document. It included demands for the recognition of Soviet Russia and the cessation of intervention against it, for recognition of the principle of self-determination for all oppressed nations, for democratization of the American political system, and for equal rights for Negroes. Basically, the Labor Party forces were strong enough to withstand the efforts of the Committee of Forty-Eight and other liberal reformers to water down the FLP platform.[54]

Governor Frazier of North Dakota, a leading figure in the Non-Partisan League, was reported to be the first choice for a presidential nominee of the new party. However, after his withdrawal from the convention, representatives of the Committee of Forty-Eight and some farmer delegates urged the convention to ask Senator Robert M. LaFollette to head the FLP ticket, but nothing came of this. In the end, the delegates chose Parley Parker Christensen, an attorney in Salt Lake City, as the party candidate for president and Max S. Hayes as his running mate. (John Fitzpatrick was nominated for senator from Illinois.) Christensen was a Utah lawyer who had gained a reputation with labor unions for his defense of trade unionism. Hayes was a Cleveland Socialist and had to resign from the Socialist Party in order to accept the nomination.[55]

Lacking funds and strong local organizations in many parts of the country, the Farmer-Labor Party was handicapped from the very outset, but the 265,000 votes Christensen received was even less than expected. Fitzpatrick polled only 50,749 in Illinois, and only 4,760 of these came from Cook County. In Chicago, the Socialists replaced the Labor Party as the third party, which accounted for the small vote Fitzpatrick received in the city. Most of his vote came from miners downstate.[56]

In the state of Washington, the Democrats had been reduced to insignificance in the September primaries and the Republicans and the Farmer-Laborites were the major contenders in the presidential and gubernatorial election of November 1920. With little money for campaigning, inadequate newspaper support, and labeled by the state's powerful newspapers as "disloyal, radical, subversive, and un-American," the Farmer-Labor Party faced incredible odds. Although the Farmer-Laborites were engulfed by the Republican Party, they captured a majority of the labor vote.[57]

GOMPERS AND THE LABOR PARTY MOVEMENT

The 1920 returns for the Farmer-Labor Party may have disappointed the militants, but they made Gompers jubilant. He called the "Farmer-Labor experiment...neither farmer nor labor, but merely a combination of foolishness and presumption."[58] As far as he was concerned, the returns fully justified the warning he had given those who favored a labor party. Addressing a labor conference in New York City on December 8, 1918 before leaving for the Peace Treaty meeting in Europe, Gompers had entitled his speech, "Should a Political Labor Party be Formed?" His answer was that, in view of the history of such ventures in both the United States and Europe, such a move should not even be considered. He insisted that all of these experiments, with no exception, had failed, and where some successes seemed to have attended their efforts, as in the case of some European countries, the trade union movement had found itself saddled with political issues which were often detrimental to labor's cause. The AFL's tried and proven policy of non-partisan political action, Gompers concluded, was the only effective path for labor to follow in the political arena.[59]

Gompers continued his attack on the idea of a labor party after the party became a reality in the fall of 1919. He brought pressure to bear on labor leaders of the AFL who espoused the labor party cause. A few days after the launching of the national Labor Party in December 1919, Gompers called a conference to mobilize support for the traditional non-partisan policy. Eighty-nine national and international unions affiliated with the AFL, together with the four Railroad Brotherhoods, were represented. The conference chose a special "non-partisan campaign committee" composed of the AFL Executive Council and the heads of its departments. One scholar has called this "the most extensive political campaign in the history of the AFL to defeat the legislative enemies of the workers and elect its friends."[60] But the principal motive behind the conference seems to have been to take the wind out of the Labor Party's sails. It was with justification that the *New Majority*, the organ of the Labor Party, declared: "The AFL is trying to scare everyone to death who dares to rise up and oppose its political ideas."[61]

Gompers also took more direct steps. The Central Federated Union of New York had endorsed the Labor Party by referendum. Gompers thereupon induced the Brooklyn Central Labor Union to withdraw its support and to maneuver to bring about the abandonment of the CFU's endorsement. By a vote of 22 to 18, conservatives in the CFU carried a motion repudiating the earlier endorsement of the Labor Party and supporting the non-partisan policy of the AFL.[62]

When the Indiana Labor Party dared to criticize the AFL's non-partisan political policy after it had been sharply criticized by Gompers, the AFL Executive Council publicly and bitterly rebuked it:

> By what right do you assume to declare the work and the policy of the American Federation of Labor to be impractical? Surely the results achieved in the interests of the workers demonstrate the utter fallacy of your assumption....
>
> Your telegram is an affront to the labor movement and an assault upon the interests of that great body of Americans who are determined that the present campaign shall result, not in the destruction of our liberties, but in the opening of the way to national progress and the achievement of opportunities for human welfare, safety and happiness.[63]

The Chicago Federation of Labor immediately came to the support of the Indiana Labor Party, and replied: "Mr. Gompers and the executive council have confessed again and again the futility and failure of the 'defeat your friends and reward your enemies' [sic]* plan whereby Mr. Gompers seeks again to juggle the labor vote around between the old parties."[64]

THE RAILROAD BROTHERHOODS

The sad experience of the Railroad Brotherhoods in Congress with respect to the Plumb Plan aroused the normally conservative chiefs of the rail unions to action. In response to the crisis, sixteen of these leaders met late in 1919 with the leaders of the United Mine Workers and agreed to a program of political action demanding the nationalization of both the coal mines and the railroads. However, they also decided to neither establish nor endorse a labor party. Instead, they would use the direct primary to elect sympathetic senators and representatives. The six hundred branches of the Plumb Plan League provided the nucleus for an organization that would intervene in the primaries to defeat the movement's "enemies" and nominate and elect its "friends."[65]

Thus, the Labor Party movement's labor elements consisted largely of those members of the AFL and the Railroad Brotherhoods who opposed the policy of non-partisan political action. On the other hand, the top leaders of the AFL and the Railroad Brotherhoods devoted nearly all of their time in 1920 to the non-partisan campaign. The philosophy behind the campaign, of course, was not new; it was much the same as it had been ever since the AFL's first efforts along this line in 1906—"the defeat of the enemies of the people and the election of their friends." In 1920, however,

*The actual words were "Reward our friends, and defeat our enemies."

the campaign was organized more thoroughly. In January, at the request of the AFL Executive Council, Gompers established the National Non-Partisan Campaign Platform Committee, and in March, it was made a permanent standing committee of the Federation.[66]

A month later, each local union of the AFL was asked to "appoint a committee of three to work in harmony with the central labor body committees in their localities" in the forthcoming presidential campaign. Circulars such as "Legislative Achievements of the AFL" and "Forty Years of Action: Non-Partisan Political Policy of the American Federation of Labor" were mailed to all union members, as well as letters of instructions on how to vote. At the Washington office of the AFL, fifty-five questions relating to issues of interest to labor were drawn up, and both the Democratic and Republican platform committees were requested to answer them.[67]

Although neither party's answers were exactly what the AFL was looking for, Gompers concluded in a letter he mailed to the editors of all major newspapers on July 13:

> In summarizing, it is fair to say that the Democratic platform marks a measure of progress not found in the platform of the Republican Party. In relation to labor's proposals, the planks written into the Democratic platform more nearly approximate the desired declarations of human rights than do the planks found in the Republican platform.[68]

THE AFL, THE RR BROTHERHOODS AND THE 1920 ELECTION

In the columns of the *American Federationist*, Gompers was even more definite in his opposition to the Republican Party. "The Republican Party, in its platform declarations and through the political character of the candidates nominated," he wrote, "has taken its position as an unqualified defender of the enemies of Labor."[69]

As for the presidential candidates—Warren G. Harding (Republican) and James M. Cox (Democrat)—Gompers observed:

> There can be but one conclusion based upon a careful and impartial survey of the actions and declarations of the candidates. Governor Cox has shown himself possessed of a fuller understanding of the needs and of the problems of the industrial world.[70]

As the national campaign entered its final months, the AFL support for the Democratic Party and its presidential candidate became even more pronounced. Meanwhile, however, the Railroad Brotherhoods had decided to concentrate on the congressional rather than the presidential campaign. In July 1920, the sixteen heads of the railroad unions issued a "Call to Political Action." "It is of paramount importance," declared the preamble, "that a progressive Congress be elected [because] the powers of Wealth and Privilege will fight even more bitterly to elect a privilege-controlled Congress than a reactionary president."[71]

The railroad chiefs also chose a campaign committee to help elect "friendly" congressmen and to defeat anyone who had voted for the Transportation Act, and in particular its authors—Representative John J. Esch of Wisconsin and Senator Albert Cummins of Iowa.

After such extensive efforts by the AFL and the Railroad Brotherhoods, the results of the November voting must have been as disappointing to the officials of the Federation and the Brotherhoods as to the leaders of the Farmer-Labor Party. Governor Cox was able to garner only 34.1 percent of the total popular vote, resulting in a most decisive victory for Harding. Esch was defeated, but the attempt to defeat Cummins narrowly failed. Moreover, while labor eliminated a number of its worst enemies from Congress, it elected few of its friends. Even Gompers admitted that not more than 50 representatives out of 435 could be relied upon as friends of labor.[72]

Having helped to weaken the movement for labor's independent political action, Gompers had approached the 1920 election with a good deal of enthusiasm. "It is to be a wonderful campaign," he wrote to a labor official in March 1920, "something that will go down as a memorable milestone in the history of Labor."[73]

When the ballots were tabulated, however, *Labor*'s headline read: "Big Business Grabs Presidency, Senate and House." And the lead article of the *American Federationist* appeared under the caption, "Reaction in the Saddle."[74]

The Farmer-Labor Party organized at the end of the First World war never recovered from the debacle of the 1920 election. But as we shall see in our next volume, the idea of independent political action by labor, the idea of a national Farmer-Labor Party, did not die.

CHAPTER 1

1. Florence Peterson, *Strikes in the U.S., 1880-1936,* U.S. Department of Labor, Bulletin No. 61, Washington, D.C., 1938, p. 21 and Table 18, p. 39
2. *Literary Digest,* Oct. 25, 1919, p.11
3. *Outlook* 119 (Oct. 29, 1919): 224
4. Paul H. Douglas, *Real Wages in the United States, 1890-1926,* New York, 1930, pp. 57, 58
5. C.J. Hendley, "The Effect of World War on American Labor," prepared by the Workers' Education Bureau, *Labor Age,* March 1926, p. 22
6. Douglas, p. 57
7. *Industrial News Survey,* 3 (April 21-28, 1919): 1
8. Peterson, p. 391
9. Herbert Lahne, *The Cotton Mill Worker,* New York and Toronto, pp. 137-38; Robert S. Lynd, "Done in Oil," *Survey* 48 (Nov. 1, 1922): 137-46; "One Day's Rest in Seven," *Social Service Bulletin* 13 (Nov. 1923): 12-18; *Wages and Hours of Labor in Cotton-Goods Manufacturing, 1910-1930,* Bulletin of the Bureau of Labor Statistics, No. 59, Washington, D.C., 1931, pp. 2-9; "Hours of Labor in the Iron and Steel Industry," *Monthly Labor Review* 30 (June 1930): 182-97; Garth L. Mangum, *The Operating Engineers: The Economic History of a Trade Union,* Cambridge, Mass., 1964, p. 120
10. Grace Hutchins, *Labor and Silk,* New York, 1931, p. 120
11. Peterson, p. 391
12. *American Labor Year Book, 1919-1920,* New York, 1921, p. 265; V.I. Lenin, *Collected Works,* Moscow, 1965, vol. 28, p. 224
13. David Montgomery, "Immigrants, Industrial Unions, and Social Reconstruction in the United States, 1916-1923," *Labour/Le Travail,* 13 (Spring 1984): 103
14. *Labor Herald* (Kansas City, Mo.), Jan. 25, 1918
15. *Ibid.,* March 1, 1918
16. Edwin Wildman, editor, *Reconstructing America,* Boston, 1919, pp. 226-31; Elish M. Friedman, editor, *American Problems of Reconstruction,* New York, 1919, pp. 47-49
17. Wildman, *op, cit.,* p. 224
18. *New York Times,* June 25, 28, Sept. 28, 1919; *The Forum* 62 (Aug. 1919): 191
19. Ray Stannard Baker and William E. Dodd, editors, *Presidential Messages, Addresses, and Public papers of Woodrow Wilson, 1917-1924,* (New York, 1927) 1: 488
20. *New York Times,* April 13, 1919; *Monthly Labor Review,* Feb. 1919, p. 69; *Iron Age,* Nov. 28, 1918, p. 1323; E. Jay Howenstine, Jr., *The Economics of Demobilization,* Washington, D.C., 1944, p. 150; *Proceedings,* AFL Convention, 1919, p. 303
21. James R. Green, *The World of the Worker: Labor in Twentieth Century America,* New York, 1980, p. 94
22. Arnon Gutfield, *Montana's Agony: Years of War and Hysteria, 1917-1921,* Gainesville, Fla., 1979, p. 76
23. *Labor Herald* (K.C., Mo.), Dec. 27, 1918, Feb. 16, 1919.
24. Montgomery, p. 103
25. *New Republic* 13 (July 30, 1919): 405; *Literary Digest,* Aug. 30, 1919, p. 17
26. *Congressional Record,* 66th Cong., 2nd Sess., 1919, p. 6879; John Finney, Jr., "A Study of Negro Labor During and After World War I," unpublished Ph.D. dissertation, Georgetown University, 1957, pp. 253-67
27. Baker and Dodd, editors, *op. cit.,* vol. 1, pp. 588-89; *New York Times,* Sept. 1, 1919; *Proceedings of the First Industrial Conference, October 6 to 23, 1919,* Washington, D.C., 1920, p. 248
28. *New York Times,* Sept. 5, 1919
29. *Ibid.,* Sept. 18, Oct. 5, 1919
30. Haggai Hurvitz, "Ideology and Industrial Conflict: President Wilson's First Industrial Conference of October 1919," *Labor History* 18 (Fall 1977): 514
31. *New York Times,* Sept. 18, 1919
32. *New Republic* 13 (Oct. 1, 1919): 242
33. *New York Times,* Oct. 9, 1919
34. *Ibid.,* Oct. 7, 1919
35. Baker and Dodd, editors, *op. cit.,* vol. 2, p. 427
36. *New York Times,* Oct. 10, 1919
37. *Proceedings of the First Industrial Conference....,* pp. 115, 116, 145; Hurvitz, pp. 517-18
38. *New York Times,* Oct. 17, 1919, *Proceedings,* AFL Convention, 1920. p. 83
39. *The Survey,* Oct. 25, 1919, pp. 36-39; *New York Times,* Oct. 10, 17, 1919
40. *Proceedings of the First Industrial Conference....,* pp. 82, 158, 185, 196, 251
41. Hurvitz, p. 519
42. *Commercial and Financial Chronicle,* Oct. 14, 25, 1919; *Iron Trade Review,* Oct. 23, 1919
43. *Proceedings of the First Industrial Conference....pp.* 174-75, 250; National Industrial Conference Board, *Statement of Principles Which Should Govern the Employment Relations in Industry: Sub-*

mitted by the Employer Group to the Industrial Conference at Washington, D.C., Oct. 10, 1919, Boston, n.d., pp. 5-6

44. *Statement of Principles*, p. 5; *Proceedings of the First Industrial Conference....* pp. 260, 267

45. Hurvitz, p. 521

46. *Ibid.*, p. 524

47. National Industrial Conference Board, *The Vital Issues in the Industrial Conference at Washington, D.C.*, Boston, n.d., p. 15

48. *Life and Labor*, Jan. 1919, pp. 19-20; *New York Times*, March 28, 1919; *Seattle Union Record*, March 29, 1919; Elizabeth Rhodes Butler, "A Study of the Cost of Living in New York City in 1918, as It Affects the Low-Wage Working Woman," Master's thesis, Columbia University, 1919, pp. 11-12, 42

49. *See* Mrs. Rosa A. Smith, *Labor*, Los Angeles, March 6, 1920

50. *New York Times*, Feb. 8, 9, 27, 1919; *Commercial and Financial Chronicle*, Feb. 15, 1919

51. *New York Times*, July 24, 1919; *New York World*, July 23-24, 1919

52. *New York Times*, Aug. 17, 18, 19, 23, 31, Sept. 7, 1919; Alfred Harding, *The Revolt of the Actors*, New York, 1919, pp. 7-10

53. *Literary Digest*, Dec. 7, 1918, p. 17

54. *New Majority*, June 19, 1920

55. *Ibid.*, July 3, 1920

56. Stanley Shapiro, "'Hand and Brain': The Farmer-Labor Party of 1920," *Labor History* 26 (Summer 1985): 407

57. Robert H. Zeiger, *Republicans and Labor, 1919-1929*, Lexington, Ky., 1969, p. 19

58. John F. Keiser, *John Fitzpatrick and Progressive Unionism, 1915-1925*, Evanston, Ill., 1965, p. 39

59. Montgomery, pp. 105-06

60. R.A. Rosenstone, *Romantic Revolutionary: A Biography of John Reed*, New York, 1975, p. 343

61. David Montgomery, *Workers' Control in America: Studies in the History of Work, Technology, and Labor Struggles*, Cambridge, England, 1979, p. 124

62. Montgomery, "Immigrants, Unions & Reconstruction," pp. 110-11.

63. *Labor Herald* (K.C., Mo.), Jan. 31, 1919

64. Curt Gentry, *Frame-Up: The Incredible Case of Tom Mooney and Warren Billings*, New York, 1967, p. 261

65. *Labor Herald* (K.C., Mo.), Jan. 31, 1919

66. Gentry, p. 263

67. *Labor Herald*, (K.C., Mo.), May 25, June 14, 1919

68. *New York Times*, July 5-10, 1919; Montgomery, "Immigrants, Unions & Reconstruction," p. 113. For a discussion of workplace organization, *see* David Montgomery, "New Tendencies in Union Struggles and Strategies in Europe and the United States, 1916-1922," James E. Cronin and Carmen J. Sirianni, editors, *Work, Community, and Power*, Philadelphia, 1983, pp. 88-116.

69. Stanley Shapiro, "The Great War and Reform: Liberals and Labor, 1917-19," *Labor History* 12 (1971): 327-29

70. John A. Fitch, "Lawrence: A Strike for Wages or Bolshevism?" *Survey* 42 (April 5, 1919): 45

71. Report of Harvey Karture, March 7, 1919, in "Lawrence Textile Strike," RG, 65, File .3434501, National Archives; David Joseph Goldberg, "Immigrants, Intellectuals and Industrial Unions: The 1919 Textile Strikes and the Experience of the Amalgamated Textile Workers of America in Passaic and Paterson, New Jersey and Lawrence, Massachusetts," unpublished Ph.D. dissertation, Columbia University, 1984, p. 288.

72. Quoted in J.B.S. Hardman, *American Labor Dynamics*, New York, 1928, p. 12

73. *Ibid.*

74. *Proceedings*, AFL Convention, 1919, p. 272; David Brody, *Steelworkers in America*, Cambridge, Mass., 1960, p. 247

75. Donald Richberg, *My Hero*, New York, 1954, pp. 113-14; Allen La Verne Shepherd, "Federal Railway Labor Policy, 1913-1926," unpublished Ph.D. thesis, University of Nebraska, 1971, pp. 180-81

76. Plumb Plan League, *The A.B.C. of the Plumb Plan*, Washington, D.C., 1919; Glenn E. Plumb, "Labor's Solution to the Railroad Problem," *Nation* 109 (Aug. 16, 1919): 200-01

77. Shepherd, p. 182; *Railroad Clerk* 18 (Feb. 1919): 65; *Railroad Worker* 17 (June 1919): 45

78. *Labor Herald* (K.C., Mo.), Feb. 28, 1919

79. *Cleveland Citizen*, Sept. 12, 1919; Shepherd, pp. 180-81

80. Samuel Gompers, *Seventy Years of Life and Labor: An Autobiography*, New York, 1924, 2: 148, 521-22

81. Frederick C. Howe, *The Confessions of a Reformer*, New York, 1925, pp. 325-26; Shepherd, pp. 183-84; New York *Call* quoted in *Literary Digest*, Aug. 26, 1919, p. 13

82. *Railroad Democracy*, July 21, Sept. 4, 1919; *Labor*, Oct. 18, 25, Nov. 1, Dec. 27, 1919

83. *Labor Herald* (K.C., Mo.) Sept. 1, 1919
84. *Literary Digest*, Aug. 16, 1919, p. 9
85. *New York Times*, Aug. 7, 8, 9, 13, 1919
86. *Congressional Record*, 66th Congress, 1st Session, pp. 3586, 8315-25; Shepherd, pp. 187-88
87. Green, *World of the Workers*, p. 95

CHAPTER 2

1. *Labor Herald* (Kansas City, Mo.), April 25, 1919
2. Robert K. Murray, *Red Scare: A Study in National Hysteria 1919-1920*, Minneapolis, 1953, p. 82; Hugh T. Lovin, "Idaho and the 'Reds,' 1919-1926," *Pacific Northwest Quarterly* 69 (1978): 107-08, 112
3. Robert W. Dunn in *Science & Society* (1973): 246-47
4. David A. McMurray, "The Willys Overland Strike, 1919," *Northwest Ohio Quarterly* 37 (Spring 1965): 35-42
5. Murray, pp. 72-73
6. Boston *Evening Transcript*, May 2, June 15, 1919; Murray, p. 74.
7. *New York Times*, May 2, 1919
8. "May Day Rioting," *Nation* 108 (May 10, 1919): 43-45; New York *Call*, May 2, 1919; Murray, p. 75
9. Cleveland *Plain Dealer*, May 2, 1919
10. *Ibid.*; Philip S. Foner, *May Day: A Short History...* New York, 1986, pp. 85-87
11. Philip L. Cook, "Red Scare in Denver," *Colorado Magazine* 43 (Fall 1966): 316
12. *Ibid.*
13. *Ibid.*
14. *Ibid.*
15. William Preston, Jr., *Aliens and Dissenters: Federal Suppression of Radicals, 1903-1933*, Cambridge, Mass., 1963, pp. 183-84; Lovin, pp. 108-09; Cook, p. 318
16. W. Anthony Gengarelly, "Secretary of Labor William B. Wilson and the Red Scare, 1919-1920," *Pennsylvania History*, Oct. 1980, pp. 320-22
17. Preston, Jr., pp. 80-151, 183, 184
18. "Investigation Activities of the Justice Department, 1919," *Senate Document 253*, 66th Congress, 1st Session, 1919; *Report of the Attorney General, 1920*, Washington, D.C., 1921, pp. 172-73; Preston, Jr., pp. 319-20
19. Emma Goldman and Alexander Berkman to "Dear Comrades," Jan. 10, 1920, Workers Defense Collection, in Elizabeth Gurley Flynn Papers, State Historical Society of Wisconsin.
20. Constantine M. Panunzio, *The Deportation Cases of 1919-1920*, New York, 1921, pp. 18-45
21. Murray, pp. 196-97; Stanley Coben, *A. Mitchell Palmer: Politician*, New York, 1972, pp. 219-28; Robert D. Worth, "The Palmer Raids," *South Atlantic Quarterly* 48 (Jan. 1944): 1-23; David Williams, "'Sowing the Wind': The Deportation Raids of 1920 in New Hampshire," *Historical New Hampshire* 34 (Spring 1979): 20; David Williams, "The Bureau of Investigation and Its Critics, 1919-1921; The Origins of Federal Political Surveillance," *Journal of American History* 68 (Dec. 1981): 561-62
22. *New York Times*, Jan. 4, 1920
23. William Anthony Gengarelly, "Resistance Spokesmen: Opponents of the Red Scare," Unpublished Ph.D. dissertation, Boston University, 1972, pp. 110-23
24. *Survey* 43 (Jan. 23, 1920): 501-04; *Nation*, Jan. 17, 1920, pp. 249-52
25. *New Republic*, Jan. 28, 1920, pp. 249-52
26. Williams, "The Bureau of Investigation," p. 568
27. Louis F. Post, *The Deportations Delirium of Nineteen-Twenty: A Personal Narrative of an Historic Official Experience*, New York, 1970, p. 90.
28. Gengarelly, "Wilson and the Red Scare," p. 326; *Congressional Record*, 66th Congress, 2nd Session, pp. 5559-61
29. U.S. Congress, House Committee on Rules, *Investigation of Administration of Louis F. Post, Assistant Secretary of Labor, in the Matter of Deportation of Aliens*, 66th Congress, 2nd Session, pp. 74-81, 226-27
30. Gengarelly, "Wilson and the Red Scare," p. 327
31. Panunzio, pp. 180-92; Post, p. 110
32. Edward J. Muzik, "Victor Berger, Congress and the Red Scare," *Wisconsin Magazine of History* 47 (Summer 1964): 308-10
33. Julian F. Jaffe, *Crusade Against Radicalism: New York During the Red Scare, 1914-1924*, Port Washington, N.Y., 1972, pp. 30-98
34. Stanley Coben, "A Study of Nativism: The American Red Scare of 1919-1920," *Political Science Quarterly* 59 (Spring 1964): 92-95
35. Art Shields, *On the Battle Lines, 1919-1939*, New York, 1986, p. 30
36. Felix Frankfurter, *The Case of Sacco-Vanzetti*, Boston, 1927, pp. 38-40
37. *Ibid.*, pp. 68-72
38. *Boston Globe*, Aug. 24, 1977; *New York Times*, Aug. 24, 1977
39. William Young and David E. Kaiser, *Postmortem: New Evidence in the Case of*

Sacco and Vanzetti, Amherst, Mass., 1985
40. J.M. Pawa, "Black Radicals and White Spies: Harlem, 1919," *Negro History Bulletin* 37 (Oct. 1975): 129-32
41. *Revolutionary Radicalism*, Report of the Joint Legislative Committee (Lusk), April 20, 1920, Albany, 1920, vol. I, p. 14
42. *Ibid.*, pp. 958-59
43. *Ibid.*, vol. 4, p. 3282
44. *Garment Worker*, Oct. 31, 1919; Interview with J.E. Roach, in charge of New York office, American Federation of Labor, Feb. 17th, 1919, David J. Saposs Papers, State Historical Society of Wisconsin
45. *The Carpenter*, May, December, 1919
46. *Labor Herald* (K.C., Mo.), Feb. 28, 1919
47. Philip S. Foner, *Organized Labor and the Black Worker, 1619-1981*, New York, 1981, p. 5
48. Quoted in Kenneth C. Weinberg, *A Man's Home, A Man's Castle*, New York, 1971, p. 5
49. *New York Times*, Feb. 22, 1920
50. Arthur I. Waskow, *From Race Riot to Sit-In: A Study of Connections Between Conflict and Violence*, New York, 1966, pp. 4-35; William M. Tuttle, Jr., *Race Riot: Chicago in the Red Summer of 1919*, New York, 1970; *American History Illustrated* 6 (July 1971): 33-43
51. Chicago Commission on Race Relations, *The Negro in Chicago: A Study of Race Relations and a Race Riot*, Chicago, 1922
52. Lester C. Lamon, "Tennessee Race Relations and the Knoxville Riot of 1919," East Tennessee Historical Society *Publications* 41 (1969): 67-85; Lester C. Lamon, *Black Tennesseans, 1900-1930*, Knoxville, 1977, pp. 243-55
53. O.A. Rogers, Jr., "The Elaine Race Riots of 1919," *Arkansas Historical Quarterly* 19 (Summer 1960): 140-42; Walter White, "Massacring Whites in Arkansas," *Nation* 109 (1919): 715-16
54. Rogers, p. 144; "The Real Causes of Two Race Riots," *Crisis* 23 (1919): 56-57
55. Rogers, p. 145; Ida B. Wells-Barnett, *The Arkansas Riot*, Chicago, 1920, pp. 118-51
56. Wells-Barnett, pp. 144, 146-47
57. Rogers, pp. 146-47
58. *Arkansas Gazette*, Oct. 8, 1919, quoted in Rogers, p. 148
59. Rogers, pp. 148-49
60. *Ibid.*
61. *Ibid.*, p. 149
62. *Ibid.*, pp. 149-50
63. J.S. Waterman and E.E. Overton, "The Aftermath of Moore v. Dempsey," *Arkansas Law Review* 6 (Winter 1951-1952): 1-7; Wells-Barnett, 3-5
64. Rogers, p. 159
65. Quoted in *ibid.*
66. Lloyd M. Abernathy, "The Washington Race Riot of July, 1919," *Maryland Historical Magazine* 58 (Dec. 1963): 318-20.
67. *Crisis* 9 (Nov. 1919): 339
68. *The Liberator*, 2 (July 1919): 21
69. Chicago Commission on Race Relations, *The Negro in Chicago*, pp. 25-26; Waskow, pp. 88-90
70. William M. Tuttle, Jr., "Violence in 'Heathen' Land: The Longview Race Riot of 1919," *Phylon* 33 (1972): 324

CHAPTER 3

1. "The Dawn of Russian Freedom," *American Federationist*, April 1917, p. 286; *Knights of Labor*, March 1917, p. 2; Philip S. Foner, *The Bolshevik Revolution: Its Impact on American Radicals, Liberals, and Labor*, New York, 1967, pp. 14-15
2. Philip Taft, *The AF of L. in the Time of Gompers*, New York, 1957, pp. 444-45
3. Resolution adopted by meeting held at Ferrer Center, New York City, April 29, 1917, copy of leaflet in possession of author; Foner, *Bolshevik Revolution*, p. 15
4. Christopher Lasch, *The American Liberal and the Russian Revolution*, New York, 1962, p. 44; Ronald Radosh, "American Labor and the Root Mission to Russia," *Studies on the Left* 3 (1962): 42-43; *American Federationist*, Sept. 1917, pp. 744-45; George Kennan, *Russia and the West Under Lenin and Stalin*, Boston, 1961, pp. 25-26
5. William A. Williams, *American-Russian Relations, 1781-1947*, New York, 1952, p. 86
6. *Ibid.*, pp. 92-94; Foner, *Bolshevik Revolution*, pp. 17-18
7. V.I. Lenin, *Collected Works* 36: Moscow, 1964, p. 236
8. William A. Williams, "American Intervention in Russia, 1917-1920," *Studies on the Left* 4 (1963): 56
9. Benjamin D. Rhodes, "The Anglo-America Intervention at Archangel, 1918-1919," *International History Review* 8 (Aug. 1986): 370-72
10. *Ibid.*, pp. 371-75; *New York Times*, Feb. 1, 5, 8, 15, 21, 1919.
11. *Kansas City (Mo.) Star*, April 10, 1919
12. *Ibid.*
13. *Rhodes*, p. 386
14. *Ibid.*, p. 387
15. Frederick L. Schuman, *American Policy*

Toward Russia Since 1917: A Study of Diplomatic History, International Law and Public Opinion, New York, 1928, p. 137; Louis Fischer, *Why Recognize Russia?* New York, 1931, p. 248

16. Simeon Larson, "Opposition to AFL Foreign Policy: A Labor Mission to Russia, 1927," *Historian* 43 (May 1980): 346

17. Donald F. Wieland, "American Labor and Russia," unpublished M.A. thesis, University of Wisconsin, Madison, 1948, p. 10; Bernard Gronert, "The Impact of the Russian Revolution upon the A.F. of L., 1917-1928," M.A. thesis, University of Wisconsin, Madison, 1948, p. 12

18. Margaret Hardy, *The Influence of Organized Labor on the Foreign Policy of the United States*, Liege, Belgium, 1936, p. 78

19. Foner, *Bolshevik Revolution*, p. 18.

20. *American Federationist* 26 (Dec. 1919)

21. Wieland, p. 4

22. *Ibid.*, pp. 4-5

23. *Proceedings*, AFL Convention, 1919, pp. 232-34

24. *Ibid.*, pp. 225-27, 246

25. *American Federationist*, July 1919

26. *Ibid.*, Aug. 1919

27. *Proceedings*, AFL Convention, 1920, pp. 357-63, 368, 371, 372

28. International Ladies' Garment Workers' Union, *Report and Proceedings of the 14th Convention*, 1918, pp. 42-43

29. *Justice*, Jan. 23, 1920, p. 2; June 4, 1920, pp. 2, 4; June 25, 1920, pp. 2-3; July 18, 1920, pp. 6-7; Nov. 19, 1920, p. 5; *Advance*, Nov. 19, 1920

30. New York *Evening Call*, June 6, 1918

31. *Advance*, June 14, 1918, p. 1; March, 1922, p. 4; Dec. 1922, p. 4

32. Gronert, p. 16; *Garment Worker*, June 27, July 25, Oct. 20, 1919

33. Foner, *Bolshevik Revolution*, p. 40

34. Charles P. LeWarne, "The Bolsheviks Land in Seattle: The *Shilka* Incident of 1917," *Arizona and the West* 20 (Summer 1978): 107-22

35. *Seattle Union Record*, Feb. 2, 1918

36. Le Warne, p. 120; Foner, *Bolshevik Revolution*, pp. 64-66

37. *Seattle Union Record*, Sept. 20, 1919; *Industrial Worker*, Sept. 27, 1919

38. *Portland Oregonian*, Sept. 28, 1919; *Baltimore Sun*, Sept. 30, 1919

39. LeWarne, p. 120; Foner, *Bolshevik Revolution*, pp. 64-66

40. *Defense News Bulletin*, Dec. 8, 1917

41. *Industrial Worker*, Jan. 26, Feb. 2, 1918

42. *Ibid.*, May 4, 1918

43. *Solidarity*, Aug. 14, 21, 1920; William D.

Haywood, *Bill Haywood's Book*, New York, 1929, p. 360

44. Paul R. Brissenden, *The IWW: A Study of American Syndicalism*, New York, 1919, p. 373

45. Foner, *Bolshevik Revolution*, pp. 32-33

46. *The Communist*, Chicago, Ill., Oct. 18, 1919

47. *The Ohio Socialist*, Nov. 19, 1919

48. *Advance*, Nov. 19, 1920, p. 7

49. Lasch, p. 121

50. Schuman, p. 34

51. *Advance*, Dec. 17, 1920

52. *Relations with Russia. Hearings before the Committee on Foreign Relations, United States Senate, Sixty-Sixth Congress, Third Session, on S.J. Res. 164, A Resolution Providing for the Establishment of Trade Relations with Russia, And So Forth*, Washington, D.C., 1921, pp. 29, 55-60

53. *Ibid.*

54. *Tampa Morning Tribune*, July 29, 1920

55. Samuel Gompers and William E. Walling, *Out of Their Own Mouths: A Revelation and an Indictment of Sovietism*, New York, 1921, p. vii

56. *Justice*, June 25, 1920, pp. 2-3; New York *Call*, Nov. 7, 1919

57. *Recent History of the Labor Movement in the United States, 1918-1939*, Moscow, 1977, pp. 67, 68

CHAPTER 4

1. Robert L. and Robin Friedheim, "The Seattle Labor Movement, 1919-1920," *Pacific Northwest Quarterly*, October 1964, p. 147

2. *Rebel Worker*, March 1, 1919, quoted in *ibid.*, p. 148

3. Freidheim and Freidheim, *op. cit.*, p. 152

4. *Ibid.*, p. 147

5. Robert L. Friedheim, *The Seattle General Strike*, Seattle, 1964, pp. 50-57; *Seattle Union Record*, Dec. 11, 1918

6. Wilfrid Harris Crook, *The General Strike: A Study in Labor's Tragic Weapon in Theory and Practice*, Chapel Hill, N. Car., 1931, p. 530; Robert L. Friedheim, "Prologue to a General Strike: The Seattle Shipyard Strike in 1919," *Labor History* 4 (Spring 1965): 130-32

7. Friedheim, *The Seattle General Strike*, p. 71

8. *The Survey*, March 8, 1919, p. 822

9. Friedheim, *Seattle...*, p. 75; Friedheim, "Prologue to a General Strike," p. 139

10. *Seattle Union Record*, Jan. 21, 23, 1919

11. Friedheim, "Prologue...," p. 140

12. *Union Record*, Feb. 1, 1919

13. *Ibid.*, Feb. 3, 1919

14. *Ibid.*, Feb. 5, 1919
15. *Ibid.*, Jan. 26, 27, 1919; Seattle *Post-Intelligencer*, Jan. 21, 1919
16. *Post-Intelligencer*, Jan. 26, 1919
17. Quoted in Friedheim, "Prologue to a General Strike," p. 142
18. *Union Record*, Sept. 26, 1919
19. Friedheim, *Seattle..*, pp. 81-82
20. *Post-Intelligencer*, Jan. 30, 1919; Friedheim, *Seattle...*, pp. 90, 202.
21. Friedheim, *Seattle...*, pp. 91-93
22. *Ibid.*, p. 111
23. Harvey O'Connor, *Revolution in Seattle: A Memoir*, New York, 1964, pp. 132-33, 143; Friedheim, *Seattle...*, p. 101
24. Friedheim, *Seattle...*, p. 107
25. O'Connor, p. 150
26. Anna Louise Strong, *The Seattle General Strike*, Seattle, n.d., p. 23
27. *Ibid.*, pp. 24-26; Friedheim, *Seattle...*, pp. 118-21
28. Friedheim, *Seattle...*, p. 122
29. Crook, p. 532
30. Strong, p. 28; John S. Gambs, *The Decline of the I.W.W.*, New York, 1932, pp. 33-35; Friedheim, *Seattle...*, p. 124
31. Crook, p. 535; Strong, p. 46; Friedheim, *Seattle...*, p. 135
32. "Side Lights on Seattle Strike," *Ohio Socialist*, Feb. 19, 1919
33. Selig Perlman and Philip Taft, *History of Labor in the United States, 1896-1932*, New York, 1935, p. 443
34. Crook, p. 535
35. O'Connor, p. 138
36. Friedheim, *Seattle...*, p. 132
37. Quoted in O'Connor, p. 138
38. *Outlook*, March 5, 1919, p. 377
39. Cincinnati *Times Star*, Feb. 11, 1919
40. *New York Times*, Feb. 8, 1919
41. Friedheim, *Seattle...*, pp. 137-38
42. *American Federationist* 26 (March 1919): pp. 243-44
43. Strong, pp. 37-38
44. *Ibid.*, pp. 38-42; Friedheim, *Seattle...*, pp. 141-43
45. *Ibid.*, pp. 144-45
46. Strong, p. 39
47. *American Federationist*, 26 (March 1919): 243
48. *Ibid.*
49. Cincinnati *Times Star*, Feb. 11, 1919
50. *New York Times*, Feb. 11, 1919
51. "Side Lights on Seattle Strike," *Ohio Socialist*, Feb. 19, 1919
52. Friedheim, *Seattle General Strike*, p. 111
53. *Literary Digest*, March 1919, p. 15
54. Friedheim, *Seattle General Strike*, pp. 163-64
55. Crook, *op. cit.*, p. 540

56. Warren Stanley Grum, "Employer Association Development in Seattle and Vicinity," unpublished Ph.D. thesis, University of Washington, 1948, pp. 5-6
57. Quoted in Friedheim, *Seattle General Strike*, p. 14
58. Friedheim and Friedheim, [n.1) p. 155
59. Gregory S. Kealey, "1919: The Canadian Labor Revolt," *Labour/Le Travail* 13 (1984): 25
60. Myer Scematycki, "Munitions and Labour Militancy: The 1916 Hamilton Machinists' Strike," *Ibid.* 3 (1978): 141
61. Charles Lipton, *The Trade Union Movement in Canada, 1827-1959*, Montreal, 1967, p. 185
62. David Jay Bercuson. *Confrontation at Winnipeg: Labour, Industrial Relations, and the General Strike*, Montreal and London, 1974, p. 176
63. British Columbia Federation of Labor, *Proceedings*, 1919, Convention, pp. 28-36; Lipton, p. 188
64. Lipton, pp. 188-89
65. Interview with Fred Tipping, member of the Winnipeg Strike Committee in 1919, in "The Winnipeg General Strike: Looking Back," *Canadian Dimensions* 9 (1980): 7
66. *Ibid.*
67. Lipton, p. 189
68. *Ibid.*
69. Master, pp. 36-38
70. Lipton, p. 190
71. Master, pp. 44, 57
72. Bercuson, pp. 142-45
73. *Ibid.*, pp. 153-56
74. *Western Labour News*, May 21, 28, 29, 1919; Lipton, p. 193; Edward T. Devine, "Winnipeg and Seattle," *Survey* 43 (Oct. 4, 1919): 5-8; Murray, *Red Scare*, p. 163
75. Master, p. 71; Crook, *op. cit.*, pp. 550-52
76. Crook, pp. 552-53
77. Lipton, p. 195
78. *Ibid.*, p. 196
79. Crook, p. 555
80. *Ibid.*
81. *Ibid.*, pp. 555-57; Master, p. 102; Lipton, p. 201
82. Crook, p. 557; Lipton, pp. 201-02
83. Bercuson, pp. 201-03; Crook, p. 558
84. Lipton, pp. 209-10
85. "The Winnipeg Strike. ..," *Canadian Dimensions* 9 (1980): 9
86. Bercuson, p. 248
87. Master, p. 210
88. *Ibid.*, pp. 212-15
89. Lipton, p. 201
90. "The Winnipeg Strike....," p. 7; Kealey, *op. cit.*, pp. 28-30

91. "The Winnipeg Strike..," p. 8
92. Lipton, pp. 204-06; Bercuson, pp. 262-65; Master, pp. 219-23

CHAPTER 5

1. Paul H. Douglas, *Real Wages in the United States, 1890-1926*, New York, 1930, pp. 334, 392-93
2. Ann Worthington, "The Telephone Strike," *Survey* 42 (April 15, 1919): 146
3. *Boston Globe*, Feb. 20, 21, 22, March 13, April 12, 13, 1919
4. *Ibid.*, April 17, 1919; Worthington, p. 146; *Kennebec Journal*, April 16, 17, 1919
5. *Boston Evening Transcript*, April 18-20, 1919; *Boston Globe*, April 19, 21, 1919; *Kennebec Journal*, April 19-20, 1919
6. *Boston Globe*, April 20-21, 1919; *Kennebec Journal*, April 21, 1919
7. Worthington, p. 146; *Kennebec Journal*, April 18, 19, 20, 1919
8. James R. Green and Hugh Carter Donahue, *Boston's Workers: A Labor History*, Boston, 1979, p. 96
9. Worthington, p. 146
10. *Seattle Union Record*, Feb. 1, 1919
11. *New York Times*, April 20, 1919; *New Republic* 13 (June 14, 1919): 202.
12. *New York Times*, April 20, 1919; *Boston Globe*, April 22, 1919; *Kenebec Journal*, April 19-21, 1919
13. Green and Donahue, p. 96
14. *Boston Evening Transcript*, June 14, 15, 1919; *Boston Globe*, June 15, 1919; Thomas R. Brooks, *Communication Workers of America: The Story of a Union*, New York, 1977, p. 15
15. *Seattle Union Record*, May 24, 31, June 21, 28, 1919
16. Jack Barbash, *Unions and Telephones: The Story of the Communication Workers of America*, New York, 1953, pp. 5-6
17. Frederick Manuel Koss, "The Boston Police Strike," unpublished Ph.D. dissertation, Boston University, 1960, pp. 20-29
18. William Allen White, *A Puritan in Babylon*, New York, 1938, p. 151
19. Green and Donahue, p. 97
20. Richard C. Lyons, "The Boston Police Strike" *New England Quarterly*, XX (July 1947): 151; David Ziskind, *One Thousand Strikes of Government Employes*, New York, 1940, p. 39; Claude M. Fuess, *Calvin Coolidge: The Man From Vermont*, Boston, 1950, pp. 205-06
21. Lyons, p. 151
22. *Ibid.*; Ziskind, p. 40
23. *New York Times*, Sept. 14, 1919; *Proceedings*, AFL Convention, p. 197
24. Robeson Peters, "The Boston Police Strike of 1919," M.A. thesis, Columbia University, 1947, pp. 32-35
25. Koss, pp. 86-88
26. Francis Russell, *A City in Terror; 1919: The Boston Police Strike*, New York, 1975, p. 82; *Boston Globe*, Aug. 18, 1919
27. *Boston Globe*, Aug. 25, 1919
28. *Literary Digest*, Sept. 20, 1919, p. 2
29. Joseph Edgar Chamberlin, *The Boston Transcript: A History of its First Hundred Years*, Cambridge, Mass., 1930, p. 223; Fuess, p. 213; Russell, p. 107
30. *Boston Globe*, Sept. 9, 1919
31. Russell, p. 113
32. Peters, p. 112; Russell, pp. 118-19
33. Koss, pp. 117-19; Russell, p. 127
34. "Harvard Men in the Boston Police Strike," *School and Society* 10 (Oct. 11, 1919): 425-26
35. Koss, p. 126; Russell, p. 145
36. Russell, p. 156
37. *Ibid.*, p. 145
38. *Independent*, Sept. 20, 1919, p. 392; Russell, p. 201
39. Green and Donahue, p. 98
40. *New York Times*, Sept. 11, 1919
41. *Ibid.*, Sept. 10, 11, 13, 15, 17, 1919
42. *Literary Digest*, Sept. 27, 1919, p. 2
43. *Ibid.*
44. *Engineering News-Record* 83 (Sept. 18, 1919): 538; Philadelphia *Evening Public Ledger* quoted in *Literary Digest*, Sept. 27, 1919, pp. 7-8
45. Russell, p. 185; *Literary Digest*, Sept. 27, 1919, pp. 7-8
46. *Labor Herald* (Kansas City, Missouri), Oct. 31, 1919
47. Koss, pp. 148; Russell, pp. 175-76
48. Peters, pp. 59-61; Lyons, p. 158
49. Russell, pp. 198-99
50. *Ibid.*, pp. 199-200
51. Koss, p. 163
52. Russell, p. 207
53. Fuess, p. 227
54. Koss, p. 212
55. Calvin Coolidge, *The Autobiography of Calvin Coolidge*, Boston, 1929, p. 118
56. *Boston Globe*, Sept. 15, 1919
57. *New York Times*, Sept. 12, 1919
58. Fuess, pp. 167-68
59. Koss, p. 165; *Outlook* 123 (Sept. 24, 1919): 232
60. Knoxville *Journal and Tribune*, Oct. 27, 1919; James A. Burran, "Labor Conflict in Urban Appalachia: The Knoxville Street Car Strike of 1919," *Tennessee Historical Quarterly* 38 (Spring 1979): 70-71
61. Burran, p. 76
62. *Ibid.*, p. 77

63. Koss, pp. 188-89

CHAPTER 6
1. *New York Times*, Aug. 2, 1919.
2. Murray, *Red Scare*, p. 7.
3. U.S. Department of Commerce and Labor, Bureau of the Census, *Special Reports, Street and Electric Railways, 1902*, Washington, D.C., 1902, p. 79; U.S. Department of Commerce and Labor, Bureau of the Census, *Special Reports, Street and Electric Railways 1907*, Washington, D.C., 1910, 193, 201
4. Gary M. Fink, editor, *Labor Unions*, Westport, Conn., 1977, p. 397; *Monthly Labor Review* 7 (April 1918): 1030-32
5. Bruce Rogers, "The Street Car War in Indianapolis," *International Socialist Review*, Dec. 1913, p. 341
6. Gary M. Fink, editor, *Biographical Dictionary of American Labor Leaders*, Westport, Conn., 1974, p. 227
7. *Labor Herald* (Kansas City, Mo.), May 3, 1918
8. "Chicago Afoot," *Survey* 42 (Aug. 9, 1919): 70-3-04
9. *Denver Express*, July 12-30, 1920
10. *Denver Post*, Aug. 2, 11, 1920
11. Thomas A. Arnold, "The Trial of the Serpent," *The Tramway Bulletin* 11 (Sept. 1920): 5, 14
12. *Denver Express*, Aug. 6, 7, 9, 1920
13. *Ibid.*, Aug. 10, 1920
14. *Ibid.*, Aug. 9, 23, 1920
15. Philip I. Cook, "Red Scare in Denver," *Colorado Magazine* 43 (Fall 1966): 324-26
16. James A. Burran, "Labor Conflict in Urban Appalachia: The Knoxville Streetcar Strike of 1919," *Tennessee Historical Quarterly* 38 (Spring 1979): 66-67
17. James A. Hodges, "The Tennessee Federation of Labor, 1919-1939," unpublished M.A. thesis, Vanderbilt University, 1959, pp. 38-39; Nashville *Tennessean*, Aug. 18-29, 1919
18. Tennessee Federation of Labor, *Book of Laws of the Tennessee Federation of Labor, As Amended and Adopted, May 5, 1920, Together With Twenty-Fourth Annual Convention Held at Jackson, Tennessee, May 3, 4, 5, 1920, n.p., 1920, p. 26*, copy in State Historical Society of Wisconsin, Madison
19. Burran, p. 68
20. *Ibid.*
21. *Ibid.*, p. 69
22. Knoxville *Journal and Tribune*, Oct. 25, 1919; Burran, pp. 69-70
23. Knoxville *Journal and Tribune*, Oct. 27-

31, 1919; Burran, p. 70
24. Burran, pp. 70-71
25. *Ibid.*, p. 62
26. Knoxville *Journal and Tribune*, Oct. 28-29, 1919; Burran, pp. 72-73
27. Knoxville *Journal and Tribune*, Oct. 28-31, 1919; Burran, p. 73
28. Burran, pp. 73-74
29. *Ibid.*, p. 74
30. *Ibid.*, p.75
31. *Ibid.*
32. Knoxville *Journal and Tribune*, Dec. 21, 23, 1919
33. *Amalgamated Association of Street and Electric Railway Employes of America, Division 76 vs. The Kansas City Railways Company, Transcript of 16 September 1918 and 1 October 1918, Hearings, Docket 265*, National War Labor Board, RG 2, National Archives, Washington, D.C.
34. *Labor Herald* (K.C., Mo.), Dec. 27, 1918
35. Greenwald, *Women, War and Work...*, [Westport, 1980], p. 178
36. *Labor Herald* (K.C., Mo.), Jan. 24, 1919; Greenwald, p. 275
37. Kansas City *Times*, Dec. 11, 1918
38. *Ibid.*, Dec. 12, 1918
39. Kansas City *Times*, Dec. 12, 1918
40. *Ibid.*
41. Kansas City *Star*, Dec. 28, 1918
42. Kansas City *Times*, Dec. 21, 1918
43. *Labor Herald* (K.C., Mo.), Jan. 12, 1919
44. Kansas City *Times*, Dec. 14, 16, 1918
45. *Ibid.*, Dec. 13-15, 1918, Jan. 10, 1919
46. *Labor Herald* (K.C., Mo.), Jan. 12, 1919
47. Kansas City *Times*, Dec. 22-24, 1918
48. Kansas City *Star*, Dec. 14, 1918; Kansas City *Times*, Dec. 27, 1918; Jan. 5, 1919
49. Kansas City *Times*, Jan. 6, 1919
50. *Ibid.*, Jan. 12, 1919
51. *Labor Herald* (K.C., Mo.), Jan. 26, 1919
52. *Ibid.*, March 28, 1919
53. *Ibid.*, Jan. 12, 1919
54. *Ibid.*, Feb. 7, 1919
55. *Ibid.*
56. *Ibid.*, Jan. 3, 1919
57. *Ibid.*, Feb. 21, 1919
58. Kansas City *Star*, Feb. 16, March 17, 1919
59. *Labor Herald* (K.C., Mo.), Feb. 21, 1919
60. *Ibid.*, Jan. 3, 1919
61. *Ibid.*, Feb. 8, 1919
62. Kansas City *Times*, Dec. 14, 1918, Feb. 12, 1919
63. Greenwald, p. 179

64. *Ibid.*, p. 180.
65. *Labor Herald* (K.C., Mo.), Aug. 1, 1919

CHAPTER 7
1. Elizabeth Faulkner Baker, *Printers and Technology: A History of the International Printing Pressmen and Assistants*, New York, 1957, pp. 302-03; Seymour Martin Lipset, Martin A. Trow, and James S. Coleman, *Union Democracy: The Internal Politics of the ITU*, New York, 1956, pp. 44-45; Donald M. Crocker, "Civil War in Printerdom," *One Big Union Monthly* 1 (Dec. 1919): 18-21.
2. Baker, pp. 302-03; Lipset, Trow, and Coleman p. 44; Crocker, pp. 18-20
3. Baker, pp. 306-10
4. *Ibid.*, p. 310
5. Crocker, p. 26-30
6. New York *Call*, Aug. 12-15, 1919
7. "The Boston Police Strike," *Survey* 42 (Sept. 20, 1919): 882
8. *Timberworker Department*, March 15, 1919; Seattle *Union Record*, April 5, 1919; "IWW Headquarters Bulletin," *One Big Union Monthly* 1 (March 1919): 63
9. Seattle *Union Record*, March 3, 1917, March 9, 1918
10. *Proceedings*, Women's Trade Union League, Seventh Biennial Convention, 1919, pp. 96-97
11. Louis Levine, *The Women's Garment Workers*, New York, 1924, pp.
12. *Documentary History of the Amalgamated Clothing Workers of America, 1918-1920*, New York, 1943, pp. 4-8; Joel Seidman, *The Needle Trades*, New York, 1942, p. 141
13. *Documentary History of Amalgamated*, pp. 9-23; *Advance*, Jan. 3, 1919
14. *Documentary History of Amalgamated*, pp. 23-24; *Advance*, Jan. 10, 17, 1919
15. *Documentary History of Amalgamated*, pp. 26-28; Charles Elbert Zaretz, *The Amalgamated Clothing Workers of America: A Study in Progressive Trades-Unionism*, New York, 1934, p. 179
16. *Documentary History of Amalgamated*, pp. 34-35, 49-52, 66-67, 75-151
17. *Ibid.*, pp. 26-29
18. Levine, pp. 304-05
19. *New York Times*, Jan. 17, 1919
20. *Justice*, Jan. 5, 1919
21. Levine, pp. 308-09
22. *New York Times*, Jan. 17, 1919
23. *Ibid.*, Jan. 19, 1919
24. *Ibid.*, Jan. 21, 1919; *Justice*, Jan. 22, 1919

25. *New York Times*, Jan. 23, 25, 28, Feb. 2, 4, 1919
26. *Ibid.*, Jan. 20, Feb. 14, 1919
27. *Ibid.*, Feb. 17, 19, 25, March 3, 1919; Levine, *op. cit.*, p. 330
28. *New York Times*, March 14, April 8, 1919; *Justice*, April 11, 1919
29. *Justice*, July 4, 1919; Levine, p. 330
30. Levine, p. 330
31. Seidman, p. 142; Philip S. Foner, *The Fur and Leather Workers:...*, Newark, N.J., 1950, p. 81
32. Herbert J. Lahne, *The Cotton Mill Worker*, New York, 1944, pp. 204-05
33. *Ibid.*, pp. 42-43; George Sinclair Mitchell, *Textile Unionism and the South*, Chapel Hill, N. Car., 1931, pp. 42-43; Jacqueline Dowd Hall, Robert Iorstad, and James Lebudes, "Cotton Mill People: Work, Community and Protest in the Textile South, 1880-1940," *American Historical Review* 91 (April 1986): 265-66
34. Robert R. Brooks, "The United Textile Workers of America," unpublished Ph.D. dissertation, Yale University, 1935, pp. 69-71; David Joseph Goldberg, "Immigrants, Intellectuals and Industrial Unions: The 1919 Textile Strikes and the Experience of the Amalgamated Textile Workers of America in Passaic and Paterson, New Jersey and Lawrence, Massachusetts," unpublished Ph.D. dissertation, Columbia University, 1984, pp. 46-47
35. Brooks, pp. 43, 90; Goldberg, pp. 45, 47-48
36. Goldberg, pp. 47, 49
37. Brooks, p. 73
38. Mitchell, p. 43
39. *Ibid.*, pp. 43-45; Lahne, pp. 205-06
40. Mitchell, pp. 45-53; Harley E. Tolley, "The Labor Movement in North Carolina, 1880-1920," *North Carolina Historical Review* 30 (July 1953): 354-75; Lahne, p. 208; Philip S. Foner, *Women and the American Labor Movement: From World War I to the Present*, New York, 1980, p. 226
41. *New York Times*, Jan. 27, 1919
42. *Ibid.*, Feb. 3, 5, 1919
43. *Ibid.*, Feb. 6, 7, 1919
44. Goldberg, pp. 293-94
45. J. M. Budish and George Soule, *The New Unionism in the Clothing Industry*, New York, 1920, pp. 257-59; *New York Times*, Jan. 26, Feb. 1, 14, 1919
46. Goldberg, pp. 296-98
47. *Lawrence Evening Tribune*, Jan. 29, 1919; *Advance*, April 11, 18, 25, 1919

48. *Lawrence Evening Tribune*, Jan. 30, 31, 1919
49. *Ibid.*, Feb. 3-4, 1919; *New York Times*, Feb. 4, 1919
50. *Lawrence Evening Tribune*, Feb. 5, 1919
51. Harnell L. Rotzell, "The Lawrence Textile Strike," *American Labor Year Book, 1919-1920*, New York, 1920, pp. 172-73
52. *New York Times*, Feb. 4, 1919
53. *Ibid.*, Feb. 5, 1919. *See also Lawrence Evening Tribune*, Feb. 6, 1919
54. *Lawrence Evening Tribune*, Feb. 9, 11, 13, 17, March 12, 13, 1919; *Lawrence Telegram*, Feb. 10, 12, 13, 18, March 15, 16, 1919; *Lawrence Sun and American*, Feb. 10, 13, 16, March 13, 15, 1919
55. *Lawrence Evening Tribune*, Feb. 17, 26, 1919
56. Rudolph J. Vecoli, "Anthony Capraro and the Lawrence Strike of 1919," in George E. Pozzetta, *Pane E Lavoro: The Italian American Working Class*, Toronto, 1980, pp. 10-11
57. *Ibid.*, pp. 11-12
58. *Ibid.*, pp. 12-13
59. Goldberg, p. 339
60. *Ibid.*, p. 340
61. *Lawrence Evening Tribune*, Feb. 18, March 8, 1919; *Lawrence Telegram*, Feb. 18, 19, 1919
62. *Lawrence Evening Tribune*, March 17, 18, 1919; *New York Times*, March 18, 1919
63. John A. Fitch, "Lawrence: A Strike for Wages or for Bolshevism," *Survey* 42 (April 5, 1919): 43-44; also cited in Selig Perlman and Philip Taft, *History of Labor in the United States, 1896-1932*, New York, 1935, p. 439
64. *New York Times*, March 25, 1919; *Lawrence Evening Tribune*, April 23-24, 1919
65. *Cincinnati Times Star*, Feb. 11, 1919; *New York Times*, May 25, 1919
66. Vecoli, pp. 6-7
67. *Ibid.*, pp. 14-15
68. *Ibid.*, p. 8
69. *Ibid.*, pp. 8-9
70. *Lawrence Telegram*, May 3, 1919; *Lawrence Leader*, April 27, 1919; *New York Call*, May 7, 11, 1919; Vecoli, p. 16
71. *New York Call*, May 19, 23, 1919; Vecoli, pp. 16-17
72. Vecoli, *op. cit.*, p. 77
73. *Ibid.*, p. 10; Goldberg, pp. 340-41
74. Goldberg, pp. 378-79; Vecoli, p. 17
75. *New York Call*, May 17, 19, 22, 23, 1919; Vecoli, p. 18; Nat Hentoff, editor,

Essays of A.J. Muste, Indianapolis, 1967, pp. 17-18; *New Textile Worker*, May 31, 1919; Dexter Philip Arnold, "A Row of Bricks: Worker Activism in the Merrimack Valley Textile Industry, 1912-1922," Ph.D. dissertation, University of Wisconsin, Madison, 1985, p. 603
76. Goldberg, p. 379
77. Vecoli, p. 18
78. *Ibid.*
79. Goldberg, p. 424
80. *New York Call*, April 9, 12, 14, 15, 1919; Vecoli, *op. cit.*, pp. 18-19; Goldberg, pp. 425-26
81. Vecoli, p. 18
82. *Ibid.*, p. 19
83. Goldberg, pp. 893-94; Vecoli, p. 19
84. Vecoli, p. 19
85. Grace Hutchins, *Labor and Silk*, New York, 1931, pp. 143-45; *One Big Union Monthly 1* (March 1919): 63
86. "Paterson," *Survey* 42 (July 19, 1919): 602-03
87. Hutchins, pp. 118, 144-47; "Correction," *Survey* 42 (July 26, 1919): 638; Brooks, *op. cit.*, pp. 232-45
88. Robert Dunn and Jack Hardy, *Labor and Textiles*, New York, 1931, pp. 203-04; Marion Dutton Savage, "Industrial Unionism in America," published Ph.D. dissertation, Columbia University, 1922, pp. 250-70; *Documentary History of Amalgamated, 1918-1920*, p. 263; Goldberg, pp. 185-201
89. Budish and Soule, pp. 262-63; Dunn and Hardy, pp. 220-21; Robert W. Dunn, "Unionism in the Textile Industry," *American Labor Year Book, 1921-1922*, New York, 1922, pp. 155-62

CHAPTER 8

1. U.S. Mine Bureau, *Mineral Resources, 1922*, vol. 2, Non-metals, p. 506
2. McAlister Coleman, *Men and Coal*, New York, 1943, p. 116; James A. Wechsler, *Labor Baron*, New York, 1944, pp. 45-46; Marion D. Savage, *Industrial Unionism in America*, New York, 1922, p. 96; *United Mine Workers Journal*, Feb. 1, April 1, June 15, Aug. 1, Sept. 1, 15, 1919; Sylvia Kopald, *Rebellion in Labor Unions*, New York, 1924, pp. 5, 18, 62, 89-91, 117-19; Selig Perlman and Philip Taft, *History of Labor in the United States*, New York, 1935, pp. 435, 470
3. UMWA *Proceedings*, 1919, pp. 392-94, 868-70; Melvyn Dubofsky and Warren Van Tine, *John L. Lewis*, New York, 1971, pp. 49-50, 99

4. "How the Wheels Go Round in the Miners' Union," *Literary Digest*, Nov. 22, 1919, p. 59
5. John Hutchinson, "John L. Lewis: To the Presidency of the UMWA," *Labor History* 19 (Spring, 1978): 213; Dubofsky and Van Tine, pp. 23-24
6. Sylvia Kopald, "Behind the Miners' Strike," *Nation* 109 (Nov. 22, 1919): 658; Robert K. Murray, *Red Scare: A Study in National Hysteria, 1919-1920*, Minneapolis, 1955, p. 454
7. Hugh Archibald, *The Four-Hour Day in Coal*, New York, 1922, p. 53-68
8. Reprinted in *Literary Digest*, Dec. 13, 1919, p. 16
9. Dubofsky and Van Tine, p. 57
10. *Literary Digest*, Dec. 13, 1919, p. 26
11. *Ibid.*
12. William B. Wilson to James Duncan, April 22, 1920, William B. Wilson Papers, Pa file 13/161, National Archives; Dubofsky and Van Tine, pp. 52-53
13. Dubofsky and Van Tine, pp. 53-54
14. Murray, p. 156
15. Stanley Coben, *A. Mitchell Palmer*, New York, 1963, pp. 177-78
16. Cecil Carnes, *John L. Lewis: A Leader of Labor*, New York, 1936 p. 31; Saul D. Alinsky, *John L. Lewis: An Unauthorized Biography*, New York, 1949, pp. 30-32; Murray, pp. 155, 157; Samuel Gompers, "The Broken Pledge," *American Federationist*, January, 1920, pp. 262-64
17. Carnes, p. 35
18. Dubofsky and Van Tine, pp. 54-55
19. *Ibid.*
20. Carnes, p. 33; Dubofsky and Van Tine, pp. 55-57
21. Coben, pp. 177-78; Murray, p. 162
22. Dubofsky and Van Tine, pp. 54-58
23. Carnes, pp. 34-35
24. Dubofsky and Van Tine, p. 57
25. Coleman, *Men and Coal*, p. 98
26. Alinsky, pp. 32-33
27. Dubofsky and Van Tine, p. 57
28. *Iron Age*, Nov. 13, 1919
29. Dubofsky and Van Tine, pp. 57-58; Murray, p. 162
30. Wechsler, *Labor Baron*, p. 24; Alinsky, pp. 32-33; Dubofsky and Van Tine, pp. 58-59; Carnes, p. 44
31. Woodrow Wilson to John L. Lewis, 2 August, 1920, John L. Lewis Papers, microfilm copy in library of the University of California, Los Angeles
32. United Mine Workers, *Proceedings of the 27th Consecutive and 4th Biennial Convention: Reconvened Session*, 1920, pp. 22, 36
33. *Ibid.*, p. 59
34. *Ibid.*, p. 154
35. *Ibid.*, p. 44
36. *Ibid.*, pp. 156-57
37. Eric Haas, *John L. Lewis Exposed*, New York, 1937, p. 32; Stanley Joshua Jacobs, "Opposition to John L. Lewis Within the United Mine Workers," unpublished M.A. thesis, University of California, Berkeley, 1949, pp. 54-55
38. Philip S. Foner, editor, *Mother Jones Speaks*, New York, 1983, p. 352
39. Dubofsky and Van Tine, pp. 60-61
40. *Proceedings*, AFL Convention, 1921, p. 453; Dubofsky and Van Tine, pp. 59, 61-63, 160-62
41. David Brody, *Steelworkers in America*, Cambridge, Mass., 1976, pp. 214-18; Samuel Yellen, *American Labor Struggles*, New York, 1936, pp. 251-56; Murray, *Red Scare*, pp. 135-42; Commission of Inquiry, Interchurch World Movement, *Report on Steel Strike of 1919*, New York, 1920, pp. 3-15
42. Lewis L. Lorwin, *The American Federation of Labor*, Washington, D.C., 1933, P. 181; Raymond Patrick Kent, "The Development of Industrial Unionism in the American Iron and Steel Industry," unpublished Ph.D. dissertation, University of Pittsburgh, 1938, p. 132
43. Interchurch World Movement (IWM), *Report on the Steel Strike of 1919*, pp. 15-17, 19-21
44. *Ibid.*, pp. 22-25
45. Peter A. Sheigold, *Working Class Life: The "American Standard" in Comparative Perspective, 1899-1913*, Pittsburgh, 1982, p. 132
46. Raymond A. Mohl and Neil Betten, *Steel City: Urban and Ethnic Patterns in Gary, Indiana, 1906-1959*, New York, 1986, pp. 1-11
47. Frank H. Serena, "1919: Organization and Dashed Hopes," Paper presented at the Third Annual Meeting of the Pennsylvania Labor History Society, Pittsburgh, Pa., November 12, 1976, p. 2
48. *Ibid.*, p. 3
49. John A. Barraty, "The United States Steel Corporation versus Labor: The Early Years," *Labor History* 1 (Winter, 1960): 3-38
50. Fitch quoted in Brody, *op. cit.*, p. 214; Arthur Zipser, *Working-Class Giant*, New York, 1982, pp. 51-52
51. Quoted in David Brody, *Labor in Crisis: The Steel Strike of 1919*, Philadelphia, 1965, p. 130

52. William Z. Foster, *From Bryan to Stalin*, New York, 1938, p. 112
53. "The Steel Industry," *Social Service Bulletin* 10 (October, 1920): 1-2
54. William Z. Foster, *The Great Steel Strike and Its Lessons* (New York, 1920), pp. 16-25; Brody, *Steelworkers*, pp. 207-12
55. Ida Tarbell, *The Life of Elbert H. Gary*, New York, 1925, p. 291; Brody, *Steelworkers*, pp. 170-71; Marshall Olds, *Analysis of the Interchurch World Movement Report on the Steel Strike*, New York, 1923, pp. 74-139
56. Foster, *Bryan to Stalin*, pp. 108-12; Brody, *Steelworkers*, pp. 214-16; Brody, *Labor in Crisis*, p. 75
57. *Iron Trade Review* 55 (September 11, 1919): 675, 690; *Iron Age* July 24, 1919, p. 249; Sept. 18, 1919, pp. 781-88
58. George Soule, "Civil Rights in Western Pennslyvania," in IWM, *Public Opinion and the Steel Strike*, New York, 1921, pp. 188-96
59. *Ibid.*, pp. 200-01; Brody, *Labor in Crisis*, pp. 89-92
60. Philip Taft, *The AFL in the Time of Gompers*, New York, 1957, p. 386
61. William Z. Foster, *Great Steel Strike*, p. 21
62. *American Federationist*, September, 1919, p. 861; William E. Scheuerman, "Canton and the Great Steel Strike of 1919: Marriage of Nativism and Politics," *Ohio History* 93 (Winter-Spring, 1984): 77
63. Scheuerman, pp. 77-78
64. Brody, *Labor in Crisis*, pp. 73-78; Foster, *Bryan to Stalin*, p. 112
65. Brody, *Steelworkers*, pp. 219-22
66. *Ibid.*, pp. 231-35; William Z. Foster, *Pages from a Worker's Life*, New York, pp. 162-69; Brody, *Labor in Crisis*, pp. 92-95; Foner, *Mother Jones Speaks*, pp. 303-06; *New Majority*, Sept. 8, 1919; Foster, *Great Steel Strike*, p. 16
67. Philip S. Foner, *Women and the American Labor Movement: From World War I to the Present*, New York, 1980, p. 108
68. Foster, *Great Steel Strike*, p. 16
69. *United Mine Workers' Journal*, Sept. 15, 1983, p. 23; *Daily Worker*, Sept. 18, 1983
70. Brody, *Labor in Crisis*, p. 98; Foner, *Mother Jones Speaks*, p. 307
71. Brody, *Steelworkers*, pp. 223-24, 233; IWM *Report*, pp. 52, 119-43; Foster, *Great Steel Strike*, pp. 196-97
72. IWM *Report*, p. 148; Saposs, "The Mind of Immigrant Communities in the Pittsburgh District," in IWM, *Public Opinion*, pp. 239-48; Brody, *Labor in Crisis*, pp. 81-96
73. Whiting Williams, *Mainsprings of Men*, New York, 1925, p. 83; Brody, *Labor in Crisis*, pp. 97-98; Brody, *Steelworkers*, p. 237; *Industry* 1 (June 1, 1919): 2
74. Brody, *Labor in Crisis*, pp. 99-101; Foster, *Great Steel Strike*, pp. 76-78; *Labor Today*, December, 1979
75. Yellen, pp. 264-68; U.S. Senate, *Report Investigating Strike in Steel Industry*, 64th Congress., 1st Session, Senate Reports, vol. A, No. 289, Washington, D.C., p. 9
76. Brody, *Labor in Crisis*, pp. 45-47; *New York Times*, Sept. 19, 1919
77. Samuel Gompers to James W. Kine, September 12, 1919, AFL Archives, State Historical Society of Wisconsin.
78. Urofsky, *Big Steel and the Wilson Administration*, p. 285; Brody, *Labor in Crisis*, pp. 101-02; *Manufacturer's Record* 56 (Sept. 25, 1919):
79. *Labor Herald* (K.C., Mo.), Oct. 17, 1919
80. Brody, *Labor in Crisis*, p. 112
81. Samuel Gompers, *Seventy Years of Life and Labor* (New York, 1924) 1: 650-51
82. Samuel Gompers to M.F. Tighe, September 18, 1919, AFL Archives, State Historical Society of Wisconsin
83. William Z. Foster to the Executive Heads of all Organizations affiliated with the American Federation of Labor, September 13, 1919, copy in International Fur Workers' Union Archives.
84. Brody, *Labor in Crisis*, pp. 105, 106, 111; Foster, *Great Steel Strike*, p. 89; Foster, *From Bryan to Stalin*, pp. 115, 119
85. Saposs, "Immigrant Communities," p. 239; Brody, *Labor in Crisis*, pp. 112-15; Brody, *Steelworkers*, pp. 241-42; Raymond A. Mohl, "The Great Steel Strike of 1919 in Gary, Indiana: Working Class Radicalism or Trade Union Militancy?" *Mid-America* 63 (January, 1981): 38-39
86. Brody, *Steelworkers*, p. 250
87. Duquesne *Times-Observer*, Sept. 20, 22, 26, 1919
88. Homestead *Daily Messenger*, Sept. 27, 30, 1919
89. Soule, "Civil Rights," pp. 163-219; Brody, *Labor in Crisis*, pp. 134-35; 147-53; Foster, *Bryan to Stalin*, pp 117-19; Yellen, *American Labor Struggles*, p. 275; Robert Littell, "Under-Cover Men," in IWM, *Public Opinion*, pp. 1-86; Mary Heaton Vorse, "Civil Liberties in the Steel Strike," *Nation*, November

15, 1919, pp. 833-35; Foster, *Pages from a Worker's Life*, pp. 219-23

90. Quoted in Yellen, p. 271; Foster, *Great Steel Strike*, p. 199

91. *Iron Age Trade Review*, Sept. 18, 1919, p. 74; *Literary Digest*, Oct. 2, 1919, p. 671; Oct. 11, 1919, p. 12

92. Yellen, p. 272

93. Quoted in Brody, *Labor in Crisis*, p. 132

94. Murray, *Red Scare*, pp. 147-48; Brody, *Labor in Crisis*, pp. 132-35; *New York Times*, Sept. 30, 1919

95. Mohl, p. 39

96. *Ibid.*, p. 40

97. *Ibid.*, p. 41

98. *Ibid.*, p. 40

99. *Ibid.*; Leonard Wood Diary, Oct. 6, 7, 8, 1919, Box 12, Leonard Wood Papers, Library of Congress, Manuscripts Division

100. Mohl, p. 40

101. *Ibid.*, pp. 45, 46

102. *Ibid.*, p. 46; Leonard Wood to Elbert H. Gary, Dec. 23, 1919; Wood Papers, Box 129; Elbert H. Gary to Leonard Wood, Dec. 30, 1919, ibid.; Jack C. Lane, *Armed Progressive: General Leonard Wood*, San Rafael, Calif., 1978, pp. 230-49

103. Mohl, pp. 46-47

104. Robert K. Murray, "Communism and the Great Steel Strike of 1919," *Mississippi Valley Historical Review* 37 (December, 1951): 453; Mohl, pp. 41-42

105. IWM *Report*, pp. 31, 40.

106. *Ibid.*, pp. 177-78; Francisco A. Rosales and Daniel T. Simon, "Chicano Steel Workers and Unionism in the Midwest, 1919-1945," *Aztlan* 6 (1975): 267. Philip S. Foner, *Organized Labor and the Black Worker, 1619-1981*, New York, 1982, p. 144

107. Robert Asher, "Steelworkers and the 1919 Strike," *Pennslyvania History* 87 (Spring, 1983): 117

108. *American Federationist* 26 (November, 1919): 1061; *Proceedings of the First Industrial Conference, October 6 to 23, 1919*, Washington, D.C., 1920, pp. 102, 221

109. *Ibid.*, pp. 221-22; Foster, *Great Steel Strike*, p. 142

110. Taft, *A.F. of L. in the Time of Gompers*, pp. 302-03; Brody, *Labor in Crisis*, pp. 166-71; Brody, *Steelworkers*, pp. 256-57; Foster, *Bryan to Stalin*, pp. 115-16; Foster, *Great Steel Strike*, pp. 220-36

111. John Howard Keiser, "John Fitzpatrick and Progressive Unionism, 1915-1925," unpublished Ph.D. dissertation, North-western University, 1965, p. 48; Yellen, *American Labor Struggles*, p. 284; "The Commission's Mediation Effort," in IWM, *Public Opinion...*, pp. 332-41.

112. Keiser, p. 50; *New Majority*, Jan. 17, 1920, p. 14

113. Foster, *Great Steel Strike*, pp. 234-35

114. *Ibid.*, p. 237

115. "An Open Letter to John Fitzpatrick," Labor Herald, January, 1924, p. 6

116. James Robert Prickett, "Communists and the Communist Issue in the American Labor Movement, 1920-1950," unpublished Ph.D. dissertation, University of California, Los Angeles, 1975, p. 56

117. Foster, *Great Steel Strike*, pp. 209-10

118. William Scheuerman, "The Politics of Protest: The Great Steel Strike of 1919-20 in Lackawanna, New York," *International Review of Social History* 30 (1986): 121-46

119. Foster, *Great Steel Strike*, p. 233

120. Allan M. Wakstein, "The Open-Shop Movement, 1919-1933," unpublished Ph.D. dissertation, University of Illinois, 1961, p. 42

CHAPTER 9

1. *Manufacturer's Record* 76 (Dec. 11, 1919): 93

2. W.S. Mosher, "Open Shop in the Southwest," *The Open Shop Review* 18 (March 1921): 116; Allen M. Wakstein, "The Open-Shop Movement, 1919-1933," Unpublished Ph.D. dissertation, University of Illinois, 1961. Hereinafter cited as Wakstein, thesis.

3. *Manufacturer's Record* 76 (Dec. 11, 1919): 93; Wakstein, thesis, pp. 53-54

4. George Pattrillo, "A Strike Against Strikes," *Saturday Evening Post* 182 (Jan. 24, 1920): 50

5. Mosher, pp. 17-18; Wakstein, thesis, p. 55

6. Dr. Frederick C. Ryan, "The Labor Movement of San Diego: Problems and Development from 1887 to 1957," San Diego State College, 1959, pp. 35-36

7. *Ibid.*, p. 38

8. *Ibid.*

9. *Ibid.*, pp. 38-39

10. *Iron Trades Review* 67 (Aug. 12, 1920): 440

11. *Literary Digest* 66 (Aug. 7, 1920): 1341-45; Wakstein, thesis, pp. 89-90

12. *U.S. Fourteenth Census: Abstract*, pp. 50-72, 920-23; Wakstein, thesis, pp. 91-92

13. Citizens' Alliance of Duluth, *Citizens' Alliance Bulletin*, 3 (March 1921): 12;

Wakstein, thesis, p. 68
14. Lamar T. Berman, editor, *Selected Articles on the Closed Shop*, New York, 1921, p. 188
15. National Association of Manufacturers, *Proceedings*, 1920, pp. 330-31; Wakstein, thesis, p. 63
16. Selig Perlman and Philip Taft, *History of Labor in the United States, 1896-1932*, New York, 1935, p. 494; Savel Zimand, *The Open Shop Drive: Who is Behind it and Where is it Going?* New York, 1921, pp. 13-16
17. National Association of Manufacturers, *Open Shop Encyclopedia for Debaters*, New York, 1921, p. 61
18. *Commercial and Financial Chronicle* 103 (Nov. 20, 1920): 2004
19. Wakstein, thesis, p. 65
20. *Ibid.*, p. 69
21. *Iron Trades' Review* 67 (Nov. 11, 1920): 1341, 1344-45
22. Wakstein, thesis, p. 71
23. *Ibid.*, pp. 73-74
24. Dallas Chamber of Commerce, *Annual Report*, pp. 17-19
25. *Iron Trades' Review* 67 (Sept. 23, 1920): 920.; Wakstein, thesis, p. 21
26. *Tampa Morning Tribune*, Aug. 1, 23, 1920
27. Durward Long, "The Open-Closed Shop Battle in Tampa's Cigar Industry, 1919-1921," *Florida Historical Quarterly* 47 (1968): 111
28. *Ibid.*, pp. 103-04, 120; Federal Trade Commission, *Decisions, Findings and Orders of the Federal Trade Commission, May 22, 1922 to February 13, 1923*, (Washington, 1924) 5: 1-23
29. Robert W. Dunn, *The Americanization of Labor*, New York, p. 87
30. *Ibid.*, pp. 87-88
31. Perlman & Taft, *op. cit.*, pp. 492-93; Wakstein, thesis, pp. 77-78
32. Dunn, *op. cit.*, pp. 31-32
33. Wakstein, thesis, pp. 108-09
34. *Ibid.*
35. *Ibid.*, p. 110
36. Allan M. Wakstein, "The Origin of the Open-Shop Movement, 1919-1920," *Journal of American History* 51 (Dec. 1964): 475
37. *The Employer* 4 (March 1920): 9; Robert L. Friedheim, *The Seattle General Strike*, Seattle, 1964, p. 158
38. Allan M. Wakstein, "The National Association of Manufacturers and Labor Relations in the 1920s," *Labor History* 10 (Spring 1969): 168-69
39. *Ibid.*, p. 166

40. Clarence E. Bonnett, *History of Employer Associations in the United States*, New York, 1956, pp. 40-42, 98-133, 553-54; William Haber, *Industrial Relations in the Building Industry*, Cambridge, Mass., 1930, pp. 458-61; Louis Aubrey Wood, *Union-Management Cooperation on the Railroads*, New Haven, 1931, pp. 79-101; Wakstein, thesis, p. 127
41. *Labor Herald* (K.C., Mo.), April 5, 1918
42. Long, 101-03
43. *Ibid.*, pp. 104-05
44. *Ibid.*, pp. 106-07
45. *Ibid.*, p. 108; *Tampa Sunday Tribune*, July 11, 1920
46. *Tampa Morning Tribune*, July 7, 1920
47. Long, p. 105
48. *Tampa Morning Tribune*, July 20, Aug. 22, 28, 1920
49. *Ibid.*, Aug. 8, 1920
50. *Ibid.*, Aug. 27, 28, 1920; Long, pp. 114-15
51. *Tampa Morning Tribune*, Aug. 28, 1920
52. *Ibid.*
53. *Cigar Makers' Official Journal* 44 (Sept. 15, 1920): 4-5; Long, p. 116
54. Long, p. 117
55. *Ibid.*, p. 106, 117
56. *Tampa Morning Tribune*, Aug. 22, 1920
57. *Tampa Morning Tribune*, Feb. 5, 1921
58. *Ibid.*, Feb. 6, 1921; Long, p. 119
59. *Cigar Makers' Official Journal* 46 (Feb. 15, 1921): 2; *Tampa Morning Tribune*, Feb. 6, 1921
60. Long, p. 12
61. *Ibid.*
62. *Tampa Morning Tribune*, Feb. 5, 1921
63. Gary R. Mormino and George E. Pozzetta, *The Immigrant World of Ybor City: Italians and Their Latin Neighbors in Tampa, 1885-1985*, Urbana and Chicago, 1987, p. 128
64. Long, p. 121
65. Leo Wolman, *Ebb and Flow in Trade Unionism*, New York, 1936, pp. 16-18, 35-37, 172-91
66. *Ibid.*, pp. 16-17; National Industrial Conference Board, *Collective Bargaining Through Employe Representatives*, New York, 1933, pp. 16-17
67. Perlman and Taft, p. 492
68. Address by Samuel Gompers before Central Labor Union of Washington, D.C., November 22, 1919, Samuel Gompers Papers, Box 51, State Historical Society of Wisconsin

CHAPTER 10

1. William M. Tuttle, Jr., *Race Riot: Chicago in the Red Summer of 1919*, New York, 1970, p. 156; William Tuttle, Jr., interview with Chester Willkins, Chicago, June 25, 1869, quoted in James Richard Grossman, "A Dream Deferred: Black Migration to Chicago, 1916-1921," unpub. Ph.D. dissertation, Univ. of California, Berkeley, 1982, p. 232.
2. Grossman, p. 232; Walter Fogel, *The Negro in the Meat Industry*, Philadelphia, 1970, p. 29; David Brody, *The Butcher Workman: A Study in Unionization*, Cambridge, Mass., 1964, p. 85.
3. Grossman, p. 233.
4. Phil Bart, *Working Class Unity: The Role of Communists in the Chicago Federation of Labor, 1919-1923*, New York, 1975, p. 9.
5. *Ibid.*
6. Brody, *Butcher Workman*, p. 77.
7. *Ibid.*, pp. 83-85.
8. Grossman, p. 305.
9. Bart, pp. 8, 12.
10. Tuttle, Jr., p. 143.
11. Grossman, pp. 297-98; *Chicago Whip*, July 19, 1919; *New Majority*, (Chicago), July 5, Aug. 9, 1919.
12. *Ibid.*
13. Grossman, p. 299.
14. *Ibid.*, p. 300.
15. *New Majority*, June 21, 1919.
16. Grossman, p. 319.
17. *Butcher Workman*, June, July, August, 1919; Grossman, pp. 320-22.
18. Grossman, p. 322.
19. Tuttle, pp. 32-64; Grossman, p. 324.
20. Minutes of the Chicago Federation of Labor, August 3, 1919, in Bart, p. 11; *Labor Herald* (K.C., Mo.), Aug. 22, 1919.
21. *Chicago Defender*, Aug. 30, 1919; Chicago Commission on Race Relations, *The Negro in Chicago*, Chicago, 1920, pp. 2-3, 395-96, 399.
22. Tuttle, pp. 108-56; Grossman, pp. 324-25.
23. *Chicago Defender*, Aug. 30, 1919; Tuttle, p. 109; Grossman, p. 326.
24. Grossman, p. 325.
25. *New Majority*, Aug. 9, 1919; Tuttle, pp. 57-60; Brody, *Butcher Workman*, p. 88
26. *New Majority*, Aug. 9, 1919; Grossman, p. 328.
27. *New Majority*, Aug. 9, 1919.
28. *Ibid.*
29. *Ibid.*, Jan. 14, 1922; Grossman, pp. 327-28.
30. Grossman, p. 327.
31. *New Majority*, Aug. 2, 1919; *Butcher Workman*, July, 1919—May, 1920; Grossman, pp. 329-30.
32. Sterling D. Spero and Abram L. Harris, *The Black Worker*, New York, 1971, p. 271.
33. *New Majority*, Dec. 10, 1921; Brody, pp. 102-03; Grossman, p. 331.
34. Grossman, p. 332.
35. *Ibid.*, pp. 302-03.
36. John Kiluski and Chicago Federation of Labor Secretary Ed Nockels in *New Majority*, Jan. 11, 1919; Grossman, p. 333.
37. Quoted in Jacqueline Herbst, *The Negro in Slaughtering and Meatpacking*, Phila., 1874, p. 36; Grossman, pp. 336-37, 341-42, 364.
38. Quoted in Herbst, p. 37; Grossman, p. 306.
39. Philip S. Foner, *Organized Labor and the Black Worker, 1619-1982*, New York, 1983, pp. 134-39; Paul Worthman, "Black Workers and Labor Unions in Birmingham, Alabama, 1897-1909," *Labor History* 10 (Summer 1969): 394-95; Paul Worthman and James Green, "Black Workers in the New South, 1865-1915," in Nathaniel Huggins, Martin Kilson, and Daniel Fox, *Key Issues in the Afro-American Experience* (New York, 1971): 2: 61.
40. Philip S. Foner, *History of the Labor Movement in the United States* 2 (New York, 1955): 234-52; Foner, *Organized Labor and the Black Worker*, pp. 286-305.
41. Foner, *op. cit.*, vol. 2, pp. 263-68.
42. Foner, *op. cit.*, vol. 4, pp. 324-43; Foner, *Organized Labor and the Black Worker*, pp. 325-56.
43. Quoted by James E. Fickle, "Management Looks at Labor Problems: The Southern Pine Industry During World War I and the Postwar Era," *Journal of Southern History* 40 (Feb. 1974): 70.
44. *Ibid.*, pp. 74-76.
45. *Ibid.*, pp. 73, 76.
46. *Ibid.*, pp. 68-69; Huey Latham, Jr., "A Comparison of Union Organization in Two Southern Paper Mills," unpublished M.A. thesis, Louisiana State University, 1962, pp. 28-30.
47. Latham, Jr. *op. cit.*, pp. 31-32.
48. *Ibid.*, p. 32.
49. *Ibid.*, p. 33.
50. *Ibid.*, p. 34; Fickle, *op. cit.*, p. 69.
51. Latham, Jr., *op. cit.*, p. 24.
52. *Ibid.*, p. 35; Fickle, *op. cit.*, p. 69.
53. *The Messenger*, December, 1919, p. 4.

54. Latham, Jr., *op. cit.*, p. 35.
55. Foner, *Organized Labor and the Black Worker*, pp. 145, 149-50.

CHAPTER 11

1. *The Messenger*, December 1919, pp. 4, 17
2. Foner, *Organized Labor and the Black Worker*, p. 151
3. *Ibid.*, pp. 149-51
4. *The Messenger*, December 1919, pp. 4, 10-12
5. *Ibid.*, p. 8
6. *Ibid.*, June 1918, p. 8
7. *The Crisis* 18 (September 1919): 239
8. *Proceedings*, AFL Convention, 1919, pp. 216-17
9. *Ibid.*
10. *Ibid.*
11. *Ibid.*, pp. 227-29
12. *Ibid.*, p. 305
13. *New York Times*, June 14, 1919; *Literary Digest*, June 28, 1919, p. 12
14. *Proceedings*, AFL Convention, 1919, pp. 305-06
15. "The Negro and the Labor Union," *The Crisis* 18 (September 1919): 240; *New York Times*, June 14, 1919
16. New York *Age*, June 21, 1919
17. Reprinted in *Literary Digest*, June 28, 1919, p. 12
18. Reprinted in *ibid.*
19. Quoted in *ibid.*
20. Quoted in *Ibid.*
21. New York *Age*, June 21, 1919
22. Quoted in *Literary Digest*, June 28, 1919, p. 12
23. *The Crisis* 18 (September 1919): 239-41
24. John D. Finney, Jr., "A Study of Negro Labor During and After World War I," unpublished Ph.D. dissertation, Georgetown University, 1957, p. 319
25. *Proceedings*, AFL Convention, 1920, pp. 32-33
26. Foner, *Organized Labor and the Black Worker*, p. 154
27. *Ibid.*, p. 155
28. *Proceedings*, AFL Convention, 1920, pp. 263, 272-73
29. *Ibid.*, pp. 351-52
30. Herbert R. Northrup, *Organized Labor and the Negro*, New York, 1944, p. 10
31. *Proceedings*, AFL Convention, 1920, pp. 308, 311, 351-52
32. *Ibid.*, pp. 351-52
33. *Ibid.*, p. 309
34. *Ibid.*, p. 310
35. *Ibid.*, pp. 433-34
36. New York *Call*, June 11, 1920
37. *Ibid.*

38. *Justice*, June 18, 1920
39. *Advance*, July 15, 1920
40. Ruth Allen, *Chapters in the History of Organized Labor in Texas*, Austin, Texas, 1941, pp. 293-94

CHAPTER 12

1. *Sacramento Bee*, Dec. 18, 1917
2. *Ibid.*, Dec. 22, 1917; San Francisco *Examiner*, Dec. 23, 1917
3. *Sacramento Bee*, Jan. 20, 1918.
4. *Ibid.*, Dec. 29, 1917; *San Francisco Examiner*, Dec. 30, 1917
5. *Sacramento Bee*, Dec. 31, 1917
6. Hyman Weintraub, "The I.W.W. in California, 1906-1931," unpublished M.A. thesis, University of California, Los Angeles, 1947, p. 148
7. *Ibid.*, pp. 149-50
8. *Ibid.*, p. 150.
9. *Sacramento Bee*, Jan. 2, 1918; Weintraub, p. 151
10. Weintraub, p. 154.
11. Philip Taft, "The Federal Trials of the I.W.W.," *Labor History* 3 (Winter 1962): 78
12. *San Francisco Examiner*, Jan. 17, 18, 1919
13. *Ibid.*
14. *Sacramento Bee*, Jan. 18, 1919
15. "Amnesty for Political Prisoners," Testimony of Caroline A. Lowe, before House Judiciary Committee on H. Res. 60, 67th Congress, 2nd Session, pp. 32, 37
16. *Ibid.*, pp. 37-38
17. Clayton R. Koppes, "The Kansas Trial of the IWW, 1917-1919," *Labor History* 16 (Summer 1971): 349-50
18. *Kansas City Star*, Feb. 10, 1919
19. *Ibid.*, March 12, May 4, 1919
20. *Ibid.*, March 12, 1919
21. Koppes, *op. cit.*, p. 350
22. *Ibid.*, pp. 351-54
23. *Ibid.*, p. 356
24. Quoted in *ibid.*, p. 355
25. Earl Bruce White, "The United States v. C.W. Anderson *et. al.*: The Wichita Case, 1917-1919," in Joseph R. Conlin, *At the Point of Production: The Local History of the I.W.W.*, Westport, 1981, p. 144
26. Thomas McMahon, "Centralia and the I.W.W.," *Survey* 48 (Nov. 29, 1920): 123
27. Tacoma *News-Tribune*, May 1-2, 1919
28. McMahon, p. 124; Federal Council of Churches of Christ in America, *The Centralia Case*, New York, 1930, p. 9
29. Ralph Chaplin, *The Centralia Case*, Chi-

cago, 1924, pp. 42-43; Anna Louise Strong, "Centralia, An Unfinished Story," *Nation* 110 (April 17, 1920): 510
30. Robert L. Tyler, *Rebels of the Woods: The I.W.W. in the Pacific Northwest*, Eugene, Oregon, 1967, p. 170
31. Vernon H. Jensen, *Lumber and Labor*, New York, 1945, p. 138
32. Federal Council of Churches..., *Centralia*, p. 13; Jensen, p. 139
33. Tyler, p. 139; Seattle *Post-Intelligencer*, Nov. 12, 1919
34. Harvey O'Connor, *Revolution in Seattle: A Memoir*, New York, 1964, p. 175; Seattle *Post-Intelligencer*, Nov. 17, 1919
35. Centralia *Hub*, Nov. 5, 1919
36. O'Connor, p. 171
37. Walker C. Smith, *Was It Murder?* Chicago, n.d., pp. 39-40; Chaplin, pp. 7?-73; Portland *Oregonian*, Nov. 13-16, 1919
38. Portland *Oregonian*, Nov. 15, 1919
39. *Ibid.*, Nov. 16, 1919; Tyler, pp. 160-61
40. Smith, pp. 48-52
41. Jensen, p. 141
42. *Industrial Pioneer*, July 1921; reprinted in Joyce L. Kornbluh, editor, *Rebel Voices: An I.W.W. Anthology*, Ann Arbor, Michigan, 1964, p. 275
43. Chaplin, pp. 74-75
44. Portland *Oregonian*, Nov. 17-18, 1919; Tyler, p. 143
45. Quoted in Jensen, p. 140
46. Seattle *Post-Intelligencer*, Nov. 26, 1919
47. Tyler, p. 143
48. Jensen, p. 141
49. Seattle *Union Record*, Nov. 24, 1919
50. *Ibid.*; Jensen, p. 140
51. Seattle *Union Record*, Nov. 13, 1919; Tyler, p. 145
52. O'Connor, p. 181
53. *Ibid.*, p. 182
54. *Ibid.*, pp. 187-88
55. Seattle *Post-Intelligencer*, Nov. 16, 1919
56. Chaplin, p. 85
57. *Industrial Worker*, Feb. 7, 1920; O'Connor, p. 188; Tyler, p. 164
58. *Industrial Worker*, Feb. 21, 1920
59. Seattle *Post-Intelligencer*, March 1, 8, 1920
60. Portland *Oregonian*, March 1, 1920
61. *Ibid.*, March 2, 3, 1920
62. Seattle *Post-Intelligencer*, March 12, 13, 1920
63. Portland *Oregonian*, March 13, 14, 1920
64. Seattle *Post-Intelligencer*, March 14, 1920
65. Strong, pp. 508-09; *Survey* 44 (April 17, 1920): 115
66. *Opening Brief of Appellants in the matter*

of State of Washington v. Britt Smith, et. al. in the Supreme Court of Washington State, Cause No. 16354, p. 152; Seattle *Post-Intelligencer*, April 15, 1920
67. Seattle *Post-Intelligencer*, March 15, April 27, June 20, 1929
68. Tyler, pp. 169-74
69. Albert T. Gunns, "Ray Becker, the Last Centralia Prisoner" *Pacific Northwest Quarterly*, 59 (1968): 93-94
70. *Ibid.*, p. 95
71. *Ibid.*, p. 97
72. *Ibid.*, p. 98
73. *Industrial Worker*, Nov. 6, 1920
74. Thomas Howard McEnroe, "The Industrial Workers of the World: Theories, Organizational Problems, and Appeals, As Revealed Principally in the *Industrial Worker*," unpublished Ph.D. thesis, University of Minnesota, 1960, pp. 121-22
75. *Industrial Worker*, Nov. 6, 1920
76. *Ibid.*, Nov. 27, 1920, Jan. 22, 1921
77. *Ibid.*, Nov. 20, 1920
78. *Ibid.*, Dec. 25, 1920, Jan. 8, 15, 1921; McEnroe, pp. 126-27
79. *Industrial Worker*, May 28, June 4, 1921
80. McEnroe, pp. 131-32
81. Perlman & Taft, *History of Labor in the U.S., 1896-1932*, New York, 1935, p. 496
82. Jay M. Pawa, "British Radicals and Anglo-American Countersubversion: The Response of the United States and England to the IWW. 1918-1920," *New Labor Review* 5 (1968): 142-60
83. *Ibid.*, pp. 160-64
84. Fred Thompson, *The I.W.W.*, Chicago, 1930, p. 140
85. John S. Gambs, *The Decline of the I.W.W.*, New York, 1932, p. 57
86. *Bill Haywood's Book: The Autobiography of William D. Haywood*, New York, 1929, p. 356
87. *Ibid.*, p. 359
88. *Ibid.*, p. 359-65; Melvyn Dubofsky, *"We Shall Be All": A History of the Industrial Workers of the World*, Chicago, 1969, pp. 408, 459-60; Joseph R. Conlin, *Big Bill Haywood and the Radical Union Movement*, Syracuse N.Y., 1969, pp. 84, 197-209; Georgakas, *op. cit.*, p. 13
89. Conlin, p. 198
90. Bryan D. Palmer, "'Big Bill' Haywood's Defection to Russia and the IWW: Two Letters," *Labor History* 17 (Spring 1976): 272
91. Gambs, p. 60; Taft, p. 81; Elizabeth Gurley Flynn to "Dear Comrades," March 25, 1919, Workers Defense Union Collection, E.G. Flynn Papers, State

Historical Society of Wisconsin
92. *New York Times*, Sept. 15, 1919
93. Art Shields, "The New Turn of the I.W.W.," *Socialist Review* 1 (April-May 1921): 70
94. Richard C. Cortnew, "The Wobblies and Fiske v. Kansas: Victory and Disintegration," *Kansas History* 4 (Spring 1981): 30
95. *One Big Union Monthly* 3 (Jan., 1921): 52
96. *Ibid.*, 1 (July 1919): 31
97. *Industrial Worker*, July 22, 1922
98. Wm. Preston, Jr., *Aliens and Dissenters*, Cambridge, 1963, pp. 259-61
99. "Invitation to the First Congress of the Communist International," in *The Communist International, 1919-1943: Documents*, selected and edited by Jane Degras, London, 1956, 1 (1919-1922): 1-5.
100. *Industrial Worker*, Oct. 30, 1920; Gambs, p. 77
101. McEnroe, p. 320
102. *Solidarity*, Aug. 14, 21, 1920
103. *Bill Haywood's Book*, p. 360
104. *Solidarity*, Oct. 2, 9, 1920
105. *Ibid.*, Sept. 11, 1920
106. *Industrial Worker*, Sept. 25, 1920
107. *Ibid.*, Dec. 25, 1920; Gambs, p. 82
108. *Industrial Worker*, June 4, 1921
109. J.P. Morray, *Project Kuzbas: American Workers in Siberia (1921-1926)*, New York, 1983, p. 76
110. *The First Congress of the Red Trades Union International at Moscow, 1921: A Report of the Proceedings by George Williams, Delegate from the IWW*, Chicago, 1921
111. *Ibid.*
112. *Industrial Worker*, Feb. 11, 1922; William Z. Foster, *History of the Communist Party of the United States*, New York, 1952, p. 182
113. *Industrial Worker*, Dec. 24, 1921
114. Gambs. pp. 89, 150
115. Len De Caux, *The Living Spirit of the Wobblies*, New York, 1978, p. 128

CHAPTER 13

1. Morris Hillquit, *Loose Leaves from a Busy Life*, New York, 1934, pp. 168-69; Michael E.R. Bassett, "The Socialist Party of America, 1912-1919; Years of Decline," unpublished Ph.D. thesis, Duke University, 1963, pp. 291-93
2. *Liberator* 1 (June 1918): 33; *New York Call*, Aug. 24, 1918; *Milwaukee Leader*, July 8, 1919
3. Minutes of the Socialist Party (U.S.),

New York Local, Executive Committee, N.B. 38, Folder 1, p. 194, Tamiment Institute Library, New York University
4. *Ibid.*
5. *Liberator* 1 (June 1918): 42-43
6. Theodore Draper, *The Roots of American Communism*, New York, 1957, p. 138
7. *Ibid.*, pp. 77-79; Martin Glaberman and George P. Rawick, "The Revolutionary Age, Boston and New York, 1918-1919," in Joseph R. Conlin, editor, *The American Radical Press, 1880-1960*, Westport, 1974, pp. 155-58
8. "The Task Before Us," *Class Struggle* 1 (May-June, 1917): 2-3
9. Louis C. Fraina, "Problems of American Socialists," *Class Struggle* 3 (February 1919): 26-47. Italics in the original.
10. Leward Lindgren, "What is the Left-Wing Movement and its Purpose?" *Class Struggle* 3 (February 1919): 111-14
11. *Revolutionary Age* 1 (April 8, 1919): 2
12. Quoted in *Proletarian* (Detroit) 1 (April 1919): 296
13. *Class Struggle* 3 (February 1919): 111-14; *New York Communist* 1 (April 19, 1919): 2
14. S.M. Felshin in New York *Call*, Jan. 29, 1919
15. "Proclamation on Russia," adopted by the Conference of State Secretaries and Party Officials, August, 1918, Socialist Party Papers, Duke University Library
16. "Russia," Proclamation adopted by the National Executive Committee, January 17-21, 1919, Socialist Party Papers, Duke University Library
17. Draper, p. 151
18. Edward Hallett Carr, *The Bolshevik Revolution, 1917-1918*, London, 1950, pp. 116, 118-21
19. *Revolutionary Age* 1 (Feb. 8, 1919): 1-2; "The Left Wing Manifesto," *ibid.* (July 5, 1919): 6; Oakland *World*, April 11, 25, May 16, 1919
20. *Communist* 1 (April 1, 1919): 1; *New York Communist* 1 (April 19, 1919): 2
21. David A. Shannon, *The Socialist Party of America*, New York, 1967, p. 132; *Class Struggle* 3 (May 1919): 225-29
22. Ralph E. Shaffer, "Formation of the California Communist Labor Party," *Pacific Historical Review* 36 (1967): 64
23. John R. Ball, "After the Election," Memorandum, April 4, 1919, Socialist Party Papers, Duke University Library; Adolph Germer to Morris Hillquit, April 19, 1919, Morris Hillquit Papers, Tamiment Institute Library, New York University; Draper, pp. 188-90; Oakley John-

son, "1919: Crucial Year on the Left: A Study of the Proletarian Party," *Political Affairs*, December 1974, p. 25

24. Morris Hilllquit, *The Immediate Issue*, New York, 1919, pp. 13-15; New York *Call*, May 21, 1919

25. Minutes of the Socialist Party (U.S.) New York Local, Executive Committee, M.B. 48, Folder 2, May 20, 1919, Socialist Party Papers, Duke University Library; Bassett, p. 311

26. New York *Call*, May 28, 1919

27. Adolph Germer to All State Secretaries, May 31, 1919, Socialist Party Papers, Duke University Library; New York *Call*, May 29, 1919; *New York Times*, May 31, 1919

28. New York *Call*, July 2, 1919; Shannon, pp. 137-38

29. Bassett, p. 314

30. Shannon, p. 137

31. *Ibid.*, pp. 138-39

32. Walter M. Cook to Adolph Germer, June 2, 1919, Socialist Party Papers, Duke University Library

33. *Milwaukee Leader*, June 17, 1919; Bassett, p. 317

34. *Revolutionary Age* 1 (May 24, 1919): 3

35. *Ibid.*, (June 7, 1919): 1

36. *Ibid.* 1 (June 14, 1919): 1

37. *Ibid.*; Johnson, p. 28

38. Draper, pp. 166-69; William Z. Foster, *History of the Communist Party of the United States*, New York, 1952, pp. 165-66; Granville Hicks, *John Reed: The Making of a Revolutionary*, New York, 1936, pp. 355-56; *Ohio Socialist*, July 2, 1919

39. Bassett, p. 321; Hicks, pp. 355-56

40. Adolph Germer to Morris Hillquit, July 14, 1919, Morris Hillquit Papers, Tamiment Institute Library, New York University

41. Draper, p. 176

42. Auvo Kostianien, *The Forging of Finnish-American Communism, 1917-1924: A Study in Ethnic Radicalism*, Turku, Finland, 1978, p. 72

43. New York *Call*, June 5, 1919. See also *Milwaukee Leader*, June 26, 1919

44. Bassett, p. 321; *Ohio Socialist*, Sept. 17, 1919

45. Bassett, pp. 321-22; Shaffer, p. 69; Oakland *World*, Sept. 26, Dec. 26, 1919

46. Bassett, p. 323

47. Shaffer, p. 69

48. *American Labor Year Book, 1919-1920*, New York, 1920, p. 405-14

49. *Literary Digest*, Sept. 20, 1919

50. *Proceedings*, pp. 760-61; *Milwaukee Leader*, Sept. 6, 1919; Bassett, p. 323

51. *New York Times*, Aug. 31, 1919; Bassett, p. 323

52. Bassett, p. 324

53. Daniel Bell quoted in Irving Howe and Lewis Closer, *The American Communist Party: A Critical History*, New York, 1962, p. 370

54. *Ohio Socialist*, Sept. 17, 1919

55. Kathleen A. Sharp. "Rose Pastor Stokes: Radical Champion of the American Working Class, 1879-1933," unpublished Ph.D. dissertation, Duke University, 1979, p. 162

56. Foster, pp. 171-72

57. *American Labor Year Book, 1919-1920*, p. 415.

58. *Ibid.*, pp. 416-18

59. Foster, p. 177

60. *American Labor Year Book, 1919-1920*, pp. 416-19

61. *Ibid.*, pp. 418-19

62. *Ibid.*, p. 419

63. Philip S. Foner, *American Socialism and Black Americans: From the Age of Jackson to World War II*, Westport, Conn., 1977, p. 306

64. Max Eastman, "The Chicago Convention," *The Liberator* 1 (October 1919): 5-19

65. Robert K. Murray, *Red Scare:...*, pp. 212-17

66. Shaffer, p. 78

67. *Ibid.*

68. Foster, p. 176

69. *Ibid.*, pp. 175-76; Murray, p. 53

70. Draper, pp. 189-90; Foster, p. 177

71. *Organized Communism in the United States. Prepared and Released by the Committee on Un-American Activities, U.S. House of Representatives*, Washington, D.C., 1953, pp. 48-50; Foster pp. 180-81

72. *Organized Communism*, p. 64; Foster, p. 182

73. Draper, pp. 336-37; Foster, p. 187

74. *Organized Communism*, p. 72; *The Toiler*, Jan. 14, 1921; Foster, pp. 189-91

75. *Program and Constitution. Workers Party of America Adopted at a National Convention, New York City, December 24-25-26, 1921*, New York, n.d.

76. Foster, pp. 194-95

77. Draper, pp. 358-59; Foster, pp. 195, 215

78. Lewis Lorwin, *The American Federation of Labor: History, Policies, and Prospects*, Washington, D.C., 1933, p. 223 *n*

CHAPTER 14

1. Selig Perlman, *A Theory of the Labor*

Movement, New York, 1949, p. 219

2. Samuel Gompers, "Voluntary Social Insurance," *American Federationist* 24 (May 1916): 333

3. Michael Rogin, "Voluntarism: The Political Functions of an Anti-political Doctrine," *Industrial and Labor Relations Review* 15 (July, 1962): 530-31

4. Samuel Gompers to John Fitzpatrick, June 9, 1916, Gompers Papers, AFL Archives, State Historical Society of Wisconsin.

5. John Howard Keiser, "John Fitzpatrick and Progressive Unionism," Ph.D. dissertation, Northwestern University, 1965, pp. 125-35

6. *Literary Digest*, Nov. 29, 1919

7. Writ of Injunction Issued by the Circuit Court of Cook County, Illinois, August Term, 1917, in the case *of Morkrum Company versus Philip Renisch, et. al.*, copy in John Fitzpatrick Papers, Chicago Historical Society.

8. John P. Frey to John Fitzpatrick, July 9, 1917, John Fitzpatrick Papers, Chicago Historical Society.

9. Reprinted in *Literary Digest*, Dec. 27, 1919

10. *Ibid.*

11. John Fitch, "Labor and Politics," *Survey* 40 (June 8, 1918): 288

12. *Ibid.*

13. Keiser, p. 132.

14. New York *Call*, Sept. 17, 1918; *The American Labor Year Book, 1919-1920*, New York, 1920, pp. 199-201, Frank P. Walsh to Reed, Dec. 13, 1918, Frank P. Walsh Papers, New York Public Library.

15. Eugene Staley, *History of the Illinois State Federation of Labor*, Chicago, 1930, p. 318

16. *American Labor Year Book, 1919-1920*, pp. 200-01

17. New York *Call*, Nov. 26, 1918; "Chicago for the Workers," pp. 37-40, Copy in Tamiment Institute Library, New York University

18. *New Majority*, Jan. 4, March 8, 1919

19. *Ibid.*, March 15, 1919; Keiser, pp. 120-24

20. *Ibid.*, Jan. 18, Feb. 1, 1919

21. *Labor Herald*, (Kansas City), Jan. 24, 1919.

21. David Dolnick, "The Role of Labor in Chicago Politics Since 1919," MA thesis, University of Chicago, 1939, pp. 4-5; Harry Bird Sell, "The A.F. of L. and the Labor Party Movement of 1918-1920," MA thesis, University of Chicago, 1922, pp. 81-83

22. *New Majority*, April 5, 1919; *Survey* 42 (April 12, 1919): 84

23. Staley, pp. 361-65; *American Labor Year Book, 1919-1920*, p. 200

24. *New Majority*, March 15, 1919; Keiser, p. 123

25. *American Labor Year Book, 1919-1920*, p. 203

26. New York *Tribune*, Jan. 12, 1919

27. *Advance* 2 (Jan. 17, 1919): 1; *American Labor Year Book, 1920*, p. 202

28. J.M. Budish in *American Labor Year Book, 1919-1920*, p. 202

29. Sell, p. 86; Stanley Shapiro, "Hand and Brain: The Farmer-Labor Party of 1920," Ph.D. thesis, University of California, Berkeley, 1967, pp. 121, 161-69, 175-76

30. *New York Times*, Dec. 21, 1919

31. Herbert E. Bigelow to Amos Pinchot, Dec. 20, 1918, Amos Pinchot Papers, Library of Congress; Shapiro, *op. cit.* pp. 55-58

32. Stanley Shapiro, "Hand and Brain: The Farmer-Labor Party of 1920," *Labor History* 26 (Summer 1985): 414; T.A.H. Hopkins to George P. West, Dec. 27, 1918, Frank P. Walsh Papers, N.Y. Public Library; "What the Committee of Forty-Eight Has Done Since March 1, 1919," Amos Pinchot Papers, Library of Congress

33. *New York Times*, Nov. 27, Dec. 21, 22, 1919

34. Robert L. Morlan, *Political Prarie Fire. The Non-Partisan League, 1915-1922*, Minneapolis, 1955, pp. 60-63; Russell B. Nye, *Midwest Progressive Politics. A Historical Study of Its Origins and Development 1870-1950*, East Lansing, Michigan, 1951, pp. 314-15; Nathan Fine, *Labor and Farmer Parties in the United States*, New York, 1928, pp. 267-68, 375; James R. Shideler, *Farm Crisis, 1919-1923*, Berkeley, 1957, pp. 32-34

35. Morlan, pp. 112-15

36. Fine, p. 373; Arthur A. Bruce, *Non-Partisan League*, New York, 1921, p. 8

37. Theodore Saloutos and John D. Hicks, *Agricultural Discontent in the Middle West, 1900-1931*, Madison, Wisconsin, 1951, p. 180; Fine, pp. 384-86

38. Staley, pp. 373-76

39. *New Majority*, Dec. 6, 1919

40. *Ibid.*, April 5, 1919; *Survey* 42 (April 12, 1919): 84

41. *New Majority*, April 5, 1919

42. John Laslett, *Labor and the Left: A Study of Socialist and Radical Influences in the American Labor Movement, 1881-1924*,

New York, 1970, pp. 121, 128-31, 173, 178, 193, 218-31

43. *American Labor Year Book, 1919-1920*, pp. 437-38.
44. *Ibid.*, p. 438
45. *Ibid.*, pp. 438-39
46. Reprinted in *Literary Digest*, Dec. 13, 1919
47. Reprinted in *ibid.*
48. Reprinted in *ibid.*
49. Reprinted in *ibid.*
50. Reprinted in *ibid.*
51. *New Majority*, July 17, 24, 1920
52. Francis Tyson, "Labor Swallows the Forty-Eighters," *Survey* 44 (Aug. 2, 1920): 587-88; Fine, pp. 382-86, 389-92; Lincoln Colcord, "The Committee of Forty Eight," *Nation* 109 (Dec. 27, 1919): 821-22; *American Labor Year Book, 1923-1924*, New York, 1924, p. 144; Shapiro, dissertation, pp. 121-23
53. Shapiro, dissertation, pp. 121-23; *New York Times*, May 25, 1919
54. Shapiro, dissertation, p. 128
55. Fine, p. 392
56. *Labor*, Nov. 6, 1920; Shapiro, dissertation, pp. 142-43; Keiser, p. 136
57. Hamilton Cravens, "The Emergence of the Farmer-Labor Party in Washington Politics, 1919-1920," *Pacific Northwest Quarterly* 57 (October 1966): 148-57
58. *American Federationist* 27 (December 1920): 1082.
59. *New York Times*, Dec. 9, 1918; copy of speech in AFL Archives, State Historical Society of Wisconsin
60. *Proceedings*, AFL Convention, 1920, p. 78; *American Federationist* 26 (June 1919): 516-17
61. Staley, p. 373; Sell, pp. 112-15; *American Federationist* 26 (January 1919): 37-45
62. Fine, p. 387; *Garment Worker* 12 (May 28, 1920): 4
63. *Labor Herald* (Kansas City), March 1, 1920
64. *New Majority*, Dec. 23, 1922
65. Erik Olssen, "The Making of a Political Machine: The Railroad Unions Enter Politics," *Labor History* 19 (Summer, 1978): 374-77
66. Samuel Gompers to Anderson, March 30, 1920; Gompers to AFL Executive Council, January 15, 1920, Gompers Papers, AFL Archives, State Historical Society of Wisconsin; William English Walling, *American Labor and American Democracy*, New York, 1926, p. 66
67. Gompers to Herbert A. Yerks, April 9, 1920; Gompers to John P. Frey, April 9,

1920; Gompers to the Editor, Pittsburgh *Post, et al*, April 9, 1920, all in Gompers Papers, AFL Archives, State Historical Society of Wisconsin; "55 Questions and Answers on Campaign Issues," *American Federation of Labor Official Documents* (Washington, 1921) I: No. 21
68. *American Federationist* 27 (August 1920): 737
69. *Ibid.*, 27 (July, 1920): 656
70. *Ibid.*, 27 (September 1920): 810-23
71. Olssen, pp. 377-78
72. *Ibid.*, p. 378
73. Gompers to Ed. Anderson, March 30, 1920, Gompers Papers, AFL Archives, State Historical Society of Wisconsin
74. *Labor*, Nov. 6, 1920; *American Federationist* 27 (December 1920): 1082

INDEX